Given to me by
Kathy Lormand 11-5-2019

ANOTHER YEAR FINDS ME IN TEXAS

ANOTHER YEAR FINDS ME IN

TEXAS

THE CIVIL WAR DIARY OF

LUCY PIER STEVENS

VICKI ADAMS TONGATE

UNIVERSITY OF TEXAS PRESS
AUSTIN

Published in Cooperation with the William P. Clements Center
for Southwest Studies, Southern Methodist University

Copyright © 2016 by the University of Texas Press
Printed in the United States of America
First edition, 2016

Requests for permission to reproduce material
from this work should be sent to:
Permissions
University of Texas Press
P.O. Box 7819
Austin, TX 78713–7819
http://utpress.utexas.edu/index.php/rp-form

The paper used in this book meets the minimum requirements
of ANSI/NISO Z39.48–1992 (R1997) (Permanence of Paper). ∞

Design by Lindsay Starr

LIBRARY OF CONGRESS CATALOGING-IN-PUBLICATION DATA

Tongate, Vicki Adams, author.
Another year finds me in Texas : the Civil War diary of Lucy Pier Stevens /
by Vicki Adams Tongate. — First edition.
pages cm
Includes bibliographical references and index.
ISBN 978-1-4773-0846-2 (cloth : alk. paper)
ISBN 978-1-4773-0863-9 (library e-book)
ISBN 978-1-4773-0864-6 (non-library e-book)
1. Stevens, Lucy Pier—Diaries. 2. United States—History—Civil War, 1861–1865—
Women—Personal narratives. 3. Texas—History—Civil War, 1861–1865—
Personal narratives. 4. Women—Ohio—Diaries. I. Title.
E628.T66 2016
976.4'05092—dc23
[B]
2015024077

Frontispeice: Lucy Pier Stevens. DeGolyer Library,
Southern Methodist University, Lucy Pier Stevens Collection.

doi: 10.7560/308462

FOR GARY

CONTENTS

ACKNOWLEDGMENTS

I have often said that God simply dropped this project in my lap and told me to have fun with it, and that's exactly what I've done. However, it would never have happened without the assistance of many people who graciously went out of their way to help and encourage me. It is only fitting that I remember them now. I applaud all of my professors and colleagues who have willingly shared their knowledge and expertise with me. I am so honored to be able to say that, in many ways, I am here because of you.

Without doubt, I must first thank Professor Edward F. Countryman, who initially served as my undergraduate/graduate advisor for my work with the diary. His questions and comments challenged me as I began my research, and he was ever available to offer suggestions and guidance. Through the years, his encouragement and absolute faith in me have enabled me to stay the course, and his advice has been essential in the final stages of this project. Not only has he been a constant in my work with Lucy, he has become a valued friend. Who could know that a chance meeting in the basement of Dallas Hall would lead to this? "Thank you" hardly seems adequate.

I also count it a high privilege to have been a student of the incredible David Weber, founding director of the Clements Center for Southwest Studies at Southern Methodist University. As my professor and one of my thesis advisors, he challenged me to continue working on the diary and opened doors of opportunity for me. I am only sorry that I could not finish this project before his death.

Russell Martin, director of DeGolyer Library, has been my advocate, and I can never thank him enough for his unwavering support—even when it appeared that the project had ground to a halt. His willingness to intercede for me and keep Lucy's name in the forefront has yielded immeasurable results. Thank you, Russell, for remaining so patient and gracious when the project moved so slowly.

Andrea Boardman, former executive director of the Clements Center for Southwest Studies, holds the honor of first introducing me to Lucy, and without her continuing faith and backing, I doubt that I would have ever finished this work. She has offered perceptive insight and constant encouragement as she has led me into new ways of viewing and sharing Lucy's story. Her confidence in me has frequently exceeded my own. Thank you so much for being my cheerleader, Andrea—I still marvel at your faith in me.

My colleagues in today's Clements Center—Andrew Graybill, Sherry Smith, and Ruth Ann Elmore—have been ever supportive and have gone out of their way to assist me as well. Thank you all for the help you have given me.

My editor and advocate at the University of Texas Press, Casey Kittrell— how can I ever thank you for believing in the importance of Lucy's story and taking a chance on me? Your willingness to shepherd me through this new terrain keeps me steady. Thank you so much; your confidence honors me. Angelica Lopez, Victoria Davis, Jan McInroy, and others at UT Press have been invaluable in their assistance during the production phase of the book—thanks to all of you. And Molly O'Halloran—the map is wonderful!

From the earliest days of this project, David Farmer, former director of DeGolyer Special Collections Library, generously gave me free rein to work on the diary. His assistants, Kay Bost and Betty Friedrich, graciously provided a space where I could work and "play with Lucy." I will always remember their kindnesses. Most recently, Pamalla Anderson and Terre Heydari of DeGolyer have assisted with digitizing the images in Lucy's photo album—a heartfelt thank-you goes to them as well.

Many others have challenged me and cheered me on since I began this work as a thesis project in 1999: Professors Nina Schwartz and Willard Spiegelman, who served on my thesis committee and who have my enduring thanks for expecting more of me than I ever thought possible; Dr. Andrea Hamilton, who first introduced me to the scholarly study of diaries with the reading of Laurel Thatcher Ulrich's *A Midwife's Tale*; Stephen Shepherd, who approved my original thesis project; Michael Holahan; Margaret Lawhon; Beth Newman; Alexis McCrossen—the list extends. I take great joy in thanking you all for your unflagging support.

There are others outside the SMU community who must be remembered as well. In Bellville, Bill Hardt gave so generously of his time, serving as "tour guide" and historian for my husband and me as we began our search for information. Dr. Kevin Chrisman, vice president of the Institute of Nautical Archaeology at Texas A&M, spent time with me talking about blockade runners. Robert and Cristy Pier opened their home to me as well, sharing documents and family stories. Gil Pier frequently sent pieces of information that have opened new doors of possibility. Joy Neely of the Bellville Historical Society provided information I might never have found otherwise. There are countless other individuals across the country who graciously responded to requests for information—my appreciation is immense.

I especially want to thank my children, Jeff, Melissa, and Brian, as well as my in-law children, Todd and Diana, for they have loved me, encouraged me, and yes, patiently endured my Lucy stories. During the Lucy years, we have been blessed to add four grandchildren, Noah, Emma, Gabby, and Jeffrey, to our family, and they know Lucy too.

Most of all, I want to thank my husband, Gary, for his unwavering love and encouragement through the years of this journey. Although this project has started and stopped numerous times, he has never, NEVER lost faith. He has been my companion detective, my sounding board, my advisor, my champion, and my most ardent fan. Without his strength and unending support, this project simply would not be. God has truly blessed me, and I am very grateful.

Lucy Pier Stevens left behind an articulate account of her life in Civil War Texas, and I have attempted to preserve the flavor of the original text so that her words might be read in the same manner in which they were written. The diary's original spelling and grammar have been retained unless they are so eccentric that they distract the modern reader. Phonetic spellings that are consistent throughout the diary, such as "peice" (piece), "fedral" (federal), and "sevral" (several), have been maintained. Other words that Lucy might have misspelled have been silently corrected. If a word has been misspelled in the text, such as the word "scarred" in Lucy's entry of January 1, 1863, the correct version (here "scared") has been placed in the text in brackets. If a word or phrase is missing and is needed for clarification, the necessary words have been added in brackets. Accidental repetitions of words and letters have been eliminated and/or silently corrected. Lucy's use of the "eszett," a distinctive German letter for "double s," has been amended to the standard "ss" found in English.

Lucy's punctuation was erratic, and where its absence is an obstacle to ready comprehension, punctuation has been added. On occasion, commas and periods have been placed within the text for the sake of readability. Capital letters have been added at the beginning of sentences since Lucy used them inconsistently; otherwise, words written in lowercase, such as the days of the week, have been left unchanged. Lucy often ended a thought with a flourishing dash instead of a period, and to a degree, this practice has been retained, using the tilde symbol (~) to more nearly duplicate Lucy's style. Strikeovers in the printed text are those that Lucy herself marked out. On occasion, however, the diary contains lengthy passages that have been crossed out but that are still legible. In these cases, I have preceded the strikeover with "following passage crossed out;" then, if the passage is legible, I have provided it without the strikeover and followed it with "end of crossed-out passage." Lucy's marginalia are inserted on separate lines, centered, bracketed, and designated "[Marginal Note: . . .]." Book titles are regularized, as are the names of periodicals, newspapers, ships, etc.

Lucy read extensively and habitually recorded plot summaries within the text of her diary. To save space and keep the focus on the diary, I have omitted these summaries. I have included the first as an example; other summaries will be available for examination in the unexpurgated text housed in DeGolyer Library, Southern Methodist University in Dallas, Texas.

Countless people move through the pages of Lucy's diary. Those who are central to her story are mentioned in footnotes; however, many extraneous characters in Lucy's world remain unidentified. By excluding them from my annotations I am not commenting on their relative worth, but merely recognizing the transitory nature of their involvement in Lucy's life. Due to the length of the book, I have omitted sources in annotations supplying background information when the facts can be readily found in dictionaries or in standard reference works such as the incredible *Handbook of Texas Online*.

Much general contextual information and analytical commentary have been included in an introductory essay, and for the most part, I have attempted to incorporate pertinent information in footnotes or in consolidated commentary situated at the beginning/middle/end of each month's entries. However, the backstory *is* part of Lucy's story; thus, as her sojourn in Texas ends and she begins her journey northward, additional commentary will be used to properly introduce new characters and situate them within both Lucy's saga and their appropriate place in history.

Lucy was a prolific diarist, and the multitude of her entries could easily occupy several volumes. Therefore, careful and consistent editorial decisions have been made. Because early diary entries set the tone for the entire text and introduce Lucy's voice, as few as possible will be excluded. However, entry sequences that become repetitious and offer little new or enhanced understanding of Lucy's ongoing narrative will be silently omitted. Keep in mind that these omissions in no way compromise the value of Lucy's observations or perceptions. Nor will any understanding of Lucy's "story lines" be sacrificed. The amendments are a regrettable, but necessary, concession to editorial constraints, but are not intended to privilege information, obscure Lucy's meanings, or otherwise bias the text. Even Lucy acknowledged that the days (hence, the diary entries) could be repetitive, for she recorded in her earlier journal that "this is one of the days in which the sayings and doings are so monotinous that my poor journal will suffer; sometimes I think I will not pretend to keep one then again I think it may afford me some pleasure to look over when at home" (Lucy Stevens, 2/7/61). Thankfully, she decided to continue, and her abundant records offer us a full, rich picture of her life in Texas.

DRAMATIS PERSONAE

FAMILY

James Bradford Pier (Uncle Pier)
Lu Merry Pier (Aunt Lu)
Lucy's mother's sister

CHILDREN
Sarah Pier (Cousin Sarah)
Sammy Pier (Cousin Sammy)
Lu Pier Cochran (Cousin Lu)

SLAVES
Dick, Parrot, Winnie, Ellen

Waller Cochran (Cousin Waller)
Lu Cochran (Cousin Lu)
Daughter of J. B. & Lu Pier

SON
Willie Cochran

SLAVES
Catharine, Lucinda, Sally, Ike,
George, Rose, Beckie, Willis

Uncle Martin Merry
Aunt Hannah Merry
*Aunt Lu's brother; Lucy's
mother's brother*

FRIENDS

Mr. Bell & Elizabeth Bell
    Callie, Sack, Newt, Jane,
    Shiloah, Sallie Lu
George Bell
Mr. & Mrs. Brewer
    Lissie, Mollie, Elizabeth,
    Sallie Pier
Mr. & Mrs. Buck
    Bella
Mrs. Cameron
    Artie, Willie
Mr. & Mrs. Cyrus Campbell
    Austin
Mr. & Mrs. Rufus Campbell
    Sarah
Mr. & Mrs. Catlin
    Sallie Lou, Todie, Sukie
Mr. & Mrs. Chapman
    Charley
Mrs. Clemmons
    Sallie, Jimmy
Mr. & Mrs. Cleveland
    Annie, Caroline
Mrs. Cochran
    Nehemiah (Neh), Emma,
    Jimmie, Mollie, Tallie
"Uncle" Jimmy Cochran

Mr. & Mrs. Darnman
    Lulu
Lydia Francis
Anson Harvey
Lissie Jackson
Sallie Kavanaugh
Kate Kenney, Sue Kenney
Dentist Lee
Mr. & Mrs. Lott
    Emily
Dr. & Mrs. McLarin
    Sallie, Bolie, Sue, Fannie
Mollie McNeese
Mr. & Mrs. Middleton
Annie Roach
Bracey Roach
Mrs. S
    Joe, Ruf, & Ino Campbell
Grandma Swearingen
Sallie Swearingen
Sallie T.
Sis Torrence
Tom
Sue Wilson

SOLDIER BOYS

George Bell
Joe Blakley
Harry Bracey
Benton Brewer
Rufus Brewer
Jim Brewer
William Brewer
Trav C
Cy Campbell
Joe Campbell (died)
Ino Campbell
Mack Campbell
Jake Catlin
Mr. Chesley (former teacher/Travis)
Jimmy Clemmons
Nehemiah (Neh) Cochran
Jack Cochran (died)
Hez Collins
Kinch Collins
Ino E
Billy Fordtran
Stickney Fowler (died)
Jimmy Francis (died)
John Harvey
Ino Harvey
Captain Hunt
Martin Kenny
Nick Merry (deserted)
Robert Minton
Sammy Pier
Charlie Uckert
Henry P. Wiley

ACQUAINTANCES

Marion Adams

Captain S. Adkins (aboard the *Fox*)

"Aunt" Violet & "Uncle" Frank
  (lost home in fire)

Lieut. Baldwin (visiting Havana)

Mr. Baldwin & Bessie (friends of Uncle
  Martin)

Mr. & Mrs. Harry Bracey

Mr. & Mrs. Bush (residents of
  Hempstead)

Mrs. George Chambers (friend of Mrs.
  Peebles)

Mrs. Clark (friend of Mrs. Peebles)

Dr. & Mrs. Cocke, Willie

Louise (a slave)

Mrs. Day, Fanny

Mr. Dunn

Mrs. Fadi (resident of Hempstead)

Mr. Ferris (resident of Galveston)

Mr. & Mrs. Billy Francis (lived near
  Cousin Lu)

Mr. Groves (resident of Hempstead)

Mr. Joseph Hendley (Galveston)

Mr. William Hendley (Galveston)

Parson Kenney

Mr. Linn

Mr. & Mrs. Mason (residents of
  Galveston)

Miss McHenry

Mr. & Mrs. Jim Middleton

Jennie Minton

Mr. Murdock (aboard the *Fox*)

Mrs. Paine

Dr. & Mrs. Peebles

Maggie, Rachel, Samie

Mr. & Mrs. Pilley

Mrs. Purcell, Sue

Dr. & Mrs. Richie

Mrs. Scranton (resident of Galveston)

Mr. John Sleight (Galveston)

Miss Mary Smith

Bell Snood

Mrs. Stevens, Ella

TIMELINE

1863

	TEXAS (THROUGH LUCY'S EYES)	TRANS-MISSISSIPPI THEATER	MAIN EASTERN AND WESTERN THEATERS
Ch.1 January 1863	*Lucy writes about capture of *Harriet Lane* in Galveston Bay and a feared slave insurrection *Much visiting with friends	*Grant begins Vicksburg campaign (Dec. '62) *Conf. Gen. Marmaduke begins campaign into MO	*Lincoln issues Emancipation Proclamation *Battle at Murfreesboro *Burnside, Commander of Army of Potomac resigns following Fredericksburg
Ch.2 February 1863	*Rainy weather limits visits with friends *Much time spent in clothing production (consistent in entire journal) *Reading	Gen. Richard Taylor's troops capture Union gunboat *Queen of the West* near Fort DeRussy, LA	Gen. Joe Hooker reinvigorates Union troops after his appointment as commander of Army of Potomac in January
Ch.3 March 1863	*Letters received from soldiers/written from New Iberia, LA *Reading Sir Walter Scott's *Waverly* novels	*Lieut. Gen. Kirby Smith appointed commander of Trans-Mississippi Department *Troops from TX & LA capture gunboat *Diana* at Berwick's Bay, LA	*Fighting accelerates on all fronts with coming of spring *North institutes conscription with Enrollment Act of 1863
Ch.4 April–May 1863	*Deadly measles epidemic strikes *Letters received reporting fighting in LA (previous month) *Fair planned to raise funds for soldiers	*Confederate defeats at Brashear City, Fort Bisland, Irish Bend, & Vermillion Bay, LA *Banks's army begins 48-day siege of Port Hudson *Following several battles, Grant begins siege of Vicksburg	*Battle at Chancellorsville; "Stonewall" Jackson killed *Battle at Fredericksburg *Rioting in Richmond by women demanding food

Ch.5 June–July 1863	*No Fourth of July celebration *Stickney Fowler dies *Regional war news arrives; much is erroneous	*Siege of Vicksburg ends in Confederate surrender *Siege of Port Hudson ends, opening entire Mississippi River to Union troops	*Battle of Gettysburg *Rioting in New York City over conscription
Ch.6 August–September 1863	*Lucy begins teaching school *Buckhorn revival takes place *Grim details of Vicksburg siege arrive *Gloom/weariness descends on area	*Battle at Sterling's Plantation, LA *44 Confederate troops repel Union invasion of Texas at Sabine Pass, TX	*Southern inflation spirals out of control *Major battles at Chicka- mauga, GA & Chattanooga, TN
Ch.7 October–December, 1863	*Local violence in Hempstead *Dr. Peebles arrested *Soldiers arrive home on furlough	Tom Green's cavalry surprises Union troops in attack at Bayou Bourbeau, LA	Battles at Chattanooga, Lookout Mountain & Missionary Ridge

1864

	TEXAS (THROUGH LUCY'S EYES)	TRANS-MISSISSIPPI THEATER	MAIN EASTERN AND WESTERN THEATERS
Ch.8 January–February, 1864	*Soldiers leave for LA *School resumes *Worries over smallpox vaccinations	General Dick Taylor begins preparing for coming invasion and battles in LA	Northern plans for invasion of TX via the Red River begin to take shape
Ch.9 March–April, 1864	*Soldiers back home for final furloughs before LA fighting commences *Many parties to honor soldiers *Cousin Sarah engaged	*Red River Campaign rages *In heavy fighting, culmi- nating in decisive victory at Mansfield, LA, Gen. Richard Taylor thwarts Banks's plans to invade TX	Grant becomes general in chief of all Union armies
Ch.10 May–June, 1864	*Lucy attends closing exercises at Chappell Hill *Miss Mary Smith departs, attempting to travel to the North *Illness rampant	Union forces burn Alex- andria, LA, as they retreat following collapse of Red RiverCampaign	*Major battles in the Wilder- ness & Spotsylvania, GA *Campaign for Atlanta begins

Ch.11 July– September, 1864	*Local feuds/violence on rise *Lucy becomes critically ill	Confederate general Sterling Price begins expedition into MO	*Battles for Atlanta, July 20–Sept. 1 *Atlanta falls, Sept. 2 *Sheridan conducts Shenandoah Valley campaign
Ch.12 October– December, 1864	*Little war news; conflicting rumors increase *Miss Mary Smith sends word of safe arrival	Price's expedition into MO ends in defeat	*Lincoln wins re-election, beating Democratic "peace" candidate *Sherman begins "March to the Sea," burning Atlanta on Nov. 15

1865

	TEXAS (THROUGH LUCY'S EYES)	TRANS-MISSISSIPPI THEATER	MAIN EASTERN AND WESTERN THEATERS
Ch.13 January, 1865	*Sarah marries *Lucy receives letter from Ohio	Bands of outlaws/gangs roam countryside	US Congress passes Thirteenth Amendment, abolishing slavery
Ch.14 February– March, 1865	*Much local violence *Realization of Confederate defeat widespread *Soldiers arriving home, making plans to marry *Lucy plans return to Ohio	*Fighting has ceased *Troops withdrawn & sent to other areas	*Lincoln inaugurated/begins second term *Charleston burned in Sherman's advance to the sea
Ch.15 April 1–16, 1865	*Lucy tells TX family & friends good-bye *Lucy leaves Travis, travels to Houston, then Galveston	At war's end, Confederacy still controls "90% of Louisiana, all of Texas except for Brownsville, and most of Arkansas," making Trans-Mississippi the only district "not conquered by force of arms"*	*Grant takes Petersburg *Richmond falls *Lee surrenders to Grant at Appomattox Courthouse on April 9 *Lincoln assassinated April 14
Ch.16 April 17– May 4, 1865	*Lucy travels to Havana, then sails to NYC *Journal ends May 4; last entry written on train to Ohio	*General Edmund Kirby surrenders Trans-Mississippi army, May 26 *Confederate forces defeat Union soldiers at Palmito Ranch, in south TX, in last battle of Civil War	*Gen. Richard Taylor surrenders remaining Confederate forces east of Mississippi, May 4 *Jefferson Davis captured May 10

*Thomas Ayres, *Dark and Bloody Ground*, 263.

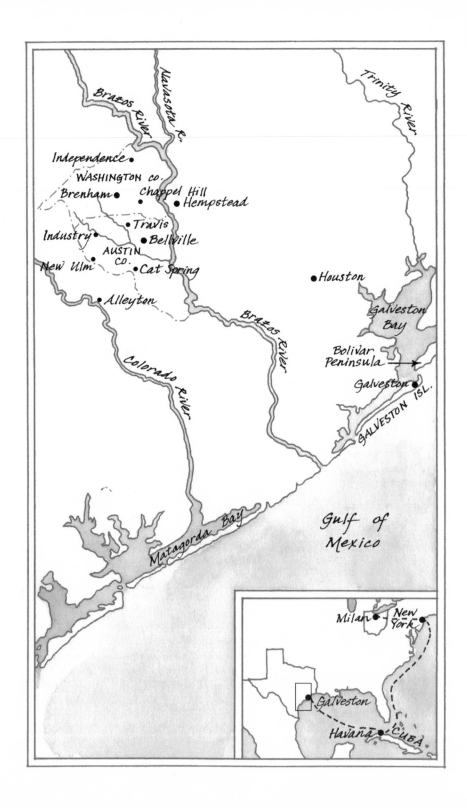

LUCY

Herself, Her Family,
Her Friends

LUCY PIER STEVENS weighed her options and impetuously made her decision—she decided to sneak out of Texas! At twenty-six, she had lived for more than five years as an unintended resident of the state, caught within the web of the Civil War, far from her home and her immediate family in Ohio. Now, unable to obtain permission to openly travel north, she took advantage of an unexpected opportunity, risky though it might be, to escape on a Confederate blockade runner's ship. And on April 17, 1865, with fifteen minutes' notice, Lucy Stevens sailed out of Galveston Bay, leaving behind extended family and a multitude of friends who had embraced her as one of their own. But why would she do such a thing when Lee had surrendered more than a week earlier? The answer is clear—she simply didn't know. Although the battlefield had grown silent and the ink had dried on the papers signed at Appomattox, neither Lucy nor anyone around her knew that the war was over. And that's not all she didn't know. As Lucy boarded the blockade runner *Fox*, risking everything to go home, she had no idea that she was sailing into history, for as an undocumented passenger on the ship, she may well have been along for the ride on the last blockade run of the Civil War.

But Lucy's story, recounted in her own words, begins much earlier, on a lighthearted journey down the Mississippi River with her cousin Sarah and several friends. Arriving in Texas on Christmas Day, 1859, Lucy came to visit her mother's sister, Lu Merry Pier, and other family. Fortunately, the diaries of Aunt Lu and her daughter Sarah, both housed in the Texas Collection at

Baylor University, provide additional details regarding the visit. It seems that Sarah, who was two years younger than Lucy, had traveled to Ohio for a visit in June 1859, and Aunt Lu recorded on October 5, "Got a letter from Wm. B. Stevens dated Sept. 20th Sarah wrote some in it too—says he wants Sarah to stay there and go to school." With no further reference to the offer of schooling, Aunt Lu later recorded that Sarah had written home, telling them, "Lue Stevens thinks some that she will come home with [me]" (11/4/59). Since Lucy Stevens's main diary commences on January 1, 1863, this information from Lucy Merry Pier's diary explains Lucy's presence, providing background and helpful details. However, an entry written in Lucy's own hand provides additional insight into her visit, even as it raises questions. In the 1860–1861 volume of her diary, which surfaced only recently, Lucy wrote:

> My mother knew full well to whom she was giving the care of her to often erring daughter but thanks to that gentle teacher who always advised me to listen to the instructions of truth & wisdom; I am willing to be told my faults and will try to correct them.
>   Lucy Stevens, 6/7/61

Lucy provided no further detail regarding the circumstances that precipitated her journey to Texas, and no inferences of wrongdoing should be entertained; Lucy's own perspectives, revealed over time, in fact, uphold her sense of propriety and her strong morals, even as they reveal her maturation from girl to woman. This maturing could perhaps be one of the most significant aspects of the earlier text. With the carelessness of a young girl, the earlier journal includes sporadic entries, with large gaps of time in between, while the later volumes, written between 1863 and 1865, indicate much more discipline, with few lapses of time, and those due only to illness. The stresses and strains of the Civil War no doubt enhanced a contemplation naturally occurring with maturity, and in those instances when Lucy recorded not just the daily events, but her responses and reflections as well, the heartbeat of a strong young woman can be measured.

Just who was Lucy Pier Stevens, and why was she in Texas? The fifth of six children born to Jacob and Mary Stevens, Lucy began her life in a small town in Ohio on June 6, 1838. The town, Milan, is located near the southwestern shores of Lake Erie, and Lucy's grandparents were among its founders. Scattered from Ohio to Texas, Lucy's family was large, and despite long distances and slow travel, they expended much effort in keeping close ties with each branch. Whether by letter or by personal visit, the Texas family and the Ohio family stayed in frequent contact. Lucy's mother, Mary Merry Stevens, in fact, had two siblings in Texas: her sister, Lucy Merry Pier, and her brother, Martin Merry. Uncle Martin and his wife, Aunt Hannah, as Lucy called them, however, lived some distance from the Piers, and Lucy's diary focuses more sharply on her involvement with Aunt Lu and her family.

James Bradford Pier and his bride, Lu Merry Pier, had come to Texas from Ohio in 1835, only one year after their marriage, having been attracted to the region by the reports of Moses and Stephen Austin.[1] As a young couple, ages twenty-two and twenty-one, respectively, they had forged a life for themselves in a land that successively took the name of Mexican territory, republic, and state. James Bradford Pier, in fact, had been required to obtain a Mexican passport at New Orleans to enter this land. The passport, dated February 5, 1835, enabled them to travel inland from the mouth of the Brazos River, eventually settling in what would become the early town of Travis, Texas. Soon after their arrival, Texas declared its independence from Mexico, and hostilities ensued. Pier volunteered to aid in the fight, and on March 1, 1836, he left home with neighbors to assist in the relief of the Alamo. En route they learned that the mission/fortress had fallen, and they quickly returned home to relocate their families to a place of safety. Then, "when the advancing Mexican armies threatened their new homes, James Pier and his neighbors joined Sam Houston's army for their defense."[2] Houston's army had retreated through Austin County, Pier's home area, on their trek northward up the Brazos, and Pier joined them once again. After the victory at San Jacinto, Pier wrote proudly to his wife of the victory, telling her, "This Country is ours."[3]

On January 11, 1838, Pier appeared before the Board for Land and was given a league and a labor of land for his service in the war for independence.[4] A league encompassed 4,428 acres and a labor covered 177 acres, with the value of a league in Texas being roughly comparable to 80 acres in the states.[5] Pier then received "640 acres of donation land from the state of Texas in 1854. He also received two bounty warrants for 320 acres each for further service to the Republic of Texas."[6] This amount of acreage enabled Pier to become

1. Robert J. and Cristy Pier, Bellville, Texas: Pier Family Genealogical History.

2. Ibid.

3. James Bradford Pier, Pier Family Papers (Texas Collection, Baylor University, Waco).

4. *Austin County Texas Deed Abstracts, 1837–1852, Republic of Texas, State of Texas*, Abstractor, Joyce Martin Murray (Wolfe City: Henington Publishing, 1987).

5. Elizabeth Silverthorne, *Plantation Life in Texas* (College Station: Texas A&M University Press, 1986), 11–15.

6. "James Bradford Pier," *The Handbook of Texas Online* (Texas State Historical Association).

James Bradford Pier. DeGolyer Library, Southern Methodist University,
Lucy Pier Stevens Collection.
—

a prosperous farmer and storekeeper, as well as a leader in his community, serving as justice of the peace for Austin County in 1843, as the first postmaster of Travis, and as Confederate postmaster during the war. Because of these contributions, James Bradford Pier was accorded "historical" status, and appropriate markers at his gravesite and near the site of Travis were erected in the 1980s.

Lucy Merry Pier bore five children, three of whom survived to adulthood: Lucy Eliza Pier, born at Travis on May 7, 1837; Sarah Charlotte Pier, born at Travis on November 7, 1840; and Samuel Bradford Pier, born July 22, 1844, at Travis. By the time Lucy began keeping her 1863 diary, Lucy Eliza (Cousin Lu) had married Waller Cochran and was the mother of a little boy, Willie. Sarah remained actively occupied at home, helping her mother in the running of the household, and Sammy was a foot soldier in the Confederate army.

The Piers had ultimately settled in the south central region of Texas, in the area chosen by Stephen F. Austin for his original colony. Watered by the Guadalupe, Colorado, and Brazos Rivers, the land was entirely arable, with rich soil providing the basis for a wide variety of crops. In 1882, A. W. Spaight, then commissioner of insurance, statistics, and history in Texas, described the seven hundred square miles of the Gulf plain of Texas as containing forest land and rolling hills with many streams breaking up the bands of timber. The northern part of the country was covered by post oak, while a wide variety of oak, elm, walnut, and pecan trees dotted other portions of the land. Wild land could be purchased for one to ten dollars an acre.[7] Tiny communities, sometimes no more than a cluster of farmsteads scattered around a post office and a general store, sprinkled the countryside, with less than 5 percent of the population living in any kind of urban area.[8] Small farms, averaging approximately sixty acres, dominated the landscape. Hempstead, the only town of any size in the region, was a center of commerce, thanks to the rail system. Other small towns in the area included Industry (founded in 1831 as the first German settlement in Austin's colony),[9] Brenham, some twenty miles away, and Bellville, settled in 1822 by two of Austin's original Old Three Hundred.[10] Perhaps one of the best descriptions of Bellville comes from Lucy herself. Soon after her arrival, she made her first visit to Bellville and noted with delight the beauty of the small town, recording,

---

7. A. W. Spaight, *The Resources, Soil, and Climate of Texas* (Galveston: A. H. Belo and Company, Printers, 1882), 11–13.

8. Allen P. Ashcraft, *Texas in the Civil War: A Resume History* (Austin: Texas Civil War Centennial Commission, 1962), 7.

9. Kathleen St. Clair, *Little Towns of Texas* (Jacksonville: Jayroe Graphics, 1982), 448–449.

10. Ibid., 89–90.

the morning was fine and the ride delightful we arrived at Mr. Mannings door at an early hour and so had time to sit awhile before church . . . [I] went out on the front gallery to take a general survey of the town which is a very sandy place on a gradually rising point of ground so that you can look down on a surrounding country of cotton fields and open prairie covered with vast herds of cattle. In the central part of the village and in the center of the public square stands the court house a fine two story brick building with green blinds and surrounded by shade trees. It is the finest building in the village and is quite an ornament to the place. The negroes are all out in their holy day costumes and this part of town presents the appearance of a gala place. The church is west of the court house a white frame building and unfinished. The inside of it reminds me very much of an unfurnished cabinet shop; in the front end stood a long desk table with a violin box on it and in front of that was two officiating clergymen . . .

    Lucy Stevens, 3/4/60

As a newcomer, Lucy viewed the scene with a freshness long forfeited by the time she commenced her 1863 journal.

Travis, the home of the Pier family, was an even tinier town near Bellville. Founded in 1837, it boasted its own post office from 1839 until June 1870.[11] Today the town no longer exists, and it is necessary to refer to maps dated in the late 1800s to locate the hamlet.[12] The railroad bypassed the community, and according to Robert J. Pier, a descendant of James B. Pier, the town was never rebuilt after a fire destroyed it in the late 1870s.[13] All that remains today is tiny Travis cemetery on a ridge overlooking the rolling hills that surround Buffalo Creek where the gravesites of James B. Pier, Lucy Merry Pier, and others are carefully maintained. A marker designating J. B. Pier a "Citizen of the Republic of Texas" adorns his grave.

Unlike many other Texas households who suffered desperate hunger and deprivations due to the absence of their men during the war years, the Pier family enjoyed self-sufficiency and abundance. Evidence of both can easily be detected in Lucy's references, sprinkled throughout her journal, concerning expansive meals. From special birthday meals to Christmas dinners, Lucy's

---

11. William Hardt, Bellville Historical Society at Bellville, Texas, personal interview with Vicki Tongate, February 5, 2000.

12. Adolf Stieler, *Adolf Stieler's Hand Atlas* (Germany, 1896).

13. Robert J. Pier, telephone interview with Vicki Tongate, February 6, 2000.

Lucy Merry Pier. DeGolyer Library, Southern Methodist University,
Lucy Pier Stevens Collection.
—

menus and lists imply the bounty the family enjoyed. Lucy's notes concerning the abundance of food were corroborated just a few years later, when A. W. Spaight observed,

> With an average sized family, a farmer growing his own vegetables, meat, milk, butter, eggs, poultry, fruit, sugar, molasses, vinegar manufactured from sorghum, and wine from grapes and tomatoes, together with sufficient feed for his stock for the short period of the year when feed is necessary, can live in comfort, and even luxury, with a very small expenditure of money, the amount, of course, depending on his style of living.[14]

In addition to the basic foodstuffs, treats such as cakes, pies, cookies, and candies were often prepared for the family and as gifts to neighbors, and records from the period abound with standard recipes. One such compilation is Katherine Hart's *Pease Porridge Hot*, which lists a favorite of Lucadia Pease, wife of the governor of Texas in the 1850s. Mrs. Pease's recipe for sponge cake calls for: "2 cups full powdered sugar; 2 cupfuls flour sifted; 2 teaspoonfuls baking powder, 4 eggs, ¾ teacup boiling water, a pinch of salt and lemon to taste."[15] Special family dinners often included wine, and this too was made at home. In February 1863, Lucy noted that she had been treated to a "nice glass of wine," and on July 18 of the same year, Aunt Lu recorded, "Mr. Pier has the Negroes gathering grapes to make wine." Even so, as much as Lucy enjoyed a "nice glass of wine" or a "nog," nothing compared to a cup of "sure-enough coffee."

Lucy and Cousin Sarah were fast friends and spent as much time together as possible. Lucy complained about loneliness when Sarah was gone from home, and the two were often seen about the area, visiting friends, attending small gatherings, and even sharing in nursing duties when the situation warranted. Much insight into Lucy's person can, in fact, be gleaned by the contrasting responses that surface in their respective diaries. From time to time, for example, Sarah cited Lucy's enjoyment in social settings, noting on December 30, 1863, "Cousin Lue, Sallie, Jane, Mr. Wiley and Waller and Sis a little played cards and had a great time. Cous Lue is in great spirits—I think I never saw her more gay and lively." Lucy, outgoing and fun-loving, participated fully, using the parties as a social diversion and as a coping mechanism, while Sarah, more serious and contemplative, expressed reserve regarding her own involvement in the activities, writing:

---

14. Spaight, *The Resources, Soil, and Climate of Texas*, 13.
15. Katherine Hart, *Pease Porridge Hot* (Austin: Friends of the Austin Public Library, 1967), 27.

We have passed the time off very pleasantly however. Have music and card playing often—I never indulge in the latter amusement excepting once in a great while to please the rest I play "Old Maid" and played with them tonight having Jim for an *assistant*. Card playing is something that has no charm for me. I never tried to learn anything about it because I did not wish to. The mere playing is nothing more injurious to a person than playing backgammon or draughts but so much evil springs from it that I do not approve of it.

Sarah Pier, 12/30/63

Sarah's hesitation did not stop here, however. On New Year's Eve, she wrote, "the good folks had an egg nog today but that also I never indulge in although I dearly love the taste of it. And of liquor in any form but I *preach* against the use of such things only as medicine and therefore, I try to practice the rule I would have others follow" (12/31/63). Lucy, on the other hand, loved eggnog and had no qualms about enjoying that special treat.

From permissible social activities to choices in books, and even to religion, the young women held widely differing views. The choice of appropriate reading material, for example, aids in understanding the personality types of Lucy and Sarah. Lucy, a commonsense realist, took public opinion to heart and believed in the prevailing mores guiding her society. However, she made room for practicality and for preferences. She obviously saw no harm in the novels available to her and enjoyed them tremendously. Sarah, on the other hand, was an idealist, extremely sensitive to the moral codes of her faith and her community. Needing a justification that would legitimize these activities, Sarah made excuses and listed reasons that allowed for exemptions from censure. Constantly torn between guilty participation and moralistic abstinence, Sarah battled to find a level middle ground upon which to comfortably balance her principles and her practices. On occasion, she gave grudging approval of certain texts, writing,

Cousin Lue has been reading *Kenilworth* (one of the Waverly novels) to us today—it is very interesting—full of historical facts. I intend to read them all as I have an opportunity, although I am not in favor of much novel readings—but these novels are very useful I think—they give a person a better insight into the character and manners of people of Scotland and Eng. Than almost any other books and then they contain a great deal of history.

Sarah Pier, 3/24/63

Lucy's strong, independent personality, however, enabled her to enjoy herself without recriminations or regrets.

But Sarah was not alone in her quandary. Many wrestled with the same question. Since novels had been blamed for everything from moral decay to poor health among women, it is little wonder that such ambivalence could exist within the same household. Others in and around Travis shared Sarah's sentiments and wrote about their feelings accordingly. Among the items in the Robert J. and Christy Pier Family Papers are two essays that verbalize many of the same sentiments that Sarah expressed. One, signed by Emma Cochran, asks the question:

"What Shall We Read"

This all important question may be answered in various ways. Some may say read that which is interesting and pleasing. Others may say read extensively the works of the best authors. This however would be my advice, It is wrong that young persons should indulge in trashy worthless reading. Here may be mentioned the greater part of novels which forever ruin the mind and taste. We should ever be in search of Knowledge—such as will be useful in after years. This can only be gained by an attentive study of the works of our best authors. The advantages of reading extensively are innumerable, We would by no means pass over the "Book of Books" the Bible. There we are taught our duties and obligations to God & to man. We should read it with a view to put its precepts & truths to practice. Persons very often prefer spending their time in idleness in preference to reading & improving the mind. This should not be so. If one is afflicted & unable to work, there is one consolation there are books of any kind that would please them.

Emma Cochran[16]

Lucy believed in her own good sense as a woman, however, and despite cultural constraints, had little use for anything or anyone who demeaned a woman's independence. At one point, she recorded that she had read a friend's love letter in which the friend's suitor expressed his admiration for her independent character. The suitor, however, tempered his admiration with rebuke by telling the lady that "he did not deem it [her independent character] prudent" (4/9/63). Lucy's response to the situation can be measured not by her words, but by her sarcastic use of punctuation to indicate her disgust. On

---

16. Robert J. and Cristy Pier, Pier Family Papers.

other occasions, she candidly noted her disagreement with certain church leaders over dancing and even wrote that she had stopped attending Sunday School because she had decided it "did not pay" (6/14/63). These gentle rejections of prescribed behavior signal a strength of character embedded in Lucy, and it appears in small decisions and quiet opinions throughout her journal. Although she readily subscribed to the commonly accepted conventions of womanhood, she was clearly a strong, self-directed woman who had no qualms about charting her own course. Yet even as we see this in many small ways throughout the diary, nowhere is her autonomy projected as clearly as when she quickly decided, despite the misgivings of her friends, to take her chances aboard the blockade runner *Fox*. And in that moment, in that one decision, Lucy demolished any doubt of her own independence and secured for herself a place in Civil War chronicles. For not only did she sail with one of the South's most noted blockade runners on his only trip into Galveston, but the *New York Times* in 1892 indicated that Captain Adkins's foray into Galveston may well have been "about the last run of the war."[17] Lucy's impetuous decision, then, to "hitch a ride" situated her as an unintended participant in history. As far as is known, no logs or official records showing Lucy's presence aboard the *Fox* exist. But for her own detailed account, the fact that one of the last blockade runs of the Civil War carried as a passenger a young civilian—a woman alone—would have remained hidden.

Lucy's more flexible opinions must not, however, be mistaken for weakness of character. She held strong views on issues such as drunkenness and, on occasion, railed about another's lack of self-control. In one entry, Lucy noted with censure the inebriated state of Mr. Banks, and with a tone of disdain, unmistakably expressed her convictions on drunkenness. Clearly in keeping with the nineteenth-century stance on temperance, Lucy had no use for such a wastrel. She had recently noted, without comment, that Mr. B had come home "boosy," but now she gave vent to her disgust.

These ideas echoed public opinion that predated the Civil War. Temperance groups had found their beginnings during the 1830s in the aftermath of the Great Awakening, when women had exercised their communal voice to attempt to stamp out alcohol abuse. Sara M. Evans, author of *Born for Liberty*, claims that this "politicized domesticity" sought to implement programs through the churches such as missionary societies and Sunday Schools. In the process, moral reform covering everything from temperance to prostitution

---

17. "Running the Blockade: Exciting Experiences of Those Who Made It a Business," *New York Times*, October 2, 1892, New York Times Article Archive.

to abolition became the cry of the day. Names such as Catharine Beecher, Susan B. Anthony, and Elizabeth Cady Stanton became familiar as these women took up the call for female education, suffrage, and property rights.

With the coming of the war, however, these focused efforts were sidelined in favor of women's aid societies, organizations designed to provide supplies and funds for soldiers on both sides of the conflict. Yet the hiatus was only temporary. By the early 1870s, Evans notes, "women took to the streets, picking up the thread of temperance activism from the pre-Civil War years" (125). The Women's Christian Temperance Union, under the leadership of Frances Willard, came to the fore in 1873 in an effort to stamp out alcohol consumption, as women across the country saw an opportunity to make their voices count in a public setting.[18]

Lucy was surely cognizant of these events—a women's rights convention staged in her home state of Ohio in 1851 had seen the emergence of Sojourner Truth, a former slave woman whose "Ar'n't I a Woman" speech had stunned and inspired attendees—and, given her views expressed here, Lucy may very well have participated in some of the rallies herself. However, in a departure from rigid temperance standards, Lucy's views on drinking differed from her views on drunkenness. In other entries, Lucy clearly indicated that she enjoyed a glass of wine or eggnog. For her, moderation was key, and with her usual circumspect style, without hypocrisy, she downplayed one and degraded the other.

That Lucy was an autonomous and self-directed decision maker cannot be disputed. However, her enjoyment of her own femininity is equally clear. Lucy loved clothes! The need to look fashionable in spite of clothing and cloth shortages remained uppermost in her mind, and she perused old issues of *Godey's Lady's Book*, the fashion bible of the 1860s, adapting her wardrobe as nearly as possible. She frequently mentioned what other young women were wearing, cognizant of the idealization of "homespun" cloth and ever aware of the popular hoop skirt. The styles that had evolved in Texas included the "huge hoop-skirted dress designed by the romantic Victorians of the fifties and sixties," which, as David Holman reports, supported voluminous skirts with circumferences up to thirty feet and weights of as much as fifteen pounds.[19] Often men were flabbergasted by the popularity of the style. In 1858 Sam Houston wrote to his wife and mentioned the hoop skirt, stating

---

18. Sara M. Evans, *Born for Liberty: A History of Women in America* (New York: Simon and Schuster, 1997), 75, 101, 125–127.

19. David Holman, *Buckskin and Homespun: Texas Frontier Clothing, 1820–1870* (Austin: Wind River Press, 1979), 28.

that it was "difficult to say what side should go before. My only object is to keep out of their way, and as the sailors say 'give them sea way.'"[20]

However, while women coveted the cumbersome contraptions and men looked upon them as a nuisance, contemporary critics assign a darker meaning than simply fleeting fashion. Helene Roberts maintains that types of clothing "signal to the world the role the wearer may be expected to play and remind the wearer of the responsibilities of that role, its constraints and limitations."[21] Holman concurs, asserting, "A woman was idealized as a helpless, fragile 'angel' whose duty was to marry a brave and handsome 'prince' and whose sole responsibility was to her 'castle.' Her passive role in society was depicted by her restricted movements."[22] Sometimes referred to as a cage, the hoop visualizes the language of Coventry Patmore's sentimental Victorian poem "The Angel in the House," in which he compares a young woman to a caged bird, fearful of freedom until her protecting lover opens the door.[23] Styling prescriptive Victorian behavior into romantic eloquence, Patmore reinforces by word the responsibilities of the woman's dependent role in society. By the very limitations they impose on the wearer, the hoops, then, reinforce by sight this same responsibility. Nonetheless, while Lucy subscribed to the nineteenth-century expectations of her sex and even enjoyed the accoutrements of that society, she would have disdained the generic social commentary assigned to her simply because of her choice of fashion.

As young women of similar age, Lucy and Sarah enjoyed each other's company immensely; however, theirs was not an exclusive bond. Their feminine network spread throughout the community to include women of all ages. Lucy and Sarah both held firmly to the nineteenth-century convention of a separate feminine sphere, consisting of a large array of both intimate and casual associations with other women. They used the "institution of visiting—that endless trooping of women to each other's homes for social purposes"[24] to reinforce the strength of the network. Laurel Ulrich identifies

20. Ibid., 84.

21. Helene E. Roberts, "The Exquisite Slave: The Role of Clothes in the Making of the Victorian Woman," *Signs: Journal of Women in Culture and Society* 2, no. 3; reprinted in *Course Reader English 3341: Women in the Age of Victoria*, ed. Beth Newman (Southern Methodist University, Dallas, Fall 1998), 55.

22. Holman, *Buckskin and Homespun*, 68.

23. Coventry Patmore, "The Angel in the House," *Poems*, 4th ed. (London, 1890). Reprinted in Newman, *Course Reader*, 1.

24. Carroll Smith-Rosenberg, "The Female World of Love and Ritual: Relations between Women in Nineteenth-Century America," in *Women's America: Refocusing the Past*, ed. Linda K. Kerber and Jane Sherron DeHart, 4th ed. (New York: Oxford University Press, 1995), 173.

this custom as "gadding," a form of networking, not about "intense and sentimental relations with a few persons, but about intermittent and seemingly casual encounters with many," and documents it as a prevalent convention during the eighteenth century.[25] Although Lucy never appropriated the term, she repeatedly verified the continuation of the practice. Her diary, in fact, opens with an account of visiting in which the guests came prepared to stay, bringing their knitting with them and sharing a meal, and these types of references continue throughout. There was little segregation within or among age groupings; young and old alike enjoyed one another's company and congregated in their homes to pass the time with friends and acquaintances. Through these networks of care and common ground, they traded local gossip, household hints, and always, of course, war news and concerns. On those rare days when no caller graced the doorway, Lucy took care to note the event in her journal. Other mentions of quiet time were recorded as well, for even Lucy occasionally grew weary of the constant parade of visitors. She was not alone in her visitor fatigue—other diarists of the period recorded similar frustrations, often with more feeling than Lucy did. Kate Stone of Tyler confided her own resentment, writing, "Spending the day is my perfect aversion. Whoever started the trying fashion of spending the day? It is too much of a good thing."[26] However, since Lucy enjoyed people and activity, her "aversion" was much milder and shorter in duration. She merely relished the time alone as brief intervals between periods of enjoyable fellowship.

The countless references in the diaries to "us girls" point to the importance of these associations in Sarah's and Lucy's lives, and their many relationships reflect the size of the spreading system that defined Travis. Kinship ties formed the basic pattern of the network. Aunt Lu, her daughters, Lu and Sarah, and Lucy Pier Stevens stood at the center of their group, despite Cousin Lu's nonresidential status. Carroll Smith-Rosenberg stresses that the "emotional ties between nonresidential kin were deep and binding and provided one of the fundamental existential realities of women's lives."[27] From within this tight-knit unit, the strands spread among friends and interlocked with other core family units. As women helped one another with chores and projects, and aided their neighbors in times of sickness and sorrow, the ties grew stronger, transcending space, time, and age to form an integral part of their lives. Visits lasted days, even weeks, as women shared the understanding and emotional support they craved. Many times women stayed with one another

25. Laurel Thatcher Ulrich, A Midwife's Tale (New York: Vintage Books, 1990), 93.

26. John Austin Edwards, "Social and Cultural Activities of Texans during the Civil War and Reconstruction, 1861–1873" (PhD diss., Texas Tech University, 1985), 31.

27. Smith-Rosenberg, "Female World of Love and Ritual," 173.

for extended periods during their husbands' absences; thus, Lucy's mention of Mrs. Buck's insistent invitation for "some of us [to] go stay all night with her, as Mr B was gone to Houston" was entirely unremarkable (7/14/63).

The feminine network associated with the doctrine of separate spheres, or the "Cult of Domesticity," as it has also been called, had originated in the Northeast, finding its roots in the beginning of the nineteenth century. Women, eager to be a part of the new republic, found new power and authority in the home as they endeavored to raise virtuous and responsible citizens to populate the newly independent country. They played a supportive, background role within the seclusion of the home, while their husbands carried out their breadwinning responsibilities in a public, commercial environment. And although the women had no public role, the charge of raising the next generation of leaders for America gave them an increased sense of their own worth and propelled them into a more forceful role as wives and mothers.

A primary supporter of the concept of separate spheres and one of the most public women of her day, Catharine Beecher believed that women could sustain social order by nurturing their children and submitting to their husbands' authority. Thanks to Beecher and other proponents, domestic responsibilities came to be seen as morally uplifting, a means by which patience and perseverance could be developed. Accomplishments such as needlework and floral arranging were extolled as activities engaged in by "True Women" as they sought to promote peace and beauty within the home. They were known for their virtue, as demonstrated by piety, purity, submissiveness, and domesticity.[28] The appellation of "True Woman" came to be regarded as the comforting mark of stability in a rapidly changing society. That this was a common perception is exemplified by Aunt Lu's remarks early in 1863. Her skill in needlework qualified her as expert, and it was high praise indeed for her to comment, "Mary Cameron helped me on Waller's coat yesterday we got along with it finely she is such good help and such a true woman" (Lu M. Pier, 1/6/63). Typical of Aunt Lu's style, the compliment came as recognition of Mary Cameron's household abilities, not her personality.

But how did the concept of separate spheres fare in Texas? Barbara Welter proposes that both westward expansion and the Civil War undermined the Cult of Domesticity. Both forces "called forth responses from woman which differed from those she was trained to believe were hers by nature and divine decree."[29] Although the Northeast served as the preliminary paradigm for

---

28. Barbara Welter, *Dimity Convictions: The American Woman in the Nineteenth Century* (Athens: Ohio University Press, 1976), 21–39.

29. Ibid., 41.

women's social behavior, adjustments were necessary to include the variations found in other regions. Mary Beth Norton concurs, stating, "Studies of the diaries of pioneer women show how the sex roles learned in eastern areas broke down under the stresses of frontier life."[30] Thus, while the basic tenets of separate spheres held firm, even in places like Travis, many adaptations were necessarily made to accommodate a rural, rustic life.

All three Pier family diaries offer evidence of the accommodations made to life in Texas, with some precepts being validated and others being amended, or even discarded. The lack of industrialization in Texas retarded the development of a separate masculine sphere in which men left home for a workplace elsewhere. In the rural domestic economy of Travis, men like James Bradford Pier ran the post office or the general store, but this was in addition to the main enterprise of farming. The women's responsibilities centered around the house, with food preparation and clothing manufacture being their dominant responsibilities. According to Aunt Lu's entries, even major responsibility for the garden fell under Uncle Pier's jurisdiction, and it took a catastrophe on the order of a severe hailstorm to draw the girls to the fields for inspection. Early in Aunt Lu's diary, she had noted that all were picking cotton (10/7/59). Within a few years, however, the designation had changed, and she specified, "The Negroes that are well are picking cotton" (8/20/62). It is certain, however, from Lucy's diary that even if the female members of the household were included in field labor in the early years, by 1860, when Lucy began her journal, the division of labor was complete. Even though it is highly probable that Aunt Lu had spent her share of time in the field, by the time her daughters were grown, the situation had changed.

Sandra Myres, author of *Westering Women and the Frontier Experience*, notes, "The frontier, like the trail, tended to blur sex roles . . . from the earliest colonial frontiers, women worked beside their men to help clear the land, fell trees, construct a shelter, and plant and harvest crops."[31] While men and women like the Piers brought with them their preconceived ideas of roles and responsibilities, these necessarily required adaptation to meet the unique needs of their own locale.

Thus, the "world" of Texas to which Lucy Stevens came in 1859 seems to be more of an accommodation of the aspects of various times and places than a specifically prescripted existence, labeled according to the theoretical

---

30. Mary Beth Norton, "The Paradox of 'Women's Sphere,'" in *Women of America: A History*, ed. Carol Ruth Berkin and Mary Beth Norton (Boston: Houghton-Mifflin, 1979), 142.

31. Sandra Myres, *Westering Women and the Frontier Experience, 1800–1915* (Albuquerque: University of New Mexico Press, 1982), 160.

definitions of one dominant philosophy. In addition to a melding of the social constraints of the Northeast and the plantation economy of the South, life in Texas also included a resemblance to the paradigm of the Midwestern farming family. Farm life in the Midwest was based on the cycle of the seasons. Work was shared by all, and common goals were achieved by the fulfillment of different responsibilities. Men were not the sole breadwinners in this domestic economy of farming; they were partners in production with their wives.[32] This cultural construction bears many similarities to Hallowell, Maine, where, Laurel Ulrich contends, "Martha's diary shows how women and men worked together to sustain [the] eighteenth-century town."[33] The "neighborly exchange"[34] carried on by Martha and her counterparts, a bartering type of trade-off among neighbors, was based on a gender division of labor that guaranteed women a place in the economy. Many of the same types of activities are found in the Pier and Stevens diaries, as neighbors assisted neighbors, doing whatever they could to help one another successfully negotiate their lives.

Sandra Myres also argues that many women's diaries reflect a sense of self-esteem connected with women's work and a true respect for the contributions that women made to the partnership of the home. The entries show an understanding of the farm's economic position and indicate that husbands and wives regularly discussed farm-related topics. She asserts, "Many women considered theirs a cooperative rather than a competitive enterprise, and they certainly did not view their position as 'second class.'"[35] Sarah's and Lucy's diaries show little indication of concern about matters relating to an economic hierarchy; however, Aunt Lu's diary validates Myres's claim. Her journal indicates a partnership relationship with Uncle Pier, one in which views were expressed and differences resolved. The two of them worked at keeping communication flowing smoothly, and they moved swiftly to resolve tensions. On March 20, 1860, Aunt Lu confided, "I said something that offended him . . . had an explanation of matters." While she omitted any references to the source of the tension, the matter was important enough to her to mention in her diary. Equally important to her was the successful discussion that followed, resolving the issue. Their partnership efforts paid dividends as together they surveyed the fruit of their labors. Repeatedly, Aunt Lu wrote of

32. John Mack Faragher, "The Midwestern Farming Family," in *Women's America: Refocusing the Past*, ed. Linda K. Kerber and Jane Sherron DeHart, 4th ed. (New York: Oxford University Press, 1995), 119–126.

33. Ulrich, *A Midwife's Tale*, 30.

34. Ibid., 76–77.

35. Myres, *Westering Women*, 165.

the two of them walking together around the fields, examining with satisfaction the results of their hard work.

Lucy, with her gregarious personality, did not simply limit herself to her female friends. Her network extended to include the young men of the area as well, the young men who were now soldiers in the Confederate army. She had been quickly accepted into the circle of young people and had come to know and love these soldier boys deeply. The Piers' son, Sammy, topped Lucy's list of local boys who had left the area to fight for the Confederate cause. Sammy, who had enlisted in the Confederate army on his seventeenth birthday, represents the involvement of thousands of teenage boys in the effort. In his book, *Embattled Courage*, Gerald Linderman reports that the soldiers of both armies, North and South, were mostly young boys fresh from home. During the first year of the war, the largest single age group represented in the military was that of eighteen-year-old young men; however, boys as young as twelve participated. Linderman explains that in this setting, the conflict that separated not only "courage from cowardice, came also to separate manhood from boyhood."[36] Lucy's recognition of Sammy's maturity bears witness to Linderman's claims. When Sammy returned to Travis for a short furlough in January 1864, it is not surprising that Lucy commented that he seemed much more manly.

Yet Sammy was not the only young man who garnered Lucy's concern. In her earlier diary, she entered a list of the local boys who had enlisted in 1861, then proceeded to keep ongoing records of their whereabouts and their struggles. One of the young men, Nehemiah Cochran (Neh), ranked high in her esteem, and her affection for him was apparent throughout the pages of her diary. Nehemiah had accompanied Lucy and Cousin Sarah on their trip down the Mississippi River as Lucy began her "visit" with her Texas relatives. Although there is no evidence of a romantic connection between them, Lucy referred to him as "brother Neh," "big buddy," or her "good Texas brother." Her wishes for his success were eventually fulfilled, as he returned from the war after serving under General Thomas Green and was elected the Austin County representative to the Texas Legislature in 1866.

Lucy's affection and concern for Nehemiah and a number of the other local soldier boys, in fact, provide a major theme throughout her diary, for she expended much effort chronicling the battles in which they participated and the experiences they recounted to her. For this reason, we are able to

---

36. Gerald Linderman, *Embattled Courage* (New York: Free Press, 1987), 26.

learn much about the furthest reaches of the war and what many of the soldiers endured. To a great degree, Lucy viewed the war from the local level,
and her concerns were continually with the soldier boys she had come to
love. Yet she never allowed herself a serious romantic relationship during
her time in Texas, for although she had her favorites, she knew that her stay
was temporary. Her intermittent references to "my old man" do indicate that
there was a young man with whom she shared some degree of fondness.
However, because Lucy used this somewhat flippant allusion within a more
casual setting and, more importantly, because she never identified the young
man or wrote of him in a romantic context, it is unclear just how deeply this
affection ever developed. Then, as now, well-meaning friends loved to play
matchmaker. Thus it is reasonable that Lucy's pet name "my old man" could
suggest some sense of public association and/or social expectation without
any sense of romantic involvement.

That Lucy had left behind a suitor in Ohio is entirely possible as well.
Entries from her earlier journal allude to such a young man, but are shrouded
in mystery. Months after her arrival, she had written,

> Although far from the loved ones at home my thoughts involuntarily
> [turn] to those most dear and much don't I wonder why they neglect
> to write me. How often "home sweet home" comes to my mind. This
> eve I am thinking of you Delia and of the eve Sunday you spent with me
> and of one who is dear to me but ought not have his name mentioned
> in my memorandum he has been so naughty. No matter my dear sir if
> you are not careful I will not think of you always as the one who reigns
> uppermost and first in this heart of mine. Seven months and ½ and how
> have you treated my correspondence I did think I had found one true
> in thought and act and hope I may not be obliged to ever feel otherwise
> . . . Delia do you ever think of one [of] your childhoods most cherished
> friends who is now a wanderer I once thought ours was a changeless
> love and I believe mine to be although there are circumstances that keep
> me from expressing myself fully except in this memorandum. You have
> wounded my feelings deeply yet I can not give you up. If ever I have
> wounded yours it is not because I have loved you less or intended my
> heart to do so.
> Lucy Stevens, 7/30/60

In these carefully phrased musings, Lucy remained purposely vague; however, her vulnerability to a childhood friend, Delia, an unnamed young man, and an unspecified heartache slips through the veiled references. There is little doubt that Lucy cared deeply for the young man, for months later, on February 15, 1861, she wrote that she longed to hear from "her beloved," ascribing to him an appellation reserved for one quite dear. Yet Lucy's journal remains silent as to both the young man's identity and the resolution of any relationship.

From the poignant "beloved" to the facetious "my old man," Lucy's assigning of pet names is entirely consistent with the use of pet names in love letters, a practice that was quite common during the nineteenth century. Karen Lystra, author of *Searching the Heart*, holds that "pet names were the most unambiguous emblem of a privileged relationship" and that "the opening form of address [in love letters] often indicated the level of intimacy between correspondents" (19).[37] Although there are no love letters associated with Lucy's diary, her use of this term corresponds to the convention of which Lystra writes. However, while Lystra goes on to include examples such as "my dearest" and "my darling," leaving little doubt as to the degree of romance and emotion, Lucy's facetious allusions, on the other hand, downplayed any real courtship scenario. As time went by, in fact, the references to "my old man" occurred less and less often, but the "relationship" apparently never even rated enough emotional investment for Lucy to make any note as to when it ceased to matter to her at all. Lucy was sure that someday she would marry, but as yet she had not found the right person. Neither was she in a hurry to develop a permanent relationship in a land so far from her real home.

This reticence regarding romantic alignments never precluded Lucy's enjoyment of the local young men, however, and her journal provides important information concerning the social customs of the day. Whenever the "soldier boys" came home on leave, parties and impromptu gatherings were a pronounced part of the social setting. The absence of armed conflict in Texas, in fact, permitted life in Travis to move on much as it had before the war, and the networks of social circles continued undaunted. John Austin Edwards contends that "the war itself seemed to enhance the spirit of party giving throughout the state. The optimistic mood of Southerners generally may have been more pronounced and continued longer in Texas because of the state's distance from early battles."[38] Lucy provides evidence of this, for she recorded many instances of gatherings, planned as well as impromptu.

---

37. Karen Lystra, *Searching the Heart: Women, Men, and Romantic Love in Nineteenth-Century America* (New York: Oxford University Press, 1989), 19.

38. Edwards, *Social and Cultural Activities of Texans*, 35.

Throughout her diary, Lucy recorded many evenings spent playing cards or parlor games such as "Pullin Taters," "Smut," and "Hull-Gull." Hull-Gull, or Hully Gull, was a favorite of the time, a game in which each player received the same number of pecans, corn kernels, etc., as tokens. The first player held a secret number of pecans in his closed hands and extended his fists to player number two, who said, "Hully Gull." Player two then guessed the number of pecans hidden in the first player's hands. If correct, player two was awarded all the pecans; if incorrect, player two was required to "pay" player one the difference and then become "it." The game continued until one person won all the pecans.[39]

Many of the festivities that occupied the young folks' attention fell under the category of "play parties," which involved singing, games, and dancing. However, dancing could not be named since many churches considered it sinful. A Baptist church in the vicinity issued a statement condemning such pursuits: "Resolved that we the Baptist Church of Christ on Walnut Creek— give our judgment that Social Card playing and attending dancing parties are unprofitable to the members of the Church—and recommend to our Brethren and Sisters to abstain from such amusements."[40] Lucy's diary indicates that the little church at Travis held this attitude as well. Interestingly, Francis Abernethy writes that no one condemned the young people for the dancing "until instrumental music was added. The old folks drew the line there. When a fiddle and guitar were used, it was no longer a game; it was dancing, and that was a sin."[41] Lucy's family did not seem much concerned with the technicality regarding musical instruments, however, since she wrote frequently of Uncle Pier playing his fiddle for the girls to dance.

Always a highlight in the community, weddings provided a social setting for the young men and women, drawing the interest and attendance of friends and family alike. Long engagements were rare, and wedding dates were set according to the availability of a preacher.[42] For example, Cousin Sarah married Henry P. Wiley on Wednesday, January 25, 1865, after finally agreeing to the marriage on Monday, January 23. Preparations commenced with a flurry, and Lucy's diary records the details of the occasion. As an important aside, it should be noted that in this community weddings rated a celebration by both black and white. When a couple married on March 26, 1864, Sarah and Lucy both wrote extensive entries, with Sarah noting that

---

39. Francis E. Abernethy, *Texas Toys and Games* (Dallas: SMU Press, 1989), 106.

40. Edwards, *Social and Cultural Activities of Texans*, 114.

41. Ibid., 193.

42. Wilfred O. Dietrich, *The Blazing Story of Washington County* (Dietrich, 1950), 40–41.

the white folks ate prior to the ceremony, then adding that she helped to wait tables for white and Negroes alike. The wedding itself was conducted by Parson Glass, who performed a Confederate wedding ceremony of his own "getting up" and one that, according to Sarah, was

> worth walking some distance to hear. He began by giving them good advice instructing them how to live etc. and wound up after exacting other promises from them by asking Nellie if she would wash mend patch, etc for Bob. I never was more amused in my life and every one enjoyed it even the parson himself could not help smiling.
> Sarah Pier, 3/26/64

Sarah went on to write of watching the guests dance, and again, she was a spectator, while Cous Lue was one of the "principal dancers." The details included by both girls about bridesmaids, flowers, candles, and food indicate that even in such a rural setting the conventions of a wedding were observed as much as practical, making do with things at hand. The rustic setting in no way diminished the sense of celebration and joy.

Weddings were not the only occasions for gatherings. Christmas, as the most popular holiday of the nineteenth century, continued to be celebrated during the war, even though the celebration was toned down. John Austin Edwards relates that in 1861, the editor of the *Marshall Texas Republican* wrote, "The first Christmas in the new Confederacy although not as gay as in former times, has not been devoid of interest. Relatives and friends, it is true, are in the Army ... This year it is serious and solemn, but not altogether gloomy."[43] Turkey remained the staple of Christmas dinner, and eggnog the standard drink. Fireworks maintained their prewar favor as a method of celebrating to the point that the editor of the *Bellville Countryman* complained "that 'boys will be boys' at Christmas, with their shooting firecrackers and swapping business signs in the town."[44] Lucy recounted special preparations and festive meals associated with the holiday, and noted in her journal that special plans were always made to include "the darkies." However, as time passed, the war took its toll. One year later, Sarah noted in her diary, "No stocking hung up tonight for the first time, Santa Claus cannot run the blockade" (12/24/64).

In contrast, the observance of the Fourth of July virtually disappeared during the war years. While 1861 saw commemorations of national independence and Southern dominance, the practice faded as the years went

---

43. Edwards, "Social and Cultural Activities of Texans," 41.
44. Ibid., 48.

on.[45] Lucy wrote extensively of the Fourth of July picnic in her 1861 journal, but made no note of any succeeding celebrations. However, on July 4, 1864, she noted the day, and in one of her most eloquent entries, she called on a divided country to remember the sacrifices of the early patriots.

In addition to the local celebrations that Lucy and her friends enjoyed, she wrote of several outings to nearby colleges, and her detailed information sheds important light on the availability of higher education for women at that time. Lucy wrote at length of the closing exercises at Chappell Hill in June 1864, but these were not the first she had attended. In 1861 she had recorded in detail an outing to observe the closing exercises at Baylor University, where Sarah had earlier attended.

Baylor University was chartered by the Republic of Texas, with organizational meetings held as early as 1840 in Sarah's hometown of Travis.[46] The school was ultimately located at Independence, Texas, in 1845, and from its inception, included provisions for a "female department."[47] Records indicate that Sarah attended Baylor from 1857 until the spring of 1859, and a catalogue located in the Texas Collection at Baylor lists Sarah as an undergraduate student in the School of Music.[48] The catalogue, in fact, belonged to Cousin Sarah, for in the front of the book is a penciled inscription, "Sarah C. Pier, Travis, Austin County, Texas—now Mrs. S. C. Wiley, Waco." The catalogue lists a wide array of both preparatory and advanced courses, including moral and intellectual philosophy, ancient languages, math, English language and literature, modern languages (French, German, and Latin), gymnasium and ornamental endeavors (drawing, painting, wax work, and embroidery). Sarah was one of 150 undergraduates in a total female class of 165.[49]

That Sarah enjoyed the opportunity to attend college is significant, for women's access to higher education in the United States was quite limited at that time, with few universities offering such a program. However, the principal of the Female Department at Baylor, Horace Clark, argued fervently for the education of women, writing in the 1857 catalogue:

> It is always better to let facts speak in such questions, than theories. It is enough to know that whenever woman has been called by the events of Providence from her own sphere to act in that which seems to be

---

45. Ibid., 50–51.
46. Lois Smith Murray, *Baylor at Independence* (Waco: Baylor University Press, 1972), 15.
47. Ibid., 67.
48. *Catalogue of the Trustees, Faculty and Students of Baylor University, Female Department, Independence, Texas* (Waco: Texas Collection, Baylor University, 1857), 10–12.
49. Ibid.

especially the sphere of manhood, she has proved herself equal to the emergency . . . It is enough, then, if it be conceded, that she is entitled, equally with man to such mental culture as will discipline her mind . . .[50]

Thus the successful negotiation of the rugged, rural life of Texas provided the rationale for the higher education of its women, entitling them to opportunities decades before the same would be offered in other, more "civilized" sections of the country.

The catalogue promoted its faculty of one principal and nine instructors as superlative, then explained that the courses for the young ladies were both disciplinary and practical. It followed with a most interesting disclaimer, which warned,

> But we wish to be understood: We do not promise, under all circumstances, to make thorough scholars; we cannot create mental ability, nor the disposition to use it; and where either of these is largely wanting, but slender attainments will be made.[51]

While the entry may seem like an odd statement to be included in a publication meant to attract students, it may be indicative of some condescension toward education for women. Despite the efforts of women like Catharine Beecher, many felt, even until the close of the century, that education was detrimental for women. Many doctors saw the feminine constitution as frail, debilitated by the menstrual cycle—a condition worsened by education. Some even believed that education was dangerous to women because of the lesser weight of the female brain.[52] Barbara Welter cites Dr. Edward Clarke, a prominent physician of the era, who wrote that during their menstrual periods, women should avoid intellectual pursuits. In his treatise *Sex in Education: or, A Fair Chance for Our Girls*, Dr. Clarke asserted that many common maladies were the result of overextension during the monthly period. He believed that in pursuing intellectual or vocational tasks during this time of the month, "the stream of vital and constructive force evolved within [women] was turned steadily toward the brain, and away from the ovaries and their accessories."[53] Fortunately, these theories carried little weight in Travis, and girls like Sarah and Lucy were allowed to both pursue and share various educational opportunities with little resistance.

---

50. Murray, *Baylor at Independence*, 153.

51. *Catalogue, Baylor University*, 22.

52. John S. Haller, Jr., and Robin M. Haller, *The Physician and Sexuality in Victorian America* (Urbana: University of Illinois Press, 1974), 35–39.

In Lucy's earlier journal, she had recorded that she, Sarah, Sammy, and Mack had attended Baylor University's commencement exercises on June 28, 1861. She paid great attention to the campus, writing that she "was delighted with the beauty of the surrounding scenery," and noting that "the two cottages, male at one end and female at the other are the principle buildings and both are very nice."

On Wednesday and Thursday of that week, the young people attended a number of closing exercises, including examinations in composition, vocal, and instrumental music. Lucy met Governor Edward Clark, describing him as "a gentleman of about thirty eight years of age, about 5 ft 8 inches in height, the front part of his head bald, hair sprinkled with grey & whiskers quite white & remarkably pleasant countenance." The next morning, Lucy's group sat with the principal of the Female Department, Horace Clark, on his private gallery, watching a military review. Again, her journal descriptions paint a vivid portrait of the event: "The infantry had a uniform of black coats striped with yellow & jackets (blue with brass buttons) ~ the cavalry wore black pants striped with red & white & white waists ~ After the review the Gov addressed them then company disbursed."

However, Lucy saved her most detailed descriptions for the drama that the students presented at the Grand Concert following the graduation exercises. In what Lucy called the "Secession Play," she not only recorded the day's highlights but unknowingly captured for a future audience the essence of Southern resolve:

> Another scene was the Secession states ~ first one that came out was a young lady dressed in deep mourning with the American flag with mourning dress also crape on her arms and a black crown on with liberty written in gilt letters on it ~ She was lamenting our lost liberty ~ The next came Miss Montgomery with a banner of Southern rights ~ white with gilded lettering ~ She and all the rest were dressed in pure white ~ Then came Miss Ella Chase representing South Carolina the first of the seceding states ~ then the other states in their order ~ with music (instrumental) between the coming of each after three or four had seceded ~ came the Southern confederate flag ~ when Virginia came Lincoln's long and heart piercing wail was heard & soon after he tried to swear Missouri to the constitution ~ but her cries went up to the helpers of the feeble that she should never be a slave and then calls for aid from her sister states represented by a young lady's coming out and kneeling with

---

53. Welter, *Dimity Convictions*, 63.

both hands uplifted & crying help my sisters! For the love of mercy ~ As she came there was a great rattling of chains and Lincoln's Proclimation for the rebels to disperse ~ I give you twenty days to return peaceably to your home but at last she arose freed with her banner though sadly torn still floating in the breeze.

Lucy Stevens, June 28, 1861

Lucy's description vibrantly captures the passion and righteousness of the early days of the war, yet for current historians the play itself vividly portrays the Confederate use of the female to effectively "market" the war. In her book *Confederate Reckoning*, Stephanie McCurry discusses the image of the state as female: "Women figured centrally, indeed ubiquitously, as embodied symbols of the property and rights at risk in the crisis"—scattered, vulnerable, and weak, to be protected at all costs, against all foes.[54] However, in a powerful reversal, the play presented at Baylor in 1861 also presents the female as state, ascribing to her unity, strength, power, and, ultimately, victory.

HER TEXAS WORLD

In Lucy's world, the seasons were the guideposts by which farmers "tried to unite their efforts with the natural order of things."[55] In an agrarian, domestic economy that, for the Pier household, was almost self-sufficient during the war years, all of life revolved around seasonal changes. Here, as in the rest of "the overwhelmingly agricultural South the individual household was the fundamental unit of what scholars have called 'production and reproduction,' the place where the most important economic as well as social and cultural work of civilization took place."[56] In the domestic economy of Travis, life was ruled by the cycle of the seasons. Preparations began in winter, and planting commenced by mid-February. Lucy noted this sequence in early 1864. On January 18, she wrote of beginnings, and her entry dated two weeks later followed the progress as planting began. Here again, the weather played a significant role. Less than three weeks later, a winter storm known as a norther blew through, irreparably damaging the oats and corn. Lucy noted the loss and chronicled the damage done, but also went on to list the garden crops

---

54. Stephanie McCurry, *Confederate Reckoning: Power and Politics in the Civil War South* (Cambridge: Harvard University Press, 2010), 26–27.

55. Silverthorne, *Plantation Life in Texas*, 106.

56. Drew Gilpin Faust, *Mothers of Invention* (New York: Vintage Books, 1996), 32.

that were planted the same day. As she documented various agricultural tasks and events throughout the year, her journal validates the farming calendar modeled by twentieth-century researchers to track farming practices.

Lucy also attempted to keep a record of the various crops that local farmers were planting. In Texas, similar to other areas of the country, the end of winter and the beginning of spring signaled the new year of cultivation, with field crops and early gardens being planted. Corn, along with oats, barley, and peas provided the basic staples of sustenance. Peas, beans, potatoes, small fruits and berries, and vegetables all added to the variety of crops that farmers grew. With summer came the planting of a second round of crops, even as grains were simultaneously being cut and harvested.[57] Lucy wrote with delight about the berrying expeditions that she and the other girls enjoyed, and the summertime routine was not complete without peach drying. During the fall, corn and other crops were gathered, sugarcane was cut, and pecans were picked. Hay and wood were cut, feed was laid aside for the stock, and fruits were dried. After drying, the preserved food was put away with "chinaberry leaves placed between layers to discourage insects and worms."[58] Finally, in winter, as fields lay dormant, farmers caught up on tasks reserved for colder weather. The holidays offered little respite from seasonal chores. Although much of the farming work had been completed for the year, fences and outbuilding were mended, hogs were butchered, and preparations were made to begin the cycle again. As described in *A History of Waller County*, something always needed doing, and hands never remained idle.[59] Lucy's journal gives a thorough account of the ongoing work as she regularly recorded these different practices, providing detailed descriptions of the daily activities of farm life in Texas and giving credence to the cyclical and ongoing nature of an agrarian world.

In the rural domestic economy of Texas, cotton was the doorway to prosperity, and slave labor was the key. Cotton provided a variation of the seasonal progression of farming, and cultivating it was a yearlong effort. The ground had to be prepared, the seed planted, the plants tended, the bolls picked, the fiber ginned, and the bales packed.[60] All of this effort required many hands, and as early as 1825, Stephen F. Austin recognized that "the protection of slavery was 'a matter of greatest importance.'" Without slavery, he wrote, Texas could not attract the people to make it a land of sugar and

---

57. Silverthorne, *Plantation Life in Texas*, 106–107.

58. Ibid., 92.

59. Waller County Historical Survey Commission, *A History of Waller County, Texas* (Waco: Author, 1873), 112–113.

60. Silverthorne, *Plantation Life in Texas*, 127–141.

cotton plantations and would instead be populated by shepherds and the poor."[61] The concept that holding slaves produced success was accordingly perpetuated, and Randolph Campbell reports that years later, in 1858, "the *Matagorda Gazette* told its readers that 'a successful planter could have field hands pay for themselves,'" multiplying his holdings in land and property, thereby making him a wealthy man.[62] Campbell goes on to explain that in 1860, 27.3 percent of families in Texas owned slaves, with 3 percent owning twenty or more, officially affording them planter status.[63]

Thus, by the time Lucy arrived, at the end of 1859, slavery was entrenched and accepted without question as a way of life. *The Handbook of Texas Online* indicates that Austin County, including Travis, where the Piers made their home, boasted 324 slaveholders and was one of seventeen counties where the average number of slaves per owner was greater than ten. According to early tax records, in 1860 James Bradford Pier owned eleven slaves, and by 1864 this number increased to fourteen, granting him prosperity and position within his community.[64]

Yet regardless of the contribution of slave labor to economic prosperity in Texas, investment in cotton became less and less cost-effective as the war progressed. Thanks to the naval blockade of Galveston, shipment of cotton was almost impossible, and Texans looked for other ways to market their crops. In 1863, Lucy wrote of her uncle Martin hiring men to take his cotton to Matamoros; Cousin Lu's husband, Waller, would also make the trip. However, by the time another year had passed, thanks to the blockade, many had turned to other crops for cash. As Lucy chronicled the planting of new spring gardens in 1864, she noted that "very few round here are thinking of planting cotton this season." The income potential could not justify the expense—thanks to the war, it was simply too risky an investment. Other planting, however, was ongoing and essential because the ability to produce a variety of other crops and the existence of raising stock in concert with farming combined to allow a high degree of independence for the Texas farmer and planter.

Lucy's entries regularly reference some aspect of clothing production; almost daily, she recorded details about mending, laundering, weaving, sewing—all of the tasks needed to keep the family clothed. From her records, we can learn much about the daily activities and responsibilities of women within

---

61. Randolph B. Campbell, *An Empire for Slavery: The Peculiar Institution in Texas* (Baton Rouge: Louisiana State University Press, 1989), 18.

62. Ibid., 68.

63. Ibid., 69.

64. Austin County, Texas, *Austin County Tax Rolls*, 1860–1865, Dallas Public Library.

the household; it quickly becomes apparent that care of clothing ranked at the top of the list. Because dry goods were so scarce during the war, mending old pieces to extend their serviceability took up much of Lucy's time. She recounted many attempts of mending and spent great effort, as well, remaking existing dresses, bonnets, and even shoes. Maintenance and preservation of clothing was imperative, and at one point Lucy wrote that Lu's sick slave woman, Lucinda, had been washing that day and the day before. In spite of her illness, the task had to be completed, cumbersome and tedious though it might be. Laundering clothing required an all-day effort, and Sandra Myres explains that it was the most dreaded of chores, for "no satisfactory mechanical aids for laundry were developed until after 1900, and women universally despised the long, hard hours spent over wash tubs and soap barrels."[65] After the water had been hauled, the clothes had to be sorted and soaked, and the white garments had to be boiled over a hot fire. The pieces were scrubbed, even beaten with a stick; then they were rinsed, wrung out, starched, and hung or spread out to dry.[66] Katherine Hart's research shows that even the soap was often homemade.[67]

Making soap continued to be a time-consuming endeavor, and people were always interested in newer, more efficient methods. The August 16, 1864, edition of the Bellville Countryman ran an article on its front page that gave detailed instructions and a "receipt for making soap out of materials that [could] always be obtained in spite of the blockaders." Steps included boiling a combination of lye and lard for several hours. Afterward, the liquid was removed from the fire and salt was added. The concoction was then boiled for an additional amount of time, and brine was added. Once this mixture was removed from the fire, the soap would "rise like foam to the top" and be skimmed off. The article went on to give precise instructions for adding fragrance and/or coloring for aesthetic appeal and concluded that once the soap had hardened, it could be cut into smaller cakes and stored.[68]

Production of new clothing was even more involved. Fabric and ready-made clothing had become increasingly expensive as time passed, and both were often completely unavailable. From underwear to coats, if the items were to be had, they had to be made. Because of these shortages, women in Texas, like women in other parts of the South, resumed the practice of home production in order to clothe their families. By 1862, the shortages

65. Myres, Westering Women, 151.

66. Ibid., 152–153.

67. Katherine Hart, Pease Porridge Hot, 27.

68. Bellville Countryman, August 16, 1864, Texas and Other Southern States Civil War Newspapers/Newspaper Research, 1861–1865.

were widespread. One Arkansas woman wrote: "There is very little if any cloth in the stores throughout the country now. It has all been sold and very near all mad[e] up and is now worn. There are families that have no cloth to make up and not enough clothes for their children . . . All the old looms have been fixed up."[69] Texas women brought antique spinning wheels out of storage and relearned the art of spinning and weaving. In her memoirs, Mrs. Ottilie Goeth recalled, "Only those who experienced those rough times can understand the difficulties of the war years for the women. There was practically nothing left to buy. One turned again to spinning and weaving in order not to go about in rags."[70] The Pier household was no different.

In the beginning, records indicate, home production of clothing was seen by many in the South to be demeaning. Initially viewed as appropriate only for slave women, the revival of home production met with some resistance. From the front, Will Neblett wrote to his wife in Texas, "I do not like the idea of your weaving. It is mortifying to me. I wish you not to do it."[71] Yet, even though the practice clouded the distinction between owner and slave, circumstances gave little option. For Aunt Lu and her household, there was no time wasted questioning the propriety of cloth production. Everyone needed clothes, and these women met the need. One result was known as homespun, which eventually came to be seen as the emblem for Southern virtue and industry.[72] Where once such a material would have been discounted as shabby, it now was upheld as the essence of femininity. On many occasions, Lucy admired someone's homespun costume and noted it in her journal.

In his book *Buckskin and Homespun*, David Holman gives an excellent description of the production steps that would furnish the clothing needed by the family. To prepare the cotton for spinning, the fibers had to be separated from the seed, a slow process until the advent of the cotton gin in 1793. It then had to be washed, greased, and carded. Cards came in pairs, each one consisting of a thin piece of wood attached to a handle. One side of the wood was covered with wire bristles mounted on a leather covering. The cards were used as follows: "The worker placed a warm piece of cotton or wool on the bristles of the card in her lap, and drew the second card across the first with a downward motion," separating the fibers and aligning them in parallel rows to be spun.[73] Carding was essential to create the thread that would be woven into cloth, and these cards became prized possessions during the war

---

69. Lois Myers, *Letters by Lamplight* (Waco: Baylor University Press, 1991), 24.

70. Holman, *Buckskin and Homespun*, 28.

71. Faust, *Mothers of Invention*, 47.

72. Ibid., 27.

73. Holman, *Buckskin and Homespun*, 31.

because of their scarcity. Aunt Lu wrote repeatedly of sending first to one place, then another, hoping to acquire the precious tools. She even wrote of the slave women being punished for ruining a pair of cards, noting: "Winny [one of the slaves] got whiped for fighting with Henry and mashing my new cards" (1/3/64).

Spinning followed carding and was done on a walking or a sitting wheel.[74] After spinning was completed, and before the thread could be woven into cloth, it had to be colored according to preference and the availability of dye. As Elizabeth Silverthorne points out in *Plantation Life in Texas*, this process was quite intricate; before 1870, most dyes were made from natural substances such as leaves, blossoms, berries, nuts, roots, bark, and wood. Indigo, found in several plants, produced a dark blue color, and small amounts were always included in the mixture to ensure that the dye would be colorfast.[75]

It is at this point that Aunt Lu's diary, not Lucy's, offers the voice of experience, as she recorded her use of various preparations for dyeing the cloth. She wrote of trying to color wool with moss (2/19/62) and of using plum roots for plum color (1/2/63). Two weeks later, she noted, "I took some hickory bark and colored some blue yarn. I had sea green, set the yellow with copperas" (1/19/63). Setting the color was imperative; otherwise, colors would immediately begin to fade away, and the entire tedious procedure would be for naught. Lu Merry Pier had mastered this endeavor, and other women in the community appreciated her expertise and advice. On October 15, 1862, Aunt Lu recorded that "after dinner Miss Sallie Tomlinson came and wanted to know about coloring"; others came frequently for help as well.

Weaving the thread into cloth required large looms, and both Sarah and Lucy kept records of how much cloth they wove in a day. The local women sometimes turned the tasks into a competition of sorts. In a friendly neighborhood rivalry, they kept up with the amounts of thread they could spin or the lengths of cloth woven and reported the results of their labors. Sarah, who had begun to spin only in 1862, in fact, became well known in the area as an expert weaver. Her skill is acknowledged by David Holman, who reports, "During the Civil War, a young weaver from Bellville, Sarah Wiley [Sarah's

---

74. Ibid., 31–32. Holman explains the difference between the two wheels, stating that the walking wheel was about five feet tall, while the sitting wheel was only about three feet high. The major part of the process involved the spindle, which was rotated by the big wheel, turning and twisting the fibers into thread. Holman explains that because the finished product had to be long, even thread, "spinning required coordination, timing and patience." After spinning was completed, the thread was wound into balls or skeins, the balls for immediate use, the skeins for storage.

75. Silverthorne, *Plantation Life in Texas*, 104.

married name], wove a twilled 'negro cloth' from hemp and cotton, the cotton dyed indigo blue."[76]

Negro cloth, a roughly woven blend known for its service and durability, was a mainstay of the slaves' clothing, and with the approach of winter weather, the women of the household focused more heavily on producing this fabric. Work had continued throughout the year, and with a flurry of activity at Christmastime, Aunt Lu and the girls struggled to finish the slaves' clothes in anticipation of the holiday. On larger plantations, meeting that need might fall to the slaves themselves, but in the Pier household, the task was Aunt Lu's charge. Each year she spent hours, with the help of Sarah and Lucy, and even Uncle Pier, preparing the fabric and sewing the clothes for the family's slaves. Lucy wrote of this preparation, and Aunt Lu recounted the degree of effort in making the clothing. On December 22, 1860, she wrote, "With Lue and Sarah's help I have the Negro pants, children's dresses and three dresses for the grown Negroes or will have all done for Christmas."

Aunt Lu's position as supervisor manifests itself repeatedly as she gave assistance to family and friends. On January 10, 1860, she had written, "Lue and Sarah made delain and calico dresses. Johanna making a robed delain. I am helping all of them." Later, in another statement made only a few days after Lucy's arrival in Texas, Aunt Lu not only detailed her own role as mistress of the household and supervisor of those less experienced, but she also set the tone for Lucy's full involvement in the Pier family and the Travis community at large. Lucy had been in Texas a mere two weeks and was only now meeting many of the residents, yet she was already hard at work with the other women, fully immersing herself in the feminine world of her family and the community she would come to call home.

Not all time was devoted to work, however, for Lucy and her family spent many leisure hours reading. Texas was a literate land by 1860, with fewer than 19,000 white people over the age of twenty who could not read.[77] This is an impressive statistic, considering that there was a total free population of more than 431,000 in Texas in 1860.[78] Books were available in stores and lending libraries, and many enjoyable hours could be spent reading. Books were shared among family and friends, with one person often reading aloud to the others. As the war progressed, however, new books became harder to acquire, and a fresh shipment of books was worthy of note in the local news.[79]

76. Holman, *Buckskin and Homespun*, 43.

77. Edwards, "Social and Cultural Activities of Texans," 12.

78. Campbell, *An Empire for Slavery*, 55.

79. Edwards, "Social and Cultural Activities of Texans," 23.

Southerners had become enamored of English and Scottish tales set in feudal times.[80] The dominant author of this genre was Sir Walter Scott, who had risen to prominence earlier in the century. His *Waverly* series, a collection of books of his native Scotland and feudal England, initiated the genre of the historical novel. With wild adventures, beautiful heroines, and rugged heroes, the extravagantly romantic tales fired the imaginations of readers on both sides of the Atlantic. The popularity of Scott's novels in the South can be tied to the Southern plantation system and its emulation of medieval feudal society. Historian Clement Eaton asserts that "Southerners had, of course, read these captivating novels about feudal times and probably had found some justification for their own slave-based society in the chivalrous society described by the Scottish writer.[81] He concludes, "The historical novels of Sir Walter Scott fitted in perfectly with this trend of thought and feeling. Accordingly, although the Scottish writer was popular in the North, he was the rage in the South."[82]

It is not surprising, then, that Scott and his *Waverly* novels dominated Lucy's reading for 1863. Of the many volumes that she included in her reading list in the back of her journal, the great majority were authored by Scott. As time allowed, she also included lengthy synopses of the books, giving close attention to plot detail and narrative. Her reviews consumed large amounts of space in her diary, often continuing for three or more pages in the journal. With their formal sentence structure and precise grammar, the unofficial essays indicate Lucy's level of education, and serve as an implicit reminder to herself of her own abilities.

Other leisure time was spent corresponding with the boys at the front, and precious paper was conserved for this all-important task. Letters provided the main link by which families could know that their loved one was well, and Lucy and Sarah, along with the rest of the family, spent countless hours writing to Sammy and the other Travis boys. Soldier boys relished these updates, filled with news from home and marked with concern; their letters from the front became cherished possessions back home, passed around among family and friends to be read and re-read. In her journal entry on May 25, 1864, Sarah wrote, "I found 8 (eight) letters waiting for me and had a glorious letter feast for an hour or so." She then took the time to document the content of each letter, along with its author. Lucy waited patiently for letters as well,

---

80. Clement Eaton, *The Mind of the Old South* (Baton Rouge: Louisiana State University Press, 1964), 184.

81. Ibid., 186.

82. Ibid., 184.

particularly those from Ohio. However, her wait proved in vain, for communication with loved ones in the North was halted for well over two years, and she could only guess at the condition of her family in Ohio.

———

The institution of the church dictated much of the social landscape in Lucy's world. By 1860 the Methodist Church had become a significant presence in Texas and dominated all evangelical efforts there and around the rest of the country as well, with its pro-revival stance.[83] With its emphasis on personal repentance and experiential conversion, the Methodist Church became the largest Protestant denomination of the nineteenth century. In Texas, circuit-riding preachers spread the gospel to rural communities, holding both Sunday services and extended revival services, known as camp meetings, or as Lucy called them, "protracted meetings." The services included an invitation to come to the "mourner's bench" at the front of the building and pray, and great emphasis was placed on an emotional response to one's inner conviction.[84] Periods of revival services, such as Lucy documented in October 1863, formed the locus of social activity for the community. With picnicking and visiting, singing and worship, entire communities responded. But even more important than the social aspects were the deep ties to religious roots grounded in the New Testament and reinvigorated by the Second Great Awakening, which took place during the early part of the nineteenth century. For many years following that event, revival services lasting for extended periods of time were commonplace. In fact, an observer of the same revival about which Lucy wrote noted, "A revival in Bellville in October 1863 continued for more than two weeks in what an observer described as 'the greatest revival season known in Bellville for many years.'"[85]

Lucy wrote a running commentary in her journal as the revival progressed, sometimes expressing happiness over someone's possession of newfound faith, sometimes skepticism over another's public profession. Yet even as she questioned the motives of others, she held firmly to her own foundational beliefs, sometimes quoting scripture and short prayers in her diary. In times of illness and other such crises, she reached past institutional traditions to grapple with core issues of faith and doctrine. Her own experiences had moved her beyond the comfortable platitudes of pious jargon to a deeper examination of core Christian precepts.

---

83. Edwards, "Social and Cultural Activities of Texans," 66–83.

84. Silverthorne, *Plantation Life in Texas*, 104.

85. Edwards, "Social and Cultural Activities of Texans," 102.

But while Lucy's entries often imply skepticism, and even sarcasm regarding the sincerity of those who had gone forward during the invitation times, Sarah's words were perhaps more forgiving and gentle. Sarah, who earnestly incorporated her faith into every aspect of her daily life, recorded the decisions of her friends and wrote of her own part in the revival effort. From these entries, it is clear that Cousin Sarah devoutly believed in the sovereignty of God and in her own responsibility to live accordingly. From her efforts during the revival to counsel her friends, to the life-and-death realities of Travis, her diary abounds with her determination to validate her faith. On August 30, 1863, after noting that Callie had been to the mourner's bench to be prayed for every night, Sarah wrote,

> Laura, Callie & Maggie asked me a number of questions about the church rules &c today. I got the discipline and read and explained them to them. I thought they were intending to join the church & tonight Laura joined and professed religion. Artie went up to the mourner's bench tonight and Callie & Maggie. Caroline Fleitzman and a German girl from Chapel Hill.
> Sarah Pier, 8/30/63

Sarah's efforts spilled onto the pages of her journal, yielding a glimpse into her own convictions and the priority that she ascribed to spiritual matters.

Interestingly, the entries of both Lucy and Sarah closely parallel the reflections of a young woman thousands of miles away. In Ohio, Lucy's home state, Rachel Cormany, whose husband ultimately fought under the Union flag, had recorded her own perceptions during a similar revival, and the three diaries read as though the entries were written after the same church service. Yet the significance lies not in the stress that each placed on emotional responses to spiritual leanings but in the fact that the three responses resembled one another so closely. Separated by distance, politics, national loyalties, and secular ideologies, the accounts reverberated with similarities of faith. Faith, and its practices, found a common voice in disparate settings, overreaching difference to tie together believers with a common thread of response. Even as the North and South were being ripped apart by sectional loyalties, the transcendent ties of faith stretched past the variances, stitching Northern and Southern believers together in a strong seam that would hold in spite of the tension placed on it.

The other institution that shaped the social terrain of Texas was education. Across the nation, teaching primary school had become an acceptable occupation for women only in the past twenty years, thanks to the efforts of women like Catharine Beecher. Justifying this shift, Beecher emphasized that women, with their maternal instinct and nurturing abilities, were obvious choices as teachers. She also proposed that since the schoolroom ranked next to the home in maternal influence, it kept women within their separate sphere. She even went so far as to suggest the women could be paid less than men and save the school district money.[86] Using the argument that historians call "True Womanhood," Beecher maintained that because of their duty to future generations, women should seek education themselves and then provide it for the children around them.[87]

In Texas, particularly during the 1850s and 1860s, private subscription schools dominated the educational realm. In this system, a teacher was hired by the parents of the children who would attend the school, and the salary was negotiated for individual school terms. Many subscription schools were started by one family who wanted basic education for their own children and who then extended the opportunity to other children in the vicinity. Because of the private nature of the primary schools, there was little control from the state with regard to the qualifications for teachers. However, John Austin Edwards reports that "most parents and communities required some proof of a teacher's own education before they would hire that person. Usually a certificate or a letter of recommendation from another teacher allowed one easier access into the teaching ranks."[88]

Lucy had, in fact, taken and passed a qualifying examination in February 1861. Aunt Lu's diary tells us, "Mr. Pier, Sarah & Lue gone to Belleville to the examination. Teacher. Lue to be examined, as teacher" (2/23/61). Lucy's own early diary reflects her resolve *and* her nervousness as she prepared for, then took, the exam that February day. She wrote, "Spent yesterday in looking over studies preparing for today's examination but might have left it undone as well . . . After dinner went up to be examined and nearly frightened out of my sense but it was not long ere my fears vanished" (2/23/61). Lucy's fears were needless, and she obviously passed the examination, since later in 1861 she recorded that she had been offered a position. However, as that entry continues, it is apparent she was not well pleased, for she wrote, "received an offer from Mr. Day and Grace to teach for them next year and I think some of

86. Kathryn Kish Sklar, "Catharine Beecher: Transforming the Teaching Profession," in *Women's America*, ed. Linda K. Kerber and Jane Sherron DeHart, 4th ed. (New York: Oxford University Press, 1995), 162–165.

87. Nancy F. Cott, *The Bonds of Womanhood* (New Haven, CT: Yale University Press, 1977), 121.

88. Edwards, "Social and Cultural Activities of Texans, 177.

accepting it but I know if I do it will be one of the most unhappy years of my life" (10/1/61).

In addition to her successful examination, Lucy's writing skills lend credence to her own higher level of education and teaching qualifications. And although no records have been found that name her preparatory school, a likely institution was situated in her hometown of Milan, Ohio. According to the Milan-area website, the Huron Institute and Western Reserve Normal School was founded in Milan in 1832 for the express purpose of training future teachers and establishing teaching standards.[89] The school was the only school of higher education west of Cleveland, and it is entirely plausible that Lucy graduated from this local institution. This earlier training would have equipped her not only to easily pass a qualifying examination but also to undertake the challenges of a schoolroom.

Lucy had originally determined to pursue a teaching position as her visit to Texas lengthened and she began to feel restless. In her earlier journal, she had written, "Oh how I begin to wish I could get a school once more. It does not seem right for me to spend so much time in idleness and I know it is not" (2/12/1861). It was not until August 1863, however, that Lucy's teaching career received detailed documentation, as she noted with regularity her own schedule and her scholars' progress.

At any time, attendance could be affected, and school even dismissed, for a variety of reasons, including the weather, poor roads, or sickness among the students. School terms were usually arranged so that children could help with planting and harvesting, as well as other seasonal farm needs.[90] Only one month after beginning her contract, Lucy delayed the start of the school day due to Jimmy Clemmons's arrival. As she put it, "I did not commence school until after he went away ~ as we do not have soldier boys to visit us [e]very day" (9/1/63).

As a teacher, Lucy took her charge seriously, often commenting that her children had prepared their lessons well, or grumbling that they had done poorly. She organized special programs and had her students perform for the parents. The children recited and sang pieces from a variety of sources, including *McGuffey's Reader*, the most popular source for children's instruction at the time.[91] Full of moral advice and instruction, *McGuffey's Reader* provided

---

89. "Huron Institute and Western Reserve Normal School," MilanArea.com.

90. Edwards, "Social and Cultural Activities of Texans," 139–141.

91. "McGuffey's Reader," *Ohio History Central*, July 1, 2005. Between 1836, when publication began, and 1890, more than 100 million copies of the readers were sold; virtually every student was exposed to the lessons contained within.

excellent forage with which to feed young minds and build character as well as intellect.[92] The programs were well attended by parents and other adults of the community, who readily applauded the performances and exhorted the students to continue in their endeavors. From Lucy's entries, we can easily see the emphasis that the community placed on education, as adults instituted, approved, and participated in the education of their young. And Lucy's documentation of her scholars' performances presents us with an invaluable view into those early classrooms and the curriculum that was offered.

More than any invading army, disease and death proved to be the nearest and most formidable enemies that Lucy, her family, and her friends faced. Throughout her journal, Lucy alluded to maladies that continuously plagued the community. From risings (boils), which were an ongoing problem in the Pier household, to yellow fever, the ailments were chronic and consuming. Lucy afforded entries about sickness a great deal of space, often tracking a person's illness as a separate plotline in her diary for several weeks or months. Yet many of the terms that she used are unfamiliar to modern readers and need translation. The term "congestive chills," for example, was commonly used to denote malaria. "Bowel hive" represented diarrhea, and "consumption" signified pulmonary tuberculosis. The list goes on and on. Records show that summer diseases that commonly plagued Texas were dysentery and malaria, yellow fever, and cholera. Cold-weather ailments included pneumonia, pleurisy, and whooping cough.[93] Medical knowledge limited the treatments available to combat illness and ease pain, and ingredients that are now known to be dangerous, such as mercury, were used on a regular basis. Other common remedies were opium, laudanum (a derivative of opium), morphine, and quinine. Liquor, primarily whiskey, was a medicine cabinet staple.

In this little community, as in many at the time, trusted family physicians made house calls often, lending their expertise to the situation, but Randolph Campbell reports that, unfortunately, "physicians, regardless of their educational backgrounds, simply did not know very much. Some still used treatments such as bleeding, cupping and blistering, and most were powerless against many of the diseases."[94] Lucy's diary mentions the names of several physicians who were called when needed, according to their availability.

92. William Holmes McGuffey, *The Second Eclectic Reader* (Cincinnati: Truman and Smith, 1836). Harvard College Library.

93. Silverthorne, *Plantation Life in Texas*, 142–151.

94. Campbell, *Empire for Slavery*, 142.

Frequently, in the case of a critical illness, multiple doctors might be present at once, conferring among themselves about the best course of treatment.

Blistering and bleeding were both mentioned in the Pier diaries as remedies used to alleviate troublesome symptoms. Just as frequently, however, home remedies prevailed. Elizabeth Silverthorne writes that herbs, barks, roots, leaves, berries, and weeds all offered the potential of medicinal value. Teas brewed from a variety of substances promised relief for a multitude of problems. Watermelon tea soothed babies; sage and sassafras tea worked for fever and chills; butterfly-weed tea combated pleurisy, and peppermint cured indigestion. An all-purpose cure-all, known as "bitters," was used to treat vague symptoms and everyday aches. True to its name, bitters was "a popular and particularly nasty version . . . of a mix of tree bark, rust from iron nails and whiskey."[95]

From Lucy's diary, we get a glimpse of the neighborliness among the residents of the area and a sense of community that prevailed as they took care of one another. Family members nursed those who were ailing, and when necessary, the community rallied to shoulder that care. In the event of a protracted or critical illness, neighbors took turns sitting with the sick, and on occasion, a house might be overrun with sitters and nurses. Men and women alike were called upon to assist, and little impeded that call. Even on the morning after her wedding, Cousin Sarah was called upon to go and sit with an elderly patient, and she showed no hesitation in meeting that need. It was understood that neighbors helped neighbors in such circumstances.

Yet as outspoken as the diaries of Lucy and the other Pier women were concerning illness and death, they were markedly silent on matters concerning feminine health and associated problems. From their distinct dichotomy between public and private acceptability, we must decipher Lucy's remarks as they provide telling clues to the codes of early diaries. The subject of menstruation was never directly mentioned in any of the diaries, and childbirth was broached only in the most delicate fashion. Typical of Victorian reserve about sexual matters, the diaries may instead contain codes for these topics, which were known only to the authors. Lillian Schlissel maintains that contemporary readers "should anticipate reticence about subjects such as sex, childbirth and marital relationships," and look instead for patterns that silently represent the taboo subject.[96]

---

95. Silverthorne, *Plantation Life in Texas*, 151.

96. Lillian Schlissel, "Diaries of Frontier Women: On Learning to Read the Obscured Patterns," in *Woman's Being, Woman's Place*, ed. Mary Kelley (Boston: G. K. Hall, 1979), 54.

Aunt Lu, for example, left blanks in certain entries that could easily have been filled in had they not concerned matters of such a personal nature. On January 9, 1863, she wrote concerning one of the slaves, "Ellen sick to night got the _____." When this comment is compared with others that Aunt Lu made, it hardly seems likely that she was speaking of something like a cold in this passage. Usually blunt and forthright, here she seemed unable to include a term for menstrual cramps. Earlier, in 1860, she had commented, "got one of the worst _____ ever had" (9/10/60). Aunt Lu, at this time a woman of forty-six, was approaching menopause, and was probably experiencing some of the associated changes in her body. However, she could not bring herself to name her problem. The acknowledgement of "the worst _____" was as close as she could delicately go.

For all her outspokenness, Lucy, too, remained remarkably silent on the subject. As freely as she expressed herself about all manner of topics, this was one area where she would not venture. Despite her reticence, however, a close inspection of her diary entries may signal a revealing pattern. In many writings of nineteenth-century women, the phrase "being sick" implied the onset of the monthly period or pregnancy, and Lucy readily used this term.[97] At regular intervals, approximately thirty days apart, she recorded being sick with maladies such as headaches, the vapors, or other vague illnesses. Using the same code, she confided in her journal about her cousin Lu, writing, "Lu has been preparing herself today for sickness tomorrow"—quite a telling remark, considering that few knew in advance about the onset of a future illness.

Lucy, in fact, wrote with outrage when others made what she considered unseemly remarks, using her diary to vent her embarrassment, then expressed equal alarm when she herself committed the same blunder. So restrained was she about matters such as childbirth that her chagrin knew no bounds when she inadvertently allowed Mr. Wiley to read a friend's letter that gave details about a multiple birth. And it was only in passing that Lucy mentioned that "E" had just borne her fourteenth child, with no mention at all of her friend's labor and delivery (10/8/63).

It is understandable that as a young single woman, Lucy would avoid some subjects. However, it is harder to grasp such reserve when the experience was one's own, as in Cousin Sarah's case. When Sarah Pier married Henry Wiley in January 1865, she included in her journal lofty spiritual descriptions of their love and commitment. On her wedding day, she wrote, "The hour is drawing near when I will take upon me the holy vows of a wife.

---

97. Elizabeth Hampsten, *Read This Only to Yourself* (Bloomington: Indiana University Press, 1982), 105.

Tis strange how calm I am. The struggle is past—I am determined and God has given me grace to fearlessly go forward" (1/25/65). The following morning, she inscribed, "I am this morning—a wife—God help me to nobly fulfill my duty as such" (1/26/65). There are no references to the physical aspect of their union, nor should any be expected. Historian Barbara Welter explains that Victorian mentality "insisted on the utmost privacy as well as the utmost sanctity of the marriage bed."[98] Apparently Sarah felt this need for privacy so strongly that she could not even write within the pages of her own diary the details of her pregnancy, which occurred shortly after her marriage.

During this time, pregnancy was a cause for much fear and trembling. All manner of complications could accompany pregnancy, labor, and delivery, and here again, medical science had not progressed rapidly enough to ensure safety for mother or child. Expectant mothers spent their time torn between anticipation over the new arrival and fear of the impending birth. Lizzie Neblett, for example, lamented each succeeding pregnancy, as she fearfully awaited her time of travail.[99] Women had nine months to consider their own mortality since, as Judith Leavitt writes, "nine months gestation could mean nine months to prepare for death. A possible death sentence came with every pregnancy."[100] Yet Sarah never recorded fears of any kind. It is impossible even to tell when she first guessed of her own pregnancy, for she never mentioned the possibility.

Here again, however, code phrases sound the alert. Throughout the entries for the summer of 1865, Sarah repeatedly complained of feeling tired and/or being sick, yet it was not until September 3 that she gave any indication as to the cause of her problems. At the end of that day's entry she wrote, "Sis spent most of yesterday evening cutting out little clothes for me—for me! How strange!" (9/3/65). And that is how Sarah announced her pregnancy—"little clothes." There was no further mention of her condition until October 14, when she wrote, "I am sitting before the fire in the parlor (which is now converted into my sick room) near by—lying sweetly sleeping is my little one, my precious gift from heaven—I am now a mother" (10/14/65). Much later in the entry, Sarah noted that the baby, a girl, was born on September 27, almost six weeks prematurely. The silence surrounding Sarah's pregnancy and delivery make it virtually impossible to discover what, if any, concerns

---

98. Welter, *Dimity Convictions*, 14.

99. Elizabeth Scott Neblett, *A Rebel Wife in Texas: The Diary and Letters of Elizabeth Scott Neblett*, ed. Erika L. Murr (Baton Rouge: Louisiana State University Press, 2001), 12.

100. Judith W. Leavitt, "Under the Shadow of Maternity," in *Women's America: Refocusing the Past*, ed. Linda K. Kerber and Jane Sherron DeHart, 4th ed. (New York: Oxford University Press, 1995), 186.

and fears she might have had. Nor can it be determined how the labor progressed or how she fared.

Then, as now, the presence of illness and death, among all ages, was part of the fabric of life. Lucy's diary is replete with stories chronicling account after account of one person or another doing battle against the common foe. She was careful to record minute details about a person's symptoms, the prescribed treatment, and even death itself, when it came. The preservation of these details reflects a fascination with death that was common in the nineteenth century. In *The Popular Mood of Pre-Civil War America*, Lewis Saum contends that the high mortality rates and the lack of professionals who could step in at the appropriate time created an intimacy with death that extended throughout society.[101] Details of a patient's passing were of extreme importance, and nothing was too trivial to notice. Thus, when Sarah attended the passing of young Rufus Campbell, it was normal for her to note that she had fanned and bathed his face until he died and then closed his loving eyes. Later, she went on to add, "Mrs. C. & I have been busy all day arranging things. I have washed the blood and foam off Rufus face more than twenty times today—he looked dreadfully before he was buried—decomposition was going on rapidly" (9/1/63).

Again, the community responded to the bereaved family's needs, providing assistance with preparations, even the building of caskets and sitting up with the body of the deceased. Lucy's journal furnishes detailed descriptions of the practices surrounding death and mourning, allowing for a fuller understanding of the social mores of the time. Indeed, her journal validates Saum's research, which reveals that besides needing graphic details, nineteenth-century mourners commonly expressed an acceptance of death, without question and without anger. Grief was marked by a fatalistic resignation that focused on how someone had died: Was she or he a great sufferer, or did she or he die hard? Was physical anguish countered by a resigned submission to the situation, or did an agonizing death indicate a poor spiritual condition? A high compliment, indeed, was the comment that someone had died a triumphant death.[102] The Pier family, then, was typical in their response to death, as Sarah commented that Rufus had, two days before his death, asked his uncle Cyrus to pray for him, had even prayed himself, and had "made several remarks that [led] them to think he was resigned and willing to die" (9/1/63). Years earlier, Aunt Lu had written similarly, observing, "Our

---

101. Lewis O. Saum, *The Popular Mood of Pre-Civil War America* (Westport, CT: Greenwood Press, 1980), 78–88.

102. Ibid., 99–101.

brother Otis Pier in the full possession of his senses calm and resigned . . . he folded his hands upon his breast and so calm and peaceful was his departure that you hardly knew it only upon the closest observation (thus he passed away)" (9/20/52). Death was seen as instructional to the one departing and as a repository of valuable lessons for those left behind. When her father-in-law passed away, Aunt Lu wrote, "Thus passed away a very dear good man. A devoted follower of Christ. My wish is that we may all be able to profit by his example" (3/20/56). Likewise, in Lucy's final remarks following Rufus's funeral service, we see, more than a sense of grief, a philosophical acceptance of the sad loss of such a young life.

Slavery had been an integral part of life in Texas since colonization days, and it by far overshadowed any other social construction or institution present in the state. As is obvious from the earliest entries in the diary, the Pier household embraced the racial hierarchy entrenched in 1860s Texas, and they were not alone. Historian Randolph Campbell calculates that at the outbreak of the Civil War, there were nearly two hundred thousand slaves in Texas. As can be seen by the Pier diaries, the practice remained relatively untouched in many homes throughout the hostilities. Campbell believes that the reason for this can be simply explained by the lack of active conflict in Texas. He asserts, "Texas escaped any significant invasion by Federal troops, and thus the great majority of the state's slaves were not uprooted by advancing armies or given an opportunity to flee to nearby Union forces."[103] Other historians, such as Eugene Genovese and Drew Gilpin Faust, concur.[104] Without interference from Federal troops and with a rationale of necessity, Texas planters and farmers continued to work their slaves for the duration of the conflict. The threat of losing their workers, in fact, was what prompted many Texans to vote for secession in early 1861.[105] One of the earliest mentions of any type of political activity or tension in Aunt Lu's diary involves the secession vote. On the same day that Lucy took her teaching examination, Aunt Lu noted, "Election all over the state to take the vote for Union or Cecession" (1/23/61).

With the growth of the cotton economy, the value of slaves rose steadily. Campbell reports that even with "more than a 200-per cent increase in the slave population from 1850 to 1860, prices . . . nearly doubled."[106] In an entry

103. Campbell, *Empire for Slavery*, 231.

104. Drew Gilpin Faust, "Trying to Do a Man's Business," *Southern Stories: Slaveholders in Peace and War* (Columbia: University of Missouri Press, 1992), 176.

105. Campbell, *Empire for Slavery*, 229.

106. Ibid., 69.

that validates this assertion, Aunt Lu recorded in her journal on April 3, 1855, "Mr. Pier bought a Negro (Harry) in Houston paid fifteen hundred dollars for him." According to Austin County tax rolls, the Piers owned eleven slaves by 1860, valued at $8,000. The value of their real estate was $15,000, and the total value of their personal estate (which included the slaves) was $26,000.[107] By 1861, the number of slaves had risen to thirteen, and in 1864, the last year that the category for slaves was included in the tax records, their slaveholdings topped out at fourteen.[108] These numbers place the Pier family well within the top 25 percent of slave owners in the state. In her article "Trying to Do a Man's Business," Drew Gilpin Faust uses the North Texas family of Will and Lizzie Neblett to explore this issue, and the figures she presents for them indicate that the Neblett family's economic position was comparable to that of the Pier family. The Nebletts, whose real estate was valued at $12,500 and whose personal property was valued at $14,500, ranked well above the state average, owning a total of eleven slaves. Since only 3 percent of the landowners in Texas owned more than twenty slaves (the minimum that afforded them planter status), the Nebletts (and by inference, the Piers) lived within the upper stratum of Texas economic culture.[109]

However, once the war began, life for the Nebletts changed much more dramatically than it did for the Piers. Because James B. Pier was forty-nine years old when the Confederate draft was instituted in 1862, he retained reserve status and remained at home to oversee his slave population. Will Neblett, however, enlisted in the Confederate army at age thirty-seven, leaving Lizzie to manage on her own. This shift in management from male to female created a crisis of authority for Lizzie, and other women in similar positions, as they attempted to fill the gap left by their husbands' departure. Faust asserts that these wives felt increasingly overwhelmed with their new responsibilities, a problem exacerbated by the condescending attitudes of the slaves. Both blacks and whites held a hierarchical view of their society, and the slaves saw the plantation mistress's efforts as a poor substitute for the master's supreme authority. Faust finds that the slaves themselves "frequently seemed to share their mistresses' views of their own incapacities. One Virginia woman complained that the slaves 'all think I am a kind of usurper and have no authority over them.'"[110] The women's problem, in fact, found its basis in the very nature of the slave system.

---

107. *Austin County Census 1860*, Dallas Public Library.
108. *Austin County Tax Rolls, 1860–1865*, Dallas Public Library.
109. Faust, "Trying to Do a Man's Business," 178.
110. Faust, *Mothers of Invention*, 57.

Southern slavery was a patriarchal system controlled by dominant white males. Women with absentee husbands had real problems asserting an authority that was considered subsidiary at best. Additionally, many women in the South were so dependent on their slaves that they had trouble with even the most basic household chores. Elite white women who knew little or nothing about running a household could expect little in the way of automatic obedience when it came time to oversee an entire plantation.[111]

For Aunt Lu, however, neither of these situations applied. Uncle Pier was nearly always available for arbitration and/or discipline, and Aunt Lu knew the minutest details about the properties that the Piers owned. James Bradford Pier's ongoing presence enabled him to enforce the system of patriarchy that underpinned the institution of slavery. The image of the father was constantly reinforced by the planters themselves, says Randolph Campbell, who writes that the plantation owners "generally preferred to see themselves as benevolent paternalists. Their slaves, they said, were like members of their families."[112] Genovese agrees, stating that the "slaveholders meant precisely what they said when they referred, privately as well as publicly, to 'our family, white and black.'"[113]

Lucy captured this system of benevolent protection practiced by Southern slaveholders as she wrote frequently, and sometimes fondly, of reciprocal exchanges of food, shared chores, and even caregiving duties. This, of course, implied a structure that served to protect and provide for the welfare of the slaves. However, while the slave owner preferred to consider himself the "benevolent father," his actions were usually not entirely altruistic. In reality, through the provision of goods and services, the slaveholder more tightly tied the slaves to himself. By forcing the slaves' dependence for basic food, clothing, and medical care, historian Drew Gilpin Faust explains, the owner justified the unpaid labor as a "legitimate return for the master's protection and support."[114] This system of protectionism was not only a mechanism of individual slaveholders, however. Campbell explains further, reporting that the Texas Constitution of 1845 had, in fact, mandated this responsibility for the physical care of slaves, deeming negligence to provide basic food and clothing a criminal offense and assessing a fine of up to $2,000 upon conviction.[115] The Pier family ratified the system of exchange wholeheartedly,

---

111. Ibid., 78.

112. Campbell, *Empire for Slavery*, 195.

113. Eugene D. Genovese, *The Southern Tradition* (Cambridge: Harvard University Press, 1994), 69.

114. Faust, "Trying to Do a Man's Business," 174.

115. Campbell, *Empire for Slavery*, 174.

spending vast quantities of time in clothing production for the slaves and providing medical care for them as well.

In the midst of this patriarchal system, J. B. and Lu Pier shared certain duties as partners, including the management and discipline of their slaves. On March 7, 1862, for example, Lu Pier recorded, "I whipped Ellen to night—not the first time." One month later, she noted, "Mr. P whipped Ellen, Wm & Civilia to night" (4/13/62). Each retained the authority and discretion to deal with insubordination as needed. At one point, Lucy documented a dispute involving two slaves, Winnie and Parrot—a dispute that had escalated within the Pier household to involve Uncle Pier and Aunt Lu. From Lu Pier's diary, it is apparent that although she and James Bradford Pier retained independent discretion, they felt free to question each other's actions and discuss their differences. On July 13, 1863, when Aunt Lu whipped Mary and Winnie, apparently Uncle Pier questioned her judgment, for the next day she wrote, "Mr. Pier went to the store early this morn. Ask me about whipping the Negroes yesterday & thinks I am not consistent." Although Aunt Lu elaborated on neither the circumstances nor the resolution of the matter, her use of the word "consistent" brings to mind the parent/child relationship, with its attendant responsibility of instruction and discipline. Indeed, this was the prevailing perception of ordained authority and responsibility of slaveholders across the South.

Yet, while it is clear that Lu Pier frequently administered punishment to the slaves, in this instance, the slaves had apparently felt a sense of injustice and had complained. This picture of parental control resting with the father figure explains the situation that Uncle Pier and Aunt Lu faced when they had their discussion at the store. The slaves had not gone directly to Aunt Lu, but had gone "over her head" to the supreme authority of Uncle Pier. There is, however, no indication from Aunt Lu's entry that he reprimanded her or countermanded any orders that she had given. He stated only that he thought she was inconsistent, which leaves the impression not of a condescending monologue, but of a dialogue between partners. The outcome for the slaves, however, remained constant—they were located at the bottom of the hierarchy.

Lu Merry Pier's diary is, in fact, filled with accounts of punitive measures taken against recalcitrant slaves. Two of the slaves, Winnie and Ellen, seemed particularly prone to fighting with each other, and this gave occasion for repeated disciplinary measures. In August 1862, Aunt Lu recorded, "Today Mr. Pier after dinner took Winny out under a peach tree and whipt her with a strop. Ellen says Winnie cut her dress sleeve." From Aunt Lu's journal, it is apparent that the two women had a history of conflict. One or the other, it seems, was constantly in trouble. In July 1860, Aunt Lu had written ominously, "Made a discovery this morn at about 7 A.M. Gave Winny a glorious whipping in the barn and it was only half what she deserved."

This propensity for violence was neither rare nor regretted. Drew Gilpin Faust maintains that while violence was theoretically used as a last resort, in reality it was ever present.[116] Randolph Campbell concurs, reporting that violence was used frequently enough for every slave to be aware of its possibility. He also asserts that slave owners "tended to view whippings as a necessary disciplinary measure, not as cruel treatment," again much as a parent would discipline a child.[117] And as a parent would forgo regret for administering punishment in exchange for the future obedience and proper conduct of the child, for all of the mentions of whippings in Aunt Lu's diary, never did she express any remorse or any sympathy.

Although records clearly indicate that the Piers readily administered corporal punishment, on occasion they also resorted to other measures, such as imposing restrictions on the slaves' movements. For example, on May 26, 1861, Aunt Lu noted, "Harriet, Winnie and Dick went to Mrs. Cyrus Campbells to see Aunt Patsy came back and went to church without asking liberty. Mr. P. says they shall not leave the place again for one year from today which is May 26th 1861." However, there were times as well when the conflict became so intense that the slaves fled the premises entirely, as in the case involving Winnie and Parrot. Lucy merely acknowledged the situation in her journal, all over a dispute about shoes, but Aunt Lu recorded the grim details of the incident:

> Mr. Pier told Winny to stay at the house but when he came back from Brewers she was gone run away then he took up old Parrot tied him to whip him then he got loose and ran away. Mr. Pier followed him a little ways then came back. Mr. Withers went to Martin's after him & his Negro dogs but he had come up here and he told Mr. Pier that it was too warm then the dogs would not track in the heat.
> Lu Merry Pier, 7/20/63

For Aunt Lu to mention the use of dogs to track the slaves was also not unusual; she wrote of it more than once. However, she never questioned the

---

116. Faust, "Trying to Do a Man's Business," 175.
117. Campbell, *Empire for Slavery*, 146.

morality of this or any other practice associated with slave control. And as Lucy's diary indicates, this particular drama would continue for a number of days before both slaves returned and the social organization continued, unchanged.

Though Aunt Lu never questioned any practices associated with slave control, more often than not her tone conveyed mounting frustration with the entire situation. On occasion, the slaves resorted to a form of passive resistance in order to combat the demands of their owners, using illnesses of all sorts to escape many of their duties. Deborah Gray White reports that slave women were actually very good at inventing methods and schemes to win their own way. Often female slave resistance rested heavily on the female inclination to feign illness to change a work assignment, or even gain a respite.

White concludes that much of the time, this strategy of feigned illness was successful due to the reproductive capacity of the female slaves. The owners' investment had to be protected, despite the vague symptoms that often accompanied these illnesses, and the slaves' complaints were heeded.[118] Instances of illness were recorded so often in Aunt Lu's journal that this tactic must be suspected. Aunt Lu's frustration is apparent as she repeatedly recorded the illness of first one slave, then another. In a sample three-week period in August 1862, she noted six days of illness for Winnie and thirteen for Ellen. Ellen, it seems, stretched the limits of credibility so severely that even the other slaves turned on her, forcing her to leave "her nest" and return to work (Aunt Lu, 8/22/62). This type of infraction rated one of the few mentions of slave problems in Sarah's diary. With a rare note of sarcasm, she wrote, "Ellen managed to crawl out in time to help finish dinner" (7/30/62).

While the problems were ever present for Aunt Lu, Sarah and Lucy remained, for the most part, oblivious to the tension. Interestingly, Lucy remained silent concerning any ideological rejection of the hierarchical system. It would seem that since she had come into the system only recently, she would bring a distinctly Northern mind-set with her. However, no outright condemnations of slavery present themselves within the pages of her journal. Instead, she seemed to take for granted existing hierarchies, and by the time she began her 1863 journal, her implicit acceptance appears to rule. She regarded the slaves as her friends, writing of them often and fondly, as members of the family, and at one point, even writing of bringing the "darkies" into the family house to care for them. But like longtime residents of the state, Lucy made very clear and stereotypical distinctions. Her Northern

---

118. Deborah Gray White, "The Nature of Female Slavery," in *Women's America*, ed. Linda K. Kerber and Jane Sherron DeHart, 4th ed. (New York: Oxford University Press, 1995), 104–117.

roots seem to have been supplanted by the Southern philosophies that surrounded her.

On those occasions when Lucy did write of slave problems, most often it signaled a perceived threat to the safety of the neighborhood. In 1864, she wrote of slaves who had apparently stolen from a neighbor and had beaten him severely (6/28/64). Uncle Pier and the other white men of the community met to formulate a plan to capture and punish the perpetrators. As a leader in the community and as a slaveholder, James Bradford Pier had an obvious stake in maintaining the status quo. Although it is unclear if Uncle Pier was a member of an official posse or if he and the other men in the community were banding together as vigilantes, he participated fully in any correction the group deemed necessary.

What that punishment might be was clearly spelled out in the slave code that operated in Texas during the mid-nineteenth century. Randolph Campbell states that the code addressed five areas of concern: the right to own slaves, laws concerning criminal acts against slave property, conduct of slaves, laws concerning runaway slaves, and laws concerning free blacks. In the matter of slave conduct, the law was quite specific—two punishments were available: whipping or death. If the infractions were minor, whippings were administered, and often these types of violations were not even brought before the court. However, if the infraction was more serious, such as rape of a white woman or murder, the slave had the right to a jury trial; the punishment for a guilty verdict was death by hanging. These were considered capital offenses, and were to be tried in district court. Campbell goes on to state that, most frequently, slaves were presumed guilty and were frequently dealt with by "lynch law."[119]

Yet in stark contrast to the energy expended in enforcing the hierarchy, there also existed within the system a great deal of reciprocal exchange between master and slave. Rhys Isaac believes that this exchange had to be constantly maintained in order to sustain the hierarchical control of master over slave. He states that the "master's disposition of material and social resources, extending even to the domicile of the slaves, inevitably rendered him an extremely potent figure in the slaves' world."[120] From medical care to clothing, the master dispensed goods and services in a manner that, on the surface, supposedly sustained the slaves, but on a deeper level, upheld his own position of patriarchal control. For their part of the bargain, the slaves were supposed to perform the chores assigned to them, from housework to

---

119. Campbell, *Empire for Slavery*, 103–105.
120. Isaac, *Transformation of Virginia*, 339.

picking cotton. When those chores suffered, however, or another arbitrary infraction occurred, the owner exercised his "right" to mete out discipline. Yet in the midst of this dichotomy, it is apparent that a familial bond and a fondness existed between the Piers and their slaves; Lucy's notes about the toasts with the slaves on Christmas Day and her record of a dinner at Cousin Waller's for the "darkies" (12/26/63), as well as other mentions of reciprocity of goods, services, and even affection, confirm the close connections.

However, in her last entry of 1863, the afterthought with which Lucy closed the year, "Jim has been in the Woods most all the P.M.," she provides a simple yet chilling vignette from the institution at the core of the national conflict—the situation of the slave. In a firmly entrenched hierarchy, the slave had minimal recourse for grievances; regardless of the cause—whether it was mistreatment, false accusation, or conflict among themselves—slaves were at the mercy of their owners.

Ultimately, two contradictions present themselves in this picture of slavery in the Pier household. First, the Pier family had migrated not from another Southern state to Texas, but from Ohio, a free state in the North. Coming as they did from the North, where an emerging rejection of slavery was under way, they had little background from which to justify Southern acceptance of slavery. Stephen F. Austin had, in fact, endorsed a project in 1827 for colonizing farmers from Ohio to east Texas, a few short years before the Piers' arrival, noting that the "inhabitants of Ohio are known to be 'principled' against slavery, and if the government of Mexico wishes to convert Texas from a useless wilderness to a civilized state, 'sound policy, and expediency I should presume would approve of a decided encouragement of Ohio and other northern migration.'"[121] The Piers' apparent endorsement and employment of slavery therefore seems somewhat incongruous with their background, and their absolute acceptance of the system, with its attendant violence and hierarchy, reflects a possible capitulation brought on by expediency rather than philosophy.

The final inconsistency in this ongoing tug-of-war, however, is that after the Emancipation Proclamation had been read to the slaves in June 1865 (Sarah Pier, 6/24/65), several of the slaves, including Winnie and Ellen, remained with the family as paid help. Despite all of the conflict and inequity, it seems that, for these two women at least, the familiar was more comforting that the unknown, and ties between former slave and master transcended even the pull of freedom.

---

121. Campbell, *Empire for Slavery*, 22.

From the beginning of her journal until her departure from Texas in the spring of 1865, the Civil War framed every aspect of Lucy Pier Stevens's life. She felt its restrictions, endured its separations, grieved for its losses, and prayed for its end. Many of her most poignant entries center on one aspect or another of the war. While her reports of individual battles are usually sketchy, many of the best-known engagements are included in the text, with a definite emphasis on the conflict in the western theater. Not once did Lucy mention the Battle of Gettysburg, but the Siege of Vicksburg ranked high on the list of her concerns. Many of the local boys saw action in and around Louisiana, and their safety was her obvious focus. Lucy cited the capture of the Union ship *Harriet Lane* in Galveston; Stonewall Jackson's death rated a mention in her journal, and battles at Donaldsonville, "Chancy-ville," Brasher City, and New Iberia were all included. Units such as Waller's Battalion and Sibley's Brigade gained a place in the pages of the diary, as did some of the men of the celebrated Terry's Texas Rangers. However, comments regarding the activities of Union commanders were filled with skepticism, and sometimes outright disdain. Yet along with, and even more telling than, the frequent mention of the personalities and places commonly associated with the Civil War were Lucy's own perceptions of the war and its web of related crises.

In Lucy's diary, we are able to glimpse the larger historical picture through a woman's eyes, as she offered details about various battles, documenting victories and defeats, prisoners and casualties. She painted vivid images of "the soldier life" as she recorded anecdotes told by her beloved soldier boys, yet she also included details that only a woman might notice—a trinket retrieved from the battlefield, or, more importantly, anxious hours spent waiting for a soldier to arrive home. At the same time, she anguished over the carnage brought on by brother fighting brother, mourning not only for losses suffered by her loved ones in Texas but also for her own losses as she remained absent from her home in Ohio. This is only part of the picture, however, for it is the unique blending of North and South as Lucy negotiated her world in Texas, with themes of femininity and of "quasi-southernness" entwined and braided together, that heightens the value of her diary.

Lucy's journal indicates that, to a great degree, Lucy Pier Stevens "put on" Southernness, trying it on for a while, as one would wear a cloak. Even her adoption of the Texas-trademark colloquialism "fixin' to" (2/15/64) indicates the degree to which she embraced Southern culture. But her acceptance did not end with superficial modifications in speech. Many entries convey an acquiescence with Southern ideology, as Lucy groped to find a philosophy to hold as her own. Her sequestration from Northern attitudes and perceptions shaped many of her views, for she heard only the Southern perspective throughout the years of war. Most importantly, whereas Lucy knew what her Texas soldier boys were going through, she had no idea of the travails of the soldiers in Ohio. Thus, she jubilantly recorded the news, erroneous though it might be, of a "perfect slaughter" of Yankees at Vicksburg (7/1/63), and positioned herself with the Southern side, expressing not only support for the Confederate generals but also a belief in Southern propaganda and a loyalty to strong Southern sentiment. At the same time, Lucy assigned an "otherness" to Federal officers, and wrote scathingly of "Yankee" tricks. Her comments praising the Democrats' 1864 nomination of General George B. McClellan, Abraham Lincoln's former commander of the Army of the Potomac, point to Southern sympathies for the "peace candidate," and her later note regarding "that Federal president's inauguration" indicate her distrust of Yankees and their views (3/4/65).

Yet, perhaps the most enigmatic expression of Lucy's less than complete assumption of Southern sentiments was her comment following the fall of Vicksburg. As the incoming reports became increasingly grim, Lucy wrote: "The Press & People generally seemed somewhat despondent, indeed since the fall of Vicksburg that feeling seems quite plain. That God will defend the right is my wish. No doubt there are few who would agree with me in what I consider right though" (8/27/63). Even as Lucy wore Southernness on the outside, the thoughts she expressed privately indicate an absence of complete capitulation, for as she asked God to defend the right, her words imply a sense of ambiguity. Although she refrained from explicitly stating one position or the other, her words hint at the possibility of another, differing perspective—one that she guarded closely, knowing that a radical departure from Southern views would bring censure and alienation within her circle of family and friends. Instead, she chose to concentrate on her long and continuous association with the people of Travis. This, in turn, aided her in focusing on the contributions Southerners made, the dangers they faced, the sacrifices they offered, weaving them together as she navigated her terrain.

At other times, Lucy's recognition of her Northern heritage spilled forth, and she furiously wrote of prejudices she encountered. While she was willing to concede differing political views, she refused to allow others to disrespect her and her heritage, castigating them within the sanctuary of her diary. Even innocent comments might bring an acknowledgement of her Northern roots, as when she wryly recounted, "Cousin W just said, 'You scour mighty often—scoured just a week ago.' I wonder what he'd think of some of the 'Yankees'" (3/20/63). As far as we can tell, however, Lucy held herself in check, resisting her impulses to call attention to her outsider status. Rather, she used the diary to vent her frustrations and to work through her ambivalent feelings.

As a practical matter, Lucy recorded ongoing efforts intended to offset the sacrifices of the soldiers and meet their needs as the war continued. From a local fair in early April 1863, complete with baked goods and trinkets, to sewing bees concentrating on basic necessities, her journal provides solid examples of the documented efforts throughout Texas to raise funds and provide supplies as the war lengthened.[122] Women across the South had turned to sewing and knitting as important outlets by which they might show their support for the Confederacy. Uniforms and tents, socks and gloves, all came to be seen as worthy contributions for the men at the front, and women viewed their efforts as a feminine form of warfare. One woman wrote, "Our needles are now our weapons and we have a part to perform as well as the rest ... Yes, yes, we women have mighty work to perform for which we will be responsible."[123] An appeal to this domestic outpouring of patriotism can be seen in an open letter that appeared in the Bellville Countryman in November 1863. The letter, addressed "To the Ladies of Austin County," outlined an urgent plea for aid for the troops in Louisiana:

I have learned through reliable men who have recently returned from the camp of our troops in Louisiana, that there are many men in Flournoy's Regiment and particularly in Capt. Zimri Hunt's company who are almost destitute of clothing. Many of these men are not able to supply themselves, nor have they friends at home able to furnish them. These men are our friends, and neighbors, they are in the field, enduring the hardships and privations of the camp, to defend and protect us and ours. The cold blasts of winter are approaching and these men must be protected against them. I now appeal to the ladies of this county for their relief, they need socks, shoes, shirts and in fact every species of clothing.[124]

---

122. Vicki Betts, "'A Sacred Charge Upon Our Hands': Assisting the Families of Confederate Soldiers in Texas, 1861–1865," in The Seventh Star of the Confederacy: Texas during the Civil War, ed. Kenneth W. Howell (Denton: University of North Texas Press, 2009), 246–267.

123. Faust, Mothers of Invention, 24.

124. "To the Ladies of Austin County," Bellville Countryman, November 14, 1863, Texas and Other Southern States Civil War Newspapers/Newspaper Research, 1861–1865.

The plea concerned clothing for the men, but as Lucy reports in her diary, the needs continued and extended beyond clothing to basic sustenance and medical care. And, as was often the case, loved ones at home used every means possible to provide for their soldier boys, either traveling to the front themselves, sending supplies by way of a neighbor, or opening their homes to the wounded. More than once, Lucy found the house turned into a make-shift hospital, with ailing soldiers occupying her schoolroom. Far from an unusual occurrence, this type of scene played out across the country. Drew Gilpin Faust explains that there were never sufficient official facilities in which to nurse the sick and the wounded, and communities set up makeshift hospitals in public spaces and private homes alike.[125] Thus, although there was a military hospital in Hempstead, the Pier family, like many others, will-ingly opened their home to aid the effort whenever needed.

Lucy's journal offers a wealth of information concerning problems that plagued the armies of the Confederate States of America (CSA). She wrote repeatedly of conscription attempts, obliquely acknowledging serious morale problems facing the Confederate army. Both Northern and South-ern governments had adopted a system of compulsory service and insti-tuted programs to supplement enlistment rosters. In fact, James McPherson reports, Southern leaders such as Robert E. Lee saw this plan as the only way to avoid disaster. Begun in the South in 1862 with the passage of a national conscription law, the practice initially affected young men between the ages of eighteen and thirty-five, but eventually was adjusted to encompass those between seventeen and fifty.[126] Furthermore, until December 1863, substi-tutes for the regular army could be purchased for $300, creating an obvious inequity based on wealth and enabling an unfair evasion of service.[127] This caused a huge decline in troop morale that bled over into the civilian popu-lation. In February 1864, Sarah noted in her diary with a note of satisfaction that the "substitute law is done away with now and all that have substitutes have to take their places in ranks as well as the rest" (2/23/64).

Several times Lucy casually mentioned conscription attempts as well, spe-cifically those targeting one or another of the local men she knew, and when Aunt Lu reported a special draft for men over forty-five, she noted with relief in her own diary, "as Mr. Pier is postmaster he is exempt" (12/31/62). Yet even at the age of forty-nine, James Bradford Pier served in a reserve company known locally as "the Minutemen," a unit charged with the maintenance of

---

125. Faust, *Mothers of Invention*, 109–110.

126. James M. McPherson, *Ordeal by Fire*, 2nd ed. (New York: McGraw-Hill, 1992), 184–185.

127. Waller County Historical Survey Commission, *History of Waller County*, 105.

order at home and the guard of any prisoners brought into the area. For the Piers, the threat of sudden removal from the home instead lay at their son-in-law's door, and Cousin Lu worried her way through her husband's every absence. Lucy, in fact, recorded at one point, "Lu is so low spirited that W [Waller] has not come from Bellville," indicating the constant concern that Cousin Lu carried.

Coupled with the repeated conscription attempts was the ongoing problem of troop desertions, and Lucy's diary provides strong evidence of the dilemma. Statistics validate the numbers that she cited, as muster rolls show that more than half of the 400,000 soldiers enlisted in the Confederate army were absent by the end of 1864.[128] They fled hunger and illness and miserable conditions at the front, and were drawn homeward by the unbearable desperation of their relatives. Women who had fervently embraced the Cause now questioned its worth in terms of personal cost. Many calculated that prior payment, in economic and emotional scrip, had indeed exceeded the value of any moral victory over the North. In North Carolina, Sal Mabry bluntly asked her husband, "What do you think of going back into the Union? Don't you think it would be better than to have all our men killed?"[129] Even in Texas, where most families were at a distance from the conflict, many women begged their husbands to return home in spite of the stigma and penalties associated with desertion. As a refugee in Texas, Mary Pugh wrote to her husband of the extent of her own sacrifice and urgently pleaded, "The truth is . . . you must come home."[130] Drew Gilpin Faust asserts that "the risk of execution and the shame of flight now seemed acceptable in the face of almost certain and almost certainly useless injury or death at the front" (243). Thus, Lucy's entries reflect the increasing problem in the South, a problem that had become so severe that Confederate newspapers began to offer incentives to their female citizens in exchange for information. In April 1864, the *Austin State Gazette* reported:

> We omitted to inform our lady friends that some time ago Gen. Magruder issued an order, that any lady who will arrest or cause to be arrested a deserter, would be entitled to a furlough for twenty days for any one in the army—whether husband, brother or lover.[131]

---

128. McPherson, *Ordeal by Fire*, 467–468.

129. Faust, *Mothers of Invention*, 240.

130. Ibid., 241.

131. *Austin State Gazette*, April 6, 1864, Texas and Other Southern States Civil War Newspapers/Newspaper Research, 1861–1865.

Other notices were posted, addressed directly to the soldiers themselves:

> To the Absentees of "Terry's Texas Rangers:" I have returned to Texas for the purpose of collecting and returning to the command all men now absent without leave. Those who will report to me at Houston, or to Capt. Terry's Regiment at Austin, Texas, before, or punctually on the 1st of January next, will have full pardon granted them, those failing to do so will be published as deserters, and dealt with accordingly. Rangers, your services are needed with your comrades in Georgia, I appeal to your pride, report promptly and save your [illegible] from the stigma of a deserter.
> S. P. Christian, Major Terry's Texas Rangers[132]

From these accounts, it is obvious that the Confederate army had begun to fight multiple foes—Union forces, disease, and even its own soldiers, who now counted their own sacrifices as sufficient to the Cause and left their posts. In the Pier household, however, where support for the Confederacy ran high, a sense of sadness at the news of desertions displaced desperation. Ongoing reports about the men at the front superseded any long-term consideration for deserters, as evidenced in the pages of Lucy's diary. The deserters' plight was swallowed up in concern for those who stayed at their posts.

Lucy's concern for those at the front was, indeed, legitimate, even when the troops were not engaged in fighting. Gerald F. Linderman reports in *Embattled Courage* that, ultimately, deaths from disease far surpassed the number of battle deaths: "Union battle deaths—those killed in combat or mortally wounded—numbered 110,000, but twice as many, 224,580, died of disease, and in the Confederate forces the ratio must also have approximated two to one."[133] Many times, courage had by now been replaced by despair as battle and disease, hunger and deprivation, death and destruction took their toll on the soldiers. Linderman indicates that although the soldiers exhibited great gallantry and stoicism during the early years of the war, by 1864 no measures of these intangibles could offset the oppressive disillusionment that gripped many.[134] Lucy herself strongly demonstrated the shifts of perception that occurred as the war progressed, noting a distinct "war fatigue" and even sarcastically criticizing as empty and futile the comfort and courage revered in the popular songs of war.

---

132. *Houston Tri-Weekly Telegraph*, November 14, 1864, Texas and Other Southern States Civil War Newspapers/Newspaper Research, 1861–1865.

133. Linderman, *Embattled Courage*, 115.

134. Ibid., 245.

When Lucy gave details of the death of her friend Jack Cochran, on June 12, 1864, her information bears out the research regarding disease and morbidity among Civil War soldiers. Jack's death had nothing to do with battle, but resulted from his exposure to the elements in camp and during prolonged marches that rendered him vulnerable to all types of illness. Childhood diseases, such as mumps and measles, more frequently afflicted the young men from rural areas who had not developed the necessary immunities. Camp diseases, however, knew no such restrictions. Illnesses such as malaria, dysentery, and diarrhea were prevalent among all demographics. Linderman notes that the ratio of battle-related deaths to those from disease was easily two to one, and he quotes Paul Steiner, who called the diseases of the Civil War "natural biological warfare."[135] This unseen foe was responsible for Jack's death, and Lucy sadly recorded the details surrounding the death of yet another friend.

An increase in all violence became an ominous and ubiquitous by-product of the war, and Lucy's journal provides case after case. She wrote of raids being conducted far away in Missouri, with details so horrific that she felt compelled to include the information. Writing of William Clarke Quantrill and his Raiders, Lucy reported on the episode for which Quantrill is best known. Quantrill and his men raided Lawrence, Kansas, on August 21, 1863, looting the town and murdering upwards of 180 men and boys, many in front of their own families.[136] Repulsed by the gruesome incident, Lucy could draw comfort only from the fact that it occurred far away.

However, as the war progressed in its downward spiral, Lucy gave more and more space to the violence occurring in her own area, with a direct correlation to the disintegration of the former constraints upon society and the increased tension of a world upside down. Lucy wrote of episode after episode of vigilante justice in which men defined "justice" according to their own terms and administered it without benefit of law. Historian Richard Maxwell Brown contends that much of this independent action resulted from a perception of justice based on individual response that was acquired on the frontier. He explains that a "distinct regional style of violent behavior emerged . . . an ethic of individual violent self-defense and self-redress, which, in turn, made central Texas more prone to settle difficulties by resorting to violence."[137] Joe

---

135. Ibid., 115.

136. "Death Runs Riot," *The West*, prod. Ken Burns and Stephen Ives.

137. Richard Maxwell Brown, *Strain of Violence: Historical Studies of American Violence and Vigilantism* (New York: Oxford University Press, 1975), 298.

B. Frantz agrees with this concept of individual redress of wrongs, stating that the frontier mind-set extolled independent action as heroic, and uplifted the perpetrators as "men who moved in the face of danger."[138]

Lucy's diary bears witness to this concept as she repeatedly included tales of murder and vengeance for which little, if any, punishment was sought. From runaway slaves to neighborhood feuds, the atmosphere was rife with violent portent. In July 1864, she wrote of a quarrel between two neighbors, an encounter that left one man grazed and one mortally wounded. Reports from Hempstead, also known as "Six-Shooter Junction," disclosed other horrifying stories. In one account, a traveler named Mr. Thomas North disembarked at the rail station in Hempstead and heard shots ring out. However, he had been in Texas long enough to pay little attention to the gunfire, since "the feeling of terror was only a uniform matter of course."[139] The victim, Dr. O's overseer, had had a disagreement with the doctor's wife in the doctor's absence. Mrs. O promptly wrote to the doctor that the overseer had insulted her, upon which the doctor immediately left his post and returned to shoot the overseer in broad daylight. Particularly troubling to North was the doctor's total lack of remorse, for he noted that following the killing, Dr. O looked on with "nonchalance and fiendish satisfaction."[140] Even as Lucy awaited her departure in April 1865, she wrote of the slaying of Mr. Buck, a well-respected neighbor who, because of his Masonic oath, refused to defend himself against his assailant. As we examine Lucy's journal, we can easily see that the violence brought on by war only seemed to inflame an already violent land. As Brown writes, Texas was "a land without surcease from killing and . . . a distinct regional style of violent behavior emerged"; he concludes that "central Texans embraced a mystique of violence," a mystique that Lucy noted all too often.[141]

———

Although Lucy's journal is replete with references to various battles, the most important contribution that the diary makes concerning war information comes with her many entries about the purported invasion of Texas. A successful invasion of Texas and the associated extensive conflict would have changed everything for the state and its residents, and citizens rightly

---

138. Joe B. Frantz and Julian Ernest Choate, Jr., *The American Cowboy: The Myth and the Reality* (Norman: University of Oklahoma Press, 1955), 120.

139. Thomas North, *Five Years in Texas; or, What You Did Not Hear During the War* (Cincinnati: Elm Street Printing Co., 1871), 155–156.

140. Ibid.

141. Brown, *Strain of Violence*, 238.

worried about that prospect. As early as September of 1861, Lucy had heard rumors concerning an expected invasion of Texas; she anxiously wrote:

> News was received here this eve that Texas was to be invaded within sixty days. It is thought Galveston island will be evacuated before many days thinking that it is the intention of the Lincolnites to surround and bombard the city. The citizens of the state are more excited than ever about war & war news. Everyone is making preparations.
>
> Lucy Stevens, 9/19/61

Although this particular report proved false, the rumors surfaced repeatedly throughout the war years, as many in the North took up the cry for an invasion. Union strategists had urged an invasion of Texas, reciting a number of reasons why the move would prove beneficial. Ludwell H. Johnson provides a thorough rationale in his book *Red River Campaign: Politics and Cotton in the Civil War*.[142] He asserts that even before the onset of the war, many had advocated such a move, and one man, Edward Everett Hale, had even pressed for a general invasion almost immediately after Texas was annexed in 1845. Hale, a strong abolitionist, published a tract titled "How to Conquer Texas Before Texas Conquers Us," an exhortation to Northerners to settle in Texas, thus populating the state with ardent anti-abolitionists and "free farmers," a system already put in place by German immigrants to Texas.[143] Johnson reports that the same sentiments were later echoed in publications such as the *New York Times*, where an editorial called for Texas "to be colonized as well as captured."[144] From textile barons in the Northeast, whose supply of cotton had dropped precipitously, to anti-abolitionists, who believed that cotton farming could be easily expanded through more free farming, many believed that with Texas firmly occupied and controlled by the Union, final victory would be swift. Even some among Lincoln's top advisers pushed for an invasion, citing the benefit of disruption of trade on the Mississippi River and a need to end Confederate trade with Mexico. Lincoln finally capitulated when told that the French government was contemplating the annexation of Texas in conjunction with its invasion of Mexico.[145]

---

142. Ludwell H. Johnson, *Red River Campaign: Politics and Cotton in the Civil War* (Baltimore: Johns Hopkins Press, 1958), 3–48.

143. Ibid., 5.

144. Ibid., 21.

145. Ibid., 5.

A series of attempts to occupy Texas, in fact, had resulted, but each had failed. At the beginning of 1864, however, a troop surge was beginning on both sides, a buildup to what is now known as the Red River Campaign. Union forces, waiting for an increase in the water levels of the Red River, were reinforced as troops from both Sherman's and Steele's commands joined in the advance under General Nathaniel Banks.[146] James McPherson writes that Banks ultimately commanded a force of 27,000, while the Confederates had some 30,000 troops spread through the Trans-Mississippi region, with their major fighting force concentrated in Louisiana under the direction of Richard Taylor, son of former president Zachary Taylor.[147] These troops would ultimately clash in intense battles across Louisiana from March until May 1864, involving many of the soldier boys Lucy loved, and her diary would cover the contests in detail as she painstakingly recorded every bit of information that arrived.

With the beginning of the Red River Campaign, in fact, we see a distinct shift in Lucy's diary. The war, which had been held at bay, had existed only at a great distance. Living on the outer edges of the CSA, the residents of Texas had largely been insulated from the storm that raged to the east, and with the fall of Vicksburg, the CSA had, in effect, been cut in half. After Vicksburg, Texas had, for the most part, been severed from the rest of the Confederacy, and "the people living there didn't really know the extent to which the Cause was sliding into disaster."[148] From Lucy's perspective, it seemed for a time that the eastern half of the country had ceased to exist. But now the storm edged closer to Texas, and the residents there knew something of the trepidation that consumed the eastern part of the land.

In his book *In the Presence of Mine Enemies*, Edward L. Ayers examines the dilemma of two towns, one North and one South, caught in the crossfire of the Civil War. He explains that their perceptions and responses were far more complex than many contemporary Americans would assume, telling us in the preface that his study "offers a history of the Civil War told from the viewpoints of everyday people who could glimpse only parts of the drama they were living, who did not control the history that shaped their lives, who made decisions based on what they could know from local newspapers and from one another."[149] In many ways, this is an apt description of Lucy and

---

146. Ibid., 83–85.

147. McPherson, *Ordeal by Fire*, 413.

148. Edward Countryman, personal interview with Vicki Tongate, June 25, 2014.

149. Edward L. Ayers, *In the Presence of Mine Enemies: War in the Heart of America, 1859–1863* (New York: W. W. Norton, 2003), xvii.

her family in Texas. However, there exists a distinct difference between the residents of Chambersburg, Pennsylvania, and Staunton, Virginia—and Travis, Texas. The people of these two Eastern towns, on opposite sides of the Mason-Dixon Line experienced the war up close; they felt the full fury of the conflict and suffered mightily the deprivations. Ayers rightly views them through the lens of the local. And this is where the difference lies. Lucy, in faraway Texas, squinted through the prism of distance. Like the townspeople in the East, the folks of Texas could only partially glimpse the drama unfolding. Yet the view was diffused, thanks to their distant locale. Similar to the residents of the Eastern towns, they had no control of the historic events; conversely, the events had a lesser impact on them. And as restricted as the knowledge base became for the Eastern citizens, this lack must have been magnified many times over for those living so far away, so removed from the epicenter of the war.

Through Lucy's diary, we can see the increasing gap between Texas and the rest of the Confederacy, and this is perhaps one of the journal's most important contributions. Over time, we see the escalating breakdown of information, a veiling of communication that simultaneously lowered knowledge and raised tensions. Lucy's accounts, in fact, offer vivid proof of the botched information, alternating between defective and deficient, that permeated the reports coming in to the citizens of Texas. As war news began to consume more and more space in Lucy's diary, her entries became a hodgepodge of truth and trivia as she processed the events and information of her world. She wrote about news reports—reports that were frequently inaccurate and exasperating. More often than not, rumor replaced reality, and she would write with frustration of an encounter only to amend and correct the account later.

Distances were so great, and reports so tardy that many times even official notices became contradictory exaggerations and misstatements. Yet the informational breakdown can also be attributed to the naval blockade of Galveston. President Lincoln had instituted a blockade of Southern ports almost immediately when the war broke out, calling for the measure five days after the evacuation of Fort Sumter.[150] Ten ports, Galveston among them, received the Union navy's top priority for surveillance and interception. Within eleven days of its implementation, the blockade had netted its first blockade runner, a ship attempting to break through Union lines to continue the trade that the South so desperately needed, and McPherson reports that ultimately more than one-fifth of all blockade runners were captured or

---

150. Hamilton Cochran, *Blockade Runners of the Confederacy* (Indianapolis: Bobbs-Merrill, 1958), 1–46.

destroyed.[151] Yet the accompanying profits were great because of the associated danger, and many blockade runners braved the risks and continued to shuttle back and forth from Nassau, Bermuda, and Havana, with round-trips between Texas and the islands being completed in ten days if there were no delays.[152] In *Waters of Discord: The Union Blockade of Texas during the Civil War*, Rodman L. Underwood notes that Havana was a "favored port for blockade running ... [because of its] deep-water location with adequate dock and warehouse facilities" and most important, "its proximity to the Texas coast."[153]

McPherson goes on to say that during the war years, an estimated eight thousand successful runs were made through the blockade, and as "the Union tightened its blockade against the Southeast part of the Confederacy, a number of runners shifted their bases of operation to the less closely patrolled coast of Texas."[154] However, the Union soon tightened its hold there, and by the last months of 1863,

> Texas was not only close to being cut off from the Confederate States east of the Mississippi River, but her most important communication with the outer world through Mexico was in imminent danger. Galveston was so closely blockaded by a Federal squadron that entrance or exit was considered impossible.[155]

Thanks to Lucy's journal, we gain a sense of the almost total information breakdown. From the lack of information to the garbled accounts transmitted via telegraph and newspapers, we see the growing isolation of the population of Texas. Lucy herself increasingly viewed the reports as frustrating, misleading, and on occasion, laughable. Ultimately, at the end of her sojourn, the isolation of Texas was complete. For as she frantically attempted to leave Texas, Lucy had no idea that the end of the war had already come. The approvals she so desperately sought were, in effect, unnecessary, for the Confederacy had fallen, and the Union had prevailed. But neither Lucy nor anyone else knew this, and "her lack of knowledge only adds to the drama of her flight."[156]

---

151. McPherson, *Ordeal by Fire*, 182.

152. Cochran, *Blockade Runners of the Confederacy*, 64–92.

153. Rodman L. Underwood, *Waters of Discord: The Union Blockade of Texas during the Civil War* (Jefferson, NC: McFarland, 2003) 62.

154. McPherson, *Ordeal by Fire*, 182; Ashecraft, *Texas in the Civil War*, 19.

155. Cochran, *Blockade Runners*, 217.

156. Countryman, Personal interview, June 25, 2014.

The isolation of Texas on the larger scale can be compressed, however, as we examine Lucy's own increasing isolation during her sojourn in Texas. As we see her boundaries and perceptions narrow, we begin to see the parallels between the limited access that Texas had to the intricate workings of the CSA and Lucy's limited/absent contact with her home in Ohio.

Lucy's vulnerability often seeped into the pages of her diary as she contemplated her isolation from her immediate family in the North. Despite the many kindnesses of her Texas kin and the many friendships she had made there, the ties with her parents and siblings had been severed, and she was alone. Even the absent soldier boys enjoyed better homeward connections than Lucy, for as they corresponded with the homefolk, even intermittently, letters were shared and news passed along. Each time a letter arrived, family and friends rejoiced, and while Lucy shared in the exultation, a renewed sense of loneliness must have tugged at her heart as she realized anew the void in her own life.

As Lucy repeatedly indicated, her many attempts to forward letters to Ohio went unheeded. Regularly, she wrote of first one soldier, then another, carrying a letter to the front with him in an effort to send it on. Time and again, she wrote of sending letters to Mexico or Cuba to have them mailed. But as her diary reveals, she waited in vain. Her letters were never sent, and she received none in return. With the receipt of her last Ohio-stamped letter in August 1861, this silence continued for well over three years. Lucy's contact with her Northern family terminated, and she had no way to know how they fared, if they were well, if they lived.

At the same time, Lucy was fortunate to enjoy the comforts of a long-established home built by a stable family. In the midst of her "exile" in Confederate Texas, she connected with family and friends there, and became a fully accepted member of the community. Yet even as family and friends did their best to make her feel welcome, in some respects she still remained an outsider, beholden to the considerations of others, obligated to repay their many kindnesses. When Lucy gave Sammy her watch as a gift, Sarah recorded her own puzzlement over the transaction, writing, "Cousin Lu gave Sammie her watch this evening, I don't know what put her in the notion of it, she said she wanted to give him something nice that he could keep and it *was* a nice present" (3/14/64). What Sarah could not know, and what Lucy's journal divulges, is that even after more than four years in Texas, Lucy considered herself outside the circle of immediate family. Despite her full involvement in and complete access to family relationships, and despite her immersion in the community's network, she still retained a separateness that no one else could comprehend. From her perspective outside the circle of immediate family, Lucy felt a responsibility to defray her expenses; she considered herself under obligation to assist in whatever manner she could, even if it meant parting with personal treasures.

Other, less direct reminders of Lucy's isolation cropped up as well. Many times in the evenings, the family would gather to listen as one read aloud to the others. On one occasion, Aunt Lu noted that she had received a new book to be read to the family (3/5/61). The book, *The Captivity of the Oatman Children*, was an Indian captivity narrative, a wildly popular genre during the last half of the nineteenth century. The narratives foregrounded the breakup of the family unit, along with the progressively intensifying isolation of the captive and the gradual adoption of the captor's ways.[157] As the years passed and Lucy recalled the story, how she must have sensed the similarities to her own situation. And how easy it is for us, as a modern audience, to read Lucy's story as yet another captivity narrative.

The Oatman story that the Piers read told the riveting yet tragic tale of Royce and Mary Ann Oatman, who traveled west with their five children in 1850. After a savage attack by Apaches, only three of the Oatman children survived. Olive, who was fourteen years old at the time, endured five years of starvation and servitude to the Indians and quickly learned that "any expression of discontent was the signal of new toils."[158] She learned the Mojave language, and her face was tattooed in accordance with Mojave custom. Ultimately, after five long years of separation from her own people, she was released, yet she was forever changed, retaining the external scars as well as the interior marks of her captivity.[159]

Hundreds of similar tales circulated as American audiences reveled in the high adventure of the sagas. Yet the stories also revealed that many captives came to appreciate their captors' kindnesses and to adopt their customs. Many of their life habits were seen as wholesome, and their compassion toward others in the tribe did not go unnoticed. Many captives refused to leave, and those who did leave did so with great ambivalence.[160] Cynthia Ann Parker, in Texas, refused to leave her Comanche captors, claiming, "I

157. Richard Slotkin, *Regeneration through Violence: The Mythology of the American Frontier, 1600–1860* (Middletown, CT: Wesleyan University Press, 1973), 94–113.

158. Frances Roe Kestler, *The Indian Captivity Narrative: A Woman's View* (New York: Garland Publishing, 1990), 327.

159. Ibid., 299–343.

160. Ibid., 5.

am happily wedded, I love my husband, who is good and kind, and my little ones, who, too, are his, and I cannot forsake them."[161]

Like these captives, Lucy too had adopted her "captivity" surroundings, acclimating herself to a new environment and assuming the culture of Texas as her own. She had immersed herself in all aspects of life in Travis and had grown to love the people there. Surrounded by loving family and adopted friends, Lucy had put on a cloak of Southernness to help her cope with the enforced exile. Like Olive Oatman, she too had learned to be circumspect in expressing her opinions. She knew she must at all times remember her status as an outsider and respond to those around her in a judicious manner. And like Cynthia Ann Parker, when Lucy at last had opportunity to leave, she struggled to balance the anguish of leaving loved ones in Texas with the joy of returning to her home in Ohio.

Sometimes re-reading old letters and reminiscing helped bridge the gap, and even Sarah could grasp a portion of Lucy's disconnected feeling when she heard the letters read, writing, "Cous Lue has been reading over some of her old letters from home to Sarah, Minnie and me tonight. It reminds me of happy hours spent in Ohio among those I loved so dearly but those times are past—and an impenetrable barrier is raised between us" (3/6/64). Both Lucy and Sarah used the letters to reminisce about happier times, but Lucy's need of them didn't end there. She needed these dated communiqués to remind herself of her roots in Ohio and her loved ones waiting for her there.

HER DIARY

As much as Lucy needed old letters to keep herself "in touch" with her family and friends in Ohio, she needed her journal to keep herself grounded as she navigated her path in Texas. Her intimate account of her sojourn in 1860s Texas reveals her situation and, yes, her dilemma, as a young woman literally caught in the grip of the American Civil War. Yet Lucy's diary, now housed in the DeGolyer Library at Southern Methodist University, also offers rich detail regarding life in Texas during that time. Framed by the Civil War, the journal presents a wonderful glimpse into Lucy's adopted world, simultaneously documenting gender relations, racial hierarchies, social practices, and networks that linked her to the community around her. For those who require memorable persons and/or events in order to assign significance,

---

161. Ibid., 76.

there are references to many. For those who look for the ordinary along with the outstanding, there is that as well. Because of Lucy's unusual position as a Northerner in Southern lands during the conflict, her perspective contains a unique mix of Northern and Southern sentiments, a blend that she would ultimately blanket with an encompassing sense of American identity. And through her journal, we are able to sense the invisible ties that bound her to those who were near and those far away. The tapestry of Lucy's life, woven with threads of heritage, threads of kinship, threads of friendship and community, spreads over the sectionalism that ripped a nation apart. These threads interlock, forming transcendent ties that overrule the differences, binding ragged fragments together into a strong quilt in which similarities provide a dominant theme.

Other themes surface as well, as we search out patterns in the journals. Through Lucy, we see femininity displayed in conformity to cultural expectations, even as we discover an independent, strong sense of self. We also sense quasi-Southernness, layered over Northern ideals and leanings. And finally, we get a strong sense of oppositions at work: North/South, networks of friendship/isolation, prominence of the war/distance, autonomous thought/ prescribed behavior, information/ignorance. As an added benefit, Lucy also offers us a kaleidoscope of stories, stories that entwine and intrigue as they teach us about this woman, this time, this place.

Without question, Lucy wrote her diary for her own edification, perhaps allowing only her closest friends and family to read it; she certainly did not intend it for the prying eyes of an anonymous audience, an audience separated from her by more than one hundred fifty years and lacking a thorough understanding of her situation. This became abundantly clear not long ago when, after devoting more than thirteen years to the study of her 1863–1865 journal and nearing the completion of the manuscript, I found that an earlier volume (1860–1861) of her diary had surfaced. Though much of the earlier diary forecasts her later entries, there are many significant inscriptions, not the least of which is a caution written on January 18, 1861, that gave me quite a start:

> Now at the lonely hour of midnight do I devote to this my memorandum, to its pages are confided my most secret thoughts at times; and should I die and leave no word of its future, This shall be my wish that whoever chances to look over its contents would keep them secret and burn the book, as I would myself.
>
> Lucy Stevens, 1/18/61

As I read with consternation Lucy's own wishes for her journal, the degree of privacy that Lucy assumed for her work became abundantly clear.

In certain women's diaries, as in Mary Chesnut's, for example, the records have been artful documents, penned with the knowledge that others would possibly read what had been written. Chesnut, who lived among the highest echelons of the Confederacy, kept records of the powerful and the well-known across the land, giving a distinctively political and militaristic slant to her writing. Alongside her accounts of her private life, she wrote with an insider's view, acquainted with the machinations of government and the political posturing that, for her, were a way of life. C. Vann Woodward explains that Chesnut's diary provides "a keen sense of awareness of history in the making, a resolute identification with a cause, ominous forebodings about the outcome, and a wry skepticism and amusement at the participants."[162] It is as though Chesnut *knew,* in penning her private thoughts, that at some point her musings would become known by a larger audience.

More frequently, however, missives such as Lucy's have been entirely private, written for the eyes of the author only. Diaries such as those of Lizzie Neblett,[163] Henrietta Embree, and Tennessee Embree[164] give evidence for the uninhibited expression of matters of the heart and mind. These private diaries, written by women in Texas, provide further contrasts as well, as they paint far different landscapes than Lucy's did. Lizzie Neblett, whose husband left her in charge of their home, their children, and their slaves as he joined the fight, gave much more attention to her own plight than to the battles raging at a distance. Full of concern for her own struggles, she paid scant attention to the particulars of her husband's tribulations.[165] Likewise, in one entry, Henrietta Embree decried the war within the "family" of Americans as "deplorable," yet focused more on her own health concerns and, understandably, on her own waning life.[166] Perhaps because Neblett and Embree were both married women, focused more sharply on their homes and their personal responsibilities and trials, they paid less attention to the particulars of various battles and the larger implications of war.

---

162. Mary B. Chesnut, *Mary Chesnut's Civil War,* ed. C. Vann Woodward (New Haven, CT: Yale University Press, 1981), xvii.

163. Neblett, *A Rebel Wife in Texas.*

164. *Henrietta Baker Embree and Tennessee Keys Embree, Tandem Lives: The Frontier Texas Diaries of Henrietta Baker Embree and Tennessee Keys Embree, 1856–1884,* ed. Amy L. Wink (Knoxville: University of Tennessee Press, 2008).

165. Neblett, *A Rebel Wife in Texas.*

166. Embree and Embree, *Tandem Lives,* 113.

As a private citizen marginalized on the outer boundaries of the war, Lucy had no reason to think her words would ever be read. And as a young single woman deeply engaged with her entire community, she felt none of the restrictions of marriage and its associated responsibilities. She maintained connections with a multitude of young soldiers, corresponding with them regularly and including their stories in her journal. As a single woman, she had freedom to voice her concerns for all of her friends, and with her extroverted nature, she felt drawn to these young men who, like herself, found themselves far from their homes and uncertain of any return. As a result of this enlarged network, and due, in part, to her own "exile" status, Lucy's diary offers a perspective far different from those found in other women's diaries. Through Lucy's journal, we are able to grasp a larger view of the war from the home front, albeit a home front far removed from active combat. Lucy's painstaking recording of many battles and skirmishes, particularly those in the Trans-Mississippi theater, offer two advantages: first, we are able to access an account of the war through feminine eyes, and second, since she was a Northern refugee in the South, her diary offers a wider and much more informed view than others do.

At the same time, all of these various diaries give shape and meaning to the women's lives and assign to that meaning a permanence that transcends time.[167] The women become the main characters in the drama, and base all perceptions on personal preferences and perspectives. All other people mentioned in the journals, no matter how closely tied to the authors, are secondary figures, included at the authors' own discretion.[168] Ultimately, however, whether the circumstances be mythic or mundane, the desire to commit their thoughts to paper have prompted the prominent and the inconspicuous alike to record for themselves the daily occurrences that whirled around them, shaping their immediate circumstances and fashioning their characters.

When diaries are written for private edification only, what possible purpose can they serve for us, as subsequent, uninvited readers? If we come to the material with the intent of careful analytical study, much can be gleaned from close examination. A diary such as Lucy's can be an academic treasure trove, yielding gems of historical information, psychological insights, and literary composition, as well as sociological data and cultural perspectives. Thus, with a reverent respect for Lucy's assumption of privacy and with a mixture of trepidation and gratitude for her unintentional provision of

---

167. Suzanne L. Bunkers and Cynthia A. Huff, eds., *Inscribing the Daily* (Amherst: University of Massachusetts Press, 1996), 12.

168. Cheryl Cline, *Women's Diaries, Journals, and Letters: An Annotated Bibliography* (New York: Garland Publishing, 1989), xiii.

public text, this study examines her diary, holding it up against established scholarly research about the nineteenth century, both validating and refuting common generalizations about the era. It also chronicles the personal aspects of her exile, seeking codes that define and explain the woman who was Lucy Stevens. And while the Civil War forms the backdrop for Lucy's diary and permeates every aspect of life, it is the connections between Lucy's personal experiences and the documented history of the war that give the overarching history a "face and heartbeat."

Historically, a grasp of the cultural context in which a diary was written is of paramount importance, and a knowledge that the viewed vignettes can never be construed as the totality of the diarist's experience is foundational. With this in mind, diaries such as Lucy's can offer a wealth of insight into the reality of a particular person, in a particular place, at a particular time. As Kenneth Lockridge determined from his study of William Byrd's journals, "To relate the universal process of personal growth in any given time, to let those two intersect, is to understand a little of the nature of that particular time in which the process occurred."[169] This goal, therefore, of connecting a place and a process drives the social historian. In her study, she "can everywhere find traces—occasionally vivid glimpses—of people doing things."[170] Lucy facilitates the contemporary historian's search because she is so immersed in her world, doing things. Rhys Isaac explains: "Academically, the searching out of the meanings that such actions contained and conveyed for the participants lies at the heart of the enterprise of ethnographic history. Actions must be viewed as statements."[171] These statements that past actions make offer very real clues to the fabric of life at that particular time.

Those clues, however, have provided only a portion of the narrative. Until recently, when women's studies demanded a more balanced search of history, most celebrated diaries belonged to men. Women's perspectives, varying greatly from men's, were discounted and ignored, and their writings relegated to the dusty attics of their descendants. Because women participated far less in the public arena than men, and because their papers contained less of the momentous and more of the ordinary, their documents have been overlooked as having little historical significance.[172] The litmus

169. Kenneth A. Lockridge, *The Diary, and Life, of William Byrd II of Virginia* (Chapel Hill: University of North Carolina Press, 1987), 149.

170. Rhys Isaac, *The Transformation of Virginia, 1740–1790* (Chapel Hill: University of North Carolina Press, 1982), 324.

171. Ibid.

172. Hampsten, *Read This Only to Yourself*, vii.

test for historical value in past times has been whether or not the document contained notable persons or events. Therefore, most women and their personal contributions carried little weight; it was only their connection to the powerful and prominent that mattered. Fortunately, that has changed, and journals such as Lucy's can be studied and appreciated for the insight they provide on daily life. Thus, that Lucy would assign such priority to her journal and her journaling can only enhance current-day illumination into the people, places, and activities of her world.

Lucy's references to the ordinary and, yes, even her sense of sporadic monotony, offer wonderful evidence regarding the value of women's journals. Lois Myers, author of *Letters by Lamplight*, argues that "feminine testimony expands the collective view by revealing private thoughts, emotions and self-images . . . In fact, women's personal literature is often the only recorded legacy that provides insights into the intimate details of home life in the previous century."[173] As keepers of the home fires, women—young and old, single and married—had firsthand information about the challenges that society faced on a daily basis. Their contributions within the private realm bear scrutiny on their own merits, as well as for their relationship to other intersecting areas of life. Myers goes on to state that "because women's lives intertwine with home, family and social group, learning their history also reveals the past experiences of children, families, domestic life, kinship relations, homemaking skills, courtship, widowhood, and social, charitable, educational and relational groups."[174] And from these recorded experiences, the culture of a people can more fully be ascertained and measured. It is in the regularity of these days and the sometimes mundane accounts of daily activities that Lucy's diary provides snapshots for us to learn about her world in Texas.

At the same time, a common complaint concerning women's diaries, and a justification for dismissing them as unimportant, has emerged. This criticism involves the recurring interruptions found in them, which some say renders them fragmented and incoherent. However, scholars such as Margo Culley and Penelope Franklin disagree, arguing that diarists are merely exercising a required editorial authority by which they select and privilege certain details over others. Additionally, Suzanne L. Bunkers and Cynthia Anne Huff assert that "the very repetitiveness and frequent interruptions of a day's work for most women make diaries a logical mode for women writers to

---

173. Lois Myers, *Letters by Lamplight* (Waco: Baylor University Press, 1991), 4.
174. Ibid., vii.

choose to pen their life stories."[175] Rather than formally separating the mind from the tedious dailiness of life, the diary format integrates thought and task, thereby asserting individuality, in thought and experience. Rather than viewing the journals as fragments of unrelated activities, the incorporation of the specific activities and encounters can be regarded as the interlocking pieces of a puzzle. Scribbling in a diary may well have afforded a woman the only private moment of her day. Insinuated amidst the demands of her home and her family, the effort of placing her pen to paper allowed her to tie together the fragments of her day, grabbing hold of a few precious moments to gain perspective and order. Perceived independently, the recorded events bring no real understanding; considered jointly, they allow an appreciation of the overarching portrait of a woman's life. Indeed, Lucy's entries present a collage of the vignettes of her days, itemizing visits—always visits—illnesses, gossip, war news, and chores. Yet in the combination of the individual facets of these days, Lucy's diary paints the full portrait of her life, with a sometimes fragmented mixture of bold strokes and muted nuances that indicate her willing and complete participation in life there—for as long as it lasted. Much insight into the young woman Lucy Stevens can be gleaned from the format and phrasing of her diary. At the beginning of her later journal, she inscribed maxims admonishing the wise use of one's time. On the title page of the journal, where she also recorded her name and the date (1/1/1863), she wrote, "Look not mournfully into the past; it comes not back again. Wisely improve the present; it is thine. Go forth to meet the shadowy future, without fear, and with a manly heart," crediting Longfellow with the adage. This reference to a contemporary literary figure indicates an advanced level of education and an awareness of the popular literary culture of the day. Likewise, Lucy opened 1864 with an anonymous warning to "Stamp improvement on the wings of time." These quotations, along with various other entries, indicate that Lucy was quite cognizant of the passage of time. Her very presence in Texas for such a long period was, in effect, a marking of time until she could safely return home.

For Lucy to have chosen two separate passages that called for self-improvement signals an awareness of the need to strive to better herself, typical of the nineteenth-century ideal of perfectionism. Lucy's own endeavors to better herself are apparent in the very writing of the diary. Her penmanship combined practicality and art as she crowded words onto pages, making every

---

175. Cited in Bunkers and Huff, *Inscribing the Daily*, 5.

line count for two. The flourishes with which she penned her words suggest hours of practice, and grammatical constructions hint at a concentrated effort to write well. It was only in moments of stress that Lucy broke with her habit of exquisite penmanship and grammatically correct sentences. At these times, the handwriting was hurried and careless, and proper punctuation was replaced with dashes, or eliminated altogether.

On occasion, Lucy's prose simply sings! Buried in a multitude of quiet musings and straightforward records, her words, phrases, and descriptions occasionally leap from the page with an eloquence that simultaneously surprises and delights. In our own assumption of an artlessness born from privacy, we see a guileless artfulness emerge. As Lucy argues with herself, as she addresses her journal as a friend, and as she applauds the honor of her soldier boys, her writing as reflection takes on the attributes of writing as literature.

Lucy's many references to books, and her compilation of an extensive reading list in the back of the later journal, bear witness to the fact that she was an avid reader who chose her material widely and well. The register is only one of many types of catalogues that Lucy kept in her diary. Although the reading list was a formal record in a separate space, other inventories occurred within the main text of her entries. As a prolific list maker, Lucy documented everything from menus to chores, guests to gifts. Besides the usual chronicling of the day's events, such attention to detail could indicate other tendencies as well. Researchers Steven Kagle and Lorenza Gramegna assert that a diary can be a mechanism by which individuals describe or redefine their experiences in order to "reconcile their own perceptions of the world with the expectations of their social groupings . . . and are likely to be used in this way by those individuals who feel a lack of or decrease in their

[FACING] Lucy Pier Stevens, 1863 Diary Title Page. DeGolyer Library, Southern Methodist University, Lucy Pier Stevens Collection.

—

Look not mournfully into the past; it comes not
back again. Wisely improve the present; it is thine.
Go forth to meet the shadowy future, without fear,
and with a manly heart.
Longfellow

L. P. Stevens
Feb. 28th, 1863

The young who in wisdom and virtue engage
lay up comfort for manhood, and peace for old age.

Look not mournfully into the past; it comes not
back again. Wisely improve the present; it is thine.
Go forth to meet the shadowy future, without fear,
and with a manly heart.

Longfellow.

L. B. Stevens
Febr. 28th 1863

The young who in wisdom and virtue engage
Lay up comfort for manhood, and peace for old age.

control of their lives."[176] Thus, Lucy's list making could have expressed an inner desire to categorize and compartmentalize the various aspects of her life, thereby giving her some modicum of control over it.

The earlier journal has a freshness about it, particularly in the first entries when Lucy was newly arrived in Texas and still a visitor. However, by 1863, despite never expecting to remain in Texas for such a long period of time, Lucy had become a resident. And in 1863, when the later volume begins, her prospects of leaving were dim. Thus, although she could not control the circumstances of the larger aspects of her life, Lucy could manifest some semblance of control via the organization in the minutiae of her days, and many passages point to her tendency to compartmentalize the segments of her life, thus tying them together in as nearly normal a fashion as she could.

Critically examined, diaries like Lucy's can also be studied for the inner codes that order the diarist's life and form her own particular history.[177] Lucy's journal does all of this and more. She used certain names and phrases so frequently that deeper meaning must be assumed. However, contemporary readers must remember that this reconstruction of codes is speculative and suppositional, and must be undertaken with caution to preserve the integrity of the author's intent. As noted historian Rhys Isaac warns in *The Transformation of Virginia*, "Limited aspects of life may be illuminated, but the whole . . . can never be summed up in any interpretive scheme."[178] Even so, patterns can be identified that grant access to the writer's codes of conduct and ethics, her personality strengths and weaknesses, as well as her likes and dislikes, beliefs and prejudices.[179] Lucy's diary provides strong evidence in favor of these claims. As she penned her thoughts, her hopes and dreams, she exposed the patterns of her life, highlighting those events and observations that were most meaningful to her, ultimately assigning value and priority that even readers removed by some 150 years can distill. For example, we see Lucy assigning importance to something as small as a cup of coffee. During the war, coffee was scarce, and many substitutes were invented. Dried okra, potato peelings, wheat grains, and cornmeal were all used as replacements,[180] but they never satisfied like real coffee. For Lucy, there was no adequate substitute, and she differentiated between the two in her diary

---

176. Steven E. Kagle and Lorenza Gramegna, "Rewriting Her Life: Fictionalization and the Use of Fictional Models in Early American Women's Diaries," in *Inscribing the Daily*, ed. Suzanne L. Bunkers and Cynthia A. Huff (Amherst: University of Massachusetts Press, 1996), 42.

177. Lockridge, *The Diary, and Life, of William Byrd II of Virginia*, 8.

178. Isaac, *The Transformation of Virginia*, 326.

179. Lockridge, *The Diary, and Life, of William Byrd II of Virginia*, 8.

180. Silverthorne, *Plantation Life in Texas*, 92.

by referring to "sure-enough coffee," a designation that continued through-out her journal, becoming synonymous with the deprivation caused by the war, a code of sorts for the bounty of peacetime.

Other codes appear in the pages of the journal as well. Like Lucy's code for peacetime prosperity, another phrase may express a controversial per-spective on a far weightier matter. Throughout the diary, Lucy's repeated use of the phrase "God speed the right" can easily be seen as a code by which she could verbalize her ambivalence about the war without fear of recrimina-tion should anyone happen upon her diary and read it. Likewise, the phrases "many are the changes" and "old times" appear throughout the journal, indi-cating a more introspective side of Lucy, and signifying a code that she used to note her own sense of helplessness and loss. As one scholar asserts, "The life of a diary is often born of tension, a disequilibrium in the life of its author, which needs to be resolved or held in check."[181] Despite the presence of a loving family, there obviously existed in Lucy's life a high level of tension and disequilibrium over which she had absolutely no control, and which required rigid command. On occasion, however, particularly as she noted birthdays and anniversaries, we see this disequilibrium bubble to the surface as she allowed herself to contemplate her fragmented life or the larger situa-tion that framed her own position.

Occasionally addressing her diary as "Mr. Journal," Lucy elevated her journaling to that of visiting with a close and trusted friend, a friend with whom she shared an enjoyable, intimate relationship. There is little doubt that she viewed this time as indispensable and looked forward to committing her thoughts to paper. What is interesting is that Lucy ascribed to this "con-fidant" the masculine gender, rather than the feminine—perhaps a personal judgment as to her perceptions of the comparable trustworthiness and con-fidentiality of men and women. Never expecting her diary to be on public display, she bared her heart with little reservation, admonishing the journal to keep her thoughts private. At one point she wrote, "now, Mr. Journal, you know this is confidential" (5/18/64) as she recorded her less than complimen-tary views about a neighbor woman.

Whether the situation was one of potential conflict or possible embar-rassment, the diary may have been Lucy's only outlet to express her true feelings. Lois Myers explains that in a day when "cultural restraints upon emotional display and dictates of social courtesy . . . often inhibited honest expressions of tension or conflict in women's correspondence," Lucy turned

---

181. Kagle and Gramegna, "Rewriting Her Life," 10.

to her journal as an outlet for her inner feelings, with no external agenda.[182] Others agree, explaining that overt expressions of anger and ambivalence were "emotions not permitted to young women of the antebellum South, or indeed, to any woman aspiring to the 'cult of true womanhood' in the nineteenth century."[183] Most of the time, Lucy followed this protocol in her diary, using initials and leaving blank spaces instead of recording names when reporting derogatory information. For the most part, she tried to carefully veil uncomplimentary thoughts of others, but as the war progressed and tension rose, and, perhaps, as Lucy's patience with her own situation wore thin, she permitted herself to express her feelings more openly. In fact, as she spent more time contemplating the losses and the heavy toll of war, including her own exile, her diary took on a decidedly contemplative and melancholy tone.

At times Lucy pondered the transcendent hardships associated with war, allowing room to feel the pain of both Northerners and Southerners. An entry from the earlier volume echoes the sentiments of many across the land as they found themselves pitted against friends, neighbors, and even family. On September 1, 1861, Lucy sadly wrote, "It seems right hard to bid my friends farewell to go to war with other friends as I fear." Even two years later, as the war raged, she exhibited an inclusiveness that spread far beyond man-made boundaries. Lucy's unique position provided her an added lens through which to view the conflict, and enabled her to recognize devotion, be it Rebel or Yank. Near the close of her time in Texas, in fact, Lucy wrote of a neighbor woman who minimized the oath of allegiance to the Union, deeming it forced, and therefore, non-binding. To this anecdote, Lucy philosophically added, "How strange that some people can only look on one side of a question" (3/30/65).

Most of the time, however, Lucy maintained a cheerful outlook, focusing on the business of life for that day. In one of her earliest entries, she described herself as "not one to have the blues" (3/1/60), and she worked hard to maintain a positive attitude. Most indicative of Lucy's positive outlook were her frequent humorous stories and anecdotes. She often related stories that she had heard others tell when she found them humorous, and, quick to tell on herself, she also recorded incidents when she was the butt of the joke and laughingly reported all the details. A lighthearted approach and enjoyment of the offerings of the day, whether it was parlor games or the merry music

---

182. Myers, *Letters by Lamplight*, 7.

183. Elizabeth R. Baer, "Ambivalence, Anger, and Silence: The Civil War Diary of Lucy Buck," in *Inscribing the Daily*, ed. Suzanne L. Bunkers and Cynthia A. Huff (Amherst: University of Massachusetts Press, 1996), 213.

of an evening spent at home with Aunt Lu and Uncle Pier, kept Lucy's morale high and her focus on the present.

As an unexpected bonanza, we have the diaries of Lucy's Aunt Lu and Cousin Sarah from which to draw additional information and context. Housed in the Texas Collection at Baylor University, and treasures in their own right, these two accounts correlate and enhance Lucy's journal. Although Lu Merry Pier's and Sarah Pier's diaries cover different periods of time (Aunt Lu's 1852–1863 and Sarah's 1862–1867), all three diaries include the year 1863, often recounting the same material, but from different perspectives. This provides insight into all three women and gives a richer snapshot of Texas life during this period. Additionally, on many occasions each diarist privileges different information and/or details, fleshing out the accounts that Lucy offers.

Aunt Lu's diary gives wonderful insight into farm life in Texas during those years. Her perceptions obviously differ greatly from Lucy's, and the contrasts are relevant. The frontier to which Aunt Lu had come as a young bride bore little resemblance to the community that Lucy visited in 1859. Aunt Lu's own experiences and the ruggedness of the land had stamped their marks on her. Her journal entries tend to be more concise, with more pragmatic information and less sentiment than Lucy's, much like the journal entries of Martha Ballard in Laurel Thatcher Ulrich's *A Midwife's Tale*. Stressing the economic forces that shaped her daily life, Aunt Lu's journal focused on the daily routines of running a farm, with all the attendant problems. Her terseness could easily be transplanted from the late eighteenth-century New England of Martha Ballard, where few words conveyed volumes of implicit information. In an entry dated November 9, 1859, for example, Aunt Lu wrote,

> A rather cloudy warm day . . . Miss McHenry & little Mattie came to day and spent the day working on a quilt for one of Mrs. Lee's little girls. Sent Mrs. Lord's today and got 15 lbs of butter for 15 cts per lb. Johanna here to day. Negroes helping Foytashic to pick cotton.
> Lu M. Pier, 11/9/59

Awkward though this may be for twenty-first-century readers, the information contained in the entry covers a vast array of topics ranging from the weather (unusual for November), to hospitality and reciprocity among neighbors, cloth production and self-sufficiency on the frontier, economic costs and bartering, planting/harvesting patterns, crop choices and slavery.

The entry conveys little emotion or personal opinion, yet reveals much about the life of Lucy Merry Pier. Author Kenneth Lockridge stresses, "Modern observers, used to a post-romantic culture in which feeling may be and usually is expressed explicitly, cannot understand the way in which, in eighteenth-century culture, feelings were expressed by their restraint."[184] His point holds true for Aunt Lu. In a format where many meanings can be tied to few words, the clipped entries of Aunt Lu's diary offer an excellent example of deep responses conveyed by restrained language. In fact, it is only as the war progressed that Aunt Lu's diary became more emotionally expressive as she recorded her fears for her soldier-son, Sammy, and her hatred of war. Even then, the lack of detailed information requires much interpretation. As Ulrich writes of Ballard's diary, "It is in the very dailiness, the exhaustive, repetitious dailiness, that the real power of Martha Ballard's book lies."[185] So it may be said of Lu Merry Pier's diary. Both are matter-of-fact accounts of daily events, with little introspection, in a world where living equaled doing.

The diaries of Lucy Stevens and Sarah Pier, however, vary greatly from Aunt Lu's pattern. Since the girls were contemporaries, their journals serve as examples of a younger generation's attempts to document its own life experiences and perceptions. Historian Lillian Schlissel writes that many of these differences stem from a difference in circumstances and in levels of responsibility. She states, "The different responses do derive from the circumstances of the diarist's life . . . the life cycle of the diarist is the significant configuration."[186] Cousin Sarah and Lucy both participated in the ongoing duties at home, yet neither was ultimately responsible for the maintenance and success of the household and farm. Aunt Lu, on the other hand, held the title of household mistress, and the associated responsibilities fell on her shoulders. Additionally, Sarah and Lucy were both single women in their twenties whose ties to the absent Sammy were those of sister and cousin. Aunt Lu, however, was his mother, and her love and worry for her son reverberated through her writings, despite the cryptic style. Sarah and Lucy could only guess at the strength of the ties between mother and son, while Aunt Lu knew full well the concern and grief that only a parent can experience.

Age and position account for many of the differences in the diaries, yet other variations must be attributed to individual personality types. In her article "I Write for Myself and Strangers: Private Diaries as Public Documents," Lynn Bloom asserts that since diaries were most often written for the

---

184. Lockridge, The Diary, and Life, of William Byrd II of Virginia, 56.
185. Ulrich, A Midwife's Tale, 9.
186. Schlissel, "Diaries of Frontier Women," 59.

personal benefit of the author, the entries can be trusted to reveal accurately the true personality of the author. The patterns identified in diary entries offer up clues about the personality of the author, and these patterns serve as tools to determine who the diarist really was.[187] When writing about the weather, for example, Aunt Lu might record "very warm day sultry and hot" (Lu Merry Pier, 3/8/63), while Lucy might record the weather's effects by writing "no church today, it was very unpleasant" (Lucy Stevens, 1/18/63). Sarah, on the other hand, would take in her surroundings, assigning sentimental meaning to them. In her entry for February 15, 1863, she wrote,

> It is cloudy and warm this morning. Dr. Stone is to preach today. The prairies are green and covered with spring flowers. The birds are singing. The peach and plum trees in bloom and everything has the appearance of an early spring. Oh! How I used to delight in the early spring flowers, birds, etc. and how happy and light hearted I was then . . .
> Sarah Pier, 2/15/63

From the patterns displayed in these entries, it is clear that Aunt Lu was aware of prevailing conditions. But as a no-nonsense person, she wasted little time on non-essential information. Likewise, Lucy appreciated the variations in weather. However, since she liked to stay busy visiting and socializing, it was primarily for the effect that it had on her plans. In contrast, Sarah eloquently expressed the impact of the weather on her feelings and melded the snapshot of a particular day with the larger landscape of her life. While these are not constant and absolute characteristics of each woman's writing, they do represent the patterns that each followed and demonstrate the role that personality played in perception.

As a note of caution as the diary begins, there is some difficulty in keeping names straight since "Lucy" seems to have been a family favorite, and much of the activity recorded in Lucy's diary occurred at Cousin Lu's home. However, while the multiplicity of "Lu" can be disconcerting, it should not be considered an insurmountable obstacle. As Laurel Thatcher Ulrich writes, "Opening a diary for the first time is like walking into a room full of strangers. The reader is advised to enjoy the company without trying to remember every name."[188] This advice is especially appropriate in Lucy's case, for she

---

187. Lynn Z. Bloom, "I Write for Myself and Strangers: Private Diaries as Public Documents," in *Inscribing the Daily*, ed. Suzanne Bunker and Cynthia A. Huff (Amherst: University of Massachusetts Press, 1996), 25–27.

188. Ulrich, *A Midwife's Tale*, 55.

Jan. 1st Thurs — This morn, cousin Sara. Sallie Tom & myself thought to commence the year, well so twenty over. to Mrs Brooks & spent the day. Sallie & I going in the carriage in the morn. & Sara after church on horseback. Sallie & I found Lizzie & her cousin Miss Betty Griswold just making themselves beautiful. to visit my Aunt C— but as we came they deferred their visit until some other time. After we had been there awhile & was taking our work out to commence knitting, Mrs B— proposed, we should do something for her to remember our day's visit. so Sallie made one pair in a pair of drawers for Sallie Ree B's drawers & I the other had just gotten them ready to cut together when dinner was announced. We had such a nice dinner. Boiled rib, sausage, liver hash, sweet potatoes, fried eggs & egg bread, & some very good coffee. it was so nice. Just after we set down, cousin Sara Anne was rode by from the gate pretty badly scared. she not very grateful. After all that, Sallie we tried our fortunes by dropping in coffee in the pleasures & found all but Sallie was to marry early this year but she poor child was to wait eleven. After dinner Sallie sewed the facing on a dress for Mrs Brooks, Sara sewed on her name cakes for the awhile then to work. time to finish, & she played on the accordion for us. Lizzie & Miss Betty seemed to have some mysterious employment that engaged them for an hour or so. Often their cousin their appearance & so Ree B & Sallie & Betty being girls & rosy cheeks just settled a little forish some body.

On the eve as we were asking by our invited & hooded. the girls insisted on our staying a little longer & sing. the very mysterious proceeding of the afternoon was explained by their coming in with some nice tea in Mrs B new china tea cups & some nice cakes.

After tea Ree B & Pups as we were slowly home & were out till home by the lattern. Father Sara was. I found Aunt Lu & Uncle Pris library & report that Magnolia had retaken Galveston.

Jan. 2 Fri— This morn, I told B. then Sallie & I concluded to take our bonnets did not complete our task. so I spent it knitting. I on myself so Tuesday he has been raining and unpleasant and my — on work & her good humor. Sallie & I us girls finished up our millinery after dinner.

Jan. 3 — My Chesley came up from Belleville this P.M. & & gave him his needle book with which he seemed quite pleased. We had quite a favorite evening over C— has been out looking up his books & by & I. The letter we have was brought to Belleville yesterday by Col Boone from Richmond a gent from Goodbury, one from New Ulm & from other places in the county that the Dutch & negroes were about to rise & preparations were being made & I have anything like insurrection by the military though. & it is hoped there will be nothing more of it. Guns going yesterday confirming the Galveston affair. Magnolia by uniting hand & other forces succeeded in taking the Harriet Lane & my small vessels & capture 600 prisoners. New Hampshire men & other vessels disgracefully made their escape by flag of truce." The Confed. loss is said to be about 400. Theo feds about 600. Knowing it is said our gentleman with his brother and another of the troops found his own who was an officer on the H. L. spoke freely his part. We heard to say there was 1200 dutch & onorarians, some 600 negroes connected with the talked of insurrection.

We held for tea to night some crullers & grape tarts Mrs Chapman sent over for the children in quite a surprise for us. But I'm also gave us a cup of nice tea for our good behavior.

Jan. 5 Monday — Chesley left us & was this morning. Cousin Lu & Sallie & went over to Mr McLains to spend the day & after the mail came I started over on foot. The Mr hoped us on the way & being as enjoying at the creek. & before he had gotten much further he all came on. going & and comes & I am coming up to where he was, I found Sara, Raffie Tom & Sallie Mc L standing by the wreck of our buggy and looking more forlorn than ever I saw them before. It seems the boy kicked the trim at the fence gone in the house & got excited where he broke loose & ran off making general distribution as he went. suffering one, getting — him to pieces. another further up the road. the seat farther on & others which still further & the carriage turned up side down. the harness broken, & her made & in the bushes where he was standing he would again to say there was a very general excitement in regard to the Dutch. I. It is said Capt. Ree — have been sent for & will be. & the neighborhood by Thursday next.

We spent a very pleasant day at Mr McL's considering all things mentions innumerable people throughout the diary, some representing solitary encounters, others revealing lengthy associations. Due to the instability caused by war, characters float in and out in a transitory manner, making it difficult for contemporary readers to ascertain some relationships to Lucy.

The pages that follow tell Lucy's story, a story of love and laughter, heartache and longing, romance and adventure. With her own words, Lucy teaches that even during the sharpest division in U.S. history, there is room for inclusion. Her insights and opinions give the lie to the simple notion that North means "X" and South stands for "Y." The Pier household, a home maintaining a balance between peace and war, of necessity accommodated both North and South. In the process, it achieved a semblance of stability in the midst of turmoil. While "Southernness" obviously dominated, this family, like many others, refused to forget its Northern ties. Lucy's perceptions, recorded in the private pages of her diary, underscore the transcendent power of family and friends. Her observations, along with those in the companion diaries, provide a vista from which an entire landscape can be drawn. My accompanying commentary meshes these diaries with scholarly research to sharpen and delineate the pictures that Lucy paints as she provides an intimate account of life in Civil War Texas. The result is a comprehensive study of one young woman's successful negotiation of a tumultuous time, a time of transition in her own life, as well as in the life of her nation.

[FACING] Lucy Pier Stevens Diary, January, 1863 Entries. DeGolyer Library, Southern Methodist University, Lucy Pier Stevens Collection.

Jan 2nd, friday ~ This morn I patched then Sallie & I concluded "poke" our bonnets. Did not complete our task, I spent it knitting. I on my soldier socks. Thursday has been rainy and unpleasant and my self in not a very good humor.

Jan 3rd, saturday ~ Us girls finished up our millinery after dinner. Mr Chesley came up from Bellville this P.M. & I gave him his needle book with which he seemed quite pleased. We had quite a shower P.M.

CHAPTER 1

JANUARY
1863

Magruder says . . . come on [and] take it~.

LUCY P. STEVENS,
January 11, 1863

WITH THE ADVENT OF 1863, Lucy began her fourth year as a resident of Texas. No longer a stranger, she documented daily happenings as someone who was at home with the routines and regimens of life in the Pier household. Her perceptions of every aspect of her life, from incidental visits to historic war news, permeate her diary entries. Furthermore, her entries disclose a familiarity with the people and the area that had grown over time, revealing her assimilation into the structures of this land.

Always, Lucy faithfully recorded events and situations that affected life in Texas. As the new year got under way, she wrote of the contest for Galveston that had begun in the fall of 1862. According to *The Handbook of Texas Online*, on October 4, 1862, five Union steamers, including the *Harriet Lane*, brought Galveston under federal control. Three months later, on January 1, 1863, Confederate general John B. Magruder launched an attack on the *Harriet Lane*, boarding her and killing five crew members, including the captain. The rest of the crew members were taken prisoner, and the blockade was momentarily eased. However, within one week, Galveston was back under the Union blockade and remained so for the duration of the war. The impact of this was enormous, as Texas would become increasingly cut off from the other Confederate states. Not only would goods become more scarce, but information would become more and more garbled, and Lucy would struggle to separate fact from rumor. And as news became increasingly unreliable, she would frequently revisit an entry in her diary, correcting and contradicting earlier entries, sometimes adding her own comments and sarcasm.

Jan 1st thurs ~ This morn cousin Sara, Sallie, Tom & myself thought to commence the year well so went over to Mr. Brewer's & spent the day ~ We had such a nice dinner ~ Baked ribs, sausage, liver hash, sweet potatoes, fried eggs & egg bread & sure enough coffee ~ 'twas so nice. just after we set down cousin Sara came in, rode her pony & got pretty badly scarred [scared] he acted so hateful. After all had eaten we tried our fortunes by dropping coffee in the teaspoons & found all but Sallie was to marry in just one year, but she poor child was to wait eleven. After dinner Sallie sewed the facing on a dress for Mrs. Brewer, Sara worked on her namesake's panties awhile then I took them to finish & she played on the accordian for us.

In the eve as we were asking for our mantles & hoods, the girls insisted on our staying a little longer & soon the mysterious proceeding of the afternoon was explained by their coming in with some nice tea in Mrs. B's new china tea cups & some nice cake.

Met Mr. B & Rufus as we were starting home & were escorted home by the latter, or rather Sara was. Found Aunt Lu & Uncle Pier at the supper table so we went out & eat with them. Uncle Pier heard a report that Magruder had retaken Galveston.

Jan 2nd friday ~ This morn I patched, then Sallie & I concluded [to] "poke" our bonnets[1] Did not complete our task so I spent it knitting. I on my soldier socks The day has been rainy & unpleasant and myself in not a very good humor.

Jan 3rd saturday ~ us girls finished up our millennery after dinner. Mr. Chesley came from Bellville this P.M. & I gave him his neadle book with which he seemed quite pleased ~ we had quite a shower P.M.

Jan 4th sunday ~ Mr. C~ has been out looking up his books today. He tells us there was word brought to Bellville[2] yesterday by Col Pane from the Bend, a gent from Industry,[3] one from New Ulm[4] & from other

---

1. The poke bonnet, common in the later nineteenth century, was made with a small crown at the back and a wide, rounded front brim, ideal for shading the face from the hot sun.

2. According to *The Handbook of Texas Online*, Bellville, the county seat of Austin County, was established in 1838 and named for Thomas B. Bell, one of Stephen F. Austin's "Old Three Hundred." A post office was established in 1849, and at the time of this diary entry, Bellville was a transport point for the area's cotton crop.

3. Industry, established in 1831, was the first German settlement in Texas.

4. New Ulm, established in 1841, was first known as Puff's Settlement. Like much of the area, New Ulm had a large German population.

places in the county that the Dutch & Negroes were about to rise up & Preperattions being made to quell anything like insurrection[5] by the military though & it is hoped there will be nothing more of it~

News came yesterday confirming the Galveston affair. Magruder by uniting land & water forces succeeded in taking the *Harriet Lane*[6] four small vessels & some 600 prisoners, New Hampshire men. 3 other vessels "disgracefully made their escape by flag of truce." The Confed loss is said to be about 100 the fed not yet known ~ It is said one gentleman took his [ ] and another, a Mr. Len found his son who was an officer on the *H-L-*, just breathing his last. We heard today there was 1800 dutch & Moravians & some 600 negroes connected with the talked of insurrection

Jan 5th monday ~ Chesley left us soon this morning. Cousin Lula & Sallie T went over to Dr McLarin's to spend the day & after the mail came I started over on foot ~ the Dr passed me on the way & fixed a crossing at the creek ~ before he had gotten much farther he heard someone saying "there comes Pa" & soon coming up to where he was, I found Sara, Sallie, Tom & Sallie McL~ standing by the wreck of our buggy and looking more forlorn than ever I saw them before. It seems they had hitched the pony at the fence, gone in the house & got seated when he broke loose & run off making general distraction as he went, left one cushion near the house another farther up the road, the seat farther on, the wheel still farther & the carriage turned up side down, the harness broken & he made fast in the bushes where he was standing.

We heard again to day there was a very general excitement in regard to the dutch. It is said Green's Reg have been sent for & will be in the neighborhood by thursday next

5. By 1859, a mounting fear of slave insurrections grew throughout Austin County and across the region. On January 8, 1863, martial law was declared in Austin, Colorado, and Fayette Counties, and companies of General H. H. Sibley's Arizona Brigade rushed to the area for order. Lucy's mention of Moravians refers to the Czech-Moravian immigrant population in the area. As evidenced in earlier entries, the region had a large immigrant population, primarily of German and Czech descent. In the account that Lucy mentions, most arrests were of Germans, and the rebellion was quelled by January 21.

6. The *Harriet Lane*, a 619-ton copper-plate steamer, was built in 1857 as a revenue cutter and served first as part of the naval squadron sent to Fort Sumter, then as part of the West Gulf Blockade Squadron outside Mobile Bay. *The Handbook of Texas Online* reports that one of the prizes afforded by the Galveston capture of the *Harriet Lane* was a complete copy of the United States signal-service code, valuable information indeed for the Confederate forces.

We spent a very pleasant day at Dr Mc's considering all things. Mrs Clemmons came there in the afternoon and took Sallie home with her. Sara & I walked home Arrived at home we found Mrs. Cameron had left ~ Uncle P says he is thankful enough the girls were not on the carriage and the most he cares for is the harness as it is a part of the carriage harness & now they get no place until it is mended.

Jan 6th tuesday ~ Cousin Sara & I walked to Mrs Clemmons this morn & carried Sallie some of her wardrobe. Found both her & Mrs C almost down sick. They were so surprised to see us walking up there. We arrived home before dark, found Aunt Lu & Uncle P going out to tea. This morn we were getting ready to go over to Mr. Catlin's when Charley Chapman came in and asked Sara wouldn't she go with his Ma & Pa down to see Lu so we postponed our visit ~ & she has gone on the river. This is the first time Mrs C ever took Miss Sara Lu out visiting

Jan 8th thursday ~ Aunt Lu went over to cousin S to help her put in a peice of cloth,[7] so I was left by myself until about 11A.M. when Mrs Cochrane & Mollie came and just before we went in to dinner Rev Bullard S. Dunn & Capt Floyd (of an Artillery Co) came to see about some cotton. Uncle Pier had to go up to the store so I had the pleasure of waiting on the table. Poor Mollie liked to have disgraced herself by laughing at the table when Aunt Lu asked the Rev to ask a blessing. I do not like him at all or nothing like as well as his brother. He is so great an egotist & a greater puppy. I think I'd have liked the Capt better if he had been in different company. Mollie & Mrs C stayed until late this afternoon. I thought to go stay all night at Grandma's[8] but just as I was starting [I saw] Mr. Chapman's carriage coming. Sara says they were dissapointed in seeing Lu as she had gone that morning across the river but as cousin W was at home they had a tollerably pleasant visit. This morn they came on to Mrs Cochrane's and this eve as they were coming home met them this side of Mr Collin's and it [was] almost dark. Em & Tallie are coming here to school & Mollie going to Independ[ence].[9]

---

7. Here, Lucy referred to Aunt Lu helping Sarah set up the materials to prepare for weaving.

8. Many times Lucy used a family appellation such as "cousin" or "grandma" for a close friend of the family. This was possibly Mrs. Swearingen, an older woman in the vicinity whom Lucy affectionately called "Grandma."

9. Em (Emma Cochran) and Tallie were to board at the Piers' house for a time while attending the subscription school. Molly Cochran was to attend school at Baylor University in Independence.

Jan 11th, sunday ~ Mr. L left this morn about 10 ~ I was so sleepy I was
glad to see him go. Uncle Pier treated us to an oyster stew this noon.
Quite unexpected, just after dinner Sis & Sallie Swearingen came and
we made it up to all go down to Lu's tomorrow. Mr Hepp the Bellville
teacher called here to day ~ he says they have had a 3 day fight at Vicksburg with heavy losses on both sides. The Feds had been repulsed but
it was thought they would renew the fight the next day. 3 of the fedral
gun boats have been sunk. There has also been a late engagement at
Murfreesborough in which the Confeds claim a victory, they say they
have taken 1300 prisoners & killed & wounded 1300. Also Van Dorn had
retaken Memphis & that 2 fedral gun boats had landed off Galveston &
demanded the surrender a second time but Magruder says if they want it
worse than he does for them to come on [and] take it.

Jan 12th monday ~ This morn has been cloudy and dreary but nothing
daunted Maria sent Sara word they would be here by 11 P.M. I finished my
soldier socks this morn ~
    We started at the appointed time. ~~Sara started on the horse Uncle Pier~~
~~bought for Sammy but he acted so badly after we started she turned back.~~
When we came to the gate at Lu's we formed in a line & marched up like
soldiers ~ they thought they were about to be taken to see such a Reg~ of
girls coming. Uncle Jimmy[10] was from home so Sis & Sara had his room.

Jan 13th tuesday ~ This morn we were up betimes and ready for H
[Hempstead][11] altho' the prospect out of doors is not very promiseing & Cousin S and Sis went in Lu's carriage & Sara J, Cousin W and I
on horseback. Cousin Lu could not go as she was looking for Aunt B
to day. We met Mr & Mrs. Buck & Bella near H on their way home also
met Mrs. Paine's carryall coming home from taking them to the cars.
they have gone down to Houston to attend the concert given this eve for

---

10. Lucy now counted Uncle Jimmy as a dear friend, but her initial opinion of him, documented in the earlier volume of her diary, had been much less flattering. Soon after her arrival
in Texas, she had written, "home we came I riding with Uncle Jimmie for the first time. If there
was not quite so much of the old bachelor about him that he could talk a little more, and if he
would not chew quite so much tobacco he would be quite enduriable company" (2/27/61).

11. Hempstead, founded in 1856 by Dr. Richard Peebles and James McDade, at this time
was a distribution center, linking the Texas interior to the Gulf coast. It served as a Confederate supply and manufacturing center and also housed a Confederate military hospital. Three
Confederate military camps were in the vicinity as well.

the benefit of Terry's – now Wharton's Regiment.[12] As we were passing
Mr Bush's saw him penning goats and received an invite from him to
go there to dinner. Arrived in town we found the artist was not taking
types [daguerreotypes][13] now, so we had our trip for nothing. Us girls
stopped at Groves while cousin W went to find out about it and of all
the talks I ever had. Groves gave me the greatest one against the north ~
not of its polatics, but its home institutions & domestic affairs. He says
the almighty dollar weighs more in the minds of all there than all else ~
the facilities for education is nothing compared to the south ~ there are
no ladies so far as refinement is concern and education is concerned in
the north. No girl considers what education she has complete without
going into a factory or teaching school – religion was a name and that
almost forgotten ~ how I felt my face flush with anger, and when in reply
I remarked, "your conversation shows, Sir how little you know of the
north." He replied "I will tell you and let you judge," he says, "my wife
who is now I trust an angel in heaven, was a New York lady, was in principle more of a southerner than I and a more noble, religious or better
woman never lived ~ she told me more than I can tell you and was much
more bitter in her feelings ~ besides I was once in business 3 yrs in New
York had spent a summer in Saratoga and at Niagara and a year traveling, visiting some of the principle cities of the west." so I finaly concluded he was a wise fool ~ wiser in his own estimation than that of any
other person. I learned to that he seemed to have found out but to late
what a treasure he had lost in that angel wife who died with consumption. He treated her with so much brutality during her sickness that
there was strong talk of riding him on a rail. He thought not I presume
I would ever know so much of his private life. To wind up with, and in
answer to a remark I had made, he said I must not judge of the south by
that place, for the people around there were the most penurious set he
had ever seen ~ complimentary certainly ~ I shall not judge by him. He

---

12. Colonel Austin Wharton assumed command of Company B, 8th Texas Cavalry, better
known as Terry's Texas Rangers, following the deaths of Colonel Benjamin Terry on December
8, 1861, and Lieutenant Colonel Thomas Lubbock a few days later.

13. According to the *Oxford English Dictionary (OED)*, the daguerreotype was an early version
of the photograph developed by French photographer Louis J. M. Daguerre. Quickly adopted
by American photographers, it declined in popularity in the late 1850s with the introduction of
the ambrotype, a faster and less expensive method of photography.

asked us after all that and urged us to dine at his house. I'd as soon think of having my head cut off. Sara, W & I went to Mr Bush's & Sara J & Sis Torrence to Mr Young's. Mrs. Wilson gave us such a cordial welcome ~ and Sallie ~ Mrs Fadis too seemed glad to see us. Mr. W showed his trophies taken at the Galveston fight ~ an officer's coat, blue cloth trimed with brass buttons with a peice of velvet on each shoulder trimmed round with gilt cord. he also had the hat with a gilt cord & tassels on it and quite a number of letters, mostly from wives to their husbands. these letters were intended for the rest of the Reg that was to have come on soon and joined those here. Mrs Fadis also showed the Yankee breastplate of her husbands, 'twas in 14 peices~. None of the letters spoke of the war except asking of the whereabouts of Banks, &tc. but all were written in a most affectionate and kind state. We left Mrs. Bush's about 3 O'c'k called by after the girls ~ found a house full of company there that have met to sew for Mrs. Young as she has been very low and looks now as if her days were numbered ~ she is so thin & pale. It is thought she has the consumption

Jan 14th wednesday ~ Mollie & Sara J liked to have talked all night – so there was little sleeping done here by any I'm thinking. And so after our ride and all, we are not the brightest set in the world. I read some & drew off some embroidery patterns. In the afternoon Uncle Tom came in the rain after Mollie, but as she had not got through with her shoes he concluded to leave her until we went to Travis then she was to go as far as Mr Middleton's with us.

Jan 17th saturday ~ All started for home this morn ~ Lu going with us. Us girls went by Mrs Harry Bracey's this morn so I saw the bride a beautiful looking bird I can assure you Mr Journal. We girls arrived home in time to get Aunt Lu's 49th birthday supper which she would not have had if we had not gone home.

Jan 20th tuesday ~ Mrs Dr. Cocke & Annie M. Cleveland spent the day here. Annie looked so funny with her short homespun dress on & no hoops & an embroidered ruffle round the neck. This is the first time any but Mrs Cocke of that family have visited us since the barbicue the 4th of July 1861. the time Sara presented her flag.

Sis came to see could I go with her out to Lu's tomorrow, she is so anxious to get her daguerreotype taken for Mr T~. Annie M learned how to knit hoods of Sara, lamp mats of me and said she was going to bring her bonnet over for Sara to show her how to poke it. Sallie T~ has been miserable with the teeth ache most of the day. Aunt Lu on plea of coloring[14] stayed in her room. This eve I've been busy getting ready to go to Lu's ~ but at last am seated to commence with you.

Jan 21st wednesday ~ We arrived at Lu's about 1 O'c'k ~ found all well ~ Lu says she got home without any trouble ~ Lu had such a nice dinner cooked for us. This afternoon I worked on my mat & Sis on her embroidery. Lu had woven 1¾ yards before we came & after knit on some socks for Willie

Jan 22nd thursday ~ As we were all looking for Jimmy to day, going to Hempstead has been deferred until tomorrow. For all our watching Jimmy came into Uncle J's room before we knew he was on the place. We could do nothing but talk after he came, finding out about our acquaintences and hearing of his trip home &c &c. He told cousin Waller that was Ridley ~ the one that told the Arkansas lady he thot they would have to plant cotton seed in the graves out there to resurect the dead ~ was just as funny as ever

One night when it was raining the Capt (Harper) came round to enquire how they were fareing, invited someone to share his tent with him & asked for Ridley and was answered "here I am out door's trying to keep the ground dry ~ for I don't think any part of it inside that tent will be. Jimmie gave me a Confederate portmonie[15] he carried his money home in ~ 'twas made by Ino H of tarpoleon cloth. it is a curiosity certain ~ I shall keep it always

He says a Miss Eugenia Kirkpatrick & her sister Annie with their Mother used to visit the hospital often & bring books & delicacies for the sick. J came all the way on horse back, when he first started was so weak he had to get on a stump to mount his horse, but has been improving every day since, until now he looks almost well, but has a bad cough. The time he left his Reg- was on the march to reinforce Hindman: but a

---

14. "Coloring" refers to the dyeing of cloth or fibers.

15. A portmonie was a small satchel. The one to which Lucy referred was made of tarpaulin cloth, rendering it waterproof.

few days after he started the order was countermanded & so in stead of going to Ft Smith [Arkansas] they took the backward march.

Jan 25th sunday ~ read sevral peices in *Godey's* today ~ Uncle Martin[16] walked over from Dr Peebles[17] after herbs for Aunt Hannah & has gone again this eve ~. We made more molasses candy this P.M.

———

January ended much as it had begun for Lucy, always focusing on the daily: visits among good friends, talk of the weather, and most common of all, clothing production. Throughout the diary, Lucy chronicled the ongoing work of women—weaving, sewing, mending, and patching clothing for one member or another of the household as they went about the business of maintaining their world.

---

16. Uncle Martin Merry was Aunt Lu's (and Lucy's mother's) brother. He and his wife, Hannah, migrated to Texas at an earlier, undisclosed date and lived some distance from the Pier family, probably near Hempstead. Their residence was never pinpointed in the text of the diary; however, references of their proximity to Dr. Peebles place them near this town.

17. Dr. Richard Peebles, one of the founders of Hempstead and one of the richest men in Texas at that time, became quite a controversial figure during the war. As Lucy would later relate, authorities discovered that he had Union leanings and, along with several other men, attempted to distribute tracts advocating the return of Texas to the Union. For this, Dr. Peebles was arrested and exiled for the duration of the war.

CHAPTER 2

FEBRUARY
1863

St Valentines day and cloudy rainey one it has been

LUCY P. STEVENS,
February 14, 1863

THROUGHOUT THE PAGES OF HER DIARY, Lucy maintained ongoing records of weather changes and seasonal responsibilities. She documented floods and droughts, northers and heat waves, usually commenting on the impact the weather would have on life in Travis. If too much rain came, Buffalo Creek would be impassable and travel would be halted. If northers came late in the season, crops would be jeopardized. Then, as now, rain was of paramount importance, and Lucy understood well the implications of drought. Yet her continuing entries regarding daily weather patterns during the month of February, especially the last few days, reflect the tension she felt as nature restricted her activities. Lucy enjoyed an extensive network of friends, and chafed when she was unable to be with them. On a larger scale, the entries serve as continuing reminders of how much every person depended on natural circumstances for customary comings and goings.

As she turned her attention to war news, Lucy mentioned an unnamed proclamation by Abraham Lincoln, issued, according to her, only in retaliation to an action by CSA president Jefferson Davis. Her focus was clearly on a locale much closer to Travis—the situation in New Orleans concerning General Butler. Yet *Harper's Weekly* had directly connected Davis's response to emancipation, stating:

> Jefferson Davis has issued a violent retaliatory proclamation to the emancipation proclamation of Mr. Lincoln, denouncing the course of General

Butler in New Orleans in vehement terms, and dooming him and all the officers in his command to death by the halter, when they are caught.[1]

However, Lucy never wrote, nor implied, any acknowledgement of emancipation, highlighting the inaccuracy/absence of information and Texas's isolation from much of the duress. If the people of Travis knew of the Emancipation Proclamation at all, they saw little bearing on their lives in February 1863, and Lucy saw no need to reference it. Her brief comment was the closest she would ever come to mentioning Lincoln's Emancipation Proclamation.

Feb 1st sunday ~ Cousin Lu, Waller, Jimmy C~, Uncle J~, Joe, the children and myself went to Buck Horn[2] to church. Heard parson Stone preach from the text "What-must-I do to be saved." Uncle Tom left home this P.M. to go down to the old bachelor's sale and almost his last word was for none to use the carriage but before he had been gone long us girls concluded it was to pleasant to stay at home, so Mollie, Em & I took Beaureagard & Jeff D~ [the horses] and went over to Mr Wm Parson's~. Met Lydia Francis, Mrs Armstrong, Jimmy Francis, Mr & Mrs Owens (Kate Heath) & Bell Snood there. The gentlemen arranged to have a party tomorrow night—if they can not get across the river ~ Mollie, Stickney & I had quite a visit on the gallery this eve. I wrote a note to Neh this eve and enclosed it in a letter of Mrs C's & Dock Cloud took it as he called by this eve.

Feb 4th wednesday ~ It rained most of last night and a part of to day. Cousin Waller returned this eve ~ brought a blank book for Sara & a quire of paper for us girls. Met Mr Scranton on the streets ~ also saw sevral of the Fedral officers who seemed quite at home. Cousin W received a letter from Johnie to day written just after the Murfreesboro fight in which he was one of the fortunate participants ~ never received eaven a scratch. Cousin W left a package of clothing with Cushing to be sent to him. I see in to days paper Lincoln has issued a retaliatory proclimation in regard to the one issued by Davis, concerning all the officers taken under Butler &c.

1. "A Roar From Jeff Davis," *Harper's Weekly*, January 10, 1863, HarpWeek.
2. Buckhorn was a small settlement begun in the 1830s, located some seven miles from Bellville.

Feb 5th thursday ~ This morn Lu cut out 3 pr of pants and I have been helping her with them ~ sewing on a pr for Jimmy ~ A busy day made our broiled chicken at supper relish.

Feb 6th friday ~ The weather has been much pleasanter than yesterday and we are in hopes 'twill remain so ~ We finished up the pants this eve ~ I am not sorry

Feb 8th sunday ~ wrote to Nick & Mack C this morn—just as I was finishing up the letter Jim Bracey came in and handed me a note from cousin Sara ~ she says a letter was received from Mrs Sc[r]anton saying I could write home & she would see that it was sent to and mailed in Havana.

Feb 9th monday ~ Helped Lu to make a harness[3] this morn

Feb 10th tuesday ~ Helped to warp cloth[4] awhile then finished reading Rutledge.[5]

Feb 11th wednesday ~ Hemed two breadths of ruffleing for Willie. Stickney came this P.M. to tell us good bye. Stickney says he, Mollie C, Lydia F and Kinch came from Travis this morn, left all well there. Lydia, Em & Sallie are going there to board

Feb 12th thursday ~ Stickney left this P.M. I treated him to a nice glass of wine and played draughts [similar to checkers] with him this morn.

---

3. In this context, a harness was an apparatus in a loom by which the sets of warp threads were shifted alternately to form the shed, or mounting.

4. To warp cloth is to weave or twine the threads together to form the fabric. This is possibly Lucy's term for weaving. Technically, it is the act of laying on the loom the warp, or lengthwise threads of fabric that form the foundation between which the cross threads, or weft, is woven.

5. Thomas Rutledge, "The proper use and application of riches recommended. A sermon, preached at Salters-Hall, April 15th, 1791, before the correspondent board in London of the Society in Scotland . . . for Propagating Christian knowledge. . . ." By Thomas Rutledge, A.M. Published at the request of the Society, . . . London, 1791, Eighteenth Century Collections Online, Gale Group, Southern Methodist University. The identity is unclear, although possibly Lucy is referring to the sermons of Thomas Rutledge. According to the Eighteenth Century Collections Online database, Rutledge published sermons in the late eighteenth century, including "The Proper Use and Application of Riches Recommended," a sermon he preached in 1791.

the officers taken under Butler &c. Lu moved his wardrobe into the 3 state-room to day which makes his room much
pleasanter.

Feb 5th Thursday. This morn Lu cut out 2 pr of pants and I have been
helping him with them, & sewing on a fur for Jimmy &
a busy day made out. broiled chicken at Supper Relished.

Feb 6th Friday. The weather has been much pleasanter than yesterday. we are in hopes I will remain so. we finished up
the pants this eve. I am not sorry.

Feb 7th Saturday. Cousin Lu & myself have been house cleaning to day
with one the strength of it. I took a severe head ache.
Lu gave me a treat of a nice eggnog this morning quite unexpected

Feb 8th Sunday. Wrote to Aunt M. Mack C this morn. just as
I was finishing up the latter him Bracy came in, and handed
me a note from cousin Jake. the Boys & a letter was received
from Mrs Hinton saying I could write home & She would see
that it was sent out and mailed in Havana. Cousin Lu
was quite sick last night and is not well this morn.
Mr & Mrs Jim mid Alton were here this P.M. Lu gave me a

Feb 9th Monday. pair of fancy pants. The day has been cloudy with no rain
Helped Lu to make harness this morn until Uncle Jo
Mrs Brady & the children when I went to write home. Mr & Mrs
Richie have been here this P.M. but gone again.

Feb 10th Tuesday. made quite a mistake in copying for I first the I wish
well spent the night. wrote to Mrs Scranton this morn.
Helped to warp Moth a while then finished reading Bulstrode.

Feb 11th Wednesday. hemmed two breadths of ruffled for Willie
Mrs H Bracy & Lu were here awhile to day. Mr Bracy came this
P.M. will be good bye. Mrs B. went home to night.
Stickney Jay the, Nellie C, Lydia Brand & Finch came from Travis
this morn. Says all well there. Lydia, Om & B Gillis are going there

Feb 12th Thursday. Stickney left this P.M. Dictated him to a nice
glass of wine & played draughts with him this morn.

Feb 13th Friday. Aunt Sara came on horseback to see us to day. Says
Mr & Mrs Wm met a negro last Sunday coming to tell them
their father was very far induced. and he was afraid they would
not be able to get there before he breathed his last. So she
saw nothing of them until after the burying when they came
back to feast, up and move over there to Stay until
after they had made a row and a division of the property had
taken place. Lu & I went in company with Aunt Sa
a part of the way on our way home to mill, after some fellet meal
for Uncle Wm. As we were passing Mr Bradbury's saw Mr Holland
just firing off to Bellville. We asked him about the crossing at the
creek then drove on. just as he turned back to tell in his carrying
I spoke to him Coffy trotting as hard as she could go try I gave
her to understand I had a whip determined not to have company
in my comical fixe no hood on, and old riding skirt, in fact a
dirty clout, coat and Aunt Sara's knit hood. nearly off my head.
and my clothes so wet they hung tight to me. Lu left Aunt Sa
at the cross roads wondering if in her absence Uncle Tom had
been to move her to the Posey place. Joe called at Mrs Galley's
on my way back & she gave us some such nice winter grapes.

Feb 14th Saturday. St Valentine's day and a clear grainy morn. it has been
Mr & Mrs Buck called this P.M. I finished the front of my
gape like Nellie's. Jim mended a coat for Joe & this morn & a
think earlier dress skirt this afternoon. Uncle Jimmy is almost
down sick with a bad cold and fever.

Feb 15th Sunday. Read Augie Garen, or Life in Washington,
written by Miss Laselle. Doc R. Ayris & Travis this morn and handed
me a Sent he note by him. Uncle Jo is no better. It has
rained all day. She had a note from Mrs Cannan this morn.
telling the death of Maltie Bryton's little Johnie. Jam of some
From the book I read to day. As we pass & Homely is the Lest twenty
Wealth does not always bring its own joys. happiness is Good and
by done, & jolly nor another dry that their slavting. God is ever our
friend to those who seek him. Relt brings contentment &
All is not gold that glitters was taught.

Feb 16th Monday. It has been another rainy day. Uncle Jo & Aunt
are miserable day & night. I am afraid he is going to be quite
ill. I am put in the part of eye. I embroidered one flower
today. hemmed, two breadths of ruffling and put some more
on some panties then finished off some ribbed socks for
cousin Elund. so now I fixe some medicine for Uncle Jimmy.

Feb 17th Tuesday. Uncle Jo is so much better. I worked on my
band & hemmed & whipped some ruffling on tape for Willie.

Feb 13th friday ~ Aunt Sara[6] came on horseback to see us to day. Lu & I went in company with Aunt S a part of the way on our road to mill after some bolted meal[7] for Uncle M. As we were passing Mr Bradburys, saw Mr Holland just fixing off to Bellville. Lu asked him about the crossing at the creek, then drove on. Just as he turned back to get in his carriage I passed by on old Roxy trotting as hard as she could go it. I gave her to understand I had a whip, determined not to have company in my comical fix ~ no hoop on, and old riding skirt in peices, Jim's cloak coat and Aunt Sara's knit hood nearly off my head and my clothes so wet they hung tight to me. We called at Mrs Pilleys on our way back and she gave Lu some such nice winter cabage.

Feb 14th saturday ~ St Valentines day and cloudy rainey one it has been

Feb 15th sunday ~ Read *Annie Grayson or Life in Washington* written by Miss Laselle.[8] It has rained all day. Lu had a note from Mrs Cameron this morn telling the death of Mattie Boington's little Johnie ~ I am so sorry.

From the book I read today, the lessons ~ Honesty is the best Policy. Wealth does not always bring its possessor happiness ~ Good may be done by all, no matter what their station ~ God is ever the friend of those who seek him ~ Peity [piety] brings contentment & All is not gold that glitters were taught.

Feb 17th tuesday ~ Uncle J~ is much better. I worked on my band[9] ~ Lu hemmed & whipped some ruffleing on tape[10] for Willie Joe P came back this morn & brought me 3 letters, one from Nick, one from Neh & one

[FACING] Lucy Pier Stevens Diary, Feb. 8, 1863 Entry. DeGolyer Library, Southern Methodist University, Lucy Pier Stevens Collection.

———

6. Again, Lucy used a family appellation to bestow "family" status and show respect for a good friend.

7. Bolted meal was meal that had been sifted by passing it through a sieve or bolting cloth.

8. Nancy Polk Lasselle, *Annie Grayson or Life in Washington*, 1853, WorldCat. This title, presented in 1853 by Nancy Polk Lasselle, was among several works that the novelist published. Lucy's inclusion of the various themes of the novel indicates her ability to read critically and analyze a text, highlighting its various components.

9. A common sewing term, "band" refers to a thin, flat piece of fabric used to gather together and confine a dress at the waist, neck, wrists, etc.

10. Another sewing phrase, the term describes the long, running stitch (whipstitch) used to attach one piece of fabric to another, in this case a length of ruffle onto a tape or band.

from Mrs S~. Also 3 from cousin S~ for us to read & a note from Aunt Lu & cousin Sara. Aunt Lu sent us girls some such pretty home spun aprons Sara wove and she made on her sewing machine. I prize mine so much.

Feb 19th thursday ~ has been a bright pleasant day ~ Cousin Waller says he saw 7 or 8 deer in the bottom this P.M. & crippled one but enough to keep him from limping off.

The river [Brazos River] is rising rapidly and it is thought if it contin-ues to do so as fast as it has done, it will be over the banks in 2 or 3 days

Feb 20th friday ~ The morn was pleasant but this P.M. cloudy & since dark it has been raining some. Cousin W killed 2 deer & the dogs ran a 3rd through the yard. Waller says he saw 9 to day.

Feb 22nd sunday ~ Lu has been in bed again all day ~ I read several chap-ters from *The Smuggler*, one of G.P.A. James[11] novels for her benefit this P.M. Mr & Mrs Buck came over to see her this morning ~ I am so tired this evening.

Feb 23rd monday ~ Lu is up to day ~ fixed her hoop skirt

Feb 24th tuesday ~ This morning cousin Lu, Willie, Fannie & I started to Travis in the carriage & cousin Waller & Catharine on horseback. I read until we got to Center Hill. Aunt Lu was at the store with Sara, but as soon as they saw us, she came running to meet us, and Sara, after she had shut up shop, came walking down. We left home about 10A.M. & arrived at Travis at 2P.M. Tallie, Lydia F and Callie Bell are boarding at Uncles this session. I have a furious headache.

Feb 26th thursday ~ Lu has been getting ready for home. We started directly after dinner. Cousin W & I on horseback & the rest in the car-riage. The roads were so full of water we did not dare venture crossing at the old place so went out near Mr Middletons. When we got there cousin W rode in to try how deep it was ~ the water came up to the

---

11. According to the Princeton University Library Manuscripts Division, which houses an extensive collection of James's writings, G.P.R. James (not "G.P.A.," as Lucy has it) wrote more than one hundred historical novels. An English novelist, he was greatly influenced by Sir Wal-ter Scott.

saddle, he rode through twice to find the best crossing then I rode over on old Bones. Got one foot and my dress right wet, next came cousin Lu on old B~ & cousin W carrying Fannie, then he went again & brought part of the [. . .] then a fifth time & brought the rest ~ the sixth time brought W & the seventh time led Clay across & Catharine followed riding Bones crossed two other streams ~ the water run in the carriage at one. It rained hard here last night

Feb 28th saturday ~ Cousin Waller went to Hempstead this morn, returned this eve bringing Jimmy with him ~ Got five yds of domestic for me at $1.50 cts per yd and this book at $7.00 Cousin Lu has not been anything like as well to day ~ but for all her bad feeling would work on her embroidery.

CHAPTER 3

MARCH
1863

Commenced reading *Kenilworth* . . . Like it much so far.

LUCY P. STEVENS,
March 22, 1863

DURING HER QUIET MOMENTS, Lucy read as much as she could. She was an avid, prolific reader who included newspapers, letters, magazines, poetry, and novels on a reading list in the back of her diary. She also took the time to write in her journal regularly. The journal itself, much of which is transcribed in these pages, serves as a symbol for the sacrifices that Lucy and her family made as a result of the war's economic impact. The Union blockade became increasingly effective as time wore on, and prices climbed. If supplies arrived at all, long lines formed and crowds gathered. One woman reportedly paid $180 for twelve candles, one pair of shoes, and a bolt of domestic cloth.[1] More than once, Lucy bemoaned the cost of goods, but she was grateful when articles could still be obtained at all.

Many everyday items, in fact, came to have luxury status because of the scarcity. Coffee was high on the list, and Lucy's diary indicates that paper was also a prized commodity. It had, in fact, become such a highly coveted item that Lucy began keeping her 1863 journal accounts on scrap paper until a suitable book could be found. As it turns out, her journal begins with entries dating January 1, 1863, but shows the date on the cover sheet to be February 28, 1863. After paying seven dollars for the journal on February 28, Lucy then spent the entire next day, March 1, copying all of the entries from the miscellaneous pieces of paper into the new book. Additionally, to extend its

---

1. Waller County Historical Survey Commission, *A History of Waller County, Texas* (Waco: Author, 1873), 111.

usefulness, she was very careful to allocate two lines of writing to each lined space in the book. At the end of 1864, when that book was completely filled, Lucy resorted to an accounts ledger with lines and columns for her new journal, again carefully using each line for two lines of text.

Mar 1st sunday ~ Have been busy all day copying my old journal in this book. Lu is no better. Dr R & wife came this P.M. The Dr has had a blister[2] put on Lu's back.

Mar 2nd monday ~ worked on my embroidery a part of the day ~ Lu says the blister has done no good at all ~ Dr & wife left this P.M.

Mar 3rd tuesday ~ Lu is up this morn, but her back has been hurting her so badly that she has to lounge most of the time. After I put my room in order I swept, cleaned & dusted in the store-room & dining room ~ this P.M. I made some cookies for Lu hoping to tempt her to eat some.

Mar 4th wednesday ~ This morn cousin Waller, Jimmy & Uncle J came in with such a nice plate of honey ~ robbed Will's be[e] hives.
This P.M. Narcissa was here to reel her yarn[3] ~ say[s] Mae & husband are with her. After she had gone, we noticed Jim & cousin W coming back from their hunt in a lope and Lu wondering what it meant ~ ran out and found Aunt Violet's house in a blaze ~ we all went down and worked faithfully for a half hour putting it out. Poor old Aunt V & Uncle Frank lost nearly everything they had, bed, beding & .clothing. They both cried like they were heart broken. Lu sent them two comforts this evening. Lu has been up all day but not well.

Mar 5th thursday ~ this morn Lu made a cape for Aunt Violet and has been almost down sick in bed this P.M. I have been busy washing my riding skirt and sack in the morn and in the afternoon I took the congruss out of my boots, put velvet in, then cut them down in front to lace up.

---

2. According to the *OED*, a blister was a medical treatment often used to reduce inflammation. It involved the application of a poultice to supply moisture and warmth to the inflamed area. The poultice frequently consisted of a substance such as meal or linseed combined with boiling water and spread upon muslin or linen cloth.

3. To reel yarn was to wind thread or yarn onto spools or other revolving devices in order to facilitate the weaving process.

Mar 6th friday ~ This morn as I was washing &c prepariatory to going across the river, cousin Waller came and told us two carriages were coming from towards Uncle Tom's and soon after Mrs C~, Em, cousin Ann, little Kelt, Mary Emmon & Caroline came and spent the day. Then this eve Mrs C, Em & Mrs Emmon went home leaving the rest to stay a few days. Cousin Ann had five or six letters from Kelt Senior by Mr Smith, just arrived yesterday from New Iberia.[4] All the boys are well ~ are now under command of Sibley.[5] Two of the men from each company are to be furloughed for 30 days each until all have been home. Neh says he intends to come next. Uncle J has been to see Aunt Margaret who was thrown from her carriage a few days ago and had two ribs broken and two more badly shattered. Has had a high fever and is thought danger-ous. the Dr has not left her bedside since he saw her. Mrs Blassingame was not hurt so seriously.

Mar 11th wednesday ~ Jim went with me to see Uncle Martin's this morn. Found Uncle M had been having typhoid fever 3 weeks had been up but a few days, was looking badly now & says he still has fevers occasionally. They are not as comfortably situated as I had expected to find them, but they seem to enjoy themselves quite as well as we could look for them too. Dr P's [Peebles's] family have been very kind to them since they have been there, but particularly so since Uncle M's sickness.

Mar 12th thursday ~ Looked all the morn for Mrs Lipscomb, intending to come home but as she did not come and I could not persuade Jim to come home, I got Mr Clayton to come over with me. We were the first that crossed at Hill's Ferry since 'twas fixed. Found Lu had been much worse while I was gone but Aunt Sara stayed until yesterday Mrs Harry B~ come tuesday & stayed until wednesday eve & Mr. Sherwood stayed wed~ night & thursday ~ went home this eve. Mrs Buck came over

---

4. New Iberia, Louisiana, situated on the Bayou Teche, was hotly contested ground between Union and Confederate forces during the spring and fall of 1863, and many of Lucy's soldier friends fought in these battles.

5. General Henry H. Sibley led Confederate forces to victory in New Mexico in 1862, but then suffered a devastating retreat when his entire supply train was lost to a raiding party. After a summons to Richmond to discuss his poor leadership, Sibley assumed command in Louisiana in 1863. However, according to The Handbook of Texas Online, he was eventually court-martialed by General Richard Taylor for his "diminishing leadership and heavy drinking." He was ultimately acquitted, but was nevertheless removed from command.

monday & sent some custards & pies. The Dr was to see her monday &
Wednesday, so she did not lack attention and now I'm just in time.

Mar 13th friday ~ Hoping Uncle Pier & Aunt Lu would be here to day.
this P.M. Dr & Mrs Richie were here to see Lu.

    Dr. left a bottle of medacine for me to try see could I cure the Goitre.[6]
I lack faith. Lu has been up most of the day, the first one since monday.
Aunt Lu & Uncle Pier came this eve in the wagon.

Mar. 18th wednesday ~ Felt much better so that I read part of the time.
The author of *Waverly* was in infancy an invalid & left to his own choice in
selection of his book reading which comprised most of his early teaching.

Mar 20th friday ~ Have been writing off recipes, reading &c all day
instead of sewing as I had intended ~ Cousin W just said ~ "You scour
mighty often." ~ "scoured just a week ago." I wonder what he'd think of
some of the "Yankees". Lu has been preparing herself to day for sickness
tomorrow

Mar 21st saturday ~ Finished Uncle George's hat in the morn ~ put a
new breadth in my dress ~ Lu gave me the cloth. Lined a velvet belt then
patched. *Waverly*[7]—the book I finished yesterday gives a history of the
Highlanders in the day of King George who were so deeply engaged in
the effort to regain the throne for the house of Stuart ~ Prince Charles
Edward was the aspirant who led the forces from Edinborough through
Scotland crossing the Esk ~ down passing through Carlisle, thence on as
far as Derby ~ when before superior forces of Cavalry they were obliged
to retrace their steps & flee for life. [. . .] of the house of Mac Ivor, a chief
among the Highlanders was taken prisoner during an engagement on
their retreat and executed at Carlisle; after his execution, Flora the last
representative of the house of Mac Ivor retired to a nunnery to spend the
remainder of her life in devotion to God. The Prince made his escape.
Many of the Highlanders also [who] returned to their homes. It had

---

    6. A goiter is an enlargement of the thyroid gland, often visible as a swelling in the lower
part of the front of the neck.

    7. Richard D. McGhee, "Sir Walter Scott," in *Dictionary of Literary Biography*, vol. 107, *British
Romantic Prose Writers, 1789–1832*, 1st ser., ed. John R. Greenfield, 247–266 (Gale Research, 1991).
Waverly, the first in Sir Walter Scott's series of the same name, was published in 1814.

been one of the habits of the H's to take off cattle belonging to the gentry of their neighboring country and until a certain tax called by them "black mail" was paid to their chief ~ said cattle were not returned. So long as the "black mail" was punctually paid their cattle & property were left undisturbed. One of the principle persons engaged in this employ where these scenes were laid I have been reading was Dean Bean Lean.

The Baron of Bradwardine & his daughter Grace were characters. A family relic of the Baron's was the "Blessed Bear of Bradwardine" a Jobalen[8] cup used only on great occasions to insure health, long life & happiness to some favored guest.*

*[This is the first of several plot summaries that Lucy included in her diary. Other summaries may be found in the unexpurgated text housed in DeGolyer Library, SMU.]

Mar 22nd sunday ~ Commenced reading *Kenilworth*[9] No 2nd of the *Waverly* novels. Like it much so far, for much of it is true history. Was right sick an hour or two this P.M. Dr & Mrs Richie came to see Lu & find how she was prospering; stayed until nearly night.

Mar 23rd monday ~ Commenced a peice of work this morn anxious to get it done soon, but was hired by Lu to lay it aside and read, first with the promise of a dime then if I would read more I should have a nice cup of coffee, the latter being so great an inducement I would most willingly have read all the P.M. rather than missed it.

Uncle M. came over in the P.M. to see about getting the German to take his cotton to Mexico.

Mar 24th tuesday ~ Had a norther blow up last night and this is a cold clear morning. Cousin W & Uncle M rode over to see the Germans about going out to Mexico today returned in time for dinner & in the P.M. learned Uncle Jimmy how to cut out shoe soles & prepare them for sewing. I have not much enjoyed the day—having had a touch of the vapors.

---

8. In this context, Lucy could possibly mean a Jacobean cup. However, when compared with the text of *Waverly*, her meaning is unclear.

9. McGhee, "Sir Walter Scott." According to the Gale Literary Database, *Kenilworth*, published in 1821, was actually the thirteenth in Scott's *Waverly* series.

Sara says there was a runaway out there. Rufus Brewer & his cousin Bell Griswold ~ went to Parson Kenney's the night of the 17th were married then went out to Center Hill. Ran away from no one.

Mar 28th saturday ~ Sara, Jimmy & myself started for Travis about half past 9 O'c'k arrived there at 1 P.M. Found all looking anxiously for us. In the eve showers on our way and this P.M. It rained hard but find [finally] turned into a norther. All the Travisites are usuly [usually] well

Mar 29th sunday ~ Cousin Sara & myself commenced copying Lu's journal but concluded as Sallie was not going to be with us long we would not write more. Aunt Lu had some corn popped & pecans cracked for us & in the P.M. cousin Sara, Sallie, Cally & Jim went over to Mr Chapmans but it was so cold I concluded not to venture out ~ Charley came back with them to spend the night.

Mar 30th monday ~ Mr & Mrs C~ just returned from Houston ~ Mrs C met with quite a mishap on the way home from Hempstead ~ lost her sa[t]chel containing about $100, gold pen, 2 silver thimbles. Jim B's picture in a locket, Lulu D's and a great many little articles of value. We arrived at cousin Lu's about 4 P.M. found Mrs Buck, Bella & Sallie Bracey here. Lu had a nice cup of coffee in waiting for me which was very accep[t]able ~ Aunt Lu had some sure enough coffee made for us the afternoon we got home

Mar 31st tuesday. Had a heavy frost last night so it cut down about 30 acres of corn for cousin Waller ~ its too too bad We all went down into the field to see it this eve ~ Its enough to make any body that has worked hard or to see the devastation but I fear to night will still [be] harder on it for it is so cold & clear.

CHAPTER 4

APRIL–MAY
1863

Cousin Sara has some kind of a breaking out on her face this morn
which she says is the measles, but we girls laugh at the idea.

LUCY P. STEVENS,
April 17, 1863

SPRING BEGAN ITS REBIRTH IN THE AREA, and with the war far away, Lucy's diary echoes the lighthearted sense of anticipation. Residents were preparing for a fair that would benefit the military hospital. Activity flourished. Friends and neighbors crisscrossed the landscape, visiting and sharing in the hope that attends the season. As Lucy continued to chronicle her relationship with Mrs. Peebles and her daughters, her staunch support and fondness for the family become apparent. Equally clear, from the historical perspective, is the impact of the entire Peebles family on Texas. Jared Groce III, son of Mrs. Peebles from her earlier marriage, resided at Bernardo Plantation on the east bank of the Brazos River, four miles from Hempstead. The plantation had been established by his father, Jared E. Groce, who had come to Texas in the 1820s as part of Stephen F. Austin's original Old Three Hundred. The older Groce had cultivated his land with the help of ninety to a hundred slaves, and had planted what was probably the first cotton crop in Texas in 1822. By 1863, the plantation was a thriving enterprise, one of the largest in the region.

After Jared E. Groce's death, his widow, Mary Ann, remarried in 1843, and she and her new husband, Dr. Richard Peebles, became a "power couple" in the early days of Texas. They resided at her plantation, Pleasant Hill, where they went on to have nine children. Dr. Peebles, who had served under Sam Houston at San Jacinto, continued his medical practice, engaged in a variety of business endeavors, and helped found the town of Hempstead and the Washington County Railroad. According to *The Handbook of Texas Online*, by 1860, he was one of the wealthiest men in Texas. Although a slaveholder,

Peebles was not in favor of secession, and later in 1863, he would be impli-
cated in a Unionist plot. Ultimately, he would be exiled to Mexico for the
duration of the war. Regardless of the case against him, and despite the public outcries for justice, Lucy remained steadfast in her concern and her affection for this family, writing fondly of them throughout her journal.

The controversy concerning Peebles was yet unknown, however, and Lucy
focused on the happy association with his family. At the same time, with the
coming of warm weather, a lurking danger cast its shadow over the area as
cases of measles began to be reported in households around the community.
As merely an aside, Lucy began tracking the spread of measles throughout
the community and in her own household. She mentioned on April 1 several
members of a household who were near death or who had died, and on April
11, she mentioned that Bell had the measles "bad, bad." Ten days later, the diary
indicates that Lucy was personally in charge of her "measly darkies." Nursing
care of family and slaves fell under the jurisdiction of the mistress and other
women of the household,[1] and Lucy, of necessity, assisted. On April 22, she
took her turn caring for the sick slaves and managing their illness.

There was no special treatment for the fever, cough, itching red rash, and
irritated eyes that accompanied the measles; indeed, all that could be done
was to keep the patient comfortable. Highly contagious, the disease spread
rapidly, thanks to the custom of visiting the sick. Yet even before Lucy mentioned the measles in her diary, Aunt Lu noted that a neighbor, John Lott,
had stopped by and spent the day, even though he "had the roseola or camp
measles just breaking out on him" (Lu M. Pier, 3/8/63). In that same entry,
Aunt Lu recorded that two more families visited on their way to a wedding,
where still other families would be exposed.

As April progressed to May, Lucy continued her count of those succumb-
ing to the measles, commenting, "the days drag wearily along" (5/9/63).
Cataloging coughs, fevers, colds, and spots for an ever enlarging number of
patients, she worried that the patients "get along so poorly" (5/9/63). By May
11, she recorded that the measles had begun to take a fatal toll, and deaths
were being reported around the area. On May 15, Lucy noted that there were
more deaths, but Aunt Lu's diary gives the count in more graphic detail:

Just at dinner time here came Sarah and Lue up from Wallers leaving the
sick at Wallers all better they brought the news that Col Day had lost two
children with measles and three Negroes (small ones) On Sunday May

---

1. Elizabeth Silverthorne, *Plantation Life in Texas* (College Station: Texas A&M University
Press, 1986), 148.

10th little Lucy Emma died and on the Thursday following little Fannie died. The measles have been very fatal on some plantations on the river. Mr. Oliver's and R. D. And G. Mills' one is said to have lost 30, Mr. O. and the other 60. Maria had the headache very bad. Sarah is looking very bad she had the measles broke out on her good this time . . .

Lu M. Pier, 5/18/63

Sarah had, in fact, contracted the measles for a second time and suffered long-term effects from the disease. On May 4, she had written in her journal, "Had another fever today, a pretty high one. I don't see what can ail me, Waller and the rest say I am taking the measels again. If so, I wont say the measels don't hurt me again. I hate to be so no account. I came to help take care of the sick but I fear I am about to give up" (Sarah Pier, 5/4/63). As April slipped into May, the disease spread, and Lucy continued to chronicle its effects on family and friends. With each passing day, the airy sense of carefree visiting became more clouded by the foe of illness on the home front and, of course, the war, far away.

APRIL 1863

Apr 1st, wednesday ~ All were up betimes this morning as cousin W, Jimmy & the negroes are going to drive up & mark & brand cattle ~ Lu did not have me called until all the rest had eaten dinner ~ then had such a nice breakfast for me ~ she is to good to me. We, Lu, Willie, & I spent the day at Mrs Richies ~ the Dr. was at a german's all day with patients ~ one little boy died about 9 A.M. & another child about 2 P.M. 3 others were sick, & in the eve Mr. Jackson sent in hot haste for the Dr to come see a negro woman who lay at the point of death.

Apr 2nd thursday ~ Lu also has been shoemaking ~ but this P.M. read *Lindu or the Prairae Flower,*[2] not a very good story ~ casts to much reflection on the female character. Cousin W~ & Jim are after cattle again to day ~ This has been a warm, pretty day.

---

2. Joseph L. Coulombe, "Emerson Bennett," in *Dictionary of Literary Biography*, vol. 202, *Nineteenth-Century American Fiction Writers*, ed. Kent P. Ljungquist (Gale Group, 1999). This title could refer to a book written by Emerson Bennett featuring Western Americana and a frontier history of the Trans-Mississippi West. According to the Gale Literary Database, Bennett published *The prairie flower; or, Adventures in the far West* and *Leni-Leoti; or, Adventures in the far West* concurrently in 1849.

Apr 3rd friday ~ Nearly finished embroidering a scarve for Lu & do believe if it had not been for her tempting me so much with goodies to eat & goodies to drink, I would have had it quite finished; she gave me such a nice 'nog before dinner & after some nice coffee, our daily treat.

In the eve we walked down to the cow pen & round back the old road to the house; Willie, Sallie, Bracy & Tallie Merse gathered such a pretty boquet for me. Cousin W says this eve thank goodness I am done with my cattle have delivered them & mad[e] three hides off from Reub Harris ~ he cut their tales off & 3 bled to death ~ a singular way to mark anything.

Apr. 5th Sunday ~ Uncle M ~ and myself started over the river soon in the morn ~ arrived there about N[noon]. Found Aunt H very well. In the P.M. Miss Maggie, Rachel, Samie Peebles & Miss Bessie Baldwin came down & called and in the evening ~ How do I like them? The Miss Peebles I am in love with, they seemed so pleasant & friendly & anxious for me to understand, they already felt acquainted with me from Aunt H's speaking of me so often & indeed it did not seem a difficult matter to feel perfectly at home & at ease with them. I felt they were old acquaintances.

Apr 7th tuesday ~ Dr P [Peebles] was here yesterday morn & called. In the P.M. Miss L came down & set a few moments then we went home with her. Just as we got near the gate met Francis coming to tell us Mrs. P~ had sent for us to come up. All seem so kind and friendly ~ Mrs P~ & Mrs Clark equally with the others I could not feel strange at their house more than at an old acquaintance.

Apr. 8th wednesday ~ Mrs Peebles & Mrs. Catlin came down & set with us an hour or two then Mrs P~ insisted we should go up and take dinner with them & help eat their turkey, so we went ~ found the young ladies in Mrs Clark's room all busy preparing neadle books, pin cushion, lamp-mats &c for the fair that is to come off the night of the 21st for Wallers Batt.[3] So I assisted them. We finished up 4 neadle books, six tomatoes[4] & 4 lamp mats. Mrs P had some such nice poped corn, some made in candy, & some plain, the only corn candy except of my own making I've ever eaten in Texas

---

3. Waller's Battalion, as Lucy refers to it, was the 13th Texas Cavalry Battalion, under the command of Edwin Waller Jr. This unit, for whom many of Lucy's friends fought, saw action in battles in the bayou country of southern and western Louisiana.

4. The "tomatoes" were possibly pincushions formed in the shape of tomatoes.

MARGINAL NOTE: *A. S. Fowler[5] wounded near Camp [Fort] Bisland[6]*
Apr. 13th 1863

Apr. 10th friday ~ Mrs Peebles went to the depot this morn hoping to
meet her son Jarred Groce Did not return until late this eve. The girls
have been busy this P.M. fixing for fishing tomorrow ~ want me to stay
& go, but that is impossible

Apr. 11th saturday ~ I bid all good bye, & went down to Aunt H's, put my
things together and then went up to go across the river.

Arrived at home, found Lu much better than I had left her. Jimmie
came soon after I did, says he left Harry Bracey some better but still perfectly crazy. He was on his way home from Fleurnoy's Reg,[7] had gotten
nearly to Navisota [Navasota] when the horses took fright & ran away ~
he attempted to jump from the stage but fell on his head ~ was picked up
for dead & taken in to Navisota without showing by motion any signs of
life. As soon as they arrived in the village word was sent to Hempstead
(25 miles). Mr. Groce' carriage was in town & he sent right over here
after Narcissa who went down that evening ~ the next day Jimmy went
with Mrs Sherwood down & yesterday Jim Bracey went. Mr. H. B~ was
hurt on thursday. Cousin Lu is busy fixing for the fair & everybody over
here is all excitement about it. Mrs. Paine is going to make cake &c, &c

The Dr says Bell has got the measles ~ bad, bad. I must not forget
Dr. Herd's being at Dr P's on friday, and being so drunk. He is one of the
most celebrated physicians in Texas. It is too bad to see so much knowledge & worth thrown away.[8]

---

5. A. S. Fowler was Lucy's good friend Stickney. He had been part of the party that traveled
down the Mississippi River when Lucy first came to Texas with Cousin Sarah.

6. In an effort to repel a Union expedition aimed at Alexandria, Louisiana, Major General
Richard Taylor's Confederate army engaged Union troops under the direction of Major General
Nathaniel Banks at Camp [Fort] Bisland in the Bayou Teche region of Louisiana. As the fighting
began at Fort Bisland on April 13, 1863, Colonel Thomas Green's regiment, a unit of Texas soldiers, was ordered to the front to slow the enemy advance. In the end, however, the Union army
prevailed, and General Taylor ordered an evacuation of the fort, beginning a Confederate retreat.

7. Colonel George Flournoy, who had served as attorney general of Texas immediately
before the war and who was an ardent secessionist, commanded the 16th Texas Infantry Regiment, as part of the Third Brigade of Walker's Texas Division.

8. Lucy's mention of Dr. Herd could possibly be a reference to Dr. Thomas Jefferson Heard,
noted physician of the Republic of Texas and founder of the Texas Medical Association. Dr.
Heard served on the faculties of medical schools in both Texas and Louisiana, and published
several papers, including a medical history of Texas, now housed in the Texas State Archives.
He also served as Sam Houston's attending physician at the time of Houston's death.

Apr 14th tuesday ~ Cousin Lu & I went up to see Harry [Bracy] this P.M. ~ found him looking very badly, but he seemed to know us. Called Lu by name & said I used to teach school there. I fear he will never recover entirely. Its enough to make a well person deranged to be in such a heated room & have so much confusion around them. I wanted to tell Dr R. to hush his mouth. Particularly when he was telling about bringing into the world that baby that weighed 13 lbs ~ (the fool). this eve I went over to see Mrs. Buck awhile, found her right sick & alone. Before she would give up, she made 8 lbs of cake for the fair

Apr. 17th friday ~ Cousin Sara has some kind of a breaking out on her face this morn which she says is the measles, but we girls laugh at the idea. I went over to see Mrs Buck a little while this morn & borrowed some bake tins for Lue ~ found her in bed & more red spots on her face than Sara has, also has a cough; they have sent for the Dr & if he pronounces her's measles I'll say Sara's is too.

Apr. 19th sunday ~ Mrs Paine & Mrs Geo Chambers came by today & called; had been to Mrs Buck's ~ had Beckie with them, but would not bring her in on account of the measles. took all of the fair articles from both places, from Mrs B's two doll dresses, a shuck basket, two vases, & 3 pin cushions & from Lu's a pair of blue baby's shoes, a pair of boots, 2 pin cushions, a cigar case, a neadle book & us girls' things

This P.M. Lu & Mrs Darnman went over to see Mrs Buck, found her much better. Mrs D~ really opened her heart, for she gave Sara, Lu & I each 12 sheets of letter paper with black edges. She gave a pair of vases for the fair; very pretty ones.

Apr. 21st tuesday ~ All was confusion until the good people were off. I am housekeeper & have charge of the children. After they started I put the house to order went out to "lead" my measly darkies then sit down to visit with Nick, who came to spend the day. Just as I was ready to go to sewing, in came Chane with Bella Buck, saying her mistress was going over to the fair & wanted to know would I take care of her little girl, but at dinner she came back saying her mistress turned back after going a short distance

In the P.M. 3 men from Hargrove's Co came to conscript cousin W, but happily he was from home

Apr. 22nd wednesday ~ Last night I barred my doors ~ put Willie at the head of Lu's bed & Lula at the foot, had a field bed made in the corner for my four sick darkies ~ made Betsy sleep at the house to wait on them & slept soundly til broad daylight.

After giving out breakfast, straightened the house, sent the sick to the hospital & prepared for a good time generally. Was by myself until after dinner when Joe came & told me everybody I knew at the fair & a great many I did not know, about 4 P.M. the rest of the good folks came. All said they would have been most highly delighted with the fair, but that news came the same day of an engagement near New Iberia in which Wallers Batt~ & Sibley's Brigade were engaged. Confed loss in killed being 150 & in missing 600[9] Col Riley among the killed.[10] The Confed were retreating still & had been every day ~ the 11th, 12th & 13th the last heard.

Sara brought me two nice cakes & cousin W a stand of revolving dice. Lu brought Willie a trumpet & Mrs Darnman brought a little bedstead for Lula. In the eve Sara & I went over & took tea with Mrs Buck & so I had a full account of all the proceedings. Our side of the river table sold off the soonest of any & Lissie's cake sold for over $2.00 more than any other; 'twas a Boone cake.

Apr. 24th friday ~ No Waller yet & no more news from the Batt as we were in hopes to have received. We left Lu still feeling very badly. She has seven [sic] negroes down with the measles. Catharine, Sally, Ike, George, Rose, Beckie & Willis & Luce most down & a prospect of two more negroes, beside Willie, Lula & herself yet to take them. Poor Lu, no wonder she is low spirited. There were four men from Hargrove's Company here for buttermilk before N[oon] & six others came & took

---

9. Sibley's Brigade, under the command of General H. H. Sibley, saw action in the Louisiana bayou country, including the Battles of Fort Bisland and Bayou Teche. Lucy's estimates of Confederate casualties are in keeping with contemporary statistics that show 450 casualties for the Confederates and 234 for the Union forces. It was after this campaign that court-martial proceedings were initiated against Sibley.

10. James Farber, Texas C.S.A. (New York: Jackson Co., 1947). Colonel James Reily was a veteran of the Mexican War and later served in the diplomatic corps of the Republic of Texas in its dealings with Mexico. In 1863, he served under General Sibley in Louisiana as commander of the Fourth Texas Mounted and was killed in the Battle of Bisland on April 14, 1863.

dinner. While they were at the table, Aunt Lu came from Mrs Catlin's & brought word that only one out of McDades Co was hurt & that the loss was not so great as was at first reported; but the gun boats *Queen of the West, Diana* & a 3rd were lost.[11]

Apr. 26th sunday ~ I spent the morn in reading *The Antiquary*.[12] Cousin S~ went to church & Aunt Lu read Cox's (an Ohio senator's)[13] speach out loud for Uncle P's benefit. This P.M. I have brought my journal up from the 11th & a time I had of it too. We are feasting now days ~ have flour all the time

Apr. 27th monday ~ while we were all at the dinner table Ann McDade, baby & John Bell came ~ almost the first words Ann said was have you heard the news ~ Jack & Puss ~ were married yesterday. I could hardly believe it at first although I had expected they would marry some time. So one of our band is gone ~ Good bye & may yours be one of the happiest of lives ~ Your choice is wise & I do not doubt if this wretched war should not cut you with others of its fair flowers down ~ you will spend many days of domestic happiness.

Apr. 28th tuesday ~ There was a Mr Glass dined with us one that have been in Johnston's spy company[14] in Arkansas.

11. Both ships that Lucy mentioned had originally been Union vessels, captured and converted for Confederate use. Now serving as a Confederate ram, the *Queen of the West* was ordered to the Atchafalaya River section of Louisiana, and on April 14, 1863, she was attacked by three U.S. Navy gunboats at Grand Lake, set afire, and destroyed. The *Diana*, now a Confederate gunboat, also assisted in the effort, but was destroyed as the Confederate forces were forced to evacuate Fort Bisland and retreat.

12. *The Antiquary*, published in 1816, was the third in Scott's *Waverly* series.

13. Congressman Samuel S. Cox (not "Senator," as Lucy has it) served as a Democratic congressman from Ohio for thirty years. He advocated acquiescence to reasonable Southern demands and tried to reach a compromise in the secession crisis of 1860–1861. He was associated with the Peace Democrats, who wanted a negotiated end to the war.

14. Captain Alf Johnson's Independent Company of the Texas Cavalry was part of Morgan's Texas Cavalry Battalion and served in Arkansas and Missouri. Organized in 1863, it was one of many such espionage units operating across the Confederacy. However, despite some success noted among individual spies, this branch of the Confederate effort, especially the large-scale efforts, yielded few results for the Southern cause.

MAY 1863

May 3rd sunday ~ Aunt Lu & all returned this morning ~ bringing word cousin Lu, Willie, Lulu D~ & sevral of the negroes were down with the measles and we are to go down tomorrow. Uncle Pier brought news of Mr Wiley being a prisoner & wounded in the face. Mr Bowers, Hezzie Harvey, Sam Princhard, Judenswife & one other person taken prisoner from McDade's Company & also that the Confederate forces were still retreating towards Louisiana, the Fedrals in close pursuit. Green's Reg[15] was sent back to Niblets Bluff[16] to get in the rear & try & cut off the enemies stores & provisions

May 5th tuesday ~ Cousin Sara is feeling worse today ~ the rest are no better. The Dr was here

May 6th wednesday ~ Sara has been in bed all day but says she intends to go home tomorrow

May 7th thursday ~ Cousin Sara broke out thick with the measles this morn, so could not go home. So Mrs Darnman & I have our hands full. Lu & Willie have a most dreadful cough & it seems like they could get nothing to relieve them. Lulu has quite a cough too & the measles have come out on her quite thick, to our joy. This is Lu's birthday.

May 8th friday ~ Mrs Buck did not visit us to day as Bella was taken with the measles. Lu's & Willie's cough are still bad, but still all are improving. This P.M. cousin Lu received a note from Mr Day telling her little Lucy Emma was very low with the measles, impossible they thought for her to recover. Fannie also was very sick & if it was possible they would like

---

15. The First Cavalry Brigade, commanded by Colonel Thomas Green, engaged in the various battles along Bayou Teche in the spring of 1863. Colonel Green had previously assisted in the recapture of Galveston on January 1, 1863. Shortly after this entry in Lucy's diary, during May 1863, Green was promoted to general and given charge of Sibley's Brigade following Sibley's removal from command.

16. Niblett's Bluff, located in southern Louisiana near the Sabine River, provided a natural crossing into Texas and was, therefore, a likely embarkation point for a Union invasion. Confederate troops consequently gathered there as part of the Trans-Mississippi Department effort to prevent any Federal offensive into Texas.

eather cousin Sara or myself to go over there. Of course it was not, so
Lu sent word to old lady Bracey & also sent her horse & carriage for
her to go.

May 9th saturday ~ The days drag wearily along for it seems to me our
patients get on so poorly. Lu & Willie have both taken more cold & there
are now eleven of the negroes down all needing attention.

May 10th sunday ~ All were better this morn & I was thinking how
much relieved I felt & was expecting to read most of the day to cousin
Sara ~ when as is usual my anticipations of a quiet day received a down-
fall by Mr & Mrs Maning with two of the children coming to spend the
day. Lu still coughs badly but says she is better.

May 11th monday ~ Cal came home this morn & brought word little
Emma died yesterday forenoon & a little negroe in the evening.

May 12th tuesday ~ Lu & Willie were both up a little while this eve I am
so rejoiced to see them so much better

May 13th wednesday ~ All were up to day for awhile & Lu & Sara both
tried to work some. Jimmie C~ started for Mexico this morn ~ I sent a
letter of eight pages interlined for him to mail in Matamoris for Father.
This eve Mr Cochrane came after cousin W to go out to Bellville to be
examined

May 14th thursday ~ Cousin W came home this P M. Has a discharge in
full ~ we are all so rejoiced. Cousin Lu gains strength very slowly, but all
are better.

May 15th friday ~ Mr Clemmons received a letter from Jimmy saying
that he was very sorry to have to write that Nick Merry had deserted and
gone to the Fedrals. Woeful case. Cousin Waller took dinner at Col Day's
~ says poor little Fannie died & was buried yesterday. Mrs Day is almost
broken hearted. Fannie was one of the sweetest disposition children I
ever saw. They have lost two children & three negroes with measles.

May 17th sunday ~ Have been reading *The Mother in Law*[17] all day ~ this PM Mr & Mrs Buck & Bella came over & stayed an hour or so. Bella brought me a magnolia ~

May 23rd saturday ~ This P.M. Johnie Young came by brought word H. P. Wiley was wounded so seriously through the face, they did not think he could live but few days. The other Travis boys were well. We are so anxious to hear more of the particulars. Col. Boone brought with him a six shooting revolving rifle that was thrown over board by the Yankees during the fight. The next day after his arrival in Hempstead he took the gun on to Columbus to be fixed and says he is going back as soon as it is ready for use. The boys are very much scattered some at bayou Beff, some at Nacatoches [Natchitoches], some at Niblets bluff & some

May 26th tuesday ~ a letter from cousin Sammie ~ the first since the fight ~ We were all so glad to hear he was well ~ letters from Jim & Jake we read also ~ all write Mr Wiley is a prisoner.

May 28th thursday ~ We heard the news of "Stonewall" Jackson's death[18] confirmed this mail & also news came of Gen. Van Dorn being shot by Dr Peters in Columbia Tenn for improper intimacy with his wife.[19] It is

17. Joanne Dobson and Amy Hudock, "E.D.E.N. Southworth," in *Dictionary of Literary Biography*, vol. 239, *American Women Prose Writers, 1820–1870*, ed. Katherine Rodier and Amy Hudock, 285–292 (Gale Group, 2001). *The Mother-In-Law; or, The Isle of Rays*, published as a novel in 1851, was written by Emma Dorothy Eliza Nevitte Southworth (E.D.E.N. Southworth), one of the most popular American authors of the mid-nineteenth century. Southworth's work was known for its engaging adventures and exuberant characters, as well as its incorporation of moral overtones as it combined a serious treatment of female subordination with a comic examination of gender stereotypes.

18. James McPherson, *Ordeal by Fire: The Civil War and Reconstruction*, 2nd ed. (New York: McGraw-Hill, 1992), 320–321. "Stonewall" Jackson, the legendary Confederate general who earned his nickname at the First Battle of Bull Run, was accidentally shot by his own men at the Battle of Chancellorsville (May 2–6, 1863), and amputation of his left arm was required. Pneumonia set in following the surgery, and Jackson died on May 10, 1863.

19. According to *The Handbook of Texas Online*, on May 7, 1863, General Earl Van Dorn was shot and killed in his office in Spring Hill, Tennessee. Common talk associated Van Dorn's death with his reputation for drinking and womanizing. A local man, Dr. Peters, had accused Van Dorn of improprieties with his wife. However, Dr. Peters's own political support of Federal forces in Tennessee clouded the murder with a sense of mystery.

said the Fedrals have evacuated Alexandria. It is also reported Col Green
has recaptured 500 negroes & taken 60 wagons[20]

May 31st Sunday ~ In the PM. Mrs N Foster & Lissie & "Uncle Wilie"
came. So we reheard La skedaddle.[21]

20. "Capture of Alexandria," *Harper's Weekly*, May 30, 1863, 339, HarpWeek. Lucy repeatedly wrote in her journal of situations that were rumored to have occurred. Even as she wrote
here of the Federal evacuation of Alexandria, *Harper's Weekly*, in its May 30, 1863, issue, wrote of
Union admiral Porter's capture of Alexandria. In any event, the incidents that Lucy mentioned
would have taken place during the retreat following the Confederate defeats at Fort Bisland
(April 12–13), Irish Bend (April 14), and Vermillion Bayou (April 17).

21. Here Lucy referred to the Confederate retreat following the encounters in Louisiana.
The term "skeedadle," meaning to leave hastily or flee, was used commonly by the troops
themselves as they discussed the retreat.

CHAPTER 5

JUNE–JULY
1863

all feeling blue enough about the reported fall of Vicksburg which is very generally believed now. However it may be others console themselves as Uncle Pier just said that V~ *never was* considered a *very important point* by the government.

LUCY P. STEVENS,
July 18, 1863

WITH THE EASING OF THE MEASLES EPIDEMIC and the approach of summer, Lucy and her friends delightedly resumed their practice of visiting one another, having grown weary of their caregiving responsibilities. But even with the resumption of social calls, Lucy's Ohio family was never far from her thoughts. In random comments sprinkled throughout her diary, she injected repeated reminders of her isolation from her immediate family. These statements alluding to the lack of communication were nothing new. Early in 1861, Lucy had complained that she had no news from home, writing, "Poor I was doomed to meet with disappointment for I truly believed Cousin Waller would bring me some news from home and loved ones; but not one word. I can not believe they have not written me though for they must know I am anxious to hear from them" (2/5/61). That temporary frustration was short-lived, however, for the next day she recorded the receipt of five letters from home.

Yet once the war began, even in the early months, correspondence diminished, and Lucy began to feel the pain of separation more acutely. When news did come, she was happily surprised, but she realized the number of letters would necessarily dwindle. On September 28, 1861, she wrote,

On the 25th was most happily and greatly surprised by the reception of a letter from sis Jule, brother Will, James and Horace. I had not expected to have news from home in long-long months and now it seems hard

that I can not answer it but not for my own sake but that of my friends
I shall deny myself the privilege of writing them that I might hear from
there often.

Recognition that she could be placing her friends in the North at risk gave her
the courage she needed to deny herself the joy of contact with her loved ones.

But now, with all communication a distant memory, Lucy held the
thoughts of home tightly in her heart, continually seeking a way by which she
could send word to loved ones in Ohio. Repeatedly, she poignantly alluded to
attempts to send messages to her family in the North, even mentioning different routes by which mail might be sent. Each time Lucy heard of someone
attempting to travel to the North, her spirits would lift . . . she would write . . .
then wait.

In the place of happy memories, however, Lucy's diary now began to fill
with reports of fighting. With the "bloody summer" of 1863 heating up, and
the war creeping closer to the outlying boundaries, for Lucy it was as it had
been from the beginning—all about the "Travis boys." When the folks in
Travis had first begun to send their loved ones to war, Lucy had noted that
she had "heard that nine of the boys from this neighborhood were going
down to Galveston" (9/3/61). A few days later, she wrote that "Mack and Trav
started this morn ~ leaving sorrowful hearts to mourn them" (9/16/61). Her
October 5, 1861, entry places the Pier household squarely in the midst of the
turmoil, noting that "Cousin Sammy has been talking quite seriously today
of going to Galveston with Col. Kirby's company. Nearly all the boys from
about here are going. Jos~ Campbell called today and says Mack and Trav
have returned and will go to G[alveston] as the company they joined is dis-
organized" (10/5/61). Her entry clearly confirms scholarly research regarding
the confusion among the troops; it also affirms the young age of many of the
soldiers—Cousin Sammy was only seventeen at the time.

Now, two years later, the theater of fighting to which Lucy most frequently
referred was the often forgotten territory of Louisiana, for this was where
most of the young men from Travis had been sent. Many scholars offer scant
mention of the war in Louisiana, but as Thomas Ayres explains in the introduction of his book *Dark and Bloody Ground*, during the two years preceding
the Battle of Mansfield in the spring of 1864, "some six hundred clashes took
place between rebel and Union armies in Louisiana, ranging from minor
skirmishes to major battles."[1] Soldier boys like Joe Campbell sent word of the

---

1. Thomas A. Ayres, *Dark and Bloody Ground: The Battle of Mansfield and the Forgotten Civil War
in Louisiana* (Dallas: Taylor Publishing, 2001), xii.

horrific fighting in Louisiana, where the swampy bayous aligned the opposing forces within such close range that the troops resorted to hand-to-hand
combat to defend their positions and their own lives.

The August 8, 1863, issue of the *Bellville Countryman* includes an account
of the news Lucy recorded on June 15. In a report filed on behalf of Waller's
Battalion, Major H. H. Boone gave particulars of the battle "one mile below
Cheneyville on the Bayou Boeuff," stating that thirteen prisoners had been
taken, with seventeen Union soldiers killed or wounded. He went on to state
that only one Confederate soldier had been killed, with eight wounded and
two missing. Boone singled out Captain W. A. McDade for his "gallant bearing" and ended his report with glowing praise for all of his men, describing
them as "being without sabres and having but few pistols." Boone continued,
"All of my officers did their duty nobly and none the less nobly did the men
do theirs. In truth, to the bravery and good conduct of the men we owe this
little success."[2] Lucy's entry indicates that all the "Travis Boys" were among
those who had acquitted themselves so admirably and shared in the commendation that Major Boone had so publicly conferred.

And as Lucy wrote of the conflicts that the Travis boys faced, she also
addressed the news of social turmoil. The world had turned upside down,
and Lucy, who had become so accustomed to the stratification imposed by
slavery, wrote on June 17 with surprised alarm of upended hierarchies within
communities and homes. As she wrote, so Thomas Ayres confirms similar
reversals, reporting that the family of Governor Mouton of Louisiana was
imprisoned on the upper floor of their home in Vermillionville, even as
Union general Banks issued orders to take one hundred civilian hostages in
retaliation for the killing of a captain on his staff. Although these prisoners were offered freedom in exchange for information, the men, some quite
elderly, chose incarceration and remained in prison in New Orleans.[3] As
Lucy recounted these events, her tone conveyed the anxiety inflicted by a
world seemingly gone mad.

JUNE 1863

June 1st monday ~ Spent the day at Grandma Swearingen's ~ had such
a very pleasant visit with Mrs Purcell – talked over war times & of our
loved ones. I am so truly sorry for my friend in her loneliness

---

2. "Maj. Boone's Report from May 26, 1863," *Bellville Countryman*, August 8, 1863, Texas and
Other Southern States Civil War Newspapers/Newspaper Research, 1861–1865.

3. Ayres, *Dark and Bloody Ground*, 168.

June 2nd tuesday ~ Cousin Sara and myself went to visit Mrs Switzer to day ~ but not finding her at home we went on to Mr Corban's ~ then came down to Mr Miller's. Arrived at home we found two men who claim to be Scotch ~ came to America to make a fortune, were almost forced into fedral service[4] at Providence, R.I. ~ came La, deserted; got a pass from commanding general Taylor & are now on their way to Mexico to go to Europe again. Good news ~ Wiley came last night, spent about four hours here to day. Bowers also is paroled and at home ~ Hurrah! But how sad that we must hear poor Stickney had both heels wounded, is a prisoner, and his life is thought to be almost despaired of. I am so very sorry. He seems to be one of the fated ~

June 3rd wednesday ~ Us girls went this morn to see Wiley, poor fellow ~ he takes his affliction very quietly[5] says it is not more than he antici-pated. It seems so strange that a ball could pass through a persons head and not kill them.

June 5th friday ~ This morn fixed some handkerchiefs for Aunt Lu to hem on the sewing machine for Uncle P ~ then finished another half of my sleeve. Cousin Sara has been spooling some warp this PM for negroes

June 6th saturday ~ Artie Harvey was here on thursday last & I sent by her a letter for Mrs Banks to mail in Mexico for me ~ am in hopes to hear from home now as Mr Banks has an agent in Matamoris who can receive letters for me.

Just one year ago today cousin Sammie, Em, Tallie Ruth & myself went out blackberrying ~ now cousin S~ is off in La, Em sick, Ruth mar-ried ~ changes ever.

June 7th sunday ~ This is my twenty-fifth birthday, the 3rd [4th] I have spent at Uncle Piers. The first I had company to tea, the second Sara & I

4. James M. McPherson, *Ordeal by Fire: The Civil War and Reconstruction*, 2nd ed. (New York: McGraw-Hill, 1992), 353. The Enrollment Act, passed by the Union in March 1863, made every able-bodied male citizen (plus aliens who had filed for naturalization) aged twenty to forty-five eligible for the draft. The law was designed to encourage volunteering, and since every congres-sional district was assigned a quota, officials used every means available to enlist "volunteers."

5. As Lucy recorded in her May 5, 1863, entry, Henry P. Wiley had been shot in the face during the conflict in Louisiana. A fortunate survivor, he had been granted a furlough and was now at home recuperating.

visited Mrs Clemmons in the morn & today have spent the morn in letter writing. Bright & beautifully has the sun shone all day & could we make it an emblem of our future & would think this to be a very happy year.

Aunt Lu, ever thoughtful, had prepared such a nice dinner for me. A roast pig, green-corn, potatoes, succotash,[6] pickle, egg-bread, biscuit, honey, fruit & pound cake, cheese & sure enough coffee and a bottle of nice wine, the latter a present from Uncle Pier. Aunt Lu gave me a nice pair of scissors, a very useful and acceptable gift. The afternoon we had a family visit in the parlor looking over the daguerreotypes and Uncle P~ talking of old times of home and our northern friends. One year ago this eve the Dr spent with us, or rather with S~ He came in after tea & I went and brought him a plate of pie, cake, preserves and a glass of wine ~ the last treat he has ever received from me and probably the last he ever will.[7] Sallie T~ was also here that afternoon A year truly brings many changes & revulsion of feelings.

June 8th monday ~ Have been helping cousin Sara all day to get in a peice of cloth. Warped it in the morn and the afternoon, beamed & drew it through the harness, then through the reed, ready to commence weaving tomorrow morning. finished *The Black Dwarf*.[8]

June 10th wednesday ~ Callie & I walked the gallery [porch] a long time. No signs of rain yet ~ the planters are needing it much, say they will not make anything like the crop they had expected too. Some of the corn is large for roasting ears now. Cotton is some of it two feet & a half high.

June 14th sunday ~ Cousin Sara & Callie went to sunday school this morn ~ but I concluded last summer that did not pay, so stayed at home and finished reading *Old Mortality*, one of the *Waverly* novels.

---

6. According to the *OED*, succotash comes from the Naragansett Indian word *missickquatash*, and means "boiled whole kernels of corn." A Southern favorite, the dish was made from a combination of ingredients such as beans, corn, and sometimes even red and green sweet peppers.

7. Sarah apparently had been in love with a young man, a local doctor who broke her heart. Lucy obviously continued to harbor hard feelings for the pain he had caused Sarah.

8. Richard D. McGhee, "Sir Walter Scott," in *Dictionary of Literary Biography*, vol. 107, *British Romantic Prose Writers, 1789–1832*, 1st ser., ed. John R. Greenfield, 247-266 (Gale Group, 1991). *The Black Dwarf*, listed as Scott's fourth novel in the *Waverly* series, was published as part of the *Tales of My Landlord* volume in 1816.

June 15th Monday ~ A letter has been received from Joe Campbell, written the 27th saying the boys had been in a hand to hand fight with the Fedrals at Chaney-ville ~ all the T [Travis] boys were in it.

June 17th wednesday ~ read Jimmy C's letter telling of Nick's departure to the land of Nod.[9] Bowers told us of the time they had in La when the Fedrals were there, says the negroes acted like they were possessed. The gent he was staying with had eighty men to give him a French leave.[10] They would dress themselves up in their sunday clothes & strut through the yard with a silver headed cane saying ~ we're free now! Do your own work now!! See how good it is. I'll act the gentleman now ~ Some of them would curse their mistress & master in their house & order them round. Then was six of the Fedrals came up and took him prisoner and if it had not been for the Lieut in command would have taken him to N O~. They sent a negro man to order his mistress to give up the storeroom keys, but she paid no attention to him. They then sent a negro girl to get them, went into the store room & took whatever they wanted to, then left. In a house just below where P. Bowers was staying, some Fedrals dragged a sick man out of the window and took him to N.O ~. Mr B. says he hopes never to see such times again, that they were in a constant state of dread & uncertainty, not knowing what minute the house might be burnt over their heads, & that their lives were in jeopardy all the time.

June 18th thursday ~ Have got the neuraliga in my face & teeth ~ took medacine to night. Mr Slater came on out here ~ they received a letter from Neh, dated the 29th mailed at Vermillionville.[11] Sara went with Em over to Mr C's to get her trunk ~ says my old man sent word he was coming to see me tomorrow

---

9. "The land of Nod," originally referenced in the biblical account of Cain and Abel, refers to the region where Cain fled in disgrace, and as punishment, after killing his brother Abel. Here, Lucy's allusion indicates Nick Merry's exile after having deserted the Confederate army. Lucy's entry on May 15, 1863, clearly showed her feelings of revulsion as she wrote "woeful case."

10. The *OED* indicates that the term "French leave" originated in eighteenth-century France and referred to the custom of going away from a reception without taking leave of one's host. Here, Lucy used the term to refer to a soldier who was AWOL, leaving without permission or notice.

11. Ayres, *Dark and Bloody Ground*, 164–166. Vermillionville, located in southern Louisiana, was the site of a battle between Union forces led by General Banks and Confederate troops led by General Richard Taylor. Ayres reports that as the Southern army moved up Bayou LaFourche, Banks's troops were in pursuit, and the Southern forces were forced to retreat.

June 19th friday ~ Mr Wiley & Bowers ~ came by this morn on their way to Brenham, but poor I could not go out to see mine nother half ~ what a pity. Have been realy worse to day, but think the medacine helped that

MARGINAL NOTE: *Mrs H. Glass died today ~ also A. S. Fowler the latter in Franklin La, June 19th 1863*[12]

June 20th saturday ~ all left this morn for the river but I was such a beautiful bird, they concluded this was my best place ~ so I only sent love to all ~ Mr Wiley came by this eve with the mail ~ I finished *Rob Roy*[13] this eve ~ 'twas written in the day of King George – or rather the story was laid at the time.

June 21st sunday ~ Am better today ~ commenced reading *The Bride of Lammamoor*[14]

June 24th wednesday ~ It has rained most of the day cooling the atmosphere much and causing the planters to rejoice. Cousin Sara finished her peice of cloth of 52 yards today ~ came home about 4 ~ Jim wrote cousin Sammy would have been cut by a sabre if it had not been for Henry Cofield. Stickney's wound had very nearly healed but he was suffering with "two bed soars."

June 28th sunday ~ Aunt Lu ~ Uncle Pier, cousin Sara & Jane went to church this morn ~ I stayed at home and kept house ~ & so missed a lecture from Parson Kemp on dancing
    We had two soldiers to dinner from the 23rd T. Reg~ came to mail some letters ~ the company had been detailed to go up into the upper country on account of the Indians commiting depridations there ~ but found on their arrival there that 'twas nothing like as bad as they had expected.[15]

---

12. Lucy used a marginal note to record the actual date of Stickney Fowler's death. She would later write extensively about her friend in her entry of July 3, 1863, the date she actually learned of his death.

13. McGhee, "Sir Walter Scott." *Rob Roy*, published in 1818, was fifth in Scott's *Waverly* series.

14. Ibid. *The Bride of Lammamoor*, again by Scott and seventh in the *Waverly* series, was published in 1819 as part of *Tales of My Landlord*, 3rd ser.

15. According to *The Handbook of Texas Online*, problems with various Indian tribes continued until the late nineteenth century. These problems were centered far to the north and west of Travis, becoming so severe during the Civil War that areas between Gainesville and Fredericksburg were virtually abandoned by settlers, and the frontier was left exposed.

JULY 1863

Although Lucy's entries for the month of July began on a light note, with details about household chores, the availability of fresh watermelons for special treats, and even funny stories that she wanted to remember, the drama of the war was ever-present, hovering as a blurred threat just beyond the horizon. However, as she briefly mentioned the contest in Mississippi and then detailed the battles in Louisiana, the harsh realities of the conflict became more sharply focused, bringing Travis into the ruthless realm of the crisis. On July 2, Lucy mentioned Vicksburg for the first time, and like many of her other preliminary reports, her account was grossly exaggerated and erroneous. She did not actually record the Confederate defeat until July 14, and, in conjunction with the slow transmittal of information, only then did she begin to assess the details, their immediate impact, and their long-term implications as she wrote during the last days of July and August.

In a marginal note on June 19, Lucy had recorded the death of her friend Stickney Fowler, but she gave full voice to her emotions on July 3, the day she actually received the news. Obviously, the most fearful impact of the war was the injury or death of a loved one, and for Lucy, as well as for Sarah and Aunt Lu, the diaries offered a safe place to articulate the high anxiety they each experienced. Although their main worry was Sammy, their circle of concern extended to include all of the young men from the area. Lucy recorded her grief privately in the pages of her journal, as did Sarah. But Sarah also sought a public forum to express her sorrow. She wrote an anonymous obituary and submitted it to the *Bellville Countryman*, where it was published in the August 1, 1863, edition. The obituary read:

Farewell, Stickney—may thy
Sleep be sweet in thy quiet resting
Place, undisturbed by the loud boom-
Ing of cannon and the clash of arms,
And while the balmy breezes of the
South, ladened with the perfume of
Orange flowers, fan gently the turf
On thy grave—may the jeweled
Crown of the "finally faithful" rest
Lightly on thy spirit brow.

> Farewell—thou gavest thy young
> Life a sacrifice on the altar of thy
> Adopted country, and thrice precious
> Is the boon.
> A FRIEND[16]

Sarah's obituary eloquently reflected the expressions of grief that were resonating across the land for the casualties of both North and South.

Yet even as Lucy mourned the wartime loss of her friend, she omitted any reference to the significant traditions connecting his sacrifice with the next day, July 4. In the South, the observance of the Fourth of July virtually disappeared during the war years. While 1861 saw commemorations of national independence and Southern dominance, the practice faded during subsequent years.[17] In 1861, Lucy had, in fact, written about a barbecue celebration, giving great attention to detail and bemoaning the national conflict. In that entry she recorded,

The planters took great pains to have every thing pleasant and nice and were rewarded by knowing that every one enjoyed themselves and I think they must have been heathens that could have done otherwise than enjoy themselves. There were two nice arbors one for the table and another with two long rows of seats and a platform for the speakers There were four military companies present who went through with the drilling exercises and really presented quite a warlike appearance so much so that my thoughts would involuntarily turn to home sweet home and the thought that very near that sacred spot there might be a real battle enacting. Oh why! Is it that brother meets brother and friend meets friend to engage in the horrors of war!

After the exercise we all repaired—to the dinner table where we partook of nicely barbecued meats and all kinds of edibles [a] heart could wish for. After dining we listened to speaking from Col Paine, Esq Hunt, Esq Boone, Judge Chapel and Mr Campbell & Mr Cameron which were very good indeed. Mr. Hunt seems to think the "North considers the south is to good a subject to let her go until they find they are compelled to do so & find that they are . . ."

Lucy Stevens, 7/4/61

---

16. "Farewell Stickney," *Bellville Countryman*, vol. 4, no. 2, August 1, 1863.

17. John Austin Edwards, "Social and Cultural Activities of Texans during the Civil War and Reconstruction, 1861–1873" (PhD diss., Texas Tech University, 1985), 50–51.

In a January 1863, entry Lucy had again mentioned the Fourth of July bar-
beque held in 1861, but now, in July 1863, the day rated no mention at all.

July 1st wednesday ~ Mr Clemmons was here to dinner & a sadder looking man I have not seen in many a day ~ and no wonder ~ Uncle P tells
us this eve that he & his wife have parted. that Mr C says he has made all
the confessions he has to make and done all that it became a gentleman
to do~ but all to no purpose ~ and now he will do no more.

With all his sad feelings~ he tried to cover them before us girls and
told us all about his western trip, how the people lived there &c &c.
Among other things, he told us a clock tale that amused me not a little.
A gentleman who lived in the western part of the state had been urged
by his wife to get her a clock, but on account of the hard times, he had
delayed from time to time complying with her wish.

One day during his abscense a peddler came by who had clocks for
sale & proffered to take in payment anything the lady had to dispose of
that would be saleable. She had runing in the yard a motherless calf that
had proved a great pest. & so thinking it would be a good opportunity
to rid herself of it, asked the merchant would he take that in part for pay.
he assented, and next she thought of some flaxseed they had which was
sevral years old & proposed his taking that also, to which he agreed. &
the rest she was to pay in chickens any time that would suit her pleasure.
The merchant went on [to] the village which was several miles distant
~ recommended his seed as being a very superior kind and would not
consent to sell more than a pint to any one person, & so disposed of all
but one half bushel when he met up with the husband of the lady who
purchased the clock. This gentleman who was one of the prudent &
wise talked & pondered for some time but at last went to the merchant
& took one side and after great persuasion on his part ~ got him to
consent to sell the half bushel of seeds to him at an exorbitant price. Our
gentleman merchant then began to talk of his fine calf ~ Durham stock
~ which he had purchased from a foreigner at a high price ~ but he was
anxious to improve his stock, got it ~ 'twas looking badly now he had
been hauling it round so long.

At last, however, the farmer. whose powers of persuasion seemed
good, got him to part with it ~ as 'twas so far home he was afraid he
might loose it. so the farmer went on his way rejoicing ~ with seed &

calf ~ arriving at home, the first thing that met his eye was the new clock which caused him to exclaim "hurrah, old lady, a new clock" whereupon a full explanation ensued when he found to his chagrin they had now ~ seed, calf, clock & all. Farmers exit at the backdoor.[18]

July 2nd thursday ~ The telegraph says they have another engagement at Vicksburg which proved a perfect slaughter [. . .] over 10,000 Yankees fell, which was about ten times the number on our side. The engagement took place on the 27th It also says the Fedrals took possession of Yazoo city[19] on the 5th of last month the Confed forces having evacuated the place. They occupied the town but a short time, retreated to their gun boats & went up the river several miles. On the next day, the same again ~ steamed past the village and went up the river passing some sevral hundred bales of cotton which they took a good survey of & went on with the full intention of placing it on board their boats on their return, but as they came back ~ Lo, & behold! Nothing but smouldering ashes remained.

July 3rd friday ~ My dear sister Julis 19th birthday~ I am in hopes it has proved a happier one to her than the day has been to me. News came in the *Countryman*[20] that one of my best friends was dead. A. Stickney Fowler died of his wounds far from friends & home ~ after doing what he believed to be his duty, he has been a great sufferor but death came at last & relieved him. Poor Stickney ~ You had not many warmer friends who will mourn your loss than cousin Sara & myself. As long as life lasts your memory will be with us.

July 7th tuesday ~ Willie Cameron was here in the eve ~ brought me a note from his Ma with the adress I'm to give in writing home ~ how

---

18. Lucy's last comment, a tongue-in-cheek addendum to the story she had told, serves as her own signature of approval to the joke, thus furnishing a peek into a personality that appreciated humor and loved a good laugh.

19. Yazoo City, *Yazoo County Convention and Visitors Bureau.* Yazoo City, a port located on a tributary of the Mississippi River, became the scene of sporadic fighting during the war. Lucy's information corroborates the official account, which indicates that on May 22, 1863, Union soldiers forced Confederate troops back as they moved to take Vicksburg.

20. Bellville's local newspaper, the *Bellville Countryman,* was founded July 28, 1860, and carried the motto "Independent in All Things—Neutral in None." The paper was published continuously throughout the Civil War, even though distribution was curtailed from weekly to semiweekly during this time. In 1865, the paper's name changed to the *Texas Countryman,* and it was published until August 1869.

much I hope to hear from all now. Sammy says my old man had gone to Goliad[21] started yesterday morning.

July 8th wednesday ~ Ruth, Ellen & Mr Withers have been here all day ~ R & Aunt Lu have been coloring cloth.

It's almost suffocating to night ~ hardly a breath of air stiring. Uncle P~ commenced pulling fodder last week & commenced hauling it this morn. I walked through the cotton to the lower end of the plantation the other eve ~ the cotton looks so pretty now with the pink & white blossoms

Mr & Mrs McRee & Jo & Bettie Frank Foster came by yesterday evening. After they went away us girls took our evening walk & brought enough grass burs on our clothing home with us to color clothing for a Regiment ~ there are so many.

July 9th thursday ~ Mr Bowers called here this morn on his way home from seeing Sallie ~ he had expected to have gone yesterday, but hearing there was to be [a] party last eve at Mr Daughtry's was persuaded to stay and wait on Sara Jane Swearingen. He says "they danced all night til broad daylight & went home with the girls in the morning."[22]

July 10th friday ~ Cousin Sara & I went down & helped R~ put in a peice of cloth this morn. While we were there, Jane came down & told us there was company at the house, so I came back with her ~ found Mrs Mary Cameron here, & not long after, Mrs John Lott & Mrs Mattie Boington came. We spent such a pleasant day. Mrs C~ brought a letter from Johnie

---

21. According to *The Handbook of Texas Online*, Goliad, one of the oldest Spanish forts/ towns in Texas, was established in October 1749, as La Bahía. The name was changed to Goliad in 1829, and it became the center of various attempts to bring about Texas independence. In 1835, the first declaration of Texas independence, the "Goliad Declaration of Independence," was signed here, and on March 27, 1836, under orders from Santa Anna, James Fannin and approximately 340 other men were executed in what became known as the Goliad Massacre. This atrocity, coming on the heels of the fall of the Alamo, sparked American sympathy for the Texans, thus crystallizing public opinion against Mexico's Santa Anna.

22. "Daniel Decatur Emmett," *Songwriters Hall of Fame*. The song "The Boatman's Dance," which contains the lyrics quoted by Lucy, was written in the pre–Civil War era by Daniel Decatur Emmett. Emmett, who was prominent in the early minstrel shows, also wrote other well-known songs such as "Old Dan Tucker" and "Blue Tail Fly." His most notable song, however, came to be the anthem that drew the Confederacy together—"Dixie." Emmett, having sold the rights to the song for a mere $500, was "anything but a southern sympathizer" and never intended the song to serve any such purpose.

H~ to read. Mrs B was making such a pretty hat for her husband. Mrs C was making a muslin robe for John's wife, & Mrs Lott, she was the lady. There was some talking I can assure you, Mr Journal, for all were great talkers.

July 13th monday ~ We have now the full particulars of the fight at Brashire City on the 23rd of last month[23] Taylor & Mouton commanded the expedition. Hunter com[manded] the Forlorn hope that crossed Grand Lake in small boats, sugar coolers &c. Landed in a palmetto swamp, marched 3 miles & Brigadier Gen Green fired the first guns ~ attacking then by land on the left ~ the first gun being the signal for general attack. Hunter came up on the right & soon Col Majors come up on the rear. 200 fedrals were taken prisoners, 11 killed & 13 wounded, 6 of whom have since died. "on our side" but one killed & 6 wounded. The Forlorn hope was made up of Capts chosen from the different Reg's & the privates were volunteers ~ from Wallers Battallion, Capt McDade was chosen
        Sara finished reading *The Initials* today & I *Annie of Geirstein*[24]

July 14th tuesday ~ Brother Will's birthday ~ he is 31 ~ quite an old bachelor to be sure. How much I would give to see my dear good brother this eve ~ but heaven knows if ever I can see one of my dear ones again. It is reported at the fight at Donaldsonville[25] Gen Greene went in with

---

23. Ayres, *Dark and Bloody Ground*, 177. Lucy's information in her July 13 entry corroborates the official accounts of the battle at Brashear City. Ayres reports that General Taylor began assembling forces in the middle of June to mount an attack on Union troops and reclaim southern Louisiana. Ayres writes that Taylor "came up with a bold plan that, if successful, might not liberate New Orleans, but surely would scare the hell out of Nathaniel Banks" (177). Taylor combined his troops with those of Tom Green, Alfred Mouton, and James P. Major and assembled a flotilla of makeshift vessels to move the men across Grand Lake, naming their hodgepodge navy "the Mosquito Fleet." After wandering in the swamps most of the night, the men, a muddy ragtag lot, converged on Brashear City and proceeded to rout the Union forces. The resulting victory provided a large cache of supplies and a boost in morale among Southerners.

24. McGhee, "Sir Walter Scott." *Annie of Geirstein*, written by Sir Walter Scott and published in 1829, was number 22 in the *Waverly* series.

25. Ayres, *Dark and Bloody Ground*, 180–182. Ayres explains that although the town of Donaldsonville had previously been burned, Fort Butler still remained across Bayou LaFourche, guarded by the Union gunboat *Princess Royal*, a wide moat, and a number of siege guns. Despite warnings to delay the assault, General Tom Green and his forces began the attack on the fort in the middle of the night, June 28. Protected by the higher ground and the thick walls of the fortification, Union troops inflicted a brutal loss on Green and his men, the first Green had suffered. Lucy and her family were right to worry about Sammy and the others; the toll was

about 400 men and lost ~ 260 killed. We know Jack is in his old Reg and expect as Wallers Batt is attached, that the same men who went with him to Brashire City were with him there ~ McDade's Co, & if that is so, cousin Sammy was one, also Neh. *Everyone* is feeling anxious to hear.

――――――⌣――――――

It is in the margin of her diary that Lucy recorded one of the most significant events of the war as she briefly noted the most basic details of the fall of Vicksburg. The city had been under siege since May 22, following an unsuccessful assault by General Ulysses S. Grant, who was determined to wear down the Confederate troops until they surrendered. James McPherson reports that on July 4, the Confederate forces at Vicksburg, faced with starvation and exhaustion, formally surrendered, and roughly 30,000 prisoners were paroled. Then, on July 9, following its own forty-eight-day siege, Port Hudson followed suit and surrendered to Union general Nathaniel Banks. These two losses, occurring concurrently with Lee's defeat at Gettysburg, proved pivotal in the outcome of the war.[26]

Most historians agree that Grant's success at Vicksburg was "the culmination of one of the most brilliant military campaigns of the war. With the loss of Pemberton's army and this vital stronghold on the Mississippi [River], the Confederacy was effectively split in half."[27] This split would further isolate Texas, and Lucy would go on to write of the gloom that settled over the community following Vicksburg, a despondency that engulfed the South. McPherson reports that many Confederate soldiers began to foresee the end of the war, and even Jefferson Davis himself succumbed to despair. In an effort to raise their own morale and bolster their spirits, those far away from the front lines continued to put a good face on the Confederate loss at Vicksburg, claiming that it was not important. Lucy used her diary to record Uncle Pier's own comforting interpretation of the defeat, and, in her own assessment on July 27, she predicted that the defeat would ultimately work to the South's advantage.

heavy. As news of successive battles continued to trickle in, Lucy and everyone around her began to sense the perilous foothold that the Confederate troops had, one that could change dramatically on any given day. As there had been great jubilation after Brashear City, there were now fear and foreboding with Donaldsonville.

26. McPherson, *Ordeal by Fire*, 330–332.

27. "Battle Summaries by Campaign." *American Battlefield Protection Program, National Parks Service*.

MARGINAL NOTES: *Heard of the fall of Vicksburg ~ Wiley. Also that Port [Hendron?] had capitulated ~ the former on the 7th, the latter, the 9th ~ the news causes some blue faces~ Grant had command of the Fedral's and Pemberton of the Confederates ~ the conditions of surrender were that all should be exchanged & at once paroled*

July 18th saturday ~ Started for home [from Lu's] at half past five. F̶h̶a̶l̶found all well, but all feeling blue enough about the reported fall of Vicksburg, which is very generally believed now. However it may be others console themselves as Uncle Pier just said that V~ *never was* considered a *very important point* by the government

July 20th monday ~ Aunt Lu commenced peach drying today.[28] Soon this morn Winnie run away, & about an hour after, Parrot left for the woods ~ all about a pair of shoes that Winnie got Mr Brewer's Jack to make for her. They told so many stories, they got themselves into a difficulty. Aunt Lu washed out the white clothes this morn, & I my clothes. Mr Withers [. . .] for Uncle P after Mr Martin & dogs ~ but 'twas so warm he did not come 'til [entry continues next day]

July 21st tuesday ~ when he woke us all by halooing at the gate. He & Uncle P went out and rode until 10 A.M. without any success. This is Nick's twenty-fifth birthday and the 2nd anniversary of the Manassas battle. Heard from two different sources this eve that Wallers B~ had been placed to guard a point ~ were surrounded and what were not killed had been taken prisoners.

With rising hopefulness, Lucy recorded the news about Lee's engagement at Harrisburg. The continuing battle, which took place from July 1 to July 3, 1863, is commonly known to Americans as the Battle of Gettysburg. However, Lucy never mentioned that particular city, truly indicating the regional focus of her diary. The distant towns and unknown troops were a separate

---

28. "Drying Fruit," University of Georgia Extension Service, http://uga.edu/nchfp/publica tions/. Drying fruit offered a means to preserve the fruit for future use. The fruit had to be sliced, then placed on drying screens, where it was turned periodically to promote dehydration. Dipping slices of fruits such as peaches in an acidic substance such as lemon juice before drying would inhibit the darkening of the peach. Hot, dry temperatures and circulating air would assist in more rapid drying, and the fruit could then be stored and used later.

part of the war, simultaneously supporting the Southern cause, yet distinctly removed from the Texas world of Lucy. Her entry exhibits typical rumors and errors as she attributed victory to Lee and his Confederate forces. This ongoing battle, which ultimately involved the cities of Harrisburg and Gettysburg, was perhaps the most critical battle in American history. Yet, after barely a mention, Lucy shifted back to the regional theater, prioritizing the local boys' struggle above the epic battle taking place in the East.

22nd wed ~ We heard today that Lee had taken Harrisburg & Washington City ~ faces look more smiling. Mrs B~ Brewer received a letter from her husband this P.M. dated the 9th of June, just after the fight at Milican's Bend.[29] Says Benton B~ was left sick, has been sick most of the time since he went into the service. Heard farther confirmation of Waller's men being cut up & taken prisoners but do not believe it. Its ~ if such & such things happen ~ now ~ & the Western states are as badly used up as we, &c &c, somewhat of a change. This [is] cousin S~[Sammy's] 19th birthday ~ how I'd like to see him to night; how much I'd have given could he have shared the nice chicken pie Aunt Lu had made for my benefit [at] to day dinner. I trust he may spend his next birthday at home with the friends who love him so fondly & miss him so much. He is one of the best of boys and I shall ever feel interested in knowing the world fares well with him

23rd thursday ~ cousin Sara found a snake on the beam at the side of the stairs to night, and directly after, I came in our room & was stung for the first time in my life by a stinging scorpion ~ not very pleasant certainly.

24th friday ~ While us girls were cutting peaches in the dining-room, Geo Dixon & some other boys came & brought Parrot in, caught him over in mill-creek bottom. Sara sits by the stand reading *Guy Mannering*[30]

29. Ayres, *Dark and Bloody Ground*, 173–175. Here, Lucy referred to Milliken's Bend, Louisiana, where, on June 7, 1,500 Texans attacked Federal troops, who were caught off guard and unprepared. Many of the Union soldiers were black and had just received guns with which they were completely unfamiliar. Because they were told by white officers that they would be shot if captured by the South, these men consequently fought with desperation, using bayonets and rifles as clubs. The fierce hand-to-hand combat that followed resulted in a horrific bloodbath, a slaughter producing 652 casualties for the North and 185 for the South.

30. McGhee, "Sir Walter Scott." *Guy Mannering*, second in Scott's *Waverly* series, was published in 1815.

July 25th saturday ~ Embroidered all day. Capt Floyd came here soon after dinner ~ not feeling well, so Aunt Lu made a cup of coffee for him. He wrote a letter & started on to overtake his wagons that had been here this morn, loaded up their cotton & started for Allitown.[31] Had been gone about an hour when we looked out and found he had returned, feeling so sick & bad he could not go on home. So Uncle P~ got into his carriage & went for Dr Francis, The Dr says Mr F~ is worse scared than hurt.

July 26th sunday ~ Capt. F~ has been in bed until this eve. Rufus Campbell came down to see him about hauling cotton to Alleyton. Mr. Cleveland came here during negro church[32] & wanted Uncle P to go up there with him & such a scattering as there was among the colored tribe I have not seen lately.

July 27th monday ~ Aunt Lu received a letter from cousin Sammy dated the 5th of July after the battle at Donaldsonville ~ none of Waller's men were in that engagement. Cousin S~ says after the Berwick's bay fight they feasted on candy, sardines, crackers, pickles, cheese, coffee & had all the ice water they wanted [to] drink ~ says he wishes he could have sent home some things.[33] Says also the Fedrals in number were so much greater than they ~ they could have tied them ~ that they seemed

31. Alleyton, or Allitown, as Lucy spells it, was located in Colorado County, and was home to the southernmost railroad in the state. During the Civil War, Alleyton became the beginning of the "cotton road"—a destination to which planters brought their cotton to escape the Union blockade. Here the cotton was loaded on wagon trains bound for Mexico. On the return trip, these same wagon trains brought military and domestic supplies back to Alleyton, where they were shipped via rail to the rest of the Confederacy.

32. Randolph B. Campbell, *An Empire for Slavery: The Peculiar Institution in Texas* (Baton Rouge: Louisiana State University Press, 1989), 173. According to Campbell, many slaveholders allowed their slaves to attend worship services, often structured within separate churches organized for the slaves themselves. Most churches were Baptist or Methodist, the Methodist Church claiming around 7,500 Negro members in 1860 (171). Often these meetings were conducted on Sunday afternoons or evenings and were even led by black preachers. However, this leadership was enough of a concern to slaveholders that by 1860 the Texas Conference of the Methodist Church was advised to withhold approval from meetings "conducted by colored men" and discontinue "licensing or renewing the licenses of colored men to preach" (173).

33. Ayres, *Dark and Bloody Ground*, 178. The encounter at Brashear City produced such confusion that many Union soldiers broke ranks and ran, leaving behind large quantities of provisions, not the least of which was Yankee whiskey. The rebels proceeded to loot the federal commissary of its stores. The commander in charge of the strike into southern Louisiana, General Richard Taylor, later wrote of a "scene of wildest excitement and confusion," remarking that "the sight of such quantities of loot quite upset my hungry followers" (178).

to feel ashamed when they found their numbers ~ "The Yankees" had
their stores all on board the cars for N.O~, yet strange to say "they were
intending these stores for their supply during the invasion of Tx"

It is amusing to me to hear the talk of Lee's having taken Harrisburg,
Baltimore & Washington city & on his way now to Philadelphia. And
to hear the talk too that they did not think our Generals would be so
unwise as that ~ that it's the worst thing they could do &c &c. I certainly agree ~ I do not think Lee has been so unwise, but should southern forces ever penetrate into that city, I believe with them it will be the
worst thing for themselves they have ever done. It is astonishing to learn
what a great advantage the fall of Vicksburg is going to be ~ the people
are just finding it out, and it is such a great strategy on the part of our
forces. Johnson is showing now of what material he is made. He is now
to take his turn in besieging.[34] Grant will learn to his cost something of
the art of warfare.

July 28th tuesday ~ Winnie came in this P.M., went to the store first and
told her story to Uncle P~

July 29th wednesday ~ I intended to have spoken of Aunt Lu's tale she
told to Mrs Chapman of the Panoramic view exhibited in N~ Y~ years
ago that was really so. It amused Mrs C~ not a little and little Sara Lu
would stand and look at her Ma, then Aunt Lu, in perfect astonishment
until Mrs C~ stopped laughing ~ then she would commence.

In after years when I read this over, I will think how Mrs C sit in the
little stuffed rocking chair, (in the corner next [to the] parlor break-
room, Aunt Lu near by in Sara's little sewing chair (shuck bottom), Sara
Lu between them ~ cousin Sara by the rose vine window & I on the sofa.

An Irish gent who has [his] wife for assistant in arranging scenes,
prepartory to the raising of curtains. Just as he is raising it, nearby is an
oval exit ~ lady out of window, but lo, she is caught there, halfway out,
and just as gent says with great pomp, ladies & gentlemen, I now present
to your view the finest scene that ever was shown ~ comes a strong gust

---

34. McPherson, *Ordeal by Fire*, 340. McPherson asserts that Jefferson Davis had stubbornly
supported General Braxton Bragg as commander of the Army of Tennessee. He reports that it
was not until the Confederates had sustained successive defeats at Vicksburg, Chickamauga,
and, finally, Chattanooga in the fall of 1863 that Davis accepted Bragg's resignation. In his place,
Davis named General Joe Johnston the new commander of the Army of Tennessee. This same
series of battles, on the other hand, secured Ulysses S. Grant's position as the "Union's greatest
general" (340).

of wind & blew [the] ladies' clothes over her head ~ which he, still facing the audience, did not notice, and continued praising and calling their attention to the beauties & usefulness of this wonderful lake.

July 30th, thursday ~ Miss Ellen Corban, Miss Newman (Jimmy C~'s beloved), Mrs Switzer, Mrs Miller, Callie Bell & Puss spent the day with us. Sis Torrence and Mollie came over & stayed an hour or two, & in the evening Sara J Campbell, Carrie, Annie & Sara J Swearingen came and stayed an hour or two.

Cousin Sara received four letters today ~ from Mack ~ Nehemiah ~ Mr Darnman & Chesly ~ the latter is sick in the hospital at Natchitoches ~ Neh & Mr D~ were at camp Raceland on the 13th & 1st Mack at [D . . .] on the 5th, the latter has been in several engagements since we heard from him before, the first at Ashwood on the 5th of June, & at Milican's Bend on the 7th· my birthday ~ at the latter place, they were repulsed with heavy loss[35]

On July 27, as Lucy recited details from Sammy's letter, she affirmed many topics laboriously researched by contemporary historians. As Sammy told Lucy, plans for an invasion of Texas had been introduced, some recorded as early as the autumn of 1861. At that time, cotton was in such short supply in the North that many industrialists pushed for such an expedition. General George McClellan, however, opposed the move, preferring instead a plan to split the Confederacy in two. Thomas Ayres writes that McClellan convinced President Lincoln that it was more important to gain control of the Missis-sippi River and New Orleans and that Texas could be easily overcome by way of the Red River through Louisiana. Even so, Brigadier General Paul O. Hebert became so alarmed upon his arrival in Texas in the fall of 1861 that he finally wrote an open letter imploring the citizens to act. Ayres reports that Hebert wrote: "To the Men of Texas—It is more than probable that your state will soon be invaded by the sea coast . . . Yours to meet and defeat [the inva-sion] lie almost entirely in your own strong arms, brave hearts and trusty rifles." Hebert went on to challenge the Texans to organize and meet him in Galveston, reminding them of the indomitable courage many of their forefa-thers had displayed in the fight against Mexico years earlier. Ayres concludes

35. Here Lucy mentions several locations scattered throughout the central and southern parts of Louisiana where Confederate forces saw fighting. For further information concerning her reference to the battle at Milliken's Bend, see the diary entry dated July 22, 1863.

that the letter inspired some of the most daring and colorful warriors of the Civil War—the Texas cavalrymen who would defend Louisiana. To prevent the invasion of their state, they would fight in the hills, cane brakes, and bayou country of their neighbor. Their weapons were varied. Most did not have standard uniforms. Their mounts ranged from thoroughbreds to motley nags. They were cocky, headstrong, impossible to discipline, and unwilling to walk, but they would prove to be among the fiercest fighters ever assembled.[36]

Among these were Lucy's beloved Travis boys, the young men whom she had come to know and love—these were the faces that Lucy gave the war.

But, as this month began, so it ended—with household chores and lighthearted stories. In between, however, the grim realities of an encroaching war gained a stronger foothold. Lucy's journal provides important details of some of the fiercest fighting of the conflict. From Gettysburg to Vicksburg, and all across Louisiana, the conflict continued, battles raged, and the homefolk worried. Interestingly, Lucy's own perceptions of Gettysburg reverberate down through history. McPherson asserts that Lee privileged the Eastern theater with tunnel vision, contending that he did not foresee the implications of a failed invasion of the North. Ironically, Lucy concurred, for in her July 27 entry, as she voiced the concerns of her community, she wrote that she could not believe Lee would be so unwise. Even more alarming, she prophetically doomed the Northern invasion as "the worst thing for themselves they have ever done."

At last, in an almost palpable attempt to cheer herself, Lucy shifted her focus to the sweet time spent visiting with the women of her family and her community and to the funny stories that had been shared during the visit. Slipped imperceptibly among the lines of the story are her own reminiscences—a reminder to herself to remember this special time. For here, in the midst of the "bloody summer" of 1863, Lucy clung to her network of friends. With no end of the war in sight and no hope of news from home, she desperately needed these gentle reminders of stability; she promised herself that "in years after," she would revisit this entry in her diary and recall with fondness days such as this, when generations of women had banded together— just to be.

---

36. Ayres, *Dark and Bloody Ground*, 72.

CHAPTER 6

AUGUST–SEPTEMBER 1863

Come Peace at least ~ We are tired of war

LUCY P. STEVENS,
August 27, 1863

AS A NEW MONTH BEGAN, Lucy commenced a new chapter in her life. She had contracted to teach the Brewer children in a subscription school and was about to begin her duties. Sarah's diary indicates that Lucy had agreed to teach for a term of five months, at five dollars per child, "to be paid her in good money when she wants to go home" (Sarah Pier, 8/1 and 3/63). In affirmation of the endeavor, Aunt Lu also wrote about the new venture in her journal. In typical economic terms, she recorded, "Lue has taken a school at Mr. Brewer's to teach 5 months for $5 per month teaches Susan Stevens, Sallie and E. Bell's 2 children Newton and Jane commenced this morn" (Lu M. Pier, 8/3/63). Once again, all three diaries give independent accounts, each lending its own unique perspective to the narrative.

In addition to her teaching duties, Lucy began assisting Mr. Brewer as he calculated the tax rates for the residents of Austin County. In her usual fashion, she recorded details of the computations, unknowingly revealing for us the methods by which the taxes were assessed, even as she solidified her own understanding of the process. Lucy's repeated references describe an ongoing enterprise by which she and Sarah made a small income and rendered a service to the community by helping the local farmers maintain tax records and other documents.

As the months had slipped by, war news had claimed a more significant place in Lucy's journal, and now, in August, a month after Vicksburg's fall, she began to record horrific details of the siege and the state of mind of those

involved. Jimmy Clemmons had returned home, having survived the night-
mare, and bitterly reported the loss, with details of deprivation and scorn-
ful accounts of treatment by the Union soldiers. James McPherson's research
clearly confirms the situation, stating that following six weeks of intense siege,
during which time the Confederate forces were "reduced to quarter rations
[and] subjected to artillery and mortar bombardments around the clock and
sharpshooter fire during the day," General John C. Pemberton received a peti-
tion signed by the starving troops which demanded that if Pemberton could
not feed them, he had better surrender.[1] Six days later, on July 4, Pemberton
acquiesced and formally surrendered. Despite the impossible conditions,
Jimmy Clemmons and many other Southern soldier boys placed the blame
for the loss squarely on the general's shoulders, regarding Pemberton's surrender as treason and the city of Vicksburg as a commodity for sale.

Lucy went on to write of the general sense of gloom that had fallen in
the wake of Vicksburg. And for the first time, she hinted at an opinion that
diverged from the almost universally accepted stance—one that, in retro-
spect, sounds suspiciously Unionist. Even as Lucy wore "Southernness" on
the outside, the deeply personal thoughts expressed in her journal on August
27 could signal an absence of complete capitulation. She used a variation
of the title of a popular tune, "God Defendeth the Right," as she expressed
the war-weariness that the general population was experiencing. The song,
published in 1861 in Macon, Georgia, by John C. Schreiner and Sons, fur-
nished the catchphrase that resounded throughout the South, verbalizing
for Southerners their belief in the justness of their cause.[2] However, Lucy's
words reveal a deep sense of ambiguity, raising questions about her true feelings and about certain less-polarized views concerning the war. Although
she was quite fervent in her support of the local boys, this statement marks
one of her few references to a diverging opinion. It raises questions regarding
her views of the rightness of the Southern Cause and the associated institutions that the Cause swore to protect. Although she publicly refrained from
explicitly stating one position or the other, even among her most intimate
friends, Lucy's words here hint at the very private possibility of another, differing perspective, one that she would acknowledge only in carefully veiled
phrasing in the pages of her diary.

1. James M. McPherson, *Ordeal by Fire: The Civil War and Reconstruction*, 2nd ed. (New York:
McGraw-Hill, 1992), 330.

2. Hermann L. Schreiner, "God Defendeth the Right" (Macon, GA: John C. Schreiner &
Son, 1861), 19th-Century American Sheet Music, Music Library—University of North Carolina
at Chapel Hill.

AUGUST 1863

August 1st saturday ~ I proposed teaching Mrs B's & E's children and they seemed well pleased with the arrangement ~ I am to commence on monday next I am glad & yet I am sad

August 3rd monday ~ Commenced teaching this morn with my five schollars ~ am in hopes to have no trouble this session ~ Dick came over this eve & brought my sachel.

Aug 5th wednesday ~ Left every body preparing peaches to dry. Walked over to school ~ found Rufus B~ here. Had killed two deer this morn and shot a beef, so we are well supplied with fresh meat. I commenced drawing off Mr B's book of scholastic children for him this eve ~ includes all between the ages of 6 & 18 years

Aug. 6th thursday ~ Was up soon this morn & at work at my book again ~ finished it this eve. Then Mr B~ learned me how to calculate the percentage: it is 12 per cent for the first 200, then between 400 & 500 which leaves 100 more is 8 per cent ~ then 6 for the next, then between 500 & 1000 is 500 at 5 per cent & all other at 3

Aug 7th friday ~ This has been one of the cloudy & unpleasant days ~ rained in the morn. After school Mr Cleveland called to try [to] get the Edwards girls in my school, but I refused to take them.

Aug 8th saturday ~ Jimmy looks so badly ~ says he had a high fever when he got home
He told us all about the hard times they had at Vicksburg. Says that the whole of the 47 days they were besieged, they had but 3 small biscuits issued to them a day, and a part of the time ¾ lb. of flour made of peas & corn ground together. They had to drink the river water & lay in the ditches exposed to all kinds of weather. I asked him about Nick and he told me he saw him about a half hour before he left, rowing around in an old dug out ~ that no person saw him leave, but saw his dug out across the river & missed him at roll-call for the first time.[3] J~ says he does not

---

3. Here, Lucy referred to Nick Merry, whose desertion she had previously mentioned in her entries of May 15 and June 17, 1863.

think the war will last many months & that it will terminate to the disadvantage of the south.

He says the Fedrals called out to some of the pickets a few days after they had peas & corn given them to know how they liked their new rations of corn & peas ~ he says he feels confident Pemberton is a traitor & that Vicksburg was sold[4]

Aug 10th monday ~ After dinner Mr & Mrs B~ went to Centre Hill & Mr B came back boosy [drunk]. Mrs B~ got such a nice pretty set of hoops, 31 in the skirt. Lissie also had one with 16 in them.[5] This eve us girls are busy with the books

Aug 14th friday ~ Got out on the road just in time to see the Reg~ coming up from their camps at or near Mr Rufus Campbell's. Cavalry ~ 500 men on horse-back is quite an imposing sight, but to me a sad one when I know they are going to the wars. Poor fellows, few may ever return to their homes & loved ones. Mrs C~ & I waved them good wishes with our vails, & to return the compliment they played for us "the girl I left behind me"

After they had passed we went on by the Sempronius church to Mr Alex~ Cloud's ~ a member of McDade's in Wallers Batt. poor fellow he seems very low spirited ~ thinks he will never be well again, and everything around spoke poverty poverty. He showed us some Yankee letters & a dagauerreotype of a young & beautiful girl, trophies of the Berwick's bay engagement "only think their own private property to be taken ~ eaven the dagauerreotypes" but show that's the way of the world.

Mrs Banks had gone to Piedmont. Started yesterday morn, and Mr B~ [Banks] was at home in bed drunk, or just getting over tight, but hoping to find him sensible enough to tell one of receiving letters from home & where they must be directed. We went on. Old Auntie came out to the

---

4. McPherson, *Ordeal by Fire*, 313. General John C. Pemberton, like Lucy, hailed from the North. A native of Pennsylvania with two brothers fighting in the Union army, Pemberton nevertheless sided with his wife's beloved Virginia. Yet because of his ties to the North, Pemberton was subject to intense scrutiny concerning his loyalties. Although he yielded to his men's demands and surrendered to save those who had managed to survive to this point, it seems his reputation fell prey to his worst fears.

5. David Holman, *Buckskin and Homespun: Texas Frontier Clothing, 1820–1870* (Austin: Wind River Press, 1979). Holman reports that the framework of gradually enlarging circles worn under a woman's skirt in order to expand the skirt of her dress was often made from pieces of whalebone connected together with strips of material. The smallest circle, at the top, could be a yard or more across at the hip and the largest, at the bottom, three or more yards.

gate and told us her Master had been drinking, but she thought it might be he had come to his senses enough to talk to us, so Mary [Cameron] sent in word. And after much bustling and loud talking, we heard him call out ~ Mrs Cameron? ~ yes ~ tell her to come in ~ I'd rather see her than any woman in Texas. So in we went & directly after, he came down ~ red faced ~ bloted full ~ one galas[6] on, his shirt up & pants down ~ shoes unfastened, and in every look & act, the most perfect picture of a drunken sot I ever saw. He told me he would take pleasure in receiving & forwarding letters for me ~ gave me his address. Told us how well off he was, how he knew enough to look after the dimes. Treat us to a brandy toddy ~ $15. per qt &c &c

The house was a large ruin with few comforts & no attraction, except that it might be called home. The yard was full of pigs & chickens, no flowers or shrubbery, but still Mrs T. G. M. C Banks comes out carrying on her body & head the best of mantrees makers & milliners signs ~ in a fine carriage but miserable harness ~ the latter being used as frequently in gining as any other way. From there we went to old Mrs Taylors, one of Mrs C's [Cameron's] old & well-tried friends. Called there a few moments, then went on through the field to Mrs Garnet's. Stopped there and rested a little while, then Miss Savanah went with us over to Mrs C's old place.

Found everything going to ruin as fast as it possibly could do. I went into the orchard and got some nice peaches, then came back to Mrs Garnets, took a good wash. About 2 PM., Started for Mrs Cochrane's. Arrived there, we found Mrs C~ up, had been feeling better that morn than any time before since she was sick. Em, Mollie, Tallie & Mrs C~ [all members of the Cochran family] were all at home. Of the La tricks, Neh sent home an overcoat, such a nice one with brass buttons with the eagle on them, sevral pairs of shoes & boots, Hezie, three coats, a pair of boots, 32 yds of domestic, 5 of blue dennings a portable neadle case & portfolio combined, Mr G~ Harvey, an orderly sargents coat & pair of boots ~ all Yankee tricks

Mr Cloud showed us a dagauerreotype, some envelopes & some letters, also a portfolios "only think they eaven took private property" ~ but then I must be mistakened for no one but a "Yankee" would do that.[7]

---

6. According to *Webster's New World Dictionary*, "gallus/galluses," or "galas," as Lucy wrote it, was a nineteenth-century term commonly used to describe suspenders.

7. Thomas Ayres, *Dark and Bloody Ground: The Battle of Mansfield and the Forgotten Civil War in Louisiana* (Dallas: Taylor Publishing, 2001), 178–179. As Ayres indicates, the "loot" recovered from the encounter at Brashear City extended beyond the Yankee whiskey consumed in the aftermath

Ann let me read a letter from Kite of the 22nd & 23rd of July. He spoke of the fall of V and of their retreating from Brashire city. We arrived at Uncle P's just after sundown

Sara had been in bed all day with head ache ~ I hope no long columns to be added will disturb me this night ~ last night I was so busy with them that I said in my sleep ~ Yes! It makes *just* 26. Next I'll go crazy

Aug 16th sunday ~ Lounged all the morn, Sara went to sunday school & for a great wonder, no one came home with her. I am so glad ~ ditto Aunt Lu.

Aug 18th tuesday ~ My teeth are troubling me some this eve ~

Aug 19th wednesday ~ My face & teeth troubled me so much this morn that I yielded my consent not to teach and also to drinking a glass of Toddy & going to bed ~ sick with neuraliga

Aug 20th Thursday ~ Sara & I were busy at work numbering negroes, horses, cattle, sheep & money, when Sack came from school & told us Jake Catlin had come. I was so glad to see him for I truly believe him one of the best of boys although one of the hot-headed kind. He had on a silver mounted six-shooter with an American eagle & gold plate on it also 6 silver stars. He also had on a Yankee hat & plume ~ negro uniform & Yankee pants blue

Aug 22nd saturday ~ In the P.M. we girls went over to see Jake, & then all went to church. Parson Kemp preached. ~ They are going to have meetings now for some time, going to try for a revival, I believe. The house was full for night services

Aug 23rd sunday ~ Em Cochrane & Mollie Jackson came soon after ten & for the sake of their having company, I condescended to go to church with. In the eve they came home with Sara ~ say that Bolie &

---

of the fight. Ayres reports that after a short skirmish that lasted only a few minutes, "Hunter and his boys had seventeen hundred prisoners under guard and were already looting the commissary" yielding "brand-new uniforms from the Union supply depot," bottles of whiskey and "sacks of fine Yankee cuisine." Others, under Major's command thirty miles away, raided a Yankee camp, confiscating food and liquor, and as Ayres reports, "the raid became a non-stop party of fighting, looting, and celebrating" (178–179). Lucy and the others were seeing the remains of the "party," but were more than likely receiving a censored version of the account.

Sue McLarin & Fanny C got to shouting to night & Sue to dancing she got so happy

Aug 24th monday ~ Dentist Lee was here soon this morn, & I had 4 teeth extracted without stopping, but after the two first took Chloriform.

Aug 25th tuesday ~ This morn came over to teach, though not feeling very well having fasted since yester-noon, with the exception of drinking some coffee. In the PM. felt so badly, I lay down some time.

Aug 26th wednesday ~ Sue McLarin & Bolie both got to shouting last night. Sallie Catlin & Sis Torrence both joined the church greatly to my surprise, or the former was, may she prove faithful

 This eve Lissie, Sack, G~ Bell & I went to church, but as no one but Mrs Chapman once & Mr Cy~ C~ once shouted, I missed seeing a sight I have never seen. There was about fifteen went forward this eve

Aug 27th thursday ~ Read a letter from B. F Bunting to day in the paper of the 26th ~ he says their Brig were almost constantly in the saddle from the 24th of June until the 4th of June [July] during the time Shelbyville & Tullahoma were evacuated. He give the Tennesseeans "*fits*" & particularly the citizens of Bedford county, & Bragg he says has gai[n]ed a greater renown for retreating than any other Gen in the Confed.[8] The troops were, it was said, badly demoralized & if they would be divided & sent under different commands where they would do some good or not, he did not know, but thought it probable. They were, at the time he wrote, in Trenton, Georgia. The Press & People generally seemed somewhat despondent, indeed since the fall of Vicksburg that feeling seems quite plain.[9] That God will defend the right is my wish. No doubt there are few who would agree with me in what I consider right though. ~ Come Peace at least ~ We are tired of war

8. McPherson, *Ordeal by Fire*, 336. General Braxton Bragg, who commanded the Army of Tennessee, had begun a retreat from central Tennessee through Tullahoma, then Chattanooga, and ultimately, Chickamauga. McPherson records that the subsequent battle at Chickamauga "turned out to be the last significant offensive victory by any Confederate army," but that it held little strategic significance. Bragg was taken to task for his poor leadership and was replaced by Joe Johnston in the fall of 1863.

 9. Ibid., 332. Lucy's sentiments echo those expressed throughout the South. McPherson records that the "losses at Gettysburg and Vicksburg shook the Confederacy to its foundations," citing writings from all ranks of officers and enlisted men alike who articulated feelings of hopelessness and despair.

Aug 28th friday ~ Laura Dent & Angie M Cleveland went forward to night ~ Annie M seemed greatly affected ~ no doubt she felt sorry that she publicly scoffed at the mourners who presented themselves the first of the meeting

Aug 29th saturday ~ Miss Plumer, Mary Lee, Ellen Kenney & another young lady joined the church this eve. Sue Mc shouted & danced all about at a wonderful rate and Mr Atkinson walked & shouted, & such slapping of hands & beating of peoples back I never before saw. Mr Clemons went forward also.

August 31st monday ~ Mr B went to Bellville this morn to have his books examined, but found when he got there, there was a misunderstanding among the Comms [Commissioners] about the day, and so the Judge appointed a week from to day for them to meet here.

SEPTEMBER 1863

Sept 2nd wednesday ~ Rufus B & Ino E~ were among the drafted ~ went to Brenham this morn & joined a company ~ cavalry. Dr Clark has been drafted again. He has two substitutes already in the war. They must consider him extra smart

MARGINAL NOTE: *Ruf Campbell died on the 6th ~ Monday*

Sept 5 saturday ~ Aunt Lu says Mrs Rufus Campbell had a son born on Wednesday. Says Miss Mary Smith has given up going north for the present.[10]

Sept 7th monday ~ Of all the miserable nights, last night was the worst I've spent in some time. Both had the headache & the figits[11] ~ had to get up & go down stairs to light the candle to find out the meaning of a paper

---

10. Lucy's first reference to Miss Mary Smith on September 5 passed with hardly a notice in the course of her entry. However, Miss Smith would prove instrumental to Lucy's renewed connection with her family in Ohio and her subsequent return. With sporadic mentions, beginning here and continuing through 1864, the intertwining of Lucy's life with Miss Smith's may be tracked.

11. "The figits" was a colloquial term for an uneasy feeling that was accompanied by restless moving about.

rattleing ~ brave girls. Mr Catlin and I Dabney, Judge & Commissioners came during the morning, but as it required 3 to examine the books, they accomplished nothing[12] Found Shiloah on our return ~ he played all the eve for us girls to dance. After we had eaten our supper, waltzed, polka'd, danced schottische[13]

Sept 8th tuesday ~ Shiloah went to offer his service to set up with little Ruf Campbell, who was taken sick on sunday at church across the creek and was taken to Mrs Daughtry's, but was well, I supposed, until this eve. Sack came home from school at 5 & Willie Clemmons with him, they say Rufus C~ died at 1 this P.M. had the pleurisy[14] which was helped on by a large bait of plums.

Sept 9th wednesday ~ went on over with Jimmy Campbell, who had come after coffee to burn in the room where the corps lay, it had become so offensive.[15] We found the family feeling most deeply afflicted. Mrs S~ was perfectly inconsoliable and Sis too takes the death of her brother so hard. The coffin was not commenced until this morn and is not finished yet. at 12 N[oon], so there is a house full here to dinner. R~ was buried at 3 P.M. Nearly all his schoolmates were there, and every one seemed to mourn this loss. It seems hard to see a person so young & promiseing taken ~ but such is life.

I did not look at the deceased, but Sara says she never saw a person so changed ~ eyes sunken & black with mortification and the blood was oozing from both nostrils & ears. The shriek his Mother gave when she saw him for the last time told a tale of its-self. They say he was so much like her last husband ~ both in looks and appearance. It seems so very strange that the first one to go was the only grown brother that had enjoyed the comforts of home since the war. But there it is. None can tell what a day may bring forth.

12. Lucy's reference to the visit of the commissioners indicates an official audit of the tax books that she and Sarah had spent hours compiling for Mr. Brewer.

13. The schottische, a form of round dance in 2/4 time, was similar to the polka, but with a slower tempo.

14. Pleurisy, a common malady of the nineteenth century, is an inflammation of the pleura, or membranes covering the lungs, and is characterized by difficult, painful breathing. Not considered fatal on its own, it is usually a secondary complication of more-serious conditions such as viral infections, pneumonia, or tuberculosis.

15. Burning coffee or coffee grounds can serve as a natural deodorizer. This practice was apparently well known, and those in the room thought the situation warranted this remedy.

The C's~ are through the books at last.

Sept 10 thursday ~ Mr B & his Confederates went to Bellville to Court to day ~ Mr B~ came home funny ~ talking about grass-widowers[16] this eve and compared them to tadpoles & told the truth too when he said they forced their company on the girls. I speak from experience but when they do it again they will be wiser

MARGINAL NOTE: *4 years ago we all went over to the island to celebrate Perry's victory*[17]

Sept 11th friday ~ Sue had a great time about her Arithmetic lesson this morn, but as she came out conqueror ~ I do not think she regrets the trial

MARGINAL NOTE: *Joe Campbell died ~ in La the 10th*

Sept 13th sunday ~ This morn I read a condensced history of Dr Davis. One of Texas' public men, he was a native of Mass. After meeting with many reverses, he emigrated to the lone star state ~ and settled in Brazoria. He soon met with great success and of course won a great name, and the Mexican war coming on soon, fame added her laural wreath ~ he having won honor in it. After the war he served as senator, minister to the U.S., and at the time of the annexation, was President of the Republic[18]

Sept 15th tuesday ~ We had quite a rain to day ~ R.B. [Rufus Brewer] came home this eve and told his folks good-bye. It is truly sad to see friends part not knowing if ever they would see them again

---

16. The OED explains that "grass widower" was a common term for a man divorced or otherwise separated from his wife. From her accompanying remarks, Lucy had apparently been on the receiving end of unwanted attentions from such men and was now well versed in methods of deterrence.

17. Here, Lucy referred to the naval victory of Commodore Oliver H. Perry during the War of 1812.

18. Lucy wrote "Dr. Davis," then proceeded to give biographical information on Anson Jones, the second president of the Republic of Texas. According to The Handbook of Texas Online, Jones's term began in 1844, following Sam Houston's second term, and ended with the annexation of Texas to the United States. Perhaps Lucy inadvertently used "Davis" rather than "Jones" because Jefferson Davis was the president of the Confederate States of America, and his name was at the forefront of her mind.

Sept 18th friday ~ found Martin (Capt) Kenny here ~ he returned last sabbath and expects to go back to his Reg (Carter's)[19] the last of this month. He has entirely recovered his speach and is looking to be in better health than when he left here with his company. By Uncle P's request he showed us where he was wounded ~ the ball entered his throat and came out through his right shoulder. A narrow escape truly! Capt K talks rather despondingly of the southeron cause, but says they will never be a conquered people,[20] God speed the right ~ ~ ~ ~ ~ ~

Sept 20th sunday ~ It was so cool yesterday morn & this eve have had to have fires, and on Friday I had one [all] day in the school-room. I finished reading the *Heart of MidLothian*[21] this morn. Uncle P~ came home this eve, says Willie has been very sick but is better now.

Sept 21st monday ~We had great times playin "Hull-gull" &c. Sack has half a bag of pecans.

Sept 28th monday ~ Mr T~'s [letter] brought the sad news of Joe Campbell's death. Poor boy. I hated so much to hear it, but such is the fate of war. Poor Mrs S~ will feel it so much. Two in so short a time and a third with most misirable health

---

19. According to *The Handbook of Texas Online*, George Washington Carter, a Methodist minister, became president of Soule University at Chappell Hill in 1860. With the onset of war, he raised three regiments, retaining command of one, the 21st, Texas.

20. Here again, Lucy referred to a growing pessimism about the South's ultimate victory. Yet, even after the events of this bloody summer, the pessimism was mixed with a refusal to give up the Cause.

21. Richard D. McGhee, "Sir Walter Scott," in *Dictionary of Literary Biography*, vol. 107, *British Romantic Prose Writers, 1789–1832*, 1st ser., ed. John R. Greenfield, 247–266 (Gale Group, 1991). *Heart of Midlothian*, number six of Scott's *Waverly* novels, was published in 1818 as part of the *Tales of My Landlord*, 2nd ser.

CHAPTER 7

OCTOBER–DECEMBER 1863

Just four years ago today I bid adieux to home . . .

LUCY P. STEVENS,
December 13, 1863

WITH THE BLOODY SUMMER OF 1863 drawing to a close, Lucy's journal began
to address more personal issues. She continued to write about war news and
reports as she received them, but as autumn progressed, she turned much
of her attention to home and the dailiness of life in the little town of Travis.
Many of her entries included bits of information about the people she had
grown to know and love. She attempted to include as much as she could,
from chores to birth announcements, to illness and even death, first as a contemporary reminder of what had transpired on a particular day, and then,
perhaps subconsciously, as a chronicle through which she could later re-
create this period of her life, possibly for loved ones she had yet to meet.

One sad entry on October 2 pulls from events Lucy had recorded in September: first, when young Rufus Campbell had died from pleurisy, and then,
within days, when his brother Joe had died while on duty in Louisiana. As
Lucy indicated, Joe died from a congestive chill, not from an injury sustained
in battle. This type of occurrence has been well documented by historians,
who have determined that disease, not injuries, proved to be the most vicious
foe for soldiers on both sides of the conflict. Medical information was limited
to the knowledge of the time, and remedies were restricted to the medicines
of the day. Antibiotics were yet to be developed, and sanitary conditions
were often primitive. These were the circumstances in which Lucy's friend
Joe Campbell found himself, and tragically, he became one more statistic in
the gruesome toll of the Civil War.

Lucy faithfully recorded the particulars of recent battles as news began to trickle in, paying close attention to a battle at Fordoche Bridge in Louisiana. The location, which is also associated with Stirling Plantation, caught her attention since it concerned her beloved "Travis boys." But in the middle of October, violence and intrigue closer to home captured her attention. Lucy first wrote of a shooting in Hempstead, Texas, a town sometimes called "Six-Shooter Junction"; Sarah documented it as well. Both young women were appalled at the incident, and Sarah rendered her own verdict on the killing, stating "these were justifiable I believe in thus attacking the Kirbys who have become perfect outlaws and bid defiance to every officer both civil and military" (Sarah Pier, 10/16/63).

Lucy, however, quickly moved from this bit of news to the ongoing drama concerning Dr. Richard Peebles. She had readily expressed her care and concern for his family and now recorded details about the doctor's arrest. Peebles and four co-conspirators with Unionist leanings engaged in a plot to distribute pamphlets advocating an end to the war. The plot was discovered, as Lucy reported, and the four were arrested on October 11, 1863, and charged with treason by General Magruder. The newspapers of the day were not even as conciliatory as General Magruder. In an article dated October 31, 1863, the *Houston Tri-Weekly Telegraph* called for severe measures:

We publish to-day from the Houston Telegraph some important disclosures as to the existence of domestic traitors among us, brought to light by Gen. Magruder. Three of these traitors, Dr. Peebles, a wealthy planter on the Brazos, D. B. Baldwin, a prominent lawyer of Houston, and a German, by the name of Zinke, formerly from Victoria, where he published a newspaper, have been some days here, on their way to banishment in Mexico—Gen. Magruder having ordered that they should be put across the Rio Grande at Eagle Pass. We take occasion to earnestly protest against these and all other traitors being left on our defenceless border to plot their treason against us. Let them either be hung, (as they deserve,) or be put at work on our fortifications on the coast, under close guard.

S. A. Herald.[1]

We must understand, however, that although the newspapers felt no qualms in applying the label of "traitor" to Union sympathizers such as Peebles and Baldwin, support for secession was by no means universal in Texas. Pockets

---

1. *Houston Tri-Weekly Telegraph*, October 31, 1863, Texas and Other Southern States Civil War Newspapers/Newspaper Research, 1861–1865.

of Union sympathizers existed throughout the state, and records of the day furnish numerous examples of tension. Perhaps the most violent conflict came to Cooke County in northern Texas during 1862, in what became known as the Great Hanging at Gainesville, where forty suspected Union sympathizers were convicted by a kangaroo court and hanged.[2]

The episode at Gainesville provided a precedent, and the *Houston Tri-Weekly* felt no compunction in calling for the execution of Peebles and his associates, an opinion shared by many. Even Cousin Sarah wrote scathingly of the men's deeds, noting that

> a small boat containing the mail intended for one of the yankee vessels was captured off the Calcassien a short time ago and in that mail were found letters from these and other prominent men of Texas written to their yankee friends giving them information intended to injure our government and using such expressions and expressing such sentiments as proved them to be traitors to our government.
> Sarah Pier, 10/17/63

Lucy, however, could not bring herself to believe the accusations. Nor would she condemn her friend, even if the evidence proved to be true. Despite the official indictments from the military and moral outrage from the press, Lucy obviously questioned the arrest and eventual deportation of Dr. Peebles and hoped for his vindication.

Oct 2nd friday ~ Stephe brought me home this eve. Met Mr B~ on his way home from Austin ~ did not succeed in getting his wool carded. Ino Campbell was at Mr B's this eve to get a certificate from the Dr for Cy ~ He seems to feel the loss of his brothers very deeply. One died the 8th, the other the 10th.

Mr Robert Park, brother to Smith, brought the mail from Brenham this eve. One came from Jim B~ with the particulars of Joe C's [Campbell's] death in it. He says he had a congestive chill which caused his death,[3] that Mr Torrence and a Mr Davis [were] two of the best nurses

2. Richard B. McCaslin, *Tainted Breeze: The Great Hanging at Gainesville, Texas, 1862* (Baton Rouge: Louisiana State University Press, 1994), 60–83.

3. Ray Vaughn Pierce, MD, *The People's Common Sense Medical Advisor in Plain English; Or, Medicine Simplified* (World's Dispensary Medical Association, 1895), Project Gutenberg. "Congestive chill" was a term used throughout the country in the nineteenth and early twentieth centuries for ailments varying from pneumonia to malarial fever to tuberculosis. According to Dr. Ray

in the Batt and he had all the attention he could have, that they buried him [in] a nice coffin beneath the weeping willows near where they were stationed.

Oct 5th monday ~ Cousin Sara went over to Mr B's with me this morn to see Little Miss Sallie Lu P Bell, who came to town last saturday eve. Newton & Sallie met us and Newton commenced the first thing with "Miss Lu, you don't know what we have got at our house." They all seem delighted

Oct 8th thursday ~ Mr Bell arrived this eve to see his daughter. He was in such haste, he almost run over us little folks when he came and never stoped until he got into the bed-room where E was. This is the 14th E~ has had. Her & Mrs C are just eaven.

Oct 9th friday ~ My children spoke this P.M. and I invited in the good folks to hear them. All my little ones had on their clean frocks, hair combed and recited well. Sue's peice was "The Festal Board," Steve's "The Monkey, Jane's "Amelia," Sallie's "The River," & Newton's "When Little Fred Was Called to Bed." Then I had them sing "Oh Come-Come Away," "Tis a Lesson All Should Heed," "The Little Pony" & "Chick a Dee Dee." After they had done, I called on Mr Bell to address my pupils and he gave them great praise for their learning so well. All seemed highly pleased. They did finely to my credit.

Oct 10th saturday ~ They are holding protracted meeting at Buck-horn. Lydia Francis, Uncle J~ Mrs Margret Foster, Mattie Rutherford & Lis Miller have found the church, and Em C~ is quite serious. Mollie went up to the mourners bench, she says, because Parson Stone urged so hard to go. They are to have meeting in the grove tomorrow. Mrs C~ invited us all to go.

Oct 11th sunday ~ Uncle Pier & Aunt Lu arrived home at ½ past 12 N. left Lu not very well Sallie T~ and Mrs D~ have both been sick and are salivated.[4]

Vaughn Pierce, a congestive chill was believed to be caused by an accumulation of blood in the blood vessels. Often accompanied by fever, this was considered to be one of the most severe types of illness. Treatments varied, but were often ineffective, resulting in the death of the patient (406).

4. Here, Lucy says her friends "are salivated," describing an ailment that caused her friends to produce an unusual amount of saliva. The term, common in the nineteenth century, could also reflect a condition brought on by the use of mercury for medicinal purposes.

News came in the last paper of a battle near Chattanooga, where it is said Bragg defeated Rosencranz. A report also came that a battle took place on the 29th of September on Bayou Fordiche in the Parish of point Coupee. Gen Green commanding the Confed forces gained a decisive victory over Ord commanding Bank's forces. Major Boon was severely wounded and it is feared will loose an arm Green captured 2 – 12 lb Parrot guns. The principle loss in Spaight's Batt.[5]

Oct 12th monday ~ This P.M. Mrs B and myself went to see Parson Kenny as he is not expected to live but a very short time. He looks badly, is confined to the bed most of the time.

Oct 13th tuesday ~ My little name-sake [Elizabeth's baby] is getting prettyer every day and is growing so fast. This eve Sack fixed himself up with mustache and whiskers and came in where we girls were, trying to kiss everybody and making the greatest kind of a scattering among us

Oct 14th wednesday ~ Cousin S~ was not at all well, had been trying the medacine Dr McL recommended her for headache. Croton oil,[6] one half drop as a dose every half hour until you have taken three, never more than that number to be given at one time. It is one of the best of medacines for sick headache.

Oct 15th thursday ~ they have had a great shooting scrape over at H~. That on Monday, two of the Kirbys entered Jack Herbert's (Mr Lee's lawyer's) office and drew a knife across his neck. That he left his office, went home and came back with his half brother, both well armed and took their stands for the K's. Shot two of them, killed one and shot the other seriously. And that after that, all the K's left in hot haste.

The K's have shot five or six men now and I think it high time they were stopped in their career by some one. Very lately they have shot two men, one a negro belonging to Mrs Lee & threatened her life. Some time ago, Col K~[7] was trying to get up a company which B. B. Lee refused to

---

5. According to *The Handbook of Texas Online*, in the battle at Fordoche, Boone ultimately "lost his right arm and the first two fingers and thumb of his left hand." Lucy's last phrase, "principle loss in Spaight's Batt," seemingly connects back to Major Boone's injury.

6. Croton oil, a thick, bitter oil extracted from croton seeds, was used during this time as an external counter-irritant to soothe skin ailments. It was also taken internally as a strong cathartic.

7. Although the definite identity of Colonel Kirby remains shrouded in mystery, *The Handbook of Texas Online* does list a Colonel Jared E. Kirby as living in Hempstead before and during

join. That was enough and so, Col K~ finding Lee drunk in town one day stood over his nephew and saw him [. . .] his eye-ball, threatning to kill any man that should attempt to interfere. Afterward Lee attempted to shoot the Col. He [the Colonel] pulled a drunken man (Ganes Lipscomb) in the way, thus saving his own life and getting Mr L killed. Since the K's threaten and kill or shoot at almost every one they think are at all friendly to Lee; among the number shot is Ino Ferril a brother-in-law of Mrs B~ Brewer.

Oct 16th friday ~ Heard that Dr Peebles, Judge Baldwin and others who had expressed union principles had been taken up. And it is thought Judge B~ has been taken where we will never see him more and that Dr P~ has been sent across the Rio-Grande, that Ennis, a merchant of Houston, has taken french leave also the "Tafts." Mr B~ returned this eve bring[ing] a confirmation of the report, says that Judge B~ was taken saturday night. That previous to this, some two weeks ago I think, there was a fedral boat blown in over the bar near Sabine Pass. On board was found letters over the signature of these men, giving account of the movements of the Confed &c, and that another U S mail was captured or taken not long since by a Confed~ boat hoisting the British colors. And [on] it was found letters of the same import, from the same source. And it was proven by a hand-bill that made its appearance they were trying to rally the people to hold a convention to be held at Houston to cede the state over into unionism again. Whereupon Magruder had all who were concerned that he could find out [arrested] and sent across the line. ~ "God will defend the right" ~ "All things work together for our good"[8]

Oct 17th saturday ~ Mr Ayers sent Uncle P~ a paper of the 15th with an account of the taking off of those men and some of the evidences against them as follows copied on a paper extracts from letters

the war years. Kirby, in fact, was one of the wealthiest planters in Austin County, owning Alta Vista, a large plantation covering eight thousand acres and bordering both sides of the Brazos River. Violence seemed to follow Kirby; in 1865 he was murdered, allegedly by a Capt. John Steele. Fourteen years later, Kirby's son, J. E. Kirby, accosted Steele, killing him as he left services at the Methodist church in Hempstead. Ultimately, the son was tried and acquitted.

8. Here again, Lucy penned a favorite phrase, combining it with a portion of a verse from the Bible (Romans 8:28). Her use of the phrase often came during a passage that implied ambivalence toward a political stance or war sentiment.

Oct 19th monday ~ Found it right cool out so that my shawl felt very comfortable enough. E's baby was not at all well yesterday, and this eve it is much worse so that they sent for the Dr who came and stayed until bed time. As I came in from school to night, the baby looked so badly it gave me a real start. 'Twas so unnaturally white.

In the nineteenth century, pregnancy was often ignored until the arrival of the blessed event, and Lucy had recorded no mention of her friend Elizabeth's advancing pregnancy. In fact, without a close reading of her October 5 entry, the meaning could easily be misinterpreted. Miss Sallie Lu P Bell's arrival in town was actually Lucy's delicate version of a birth announcement. Lucy had been keeping track of Elizabeth's new daughter, Lucy's "little namesake," commenting on October 8 about how rapidly the baby was growing, but only a few days later, the infant began having serious problems. Reversals such as this were not at all uncommon. Tragically associated with childbirth in the nineteenth century was the high rate of infant mortality. The new mother's health was only one of the sources of worry, since infant mortality rates ran as high as 25–30 percent,[9] and sadly, the death of a newborn was often mentioned in the same breath as its birth. On October 19 and 20, Lucy commented that the baby was very sick, and on October 21, she heartbrokenly wrote of the baby's death.

Harder to read than these accounts, however, are Sarah's journal entries about her own experiences. On February 9, 1866, she wrote lovingly of her four-month-old daughter's development, "baby lies and plays with her hands. She is a very smart and pretty baby. I'm not saying that's so because she is mine either" (Sarah Pier, 2/9/66). The next entry, however, tells of the sudden heartbreak that descended on the household, an anguish far too common in nineteenth-century America. On February 14, Sarah wrote:

Four days has passed since last I wrote in my journal and O, how different are my feelings from what they then were. Now I feel sad and there is a vacancy in my heart—which time can never fill. My angel babe has been taken from me. She was too pure for earth with her sweet face and deep expressive eyes—through which her soul seemed to speak. God took her to himself again to teach us submission to His will and to draw

9. Sandra Myres, *Westering Women and the Frontier Experience, 1800–1915* (Albuquerque: University of New Mexico Press, 1982), 156.

us nearer to heaven. I feared we would never raise her—I felt it in my heart, but was not expecting to have her taken from us so soon. When I wrote last she was well, that night (the 9th) she was taken with a fever— continued to get worse until the afternoon of the 10th when she seemed better but about five Oc. She began to have spasms which continued until 4 Oc. The morning of the 11th (Sunday) when her sweet spirit was released. Oh! The agony of these hours, none but fond parents can know. But I feel that it is for the best, Tis God's will and I am resigned, but tis hard to say "Thy will be done."

Sarah Pier, 2/14/66

Despite her attempts to philosophically explain and accept in good nineteenth-century fashion the death of her precious baby, Sarah struggled. For months she mourned, noting in her diary monthly anniversaries of the baby's birth and death. Maintaining a facade of stoicism to appease a pious public, Sarah fled to her diary to pour out her private grief in its pages.

Prescripted responses to personal tragedy abounded, having been taught and embraced through generations, and as Sarah confided in her diary, so Lucy wrote of her friend Elizabeth: "it seems almost impossible for her to say ~ Thy will ~ oh God! be done." No matter the depth of spiritual maturity, it seems the social expectation of quiet resignation was insufficient in juxtaposition with a mother's loss; although the bedrock of their faith, the automatically uttered responses taught since childhood fell flat, for a time, upon the hearts of these grieving mothers. Even Lucy, who had remained detached from the deaths of the Campbell brothers, writing impassively "such is life" (9/9/63), abandoned her objective stance and brokenly sympathized with Elizabeth's anguish.

Oct 20th tuesday ~ Mrs B & I sit up with the baby last night. The medacine acted well last night. But for all that and constant attention, it was so much worse this P.M. we thought for awhile it was dying. [. . .] sent in hot haste for the Dr & Sack, the latter went for Mr Bell. ~ At 9 P M ~ little Sallie Lu seemed resting quietly, though the Dr thinks it is impossible almost for her to recover. Yet he says she may linger along for a day or two.

Oct 21st wednesday ~ After getting to sleep slept soundly, except imagining I heard the moans of poor little Sallie Lu, until about 1 o'c'k in the night when the girls came out to get something to eat, leaving E~ with the baby on her lap and the Dr in the room. I asked them how was little namesake, and they told me much better. But while I was thinking of what the Dr had said, he called to Lissie to go waken her Ma, that the baby was dead. Oh, how hard it seemed to believe that we had lost our darling baby. And the poor afflicted Mother ~ it seems almost impossible for her to say ~ Thy will ~ oh God! be done. Lissie came to let me know, & as soon as I could, went in to assist in the mournful task of preparing her to be laid out. E~ says they had thought her much better after the last spell of coughing she had & had been talking of what she was to take in the morn, when she turned her over on one side & after a few moments felt her head & found it cold. I washed & dressed the baby while Mrs Wm B~ held her, then Mrs B & I sit up til morn. After Sara came, she made a winding sheet. Scolloped it, then pinked the edges. Mr Reed made a coffin. Sara layed the baby in it. Lissie, Jane Mrs B, Susan, Newton, Sallie, Stephe, & I went to the burying. ~ How deeply the heart spoke in taking a farewell.

Oct 22nd thursday ~ The house seems so lonely and deserted, and [since] last eve, the rain still continues. Mr Bell & Sack came about half past seven. Not a question was asked, but it was unnecessary ~ for the silent group around the fire side told a tale of sorrow.

Oct 29th thursday ~ Sack & Eliz~ went to Bellville & out to Englekings Store[10] to day searching for dry goods, but did not succeed in finding anything of any consequence.

Oct 30th friday ~ Last night came up a severe norther so that we all hover round the fire to keep comfortable. The Minute men had a hard time of it last night out in the sleet. Arrived at home, found Uncle P shivering over the fire. Has not gotten over last night's & yesterday's "campaign" on piny [Piney Creek].

---

10. During the late nineteenth and early twentieth centuries, Engleking Brothers Broom Factory operated in Sealy, Texas, another town near Brenham.

NOVEMBER 1863

Nov 1st sunday ~ cousin S~ wrote the Fedrals were this side of Opelu-sas[11] & their command were ordered to be on the march by daybreak. the boys generally were well

Nov 4th wednesday ~ Last night Mr B took Cholera morbeous.[12] had it very severely and is still feeling very badly.

Nov 5th thursday ~ Dr stayed here last night ~ Mr B says he feels so well this morn he will start tomorrow.

Nov 8th sunday ~ Aunt H~ told me all about the troubles across the river. My feelings of indignation were so great I could hardly find words to express them. yet do I find more of what may be expected in future shown out than I had ever thought to see at all[13]

I never expect to see my firmness forsake me in such trials and pray God to instruct me in the way to act most wise in all circumstances. We spoke of the dark and dismal future of our hopes and fears and of their anticipation but 'tis so hard to tell what a day may bring forth that they were all indecission.

Nov 9th monday ~ Uncle M told me yesterday of Mr Bells death and found on my arrival at Mr B's ~ 'twas realy true. Poor E~ I feel so much for her ~ 'tis so hard that she is to be left so much alone again. Yet it may be best ~ we can not always see aright

---

11. Cousin Sammy's unit, attached to General Tom Green's Texas Cavalry Division, was currently skirmishing with Federal troops in the area around Opelousas, Louisiana.

12. The *OED* identifies "cholera morbus" not as the acute disease found in various parts of the world, but as a common disorder in the nineteenth century. Marked by diarrhea, vomiting, stomachache and cramping, the ailment generally occurred in late summer and early autumn, but was rarely fatal to adults.

13. Thomas Ayres, *Dark and Bloody Ground: The Battle of Mansfield and the Forgotten Civil War in Louisiana* (Dallas: Taylor Publishing, 2001), 116–117. Although it is uncertain, Lucy could be commenting on the earlier regime of the commanding Union officer in New Orleans—General Benjamin "The Beast" Butler, who had wasted no time in alienating Southerners. Ayres reports that Butler, with his "women's order" that in essence reduced the status of the women of New Orleans to that of harlots, outraged residents across the South. Ayres concludes that the act spurred a new wave of recruits, anxious to avenge the honor of Southern women.

Nov 11th wednesday ~ The girls are having great times spin[n]ing ~ had, as they supposed, filling for 211 yards ready and when they came to use it found it to coarse. Read to day of the big cake made by order of king August the Strong of Austria[14] ~ it is said to have taken 3000 eggs, a ton of butter & other things in proportion ~ was made by machineary & drawn onto the ground by eight span of horses. Had 36 bushels of flour, one ton of yeast, one of butter, one of milk and trim[m]ed with crackers & almonds

Nov 13th friday ~ Dr brought news today that Brownsville had fallen into the hands of the Fedrals and that all cotton teams in route for that place were turned back. It was evacuated by Bee after burning the forts on the 1st of Nov. On the 2nd six boats were seen & six regimental flags were counted, on the 3rd 13 vessals were lying off Brazos Santiago

Nov 14th saturday ~ This is Mother's 60th birthday, how I wish I could get her a nice dinner or that she could eat with us. I have been busy at work all day ~ ripping and turning and patching my old school dress skirt, trying to make it passible to wear this winter ~ with that & my old red dress, I expect to get along finely.

Nov 15th sunday ~ Heard to day the particulars of the fight in La on the 3rd. Franklin was in command of the Fedral forces and Majors & Green of the Confederate forces. The fedrals are reported to have been some 20 or 30 thousand strong at or near Opelusas, but were driven back 7 miles onto bayou Bordeaux where they were obliged to make a stand and ~~meeting~~ were totaly defeated which ended in a complete route. Their loss was many killed and some six hundred taken prisoners, our loss was some 30 killed & 70 taken prisoners[15]

---

14. "August the Strong," *Dresdner Christstollen*. Lucy's source for this bit of trivia remains unknown; however, her subject, King Augustus the Strong (1670–1733), was a historical figure in Germany. In 1730, during a festival designed to persuade King Friedrich Wilhelm I of Prussia to make an alliance with Saxony, Augustus ordered a giant cake, or stollen, "1.8 tons in weight, 18 cubits in length, and 8 cubits in width . . . [and had it transported by] a wagon pulled by eight horses . . . into the midst of the festival. According to the website for today's Dresden Stollen Festival, the 1730 festival, with its luxury and ostentation, became legendary as "the most tremendous baroque festivity of its time."

15. Following a series of skirmishes, to which Lucy alluded in earlier entries, General Green's Texas forces dealt a decisive blow to General Banks at the Battle of Bayou Bourbeau. According to *The Handbook of Texas Online*, in a series of four victories, Green's forces inflicted

My old man came to see me this P.M. and stayed until after 9 in the eve

Nov 16th monday ~ Went over to school by myself this morn ~ found Molllie & Bell both spin[n]ing as hard as they could

Nov 20th friday ~ Papers say Walkers Division had a fight on the 10h of this month ~ do not know the result yet ~ am in hopes we shall soon hear good news[16]

Nov 25th wednesday ~ Mrs B~ and Bell have both been hard at work at the loom house to day weaving &c, so that it has been so lonesome in the house. They [are] all so busy to get a certain quantity of work for Christmas. Bell carded and spun 3 cuts of cotton & cleared back Mrs B's threads

Nov 29th sunday ~ Yesterday *Uncle Pier went out* squirrel hunting and brought back two Moravians[17] *he says deserters*

Nov 30th monday ~ Mr McRee, Mr Reid, Mr Cleveland and Dr McLarin all took dinner here, were round after the Bohemean deserters. After they left here, they went down to take one & his wife whipped them all out ~ beat Mr Cleveland & Mr Reed with a grape-vine ~ Mr McRee with a horn & cut up Dr McL's rope ~ I never laughed more in my life

---

some 3,000 casualties, while suffering only 600. The ensuing victory put an end to Banks's attempt to invade Texas at this time.

16. Richard Lowe, *Walker's Texas Division C.S.A.: Greyhounds of the Trans-Mississippi* (Baton Rouge: Louisiana State University Press, 2004). According to Lowe, Walker's troops had been involved in the Battle of Bayou Bourbeau on and around November 3, 1863. Because much of the victory was attributed to the infantry of Walker's Division, this is likely the skirmish to which Lucy referred.

17. Lucy's comments reflect a widespread friction between Anglos and Czech/Moravian/Bohemian immigrants that reached its height during these years. Several factors contributed to this animosity. According to *The Handbook of Texas Online*,

> many recent immigrants did not fully understand the conflict between North and South, and at the same time they were suspect as foreigners. Most significantly, virtually none of them had any allegiance to the institution of slavery, not only for moral reasons, but also because the concept of slavery was alien to their system of intensive family farming.

Despite the fact that many of the Czech immigrants volunteered for military duty, much prejudice existed, and many, like Lucy's family, assumed the worst.

DECEMBER 1863

The hard-fought battles of the summer had subsided somewhat with the beginnings of colder weather, and Lucy replaced many of the horror stories from the front with the ongoing activities of the soldiers and the families who waited for them at home. Lucy used these pages of her diary for light-hearted tales, relating evenings of visiting and teasing, another indication of her ability to find the whimsical in the ordinary, the comical in the routine. She filled her entries with the coming and going of family members and friends, and a glimpse of the open-door policy among neighbors reverberates through her words.

With an attitude born of necessity in early frontier Texas, families continued to accommodate others and do what they could to help. Becoming well known for their hospitality, the Piers were always ready to set another place at the table and/or shelter an overnight guest. This attitude was obviously passed along to their children, for in March 1914, the Bellville newspaper paid tribute, writing: "The Pier family of old Travis was known always for its wide hospitality, with the latch string ever on the outside for the stranger who came that way."[18] And as Lucy's entry of December 12, 1863, indicates, Cousin Lu had been well trained by her mother, with Lu hosting fifteen people who had, for various reasons, spent the night. Most of these visits were brief, with guests quickly on their way. However, as Lucy briefly noted the illness of Mr. Darnman, she introduced a decline that she would follow for many months. Her journal reveals that Mr. Darnman and his wife would ultimately reside in the home of Cousin Lu and Cousin Waller for the duration of his illness. Cousin Lu would thus shoulder much of the responsibility for another family's care, providing shelter, food, nursing, and attention for extra members of the household, in addition to her own family duties.

Yet even as Lucy wrote of community, she repeatedly expressed her wistful desire to hear from home. But no word came, and on December 13, as she commemorated the fourth anniversary of her departure from Ohio for her visit in Texas, she wrote one of her most plaintive entries, expressing her sense of isolation and separation. Her poignant reflections not only give a sense of the history of her visit, but clearly indicate that, for all her participation in her Texas home, her heart recalled her Northern family and roots,

---

18. William Hardt, e-mail interview with Vicki Tongate concerning "100 Years Ago in the *Times*—Samuel Bradford Pier," March 29, 2014.

and she longed to return. It is in this entry that Lucy made clear the two-and-a-half-year silence that she had endured, as attempt after attempt to send letters to the North had failed. Her melancholy tone reveals that her earlier expectations of a happy visit had long ago been replaced by the realities of exile in a land wounded and grieving over the devastation of war.

Yet regardless of her longings, Lucy stayed busy with her duties. The school term had progressed well, and she prepared her students for the closing exercises, set for December 23. Programs such as this provided an excellent opportunity for local residents to visit the school and socialize. With games, refreshments, speeches, and music, the day heightened the sense of community among the residents and gave the children a chance to show off.[19] Lucy's diary offers a glimpse into her teaching curriculum, as well as her relationships with those around her. As part of the program, she had her students perform a variety of well-known poems and songs. "Oh, Come, Come Away," written by William Houser in 1848, and "'Tis a Lesson You Should Heed," written by William Edward Hickson in 1857, were both popular songs of the day.[20] "I met a little cottage girl" may have been from William Wordsworth's poem "We Are Seven," written and published in 1798.[21] Lucy prepared her scholars well, and they performed admirably for the assembled guests.

Dec 1st tuesday ~ Mrs B~ went to get some Spanish-brown[22] to color with this eve and brought me a letter from Jimmy Cochrane

Dec 10th thursday ~ Sue Purcell here last night & says her brother was well again and at camp Enterprize, Miss[23] The children went over to the

19. John Austin Edwards, "Social and Cultural Activities of Texans during the Civil War and Reconstruction, 1861–1873" (PhD diss., Texas Tech University, 1985), 161–171.

20. Hickson had, in fact, appropriated the lyric from Thomas H. Palmer's poem "Try, Try Again," published in Palmer's *The Teacher's Manual: Being an Exposition of an Efficient and Economical System of Education, Suited to the Wants of a Free People* (Boston: Marsh, Capen, Lyon, and Webb, 1840).

21. William Wordsworth, "We Are Seven."

22. "Spanish-brown" refers to a type of earth with a reddish-brown color that was used as a pigment in various kinds of dyes.

23. "The Texas Hospital and Confederate Cemetery, Quitman (Enterprise), Mississippi," American Civil War home page. Enterprise and Quitman, located thirteen miles apart in Clarke County, Mississippi, served as the general site for what became known as the Texas Hospital during the Civil War. To ensure proper medical care, especially for Confederate soldiers from Texas, citizens of Houston and Galveston helped build the hospital in July 1862. Texas physicians brought wagonloads of medicine all the way from Mexico and partnered with Mississippi

office for the mail ~ came running in to tell me Sara had sent for me, that Neh C~ was at our house. Mrs B. kindly loaned me Old Charley and over I came ~ found him looking badly, so pale & thin ~ was so very glad to see him. he left La on the 30th Nov, was just a week on the road. Neh stayed with the boys the night before he started, left all of our Travis boys well. they were acting as pickets for Walker's Division. Neh brought each of us girls an orange, they are so nice. Aunt Lu came soon after dark, says Willie has the white swelling[24] and can not go about of any consequence ~ poor little fellow, 'tis so hard for him ~ Lu was well. Mr Darnman is looking miserably and feels very low spirited. Dr Baily is visiting him.

Dec 12th saturday ~ Uncle P~ says Aunt H~ & Uncle M are both at Lu's; Willie was running all about again. Mr Chapman stayed at Lu's, they had a good house full ~ 15. Mr D~ is improving slowly.

Dec 13th sunday ~ Just four years ago today I bid adieux to home ~ and friends with a heavy heart ~ 'tis true that the good bye's must be said, but yet how happy did I then feel in comparison to the present. Youth is ever happy & gay hearted naturally, & after the partings had been given and we had gotten some distance on our journey came the anticipation of the happy meeting at home again when I should return, which I imagined would not be far in the future ~ and in the mean time I should have such a pleasant visit with Aunt Lu & family ~ making new friends; and then I pictured in my mind how often would come the happy rememberances from home in the shape of letters & while reading them I would all most think myself one of their number in pleasures & dissapointments ~ until at last it seemed there was little for sorrow. Each new object began to possess an attraction, and with most agreeable company I could not wish for a pleasanter trip than we had. Alas how great are the changes now ~ friends are scattered ~ No news been heard from home since two years ago the 19th of August & no hopes of getting any soon. Peace, prosperity & happiness then smiled upon & now our beloved country is deluged in war. Not a home but feels its sorrows, and in many instances, husbands, brothers & Fathers have been torn from

doctors to provide staffing for the hospital, which operated for almost two years during the war. Then, in February 1864, General Walter Q. Gresham, acting on orders from General William Sherman, destroyed the hospital as part of a raid into Mississippi designed to eliminate anything that might be considered an asset to the Confederacy.

24. Although there are some variations of the term, it is likely that this was some temporary form of inflammation in Willie's knee or ankle that made it difficult for him to walk.

their homes to spend their life's blood for the defense of what they feel to be a Just cause.

News came yesterday that Bragg had gained another victory over Rosencrantz army ~ the latter commanded by Thomas ~ fought from the 21st of last month until the 27th. Gen Thomas occupied the Chicka-mauga valley at last accounts[25]

Dec 18th friday ~ Mr Lee came this noon got my teeth at last, am so glad I have them before Christmas[26]

Dec 19th saturday ~ Uncle Pier got out the carriage betimes this morn for us girls to go to Mr Cyrus Campbells to spend the day. My little name-sake met me on the gallery looking so rosy and fleshy ~ she has the hooping-cough[27] but it has not made her fall off any that I can see ~ she is one of the dear sweet children

Dec 20th sunday ~ Joe P came up from Lu's yesterday eve, says Mr Darn-man is worse. Mrs Alexander came home with us to dinner. Mrs A took

---

25. James M. McPherson, *Ordeal by Fire: The Civil War and Reconstruction*, 2nd ed. (New York: McGraw-Hill, 1992), 340. Lucy slipped in a reference to fighting that had taken place at Chicka-mauga. Her conflated rendering of this most recent news actually records some of the bloodi-est and most momentous fighting of the Civil War. Beginning with Bragg's Confederate victory over Rosecrans and Thomas at Chickamauga, Georgia (September 18–20), where the opposing armies sustained a combined casualty count of more than 34,600 in three days, and continu-ing with Union victories at Lookout Mountain and Missionary Ridge (November 24–25), these battles signaled important benchmarks for both North and South. According to McPherson, not only did the Northern army redeem the defeat at Chickamauga, but it followed through with victories at Vicksburg and Gettysburg that virtually "disabled the Confederacy" (340). As a result, leadership for both armies shifted, with Bragg being replaced by Joseph Johnston as commander of the Army of Tennessee, and Grant's subsequent appointment in March 1864 as general-in-chief for all Union armies. Significantly, these Union victories along the Georgia-Tennessee line brought together in one theater the four men who would ultimately outline victory for the North—Ulysses S. Grant, William T. Sherman, George H. Thomas, and Philip H. Sheridan.

26. Lucy's diary, as well as Sarah's and Aunt Lu's, indicate that Lucy had continuing prob-lems with her teeth and suffered greatly with the available treatments. On August 24, 1863, she had four teeth extracted, using chloroform to deaden the pain for the last two extractions. She then had to wait until December to receive the replacement teeth.

27. Then, as now, whooping cough, or pertussis, was a highly contagious respiratory ail-ment, afflicting mostly children. According to the Centers for Disease Control, pertussis is especially severe among infants, and, if left alone, it can prove fatal. Because treatment options were limited at this time and because immunization was not available until the 1930s, Lucy's little friend was fortunate indeed not to "fall off any."

occasion to reprove me for encouraging her daughter in her mischief the day she had the cat in church ~ says Fannie told her about it and says: that I pulled the cat's tail ~ may be so ~ I "dinna kin"

Dec 21 monday ~ found Mr Brewer in Bell's room looking at the baby. he returned on Saturday eve, says the small-pox is raging in Houston. Bell looks as bright as you please this morn, says she intends to robe herself on Wednesday. Mr B~ heard the report of Green's men being in Texas confirmed. My children reviewed their lessons and speaches to day ~ I am so anxious for them to do well

Dec 23rd wednesday ~ Has come at last and my session closes this morn. Such sweeping & dusting & cleaning. I was quite amused this morn when looking out of the window in our room I happened to overhear Jane and Sue talking to themselves, each a sweeping in the yard as busy as bees, when Sue says something "was so much trouble." Jane says "Yes ~ we all think we have a great deal of trouble, but we are young now. we don't have any ~ when we get old, we will know what trouble is."

Mrs B~ came in to hear the children read and recite in Arithmetic. Uncle Pier and Aunt Lu came at recess. Mr Wiley came just before recess. Just before I closed school, I asked my children bible questions, then heard them sing "Oh come – come away." After dinner heard the recitations in Geography, they sung "'Tis a lesson you should heed." I had recess. After, Sue said her peice "The Festal Board," Jane "I met a little cottage girl." Then Newton "See me I am a little boy" &c. N, S, & T sung "The little pony." Sallies speech "Mary Dow" sung Chick a dee-dee, Sue & Jane "Blue eyed Mary." Heard Sallie & Newton say capitols ~ then Steves speech, sung "Before all Lands in east or west" then "The close of school." Uncle Pier talked to the children awhile, gave them some good advice, & school was out and I a free girl for a short time.

Dec 24th thursday ~ All well at Lu's except Mr Darnman, who is perfectly discouraged and low-spirited; he looks a perfect skeleton. I went over to Mrs Bucks and took the cakes Sara had prepared for the children ~ they were made in cups & painted.

Dec 25th friday ~ Another Christmas comes which finds me at cousin Lu's. Made a "Nog" this morn, brandy and eggs a present from Mrs B~

After breakfast Lu & I made another for the darkies, and each drank us a toast. One wished I might live for-ever and when called to die that I might find a seat prepared for me on the right-hand of the Savior. All wished me a good, kind husband and Lucinda wished I might be Mrs Foster soon. Mr & Mrs Buck, Missie & Bella came over and took dinner with us ~ had turkey, ham, pork & turnips, cake: pound & jelly, pie: pumpkin & minced and preserves, and sure enough coffee ~ every thing was so nice. The children had great times over their presents from St Nicholas: candy, oranges, Sara's fancey cakes, some white ones, and each a dolly & bedstead.

Dec 26th saturday ~ Cousin W's darkies had a dinner today.

Dec 27th sunday ~ Came up a norther last night so we find the fire our warmest friend. I spent the day in reading *Major Jones Courtship and Marriage*.[28] Laughed at the foolish thing until I think I weigh several pounds more than yesterday. I am afraid this norther is going to interfere with my visiting arrangements.

Dec 28th monday ~ Read a sketch of the life of "Lafitte" the Baratarian chief ~ from Fields Scrap Book[29] Cousin W~ killed twenty hogs today ~ says he puts up about 7000 lbs of pork every year. Lu is wanting to make sausage so Joe P went to Travis for her some sage

---

28. Scott Slawinski, "William Tappan Thompson," in *Dictionary of Literary Biography*, vol. 248, *Antebellum Writers in the South*, 2nd ser., ed. Kent Ljungquist, 370–377 (Gale Group, 2001). *Major Jones's Courtship*, written by William Tappan Thompson in 1844, was part of a series of stories that gained great popularity across the nation during the nineteenth century. Thompson and other Southern writers were known as "the Georgia humorists" for the satirical style with which they poked fun at contemporary society. In this story, Jones's marriage to a Southern socialite carried the underlying message that the South's best hope lay in the plantation economy and its way of life rather than in a continued alliance with the North. Stylistically, in the writing of these stories, Thompson helped develop an approach by which the main character's point of view consistently appeared in Southern dialect. This technique, ushered in by Thompson and others of the Georgia humorists, was later adopted to great effect by Mark Twain.

29. William Fields, *The Literary and Miscellaneous Scrap Book* (Philadelphia: J. B. Lippincott, 1860). According to the Brick Row Book Shop, an antiquarian bookseller in San Francisco, *The Literary and Miscellaneous Scrap Book: consisting of tales and anecdotes, biographical, historical, patriotic, moral, religious and sentimental pieces, in prose and poetry*, compiled by William Fields, was first published in Tennessee in 1833. The book, one of the earliest of its kind, contained a wide-ranging anthology of writings by famous authors.

Dec 29th tuesday ~ Mr Darnman came out and spent most of the day with us ~ took dinner at the table. In the eve we played cards and all got smutted ~ Cousin Sara has a terriable head ache ~ took Morphine for it

Dec 30th wednesday ~ Mr W and cousin Sara spent most of the morn with Mr Darnman. The old piano had to suffer this eve. Cousin W~ and Mr Wiley played at drafts most of the eve, us girls read some, played more.

Dec 31st thursday ~ Came up a norther last night & we folks came near freezing to day. Cousin Lu has been sick most of the day. Cousin W~ killed eight hogs today, the heaviest weighed 350 lbs. Jim has been in the Woods most all the P.M.

With a few incidental remarks, Lucy completed her diary for 1863. The grisly reports of faraway battles had temporarily dwindled, having been replaced by the daily details of life in this small community in Texas. Many of the soldier boys were coming home on furlough, and the holidays offered a reprieve, however brief, from the grim reality of a nation at war with itself. However, Lucy's otherwise tranquil conclusion to 1863 rings a bit false as she ominously referenced the tension that engulfed the household as they, like so many others across the South, fought to maintain the status quo.

CHAPTER 8

JANUARY–FEBRUARY 1864

Cousin Sammy left us this morn about half past 9 ~ Mr Wiley came to tell us a last
fare-well. All had gone before 11, leaving us girls to lonesome-ness and
thoughts ~ which it is not well to indulge in.

LUCY P. STEVENS,
January 17, 1864

WITH THE ADVENT OF 1864, many of the local boys arrived home on furlough, taking a much-needed break from camp life. However, they would
soon be recalled to their posts, as South met North in Louisiana, a sometimes overlooked theater of the war, in what is known as the Red River
Campaign. By mid-January, Cousin Sammy and the others took their leave
of home and hearth and began the trek toward the swamps of Louisiana to
repel yet another attempted Union invasion.

Although Texas had obviously been spared much of the fighting and
destruction that other Confederate states endured, there had nevertheless
been ongoing fears of a Union invasion. A year earlier, Lucy had written of
General Magruder retaking the city of Galveston. Other invasion attempts
had been made as well, at Sabine Pass in September and at Brownsville in
November. Now, as 1864 dawned, General Banks shifted his efforts inland
and began his Red River Campaign, a major offensive that, if successful,
would provide much-needed cotton for the textile manufacturers of the
North and a staging and supply area from which a Union army could maintain control over first Texas, then Arkansas and Louisiana.

As the spring approached, Banks's Northern forces matched themselves
against Tom Green's cavalry in battle after battle, skirmish after skirmish.
And the entries of Lucy's diary contained more and more references to the
fierce fighting in Louisiana.

JANUARY 1864

Jan 1st Friday ~ New Years day ~ Have done nothing the livelong day but read "The Missing Bride"[1] ~ played cards and in the eve that we might finish out the day well we girls all of us danced ~ Mr D seemed to enjoy ~~ourselves~~ our gaity as much as we did

Jan 6th Wednesday ~ This morn helped Sara to make out the post-office report & after dinner, mended my shoes. Had not gotten them done when we saw Neh, Em & Jennie Minton coming. Neh stayed but a short time then went to see Mr Wiley, brought him back with him to spend the night. Aunt Lu had such a nice supper for us. The boys had great times talking over their La [Louisiana] soldier life. Sara and I went and got some corn and pecans and Uncle Pier and I poped the corn.

Jan 7th Thursday ~ Neh, Em and Jennie stayed until after eleven. Brother and myself talked over old times coming down the river, about the changes of differences of opinions &c. I have got one of the best Texas brothers in the State and I most sincerely wish he might succeed in all his undertakings. Thermometer stood at 10° above zero on New Years day, at 18, Tuesday morn at 20 wednesday and today.

I am not at all well this eve have Jane's headache.

Jan 9th Saturday ~ Heard news yesterday that B~ B~ Lee was one of Jack Hamilton's[2] confederate's on his way out from Brownsville last week with mail for the Union men [who] was taken up and is now in Houston under arrest. Although report brings still further news of the

---

1. E.D.E.N. Southworth, *The Missing Bride* (Project Gutenberg), was published in 1855 by T. B. Peterson Publishing.

2. Andrew J. (Jack) Hamilton, a leader in Texas politics during the 1850s, served in the US House during the years immediately preceding the war. In 1861, as a member of a House committee assigned the task of solving the looming crisis, Hamilton made several major anti-slavery/anti-secession speeches in the North, earning him a hero's status there. According to *The Handbook of Texas Online*, early in 1862, President Lincoln rewarded Hamilton's efforts by commissioning him as brigadier general of volunteers and by appointing him military governor of Texas during the war. Hamilton accompanied Union forces on their attempted raid into south Texas during the fall of 1863, then spent most of the rest of the war in New Orleans. Following the war, he became the provisional governor of Texas. Obviously, Hamilton's secession stance and ties to the North brought him great censure among many Texans, the Pier household included.

fedrals landing along the coast, as yet we have heard of no great demon-
stration. Green's Reg~ arrived in Houston New-Years day. Wallers Batt
was at bayou Bueff~ at Pickens plantation on the 23rd waiting for two
companies to come up before they left on their homeward march. Capt
McDade arrived in Hempstead day before Christmas

Cousin S~ and myself went over to Mr Brewers this eve. Mr B~
accepted my proposition and give me $100. Left it to Mrs B~ and myself
to decide when school should commence and as the weather is now so
unsettled, and as Eliz~ is going to come down soon, we agreed on the
first monday in february[3]

Uncle Martin and Aunt Hannah came giving us all a great surprise,
quite an agreeable one. They told me of Dr Peebles ~ he is still at St Antonio Mrs P~ and Miss Rachie are with him ~ their board is $40. a day, or
$10~ a piece, gives something of an idea of the expense of every thing
now days.

Jan 10th Sunday ~ In the afternoon we girls had a good big fire made
up in the parlor and had a nice visit. In the eve my two Uncles played
a game of back-gammon. Sara read a story of Helen Mac Trevor or the
battle of Brandywine a tale of 1777, one of Milford Bard or John Lofland's
writings.[4] No preaching today.

Jan 12th Tuesday ~ Mail came at 12 brought a letter from cousin M Adams
who is now at Galveston. [He] writes quite despondingly, owing to the
fact of his wife having poor health and the probable invasion of Texas.
His own health he says is miserable and he knows not what may be the
consequences to his family should the war continue long, but dreads.

While we were at tea, Sukie Shelburn and Todie came running in to
tell us Wallers Battallion had gotten into Hempstead. Brother Jim had
got home and cousin Sammy would be here tomorrow.

---

3. The terms of Lucy's employment had changed since August. Instead of the $5 per child
each month to which Mr. Brewer agreed in August, he now proposed a flat rate of $100.

4. William W. Smithers, *The Life of John Lofland: The Milford Bard, the Earliest and Most Distinguished Poet of Delaware* (Philadelphia: Wallace M. Leonard, 1894). Among his many literary
accomplishments, John Lofland, the Milford Bard, wrote a variety of stories for *The Blue Hen's
Chicken*, a newspaper published in Wilmington, Delaware, during the mid-nineteenth century.
Lofland worked as the paper's literary editor and published several short stories in serial form.
Smithers, in his biography of Lofland, reports that Lofland, who battled opium addiction
throughout his adult life, reached the height of his fame and created great success for the newspaper through these stories.

Jan 13th Wednesday ~ Cousin Sara and I made some tea cakes for cousin Sammy this morn ~ while we were fixing them, Miss Mary Smith, Mrs Moore, little Theadore M and David Moore came to spend the day. We have been watching so close for cousin S~ that at last he slipped up on us before any one knew he was on the place. Came up to the back door and some of the negroes called out there comes Mars Sammy ~ and away we went. Sara got up on the big chest to look, Aunt Lu & Uncle Pier on the edge of the gallery and I started to run round the house. Cousin S~ has grown considerably ~ looks more manly than he used to[5]

Jan 15th Friday ~ Mollie and the others are to come here tomorrow. Mrs John Lotts baby died yesterday evening at 4.

Jan 16th Saturday ~ Went to the burial ~ In the eve America, Neh, Mollie, W~ Fordtran, Sara Catlin, Jake, Jim, Bennie, Mr Wiley, Sue, Sara Jane, Cy Campbell, Charlie Uecker & Adam Cloud were here ~ Aunt Lu had a nice supper which all seemed to enjoy. Had music and playing, but nearly every one looked sad, for all they laughed and tried to be merry

Jan 17th Sunday ~ Cousin Sammy left us this morn about half past 9, Uncle Pier and Aunt Lu going with him as far as Lu's. Not long after, Cy came by to tell us good-bye; Next Mollie, Em, Billy F~ and Neh went, then America and Jennie M. As they left, Josephine P~ came. While she was here, Mr Wiley came to tell us a last fare-well. It seemed sad to see the boys leave, yet not so much so as when they had to go to Louisiana ~ ~
       All had gone before 11, leaving us girls to lonesome-ness and thoughts, which it is not well to indulge in. Therefore we took books, and when that did not suffice I learned "Come back my Noble Warrior come." We girls dined and took our tea in the sitting room.

Jan 18th Monday ~ This morn while we were by ourselves, who should knock at the door but Capt Hunt ~ so changed in looks, he is but a shadow of his former self and seems sadder and more thoughtful than formerly. This war brings many changes ~ I'd sing war songs again if they would have similar effect. Capt H~ praises Mack C~ highly, says he thinks he will be home soon on furlough hope he may; says he thinks Chesley will get a discharge from the service. Spent a very pleasant day ~~with~~

5. Cousin Sammy had enlisted on July 22, 1861, his seventeenth birthday, and literally grew to manhood while in the army.

People are beginning to make gardens now and the planters are having cotton stalks pulled up preparing for ploughing. Very few round here are thinking of planting cotton this season.

Jan 19th Tuesday ~ We hear daily of more troops coming to Texas ~ Green's Brigade, Majors & Wallers Batt lately came and it is said Carters, Beufords & Parsons are on their way

Jan 20th Wednesday ~ went for Sara Jane to go with me out to Mr Cyrus Campbells to spend the night. Just after we got there, four men belonging to Baylor's Reg~ Hogh's or Hoghlin's company (Majors Brigade of Arizona notoriety)[6] came to stay over night. Poor fellows ~ every one sick, one with pneumonia; they all look like they had seen hard times~
They say their homes are at and near Bastrop.[7] They traveled 15 hours at one time since they started through the low flat country in La where they broke the ice at every step. Buried one poor fellow on their way in, had to throw down brush to lay him on that he should not be in the water. They told us that the hardest fight they had had was at Bordeux where they, some 1500 strong, charged the enemy, 6000 in number. Mrs C asked them were they tired of fighting and the reply went round the circle ~ yes'm I am ~ yes'm we are ~ yes'm I am.
It looks to me like every one was tired of war and if they are not, should be.
Fanny played for them in the eve: "Shiloah" and several other tunes, "Do They Miss Me at Home" for one.[8]

---

6. Harry McCorry Henderson, *Texas in the Confederacy* (San Antonio: Naylor, 1955), 95. According to Colonel Harry McCorry Henderson, James Patrick Major's brigade had merged with General Sibley's old brigade in preparation for the upcoming campaign in Louisiana. There is every probability that Lucy's derisive phrase "Arizona notoriety" comes from her knowledge of Sibley's campaign in New Mexico and Arizona during the winter of 1861–1862. *The Handbook of Texas Online* explains that Sibley's plan had been to subdue and control the western regions for the Confederacy, but following his defeat at Glorieta Pass (the westernmost battle of the war) and his loss of a crucial supply train, five hundred Texans marched east to a military prison in Illinois, and five hundred more died—an incredibly high price in the view of many, including Lucy.

7. Bastrop, Texas, located approximately thirty miles southeast of Austin, was first settled as an outpost in 1804, but saw little development until cotton and slavery were introduced in the area in 1839.

8. James M. McPherson, *Ordeal by Fire: The Civil War and Reconstruction*, 2nd ed. (New York: McGraw-Hill, 1992), 229; Will S. Hays, "The Drummer Boy of Shiloh" (Augusta: Blackmar & Bro., 1863), American Song Sheets, Duke University Libraries Digital Collections. Several

Jan 21st *Thursday* ~ I embroidered eight points today. Soldiers left soon this morn, two traded off their pony's for some fresh ones; got one of Mr C~ and one of John Edwards. The ones they brought from La look like they were hardly able to carry them they are so very poor. After dinner heard Mr J~ Edwards was to be married on sunday next ~ run-away match to take place at Mrs SinClare's

I was much alarmed, fearing the news might take my strength away so I could not walk. However, I managed to walk here after an hour or so and think I will be able to survive the terriable stroke as cousin S~ has promised to give me a dose of morphine if I begin to get to serious.

Jan 22nd Friday ~ Cousin W~ came just before dark to spend the night. Says Mr D [Darnman] is no better, Willie is not at all well. Lu is hard at work weaving jeans for W~ pants. every body in the man line between the ages of 18 and 50 met at Bellville to report to the enrolling officer and bean [be in] an examination Quite a goodly number were conscripted.

Jan 23rd Saturday ~ Mrs Jim Middleton and husband came. Mrs M~ wanted me to go stay with her a month as Mr M is going off into the army ~ would like much to do so, but do not think I can under all the circumstances

Jan 24th Sunday ~ Most of the Battallion have been dismounted for a short time, and sent below to Via Point Were dismounted to give their horses a chance to recruit.[9]

MARGINAL NOTE: *Jimmy Francis died at home Jan 24th 1864*

---

popular pieces were written around the Battle of Shiloh, which occurred in the spring of 1862 and was, as McPherson records, "America's baptism in total war" (229). The songs written in conjunction with that battle, such as "The Drummer Boy of Shiloh" and "Lucilla, the Maid of Shiloh," gained great favor with those waiting at home. Other songs, such as "Do They Miss Me at Home," enjoyed increased popularity as the war dragged on. These songs, and many others from the era, can be found in the Historic American Sheet Music collection in Duke University Libraries Digital Collections.

9. Henderson, *Texas in the Confederacy*, 95. According to Henderson, Waller's battalion left Louisiana, arriving in Houston on December 25, 1863. From Houston, the troops traveled to Virginia Point, a heavily fortified post on the mainland seven miles west of Galveston. Here they remained for a month.

Jan 25th Monday ~ Commenced making my shoes this morn, went over to Mr Withers to get him to fix the soles. While there Syvilia came to tell me Miss Lucy was at our house so I went home. Heard something of a history of the "Star" (Jim) of his writing home six letters and her not answering but one, and it was only that he was a soldier that she wrote that. Such sentences as "I shall never forget the pressure of the hand you gave me as we parted" "How I long to imprint a kiss upon thy pure and noble fore-head" &c disgusted her ~ Oh wealth, how great thy charm; and vanity, thy pride. Every day we see it proved that money makes the man. Ju[s]t before tea who should walk in but Hezzie Harvey. Says he left camps yesterday morn, came to Mr Cochranes and found that Jimmy Francis, Lydia's brother died at 10 AM on sunday after a very short illness. Was taken sick on thursday and buried today. I regret very much to hear of it for I thought a great deal of him.

Jan 27th Wednesday ~ Emily Lott was here yesterday and told Aunt Lu that Mr Darnman was very low and that on sunday he had such a severe spell they did not think he would live through it. So us girls fixed up and went down there. Met Mr Clemons negroe man who went in Mr C's place as wagoner. He told us Morins Battallion was camped on Ive's creek. Took dinner with Mr Haferd the county commissioner and Mr Stewart, a member of Morin's B~ was acting as Quarter-master

Cousin W~ sold them 4 or 500 lbs of meat, pork, bought 50 bushels of corn in the shuck and 10 bushels of meal. And the men took it upon themselves to pocket Lu's sausages, except enough for two meals of victuals.

However, neather cousin W~ or Lu took it to heart very seriously. Said they knew those men enjoyed their broiled sausage.

Jan 28th Thursday ~ The folks got back just at tea time. Aunt H~ was well, told Sara what a time she had. Said that Kinch Collins was in Mr Lee's office [the dentist] and after she [Aunt Hannah] was under the influence, she got up and went across the room to tell Uncle M~ she wanted to go out.[10] Had to whisper so loud they all heard her. Then Uncle M~ had to go to Mr Lee to find out where to go to ~ went into a back-room and sit over a crack.

---

10. Lucy's account of Aunt Hannah's "situation" was indeed one of her most personal entries.

Jan 29th Friday ~ Came home this morn ~ Mr D~ lost his mule yesterday ~ died with glanders.[11] Cousin W~ commenced ploughing two weeks ago, all the folks are making gardens down here We had card playing, seven-up[12] until ten ~ Mr C~ helped me

Jan 30th Saturday ~ Nothing would do Mrs C~ but I must stay until evening.

Arrived at home, found Mr Middleton come to see if there was no hopes for me to go to stay with his wife while he was gone [He] went over to Mr Brewers to see him and came back soon to tell me he had given his consent to my coming & he was to come for me in the morn.

Jan 31st Sunday ~ Put my dry-goods together this morn and just as I was ready, Mr M~ came for me. Found Mrs M looking for us

FEBRUARY 1864

As Jack Cochran related his tale to Lucy during their visit on February 1, he unknowingly touched on a shift of perception sweeping through armies on both sides of the conflict. "Cowardice," as he described it, was the antithesis of the attribute of courage, the quality so lauded by soldiers and civilians alike. Gerald Linderman provides an excellent discussion of this concept of courage, its uses, and its abuses in his book *Embattled Courage*. Linderman explains that the concept of courage, a "heroic action undertaken without fear," initially was linked to godliness, honor, and manliness. It exhibited the old ideals of knightliness and chivalry, a respect for one's opponent, coupled with bravery, courage, and integrity. Robert E. Lee's General Order 73 exalted this ideal as he gave lofty justification for restraint.[13] Stonewall Jackson

---

11. According to the Centers for Disease Control, glanders primarily affects horses, but can also be found in donkeys and mules. Humans can contract the disease through association with infected animals, but since the 1940s, no human cases have been reported in the United States. However, the disease is endemic among animals in Africa, Asia, India, Central America, and South America.

12. Seven-Up, also known as All Fours, was a popular nineteenth-century card game dating back to seventeenth-century England. According to the *Encyclopedia Britannica*, the game, though somewhat simple in nature, gave rise to more-complex games involving bidding and partnership play.

13. Gerald F. Linderman, *Embattled Courage* (New York: Free Press, 1987), 181. Linderman explains that Lee's General Order 73, dated June 27, 1863, required soldiers to uphold civilization and Christianity as they resisted any temptation to seek vengeance against a civilian population.

became the standard-bearer for the South in his fearlessness, yet Linderman indicates that he also became the "precursor of the way the war would eventually be fought," as he personally "sever[ed] from courage its gentler, more tolerant aspects and, two years before others, [began to advance] a war of utmost stringency."[14]

By 1864, the grim realities of the battlefield, with the gruesome deaths witnessed and the horrendous injuries sustained, had exacted a blow to the genteel concept of courage for many. A hardness among combatants, a mental and emotional insulation necessary to cope with the barrage of inhumanity, had emerged, and actions once deemed inadmissible were now commonplace. Lucy's diary contains references to foraging,[15] to mementos retrieved from fallen adversaries, unseemly social conduct, and now, with Jack's story, violence and murder. Linderman shows that these avenues of conduct were a result of a justification whereby acts "initially unacceptable and even repugnant were converted to the casually admissible." The progression created a downward spiral that broadened the scope from "foraging to looting to destruction" and led to further actions that exceeded any battlefield landscape, spilling over into civilian and camp settings. The longer the war continued, the more brutal many of the participants would become and the more widespread the atrocities. Those, like Jack, who retained vestiges of the old ideals were repulsed by the conduct of others, but even they became inured to the scenes of brutality. The tenor of Lucy's diary would reflect this shift, and as 1864 wore on, she would give space to more and more of these encounters.

At the same time, her entries reflect a hardening perception toward General Magruder. Although Texans had hailed General John Bankhead Magruder's heroism in the capture of the *Harriet Lane* and the retaking of Galveston, time had passed and situations had changed. Magruder, whose wife lived at a great distance and whose existence was not necessarily known, had a fondness for parties and dancing, and for this was awarded the appellation "Prince John." *The Handbook of Texas Online* quotes an acquaintance who reported that Magruder could "fight all day and dance all night," a delight that he did not attempt to conceal. This proclivity garnered condemnation from the public, as shown in an article in the *Austin State Gazette* in March 1864,which

---

14. Ibid., 16–17, 178–179.

15. Ibid., 184. Confiscation of the local population's supplies, also known as foraging, was practiced by both sides of the conflict. Linderman recounts that as early as 1862, Southern soldiers began to know the deprivations of food. He writes: "To go a day without food became common experience, and it was not unusual for those marching or fighting to be issued no rations for two days, occasionally three or four" (184); 190–191.

leveled a scathing criticism of Magruder's frivolous extravagances that echo Lucy's observations, reporting that "Balls and supper parties continue to be the order of the day—or rather night," and citing reports of "a most elegant affair, arranged with exquisite taste." The *Gazette* then harshly denounced Magruder's profligacy, stating:

> "Elegant affair, arranged with exquisite taste," while more than half the people in the country are suffering for the necessaries of life! While private property in Galveston is being destroyed to furnish fuel for the soldiers, balls and parties, costing thousands of dollars, are given to the commanding General and his staff, and the boats that might be employed in transporting necessaries to the troops stationed there, find constant employment in carrying pleasure parties between Houston and Galveston.[16]

The sarcastic tone of the editorial effectively conveys the *Gazette*'s censure, adding barbs to Lucy's mild observation. However, with the passing of another year, Lucy's own frustration and displeasure with Magruder would equal that of the newspapers.

———〜———

Feb 1st Monday ~ We were up betimes this morn and Mr Middleton left us at half past six. Jack Cochrane took dinner here with us ~

Jack says his Reg are all under arrest for disobeying orders. They were ordered to dismount and go to Via-Point, but they said it was not their turn now and the other two of the brigade must dismount first, as they went into the last fight on foot. McEwin then told them he would not furnish them forage. Whereupon they set out and pressed corn fodder &c until they were better supplied, he says, than they had been before since the war.

Jack also told us of a circumstance that happened in La. One of the men in Green's Brig~ took a prisoner, a Dutchman, carried [him] back to the rear and wanted the commander to give him in charge to some person else. He replied, no ~ he must take him himself. so back he went with him a ways. And then said he had walked all over Arizona, Texas & La to get into a fight, and never had been in one and now ~ damn it, he was not going to be cheated out of it. So in cold blood, shot the fellow in the back and left.

---

16. *Austin State Gazette*, March 16, 1864, Texas and Other Southern States Civil War Newspapers/Newspaper Research, 1861–1865.

Jack said he did not like such cowardice as that in any one.

Feb 2nd Tuesday ~ Mrs M~ has read all three volumes of *The Children of the Abbey*[17] since I came ~ Mrs M~ planted peper peas and mustard this eve ~ they had commenced planting corn. The prospect looks discouraging, no rain or signs of it as yet

Feb 3rd Wednesday ~ Mrs M wrote to her husband and Uncle M this morn, I wrote to Aunt H~ this P.M. Will took the letters to the office. Found Will with a letter from Mr M~ he writes from Houston. met Dr Austin there and he told him to go on to his company, apply for a discharge and if he did not get one, he would be sent to Chapel-Hill to the hospital. And there he would take charge of him and he should have a furlough which should be renewed every 3 or 4 weeks. I am in hopes he will be home soon. I am so anxious to commence school. Finished one pair of drawers yesterday and commenced the others this morning

Feb 6th Saturday ~ Mr Lee came soon this morn. Extracted fifteen teeth for [Aunt H~] and got through before eleven. Aunt H~ took whiskey and morphine, stood it extremely well. Never lay down at all until she went to bed. Mr Lee's bill for coming out and all was $50 Confederate money ~ he charged $20 for taking out the four he had extracted before, so in all 'twas $70

Feb 7th Sunday ~ Uncle M says they heard that Bragg & staff attempted to cross the Miss [Mississippi River] not long since and were captured

Feb 8th Monday ~ Aunt H~ and Uncle M came by soon this morn on their way to Chapel Hill to see the dentist: Aunt thought he had left the root of one tooth in her mouth and went to have it out, but on returning this eve found she was mistakened.

---

17. *The Children of the Abbey*, Literary Notices, *New York Mirror: A Weekly*, 6:6, August 16, 1828, C19 the Nineteenth Century Index. It is no wonder that Lucy writes of Mrs. Middleton's enjoyment of this work. *The Children of the Abbey*, written in four volumes by Regina Maria Roche and published originally in 1796, enjoyed great popularity throughout the nineteenth century. According to a review published in the August 16, 1828, issue of the *New York Mirror: A Weekly Gazette of Literature and the Fine Arts*, the work embodied an enduring and endearing quality, recalling "the delight it afforded [in one's memories of] earlier days of romance and youth."

Feb 9th Tuesday ~ Mr M~ says he heard the order that took him down was countermanded, they have no use for him. Went to Columbia, stayed over night. while there Gen Magruder & Smith passed up. Nearly every one there seemed down on Magruder. [Mr M] says that a few days before, there were 60 of Pyrons men (Arizona troops) deserted and 200 were sent in pursuit and none returned. Also, that Hollands brigade had been ordered to Cypress city, but took a different route. Said they had no use for Cypress city. He also heard that Buckell's men say their time will be up in april and that they intended to go home then. That the C~ [Confederacy] had gone up a spout and 'twas no use talking ~ *so say some*

Feb 11th Thursday ~ (Had a letter from Mack) ~ Slept with Miss E~ last night she told me great tales of Gen Magruder and some of the ladies of Houston and Richmond. Among others, Mrs Geo Chambers name was mentioned.

Mr & Mrs M came to take me home. Came in the buggy ~ broke down out in the prarie ~ but tied up our vehicle with raw-hide strings so that we came safely to Uncle P's. Found all well. Was vaxcinated[18] this eve ~ was a great bravo about it too.

Feb 12th Friday ~ Cousin Sara and myself went over to Mr B's this morn to let them know I was ready to report for duty. Found my school-room turned into a hospital ~ also a sick gentleman, Mr Wm Brown, in Mrs B's room. The gent in my room belongs to McNeil's Co and is very low indeed. Looks to me like 'twould be impossible to save him.

Lieut Cleveland came over this eve to tell Uncle P~ the "Exempts" were ordered to report in Hempstead for duty tomorrow. He has just returned from Austin, says all is as quiet as need be up there. Are not looking for or fearing Jack Hamilton's coming.

There is a sick soldier by the name of Perkins here, brought while we were gone. [He] has Sara's room, and such a turning about of things ~ the post-office is taken into Aunt Lu's room and us girls dry goods taken up stairs. Mr Chapman has another sick man at his house. Uncle P~ has had eight turkeys stolen by this company

---

18. Stefan Riedel, "Edward Jenner and the History of Smallpox and Vaccination," *Baylor University Medical Center Proceedings*, January 18, 2005. Lucy noted her own vaccination against smallpox with a lighthearted jab at her own courage. Vaccination as a way to protect against smallpox and cowpox had been available since the beginning of the nineteenth century, thanks to the work of Edward Jenner and others. However, it was still new enough that it was viewed with some ambivalence, as Lucy's entry suggests.

Uncle M told me there was two soldiers stayed at Dr P~'s not long ago who sayed that Bragg and Staff were en-route for Tex. got attempted to cross the Miss~ and were taken prisoners. That Gerard Groce was on his staff and if it was true, he had probably taken an unexpected trip to Yankie-dom. They knew G had started home. Writing the name Groce makes me think of the weding. I heard Green's men some 4 or 500 went to Col Blake's that night. Stole the groom's $200. hat, a great many silver forks from the table, a silver plate and all the blankets, saddles, bridles &c they could get. Ladies had to hide their shawls.

Feb 13th Saturday ~ Jimmy left soon this morn. Soldiers have been coming in all day. That man who was sick in my school-room died last night, was buried this P.M. Dr McLarins children all came by and went to the burying
Sallie Catlin came over this eve to spend the night. Played for our sick man and he says the music was better than all the medicine, liked to have made him forget he was sick. Cut out my coat today, so farewell to horse-back riding as I have no skirt now.

Feb 19th Friday ~ Ruf met us not far from the house. Found Jack Cochrane and Capt John at our house when I got there. Jack says one of McNellie's men killed another next day after leaving Travis.

Feb 20th Saturday ~ 'Tis still cold. vegetation seems much injured by the norther ~ all who had corn up will loose it. There was ice this and yesterday morn. A goodly number of the planters in this part of the country only commenced puting in their corn last week. Uncle Pier says he had all of his oats killed.
Finished my linen Chesterfield[19] this eve with Sara's help. She made one sleeve. Aunt Lu gave me such a pretty cord & tassil to go with it. I am so proud of it.
People commenced gardening this week ~ planted radishes, peas, and some beans.

Feb 21st Sunday ~ Wonderful ~ most wonderful ~ day has passed without any person being here to stay any time. I read most of the day ~ wrote a letter to John Harvey and a note in Saras letter to Mr Wiley.

19. A Chesterfield, according to the OED, was a long, straight coat that was often single-breasted.

Feb 22nd Monday ~ Washington's birthday, but no thoughts of festal boards as in days of yore. In its stead are daily heard reports of war, where many a field can testify of the cruel results arising there from. God grant my friends may be few who pay the dear sacrifice life for the cause in which they are engaged. Found Mrs Brewer, Eliz & Rufus in bed this morn and Lissie and Bell feeling as if that were their most comfortable place. Mr B~ was home saturday eve from Hempstead where he had been tax collecting, but went to Millheim[20] yesterday again.

This eve just after we had eaten supper, he came again, was so anxious about his sick.

Feb 23rd Tuesday ~ Mr B~ was off at two this morn. All seem to be improving. Had a letter from Mr Wiley today in answer to mine of the 14th ~ they were still at Via Point but anticipated going to the mouth of Caney soon.

Feb 24th Wednesday ~ All are up this eve, and to celebrate the event we had a dance. Sack playing the violin a part of the time and Mr Brown some. Us girls waltzed ~ danced polka & schotisch ~ then we all danced a reel. Sack knocked the bones one or two peices and Judge patted.[21] We are a lively set to night

Feb 25th Thursday ~ News came in the paper we got to day of a fight near Jackson, Miss, where Gen Lee had defeated Sherman ~ and taken 6000 killed & wounded 6000. Also a report that Knoxville was now in the hands of the Confederate forces[22]

Yankee news say that Maryland has given her majority vote in favor of Lincoln's re-election. The report we heard last week of one of McNellie's men being killed is a mistake ~'twas one of their old company at Galveston. Heard also that Carters men were bound for Texas come what would

---

20. Millheim, a German settlement approximately eight miles south of Bellville, was established in the 1840s.

21. *Webster's New World Dictionary* explains that bones, such as a pair of cow's ribs, can be knocked together as a way of keeping time or producing a discernible rhythm. "Patting" would involve a quick, gentle tap or touch of the hand, or even a pair of spoons, to the leg or a hard surface in order to keep time.

22. McPherson, *Ordeal by Fire*, 333. Again, Lucy's source provided incorrect information. As McPherson reports, Jackson, Mississippi, had been abandoned by Joe Johnston's forces in July in order to prevent another siege such as Vicksburg (331). Knoxville had likewise been secured by Union forces when, on September 3, 1863, Ambrose E. Burnside entered the city, "finally achieving Lincoln's cherished goal of liberating East Tennessee" (333).

Feb 26th Friday ~ Such weather. This week has been really warm ~ and last so cold as to kill all corn, rye, oats &c that were up.

Feb 28th Sunday ~ Cousin Waller told us of Mr Buck's having his Gin ~ 150 bales of cotton and a good wagon burned up not long since. Don't know how they come on fire. 60 bags of cotton were boiled, ready for market ~ a loss that can not be replaced these times.

Feb 29th Monday ~ A gentleman from Hargroves company came by here to spend the night. Says there [are] over 200 men who have been vaxcinated at Caney ~ suffering with fever &c caused from virus. Magruder has ordered no more shall use it. Forgot to say the cause of his returning home was on account of his arm

Lucy began February's entries with a blend of local concerns and war-related worries; she ended with anxiety over suspicious vaccinations given to the troops in northern Texas. Even as she had recorded her own vaccination with tongue-in-cheek bravado, she and Sarah both wrote ominously of perhaps one of the most foreboding rumors that circulated in the area around Travis in early 1864. While Lucy commented briefly on a report of some two hundred men in Hargrove's Company who had been vaccinated and who were now sick, she merely recorded that Magruder had forbidden the use of any further vaccine without detailing the reason behind the order. Sarah, however, gave more details in her account:

Some have suffered dreadfully from vaccination up in northern Texas and other places. A poison virus was circulated through some parts of the state—which caused the persons vaccinated to break out in ulcers and a loathsome humor and many have had their arms amputated and some have died from it. It is said, but I can't say how it is—that the Yankees had some of our prisoners vaccinated with it—on purpose . . .
    Sarah Pier, 2/23/64

With careful word choice, Sarah graphically indicated what Lucy's entry omitted—an accusation of an overt plot by the North to introduce a form of biological warfare within Southern ranks.

CHAPTER 9

MARCH–APRIL
1864

Got the papers to day ~ in one place says Lee defeated Sherman & took
2500 prisoners, ~ in another that Sherman had reinforcements and Lee had retreat.

LUCY P. STEVENS,
March 3, 1864

THE MONTH OF MARCH would claim the beginning of the Red River Campaign, but even before these battles began, reports of much-needed Confederate victories were being sounded. Lucy's March 3 entry notes these triumphs, yet cites conflicting accounts in the newspaper; unfortunately, it is impossible to corroborate her interpretation of the news, since she mentioned neither date nor title of the papers she had read. She indicated that the newspaper reported a direct confrontation between Sherman and Lee; though the newspaper did carry such a report, no confrontation actually happened. However, given the frequent erroneous information circulated via rumor and/or the press, it is quite possible that Lucy's interpretation is not as much at fault as the report itself. As she continued recording bits and pieces of war information during March and April, she very casually and unconsciously acknowledged the positioning of Confederate leaders and troops for what is now known as the Red River Campaign, the last major push by Union forces toward Texas. Many of the Travis boys would participate in this campaign as the Confederate defenders in Louisiana marshaled their forces against Banks's Union army.

But as the local boys now began arriving for a final furlough before their departure to Louisiana, the frequency and fervor of parties skyrocketed. With the coming danger to the soldiers casting a dark shadow, the need to be together was almost palpable. During the next weeks, in fact, Lucy recorded many instances of parties and gatherings that connected the young people, allowing them to draw strength from one another as they mustered the courage for what lay ahead.

The impending departure of the soldier boys signaled a distinct shift in Lucy's own thinking as well. Although she had written many times about attempting to send letters north, her entry of March 20 marks her first mention of a possible return. And although she did include the snippet of information in her journal, her casual lack of comment indicates that she did not put much credence in the idea. Yet, however insignificant the mention seemed at the time, the pieces of the puzzle were slowly beginning to fall into place for Lucy's return to Ohio. Within a year, Miss Mary Smith's departure from Texas would prove to be pivotal for Lucy's future.

MARCH 1864

Mar 3rd Thursday ~ This has been almost like a summer's day ~ 'tis so warm again. Got the papers to day, in one place says Lee defeated Sherman & took 2500 prisoners, in another that Sherman had reinforcements and Lee had to retreat. Gen Wharton has been ordered this side of the river to report to E. Kirby Smith and Gen Waul is sent to La to report [to] Gen. Walker. Mr B~ was telling us this eve of one of the Capts in Green's B~ going to Mr English's to get corn & fodder. He [Mr English] gave him some and told him he had never yet refused a soldier any, but in future, he would be obliged to do so as he had not more than enough for his own use and to plant. Whereupon the Capt laughed and told him he might as well give it as to have it taken. This made Mr E~ angry and he told him to come on, but he would warn them that the first man who touched a blade would be apt to get shot. So that eve he loaded up a six shooter, a five and a double barrelled gun and took his stand. By doing so, overheard a deserter's conversation with one of his servants. [He] distrusted the man ~ informed on him and put him into the hands of an officer.

Mar 4th Friday ~ Came home this eve, found Sara had a note from Sallie, a letter from Kate P, & one from Mr W. The latter sent word to "his old lady" her letter came safe.[1]

---

1. Carrying on the same terminology that she has used for herself and "her old man," Lucy indicated that Mr. Wiley had sent a letter to Sarah, giving substance to the suspicion that the two were, in fact, a couple. In subsequent journal entries, Lucy would track the ongoing courtship.

Mar 5th Saturday ~ Made my calico waist today and cut out two white ones ~ a swiss and jaconet.[2]

Three men took dinner here today, one from Waller's B~ and two exchanged prisoners belonging to Green's B~. [They] were taken at Camp Pratt near N. Iberia[3] in Oct. Say the Yankees did not treat them well while in N O~ but the ladies were extremely kind. Brought them clothes, food &c.[4] The man says Wallers command have gone to Columbia.[5]

Mar 8th Tuesday ~ All spining again today. After school closed I came over home. Sammy & Mr Linn. Cousin S~ received the meat Uncle Pier sent him. Came just in the nick of time, for they were nearly starved. nothing but poor beef & corn bread to eat.

Mar 9th Wednesday ~ Sue came runing in to tell me Savilia had come to tell me Sammy was home ~ so Lissie and I came to see him.

Mrs B~ told us as we started to tell Aunt Lu she had spun 6 cuts & 20 rounds today & carded it herself. Bell, 6½.[6] The reason of the boys

---

2. Lucy used several sewing terms in this entry to describe the garments she was working on and the fabrics that she was using. A "waist" refers to a blouse, and "swiss" and "jaconet" are fabrics, both of which are lightweight muslin, suitable for blouses.

3. Thomas Ayres, *Dark and Bloody Ground: The Battle of Mansfield and the Forgotten Civil War in Louisiana* (Dallas: Taylor Publishing, 2001), 191. Located on Bayou Teche in southern Louisiana, New Iberia and nearby Camp Pratt endured bursts of fighting throughout the war. Camp Pratt, a Confederate conscription camp during 1862 and 1863, trained as many as 3,000 conscripts. According to Ayres, on October 1, 1863, General William B. Franklin, working in conjunction with General Nathaniel Banks, moved Union troops toward the Red River and "two days later, occupied New Iberia without opposition" (191). The men of whom Lucy wrote quite possibly could have been captured during this confrontation.

4. Ibid., 147. Following General Banks's appointment as General Benjamin Butler's replacement in New Orleans, the population of the region enjoyed a respite from the harsh treatment they had previously endured during Butler's tenure. Ayres reports that Banks, an astute politician, "released hundreds of political prisoners, reopened churches and newspapers, and restored many private homes to their owners."

5. Harry McCorry Henderson, *Texas in the Confederacy* (San Antonio: Naylor, 1955), 95–96. Henderson reports that following a month's furlough in Texas, the regiments of Sibley's brigade, as well as Waller's cavalry battalion, traveled by rail to Columbia, Texas, on February 19, 1864, to begin their march to Louisiana.

6. Lorelei Caracausa and Margaret Humphries, Fort Worth Weavers Guild, "Yarn Sizing" (E-mail interview with Vicki Tongate, June 19, 2009). According to Caracausa, "A cut of wool is 300 yards. A turn would be 2yds. The difference is that a cut is a single thread, the initial spinning on the wheel. The turn is when you have taken that single and plied it with another like thread to create the usable yarn." Thus Mrs. Brewer managed to spin 1,800 yards of single thread and 40 yards of usable yarn that day.

coming home now is sore arms from vaccination[7] & in about ten or 15 days think they will have to start for La

Mar 10th Thursday ~ Jim came in a few moments this morn to let cousin S~ know they were ordered to report at H~ [Hempstead] at 3~ P.M., to go from there to C.H. [Chappell Hill] to the hospital to be examined and receive furloughs. Our storm turned out in a norther.

Mar 11th Friday ~ Jim B~ came this eve. Says the boys will all be here tomorrow, that the party last night did not satisfy Sammy & Jake, they were going to stay to one at Mr Ferrils to night.

Mar 12th Saturday ~ Poor Mollie, I fear her time for this world is but short. We are so often reminded that death loves a shining mark, but not more forcibly than in her case.[8]

Mar 13th Sunday ~ Cousin Sara went to see Mrs Edwards again this morn ~ found her about the same. I reread a package of Louise Stevens' letters, read one of Lotts[9] last night. It almost seemed like old times.

    As I was reading my last, this morn cousin Sammy came. [He came] from Hempstead yesterday, stayed at Mr Cochrane's last night. Just before dinner Jack and Mr Lawrance, the gentleman Jack has been

---

7. O. A. McGinnis, editor, *Galveston Weekly News*, March 16, 1864, Texas and Other Southern States Civil War Newspapers/Newspaper Research, 1861-1865. Lucy and Sarah had already written about the complication associated with the smallpox vaccinations, and it seems that the problems were widespread. The side effects of the vaccine frequently caused soreness, and many remedies were offered. In a front-page article in the March 16, 1864, edition of the *Galveston Weekly News*, O. A. McGinnis wrote of one such remedy:

> Take sage leaves and vinegar, boil together, thicken with corn meal, and make poultice, apply to the wound for three days and nights, changing morning and night for fresh one, and treat constitutionally as follows: Take 1 tablespoonful sulphur, 1 do of cream tartar, mixed with molasses, every other morning, and every other morning a dose of salts and cream tartar. When the poultice is changed, the sore should be washed with camphor. This course faithfully followed will cure the worst arm in the State in less than one week.

8. As she reflected on her friend's passing, Lucy again appropriated her knowledge of literature, quoting Edward Young, an eighteenth-century British poet who had written *The Complaint, or Night Thoughts on Life, Death, and Immortality*, following the deaths of his wife and other close family members. This line, and many others from the work, had become part of the popular culture of the time.

9. This letter from Lucy's sister Lottie would have been received before August 1861, per Lucy's entry of December 13, 1863.

nursing came. Mr L~ has seven cuts on his head and neck, the worst on the left side of his neck. He said he would not mind being cut by a white man, but to be cut by a dutchman was more than he could bear.[10]

Jimmy came while we were at dinner. Jack is on his way to his command bound for La~ Johnie Harvey came just as Jack started off. Was so glad to see him. It will be two years in August since he left

Mar 14th Monday ~ A man who says his name is Nantz from Port Sullivan Milam county, and purporting to belong to Hood's Brigade stayed here last night. He tells some awful talk, says up near where he lives, Quantril's men killed some men & burned some at the stake. I don't know if they were deserters or Jayhawkers. No I am mistakened; he says that took place in Mo. And says that they would walk up to a Dutchman, go to shake hands with him & blow his brains out, but says the Feds commenced it ~ undoubtedly. The boys are all busy fixing off for a party at Buckhorn at Mr Ringers comes off tonight.

Gave cousin Sammy my watch yesterday. I feel under very many obligations to Uncle Pier and family, and think that the little that lies within my power to do for them I should do. Uncle P will not receive a dime for my doctors bill, which was $84. Besides are all the time doing me many little kindnesses, making me presents &c

Mar 15th Tuesday ~ There is to be a party at Mr Francis tomorrow eve. Cousin Sammy came by and told us all who loved to dance were invited. So Lissie and I are going, I to see my soldier friends. Therefore have spent the eve preparing.

Mar 16th Wednesday ~ Went over to school this morn and in the eve, Sack for an escort, we went to the party. Was much surprised to find Mollie there; came from Independence[11] the day before with Nehemiah. Em too was at the party. Danced with Neh, Hez 2, Kinch 2 times, Lieut Perins,

---

10. Prejudice against the Dutch and Moravian immigrants can be inferred from the earliest pages of Lucy's diaries. Early in January 1863, she wrote of the community's fear of insurrection and linked both groups to these suspected uprisings. Fear and distrust, even hatred, consumed many in the community, and this spilled over into every aspect of their conduct and conversation, as evidenced in Lucy's entry on March 14, 1864.

11. Independence, founded in 1835, was a significant religious and educational center during the days of the Republic of Texas, winning the bid for the establishment there of Baylor University in 1845. From its inception, Baylor, a Baptist institution, included a Female Department, offering a full range of advanced courses to the young women who attended.

Jimmy C, Ino H ~ 2, Mr Rice, Jim B, Jake & Shiloah ~ thus ended. I never enjoyed myself more at a party in my life, got to dance with every one who was there that I wanted to, and one that I did not want too. Everybody seemed sociable and I felt so. Danced with Billy Fordtrans once.

Mar 18th Friday ~ Mr Wiley went over to Mr Brewers with me this morn. I had given up all idea of going to the party at Mollies, but ~~Neh~~ Mollie seemed so dissapointed and E~ told me I might take her horse & saddle, so I went. Came home directly after dinner. found cousin Sammy in a quandary, wondering if he should go or not. Was glad I came to decide the matter. Arrived at Mr Co's just after dark. They were just going to supper.

Kinch cornered Mollie back of the piano. Neh & Hez got one on one side and the other on the opposite, Ark over in the corner, just where Neh could see both of us. And by the by, he had been talking to him ~ commenced on me, and freely I admit that since my youthful days I have not been more teased. I wanted to take big-buddie out and whip him. Pulled candy with Hez, or tried too, but did not succeed. Candy was put on at 1P.M. and was not done until after 12. I don't know what we would have done if it had not been for Neh and Hez to night ~ made good wall flowers.

Mar 19th Saturday ~ Went by Mr Obryant's this morn, found Uncle M~ and cousin W there. Sue Wilson has improved so much. Mrs O~ had just received a letter from a mess-mate of her son Williams's in [. . .]. He was wounded in the battle at Sharpsburg in the hip, and fell into the hands of the Fedrals.[12]

Uncle M~ is talking of going to ~~the~~ Mexico soon ~ cousin W~ is trying to get a detail to go ~ has to raize five teams to take forty bales ~ I am so in hopes they will succeed

---

12. James M. McPherson, *Ordeal by Fire: The Civil War and Reconstruction*, 2nd ed. (New York: McGraw-Hill, 1992), 286. The Battle of Sharpsburg, or Antietam, as the North referred to it, was pivotal in the war's final outcome, and, according to McPherson, was the "bloodiest single day of the war." Tactically, the battle was a draw, but the cost to the South was irreparable. Lee's hopes of an invasion and subsequent end to the war lay in ruins. In addition to the terrible cost to the armies, this battle marked the first time that the American public was confronted with the grim realities of the carnage. McPherson states that two photographers in Matthew Brady's employ recorded the battle on film and displayed the images in Brady's studio in New York City. The stark images of the dead forced the public to abandon any romantic notions of war and accept the real suffering and sacrifice that enveloped them.

Mar 20th Sunday ~ Bid Jimmy a last good-bye as he and Neh starts tuesday; the command started on friday last.

Arrived at home, found Mr Wiley & Jake here. By going away Friday, I missed seeing Mack & Jimmy Clemons as they came to talk with us that eve. Mr Wiley says he and Mack like to have fought a duel, got so far as to order coffee & pistols for two. Mack invited him to come over with him, and he politely thanked him he had just come from here.[13]

Uncle Pier says Mr Ayers came over yesterday to let me know that there was a chance for Miss Mary Smith to go home which she meant to improve. He starts tomorrow morn for Galveston to arrange the papers, offered to see to getting some for me at the same time if I chose to go.

Mar 21st Monday ~ Lissie came and told me "Lieut Campbell had come." I was most truly glad to see him ~ it has been a year ago the 31st of last July since their command started from Hempstead and many is the weary mile they have traveled since then. However he looks none the worse for it. Mack seems so friendly, just like old times, if not a little more so. Spoke of the many changes since he left, of the unfriendly feeling existing in the neighborhood and said it marred his enjoyment much. There has been a great deal said against Mr C~ C~, but I think it will die a natural death by giving it time.[14]

I asked in regard to what Dr ~ told here at the dinner table one day ~ of what had been written him ~ to come home if he had to desert ~ he said there had never been such a thing said. I am satisfied now.[15]

---

13. "Code Duello: The Rules of Dueling," *American Experience*, PBS.org. Lucy's mention of ordering coffee and pistols indicates a variation of the formal steps associated with dueling. The Code Duello, a set of rules and regulations for dueling, was formalized by a group of Irishmen in 1777 and was subsequently Americanized in 1838 by South Carolina governor John Lyde Wilson. These rules of etiquette were strictly imposed, and despite legislation in many locales banning such customs, duels continued until public sanction of them diminished. Thanks to the duels of notables such as Alexander Hamilton and Aaron Burr, the practice had declined in the North earlier in the nineteenth century; it continued for a time in the South, however, due in part to the influence of the chivalrous novels of Sir Walter Scott.

14. At this point, Lucy did not list specific grievances; she merely referenced Mack's observations of the community. Later in the summer she would chronicle in detail the feuding and divisions among the members of "the neighborhood."

15. McPherson, *Ordeal by Fire*, 468. Lucy's implied sentiments concerning desertion fall in line with those of many other civilians during the war. Especially during the early years of the conflict, women, in particular, held their soldiers to a high standard of patriotism and duty. As the war progressed, however, many women, faced with desperation, urged their husbands and brothers to desert. As a result, desertions rose steadily until they became, as McPherson writes, an "epidemic" during the winter of 1864–1865 (468).

MARGINAL NOTE: *Neh started for La Mar 23rd 1864*

Mar 26th Saturday ~ Mr Wiley Jim B and Charlie U came by for Sammy
on their way to the hospital at Chappel-Hill[16] stayed but a few moments.
All have an invite to Bob's wedding to night. Sara and I are invited to
assist so we left soon. The boys had some of them gotten home, they
have another eight days furlough which will probably be their last.
Found all [at] Mr C~'s busy fixing bridal dress, dress for the brides maids
&c. There were two of the latter and two candle holders, all dressed in
white, the bride with white flowers and wreath, the maids of honor with
blue & white ribon ~ all low necked, white lace bertha's & white gloves

Parson Glass came in the eve and said the ceremony. Made "Nellie"
promise to "patch, wash, iron and keep Bob straight." Had the nicest
hard times supper I have eaten: four or five kinds of cake, one with a ring
in it, tarts, potato custards, roast pig, turkey, chicken, light bread & sure
enough coffee, preserves & jelly.

All us folks eat first, then the darkies. Bob had all the boys that
belongs to McD's [McDade's] company who were there to wait on him.
I went to enjoy myself, selfishly took the big rocker and stayed there and
played cards until the dancing commenced. The latter was kept up until
after eleven when we all went to see the darkies enjoying themselves at
the old store. The ribons and white dresses ~ whew! I did n't know there
was that many in the Confederacy Mr W~ came home with us. Uncle
Pier and Aunt Lu's 30th wedding day ~ celebrated it

Mar 27th Sunday ~ Cousin Sara Sammy and myself went to church to
day. It seemed quite like olden times to see so many of the Travis boys
out: Mack, cousin Sammy, Jim, Jake, Jimmy Clemons, Cy, Ino Campbell,
Mr Wiley, Mr Torrence, Trav and Charlie U. The house was well filled for
a wonder. Parson Glass took up a collection for bibles

Jim B and Mack, then Jake gave us an invite to go to Mr Ino Lott's to
a party this week ~ of course we'll go [to] any thing to please the soldier
boys with us.

16. Stephen Chicoine, *The Confederates of Chappell Hill, Texas: Prosperity, Civil War, and Decline*
(Jefferson, NC: McFarland, 2004), 99–100. Chappell Hill, Texas, approximately ten miles east of
Brenham, was selected as the site of one of the many hospitals scattered across the Confederacy.
According to Chicoine, the choice was a good one, since the area provided plenty of wood and
water, the location was "high and dry," and Soule University at Chappell Hill provided a building
with ample space—a three-story structure. Perhaps the most important reason for the selection
of Chappell Hill was that the railroad crossed the Brazos River, then passed through the town
on its way to Brenham.

Mar 28th Monday ~ Just before school closed, Mack, Mr Wiley and Charlie U came and spent the eve. Gave us an invite over again to Mr L~. Mack says provided we go on horse-back, he would like to accompany me and I could not have an escort that would better please me.

Mar 30th wednesday ~ Cousin S~ went after Em C~ and Mollie, got here before dark. Em wore a pea green wool-delain and Zouave sack[17] looks so nice. Sallie Catlin came up soon this eve and I braided her hair for her. Mary-Emily Chapel came with her. Both had on calico dresses, so persuaded Callie to go and wear hers. We started soon after dark, but 'twas dark, sure enough, 'twas so cloudy. We were all in gay spirits singing, talking &c got on nicely until after we passed Mr Clemons and got to the gulley beyond. Decided on all singing "Come Dearest, the Day Light is ~~Dawning~~ Gone"[18]

But alas for the vanity of all things. Had not much more than decided on it, when with the easiest slide imagineable, down went the wheels on one side of the carriage and landed us low on the ground. Happily however, the horse did not run so none of us were seriously hurt. Mack came down to go with me on horse-back, and as we were none of us much hurt, he joked me well about it. Said the first thing he heard was "Mr Wiley are you hurt ~ oh Mr Wiley are you hurt" all a fib. Jimmy Clemons and Mack came up while we were there and acted as pilot the rest of the way.

Jinnie and America were there, John Bell, Geo, Jim Murry & a Mr Owens ~ those three representatives from Hargrove's company, Browns Batt

~~Johnny H~~ Jimmy Clemon represented the 2nd Texas; Mack, Flournoy's R; John H, Carters R; Cousin S~, Jake & Mr W~, Charlie and Cy~ C~,

---

17. "Zouave Jacket," Apparel Search, 1860 Fashion History. The zouave sack, or jacket, became popular in America during the Civil War because of its military styling and flair. The jacket was often bright red and was highlighted with black trim, such as embroidery or braid. Worn with a skirt and blouse, and belted at the waist, the garment projected a distinctly military effect.

18. Brinley Richards, "Come Dearest the Daylight is Gone" (Baltimore: Miller and Beacham), 19th-Century American Sheet Music Digitization Project, University of North Carolina at Chapel Hill. This popular song was published before secession and was thus well known, yet the song's popularity may have endured thanks to its second verse, which reads: "Remember love I soon must leave thee / To wander mid strangers alone, / Where at eve thy sweet smile will not greet me / Nor thy gentle vision at morn; / But oh twill be sweet to remember / That though I am far, far from thee / That the hand of fate only can sever / My lasting affection from thee." These melancholy lyrics express the ongoing separation of loved ones and embody the poignant longing for their suitors' return.

Wallers B; a Mr Kennon, Elmore's Reg; Mr Jim Lott, the Militia; and John C~, a late made up spy company for the Rio G~ service. Mrs L surprised us all with a very nice supper about ten. Danced and played cards from that time until half past 3 A.M., concluding not to venture out again before 'twas light enough to see. They made up a fish fry & a dance at Nate Murrey's on friday night. Tried to persuade me to excuse school for that day, but I did not think the arrangement a wise one. So can not consent, not eaven for the sake of the soldier boys. I feel like a rest would be acceptable

Mar 31st thursday ~ Went to school this morn though did not feel much like it. Left Em~ Callie and cousin S~ in bed. Got on nicely before dinner, but after threw my wearied self on Lissie's bed and slept until half past two. Sue is sick today ~ think she has the measles.

APRIL 1864

April 1st friday ~ my gay-spiritedness received a sudden check on meeting with Uncle P~ for he told me sad news of Mollie McNese being so very nearly gone they did not think she would live til morn. Another bright jewel in my casket[19] of friends ~ alas I feel I can illy [ill afford to] give one up. None can ever fill *her* place, yet do I hope she can yet be spared, for that gentle spirit will ever cling to the slightest thread.

Many of the boys were in here yesterday Sara says, and all wanted to know was I going. Mack, Jimmy C. and Mr Wiley came by today. Sis Campbell and Sara Jane T~ went. Mr Wiley was telling us of E's asking him last night or rather night before, why he did not get married and get a detail so he could stay out of the service. Said he might get a detail to go into a tannery, and when he told her he did not understand the business she remarked he could get in with some one who did; pretty good.

April 2nd saturday ~ Mr Wiley came before eight A.M. Somebody questioned me pretty close this morn in regard to somebody else, are perhaps interested over the left.[20]

---

19. Lucy's use of the term "casket" indicates not a coffin but a small chest used for keeping valuables such as jewelry. With Lucy's high regard for her group of friends, the term is appropriate indeed.

20. When taken in concert with Mr. Wiley's information in the previous entry, Lucy's vague comments on April 2 become more clear; there are two distinct possibilities for the characters in this romantic plot. One possibility might be that Lucy's friend Elizabeth, "E," who had

Was afraid to ask after Mollie this morn, but finely [finally] concluded from appearances, nothing more serious than I knew of had
occurred. Went in to see her soon ~ and oh, what a shadow of her former self. It made me feel so sadly to see her yet was I glad that it lay in my
power to visit her, and as far as I can hope, to cheer and be a comfort. I
can never forget her looks ~ so thin, pale and nearly wasted away

April 3rd sunday ~ Mollie seems sinking slowly, but sure. It will not surprise me at any time to hear of her death.

Linda decided this morn to go be baptized. Her cousin, Sallie Fadis
joined the church last night, and both are to be immersed this morn.

Kinch came home late last night. Told us the Minute men had gone to
Brenham to guard Dr Peebles in on his way to Houston to be tried by the
military. Was acquitted by the civil authorities.

April 6th Wednesday ~ Sallie played in the eve ~ I was much interested
for the sake of letting cousin S~ and Mr W have a good time to talk,
which they seemed to improve well.

Apr 7th Thursday ~ Jake got me to write an April quiz[21] for him to Lydia
Francis. Wrote two April quizes today, one to Mack and one to Sallie
Catlin. Just after dinner, Mack came. Read his quizzes, had near a dozen.
I do not think he had an idea who sent mine. I declared it must have
been Bettie Bouldin

April 8th Friday ~ Cousin S~ Sara, Mr Kemp and I went to church today
~ fast day.[22] Uncle P~ and Mr K~ were the only ones who kept it [the
fast], though.

---

quizzed Mr. Wiley so closely the day before, was now attempting to ferret out information
from Lucy by which she could press her suit. The other possibility is that Mr. Wiley himself
was pressing Lucy for information on Cousin Sarah. Lucy's comments later in April point to,
then confirm, the latter possibility.

21. "April Fool's Day," *New York Times*, April 2, 1871, New York Times Article Archive. Certain public forums, such as the *New York Times*, took a somber, even sanctimonious, view of the
tomfoolery of April Fool's Day; the *Times* stated in its April 2, 1871, edition that "as a general
thing our people are not fond of practical jokes, and this may perhaps account for the fact of
their almost ignoring April Fool's Day. Besides, we are a practical people, and cannot find time
for such cheap and trivial amusements as delight our Old World brethren." Lucy's entries,
however, indicate no such disdain.

22. "General Orders No. 8," *Tyler Reporter*, March 31, 1864. Texas and Other Southern States
Civil War Newspapers/Newspaper Research, 1861–1865. The *Tyler Reporter* relates that General

April 9th Saturday ~ Mary E~ C~ and I cracked some pecans for the fry. Just as we finished, cousin Sara and Mr Wiley came. Jimmy C~ and Mack promised to come spend monday eve with me. Perhaps it may be the last soon ~ I do not like to believe it. I'll try my best to be good.

I came near forgetting to record the fact of my getting caught so badly yesterday eve. I have always been telling Mr W~ about Sara Minase. [I] thought to make him further acquainted, I'd show him one of her letters. Looked over one or two, but was so certain I knew what was in the next, I did not stop to read it. And if I had picked for the worst of all I could not have done worse. Told of five babies being born ~ 3 at one birth ~ horror upon horror!! It learned me one lesson I'll never forget.

In Benton B's letter he wrote on the 27th, they had been retreating since the 14th; that during that time, they had lost from 800 to 1000 men, 250 at Ft Derusia, Co E~ out of their Reg and Edgars Battery, of six peices with 200 La cavalry. They traveled two days & nights at the rate of 30 miles per day without a thing to eat. The Fedrals boast of their intended march through Texas. The three prisoners they took tell it.[23]

MARGINAL NOTES: *Mollie died at 9~ this morn ~ Sunday 10th 1864 Mack left for La the 14th thursday*

Kirby Smith declared April 8 as a day of "fasting, humiliation and prayer," with services being held around the state. The article goes on to state: "[On] the eve of a campaign in which our resources will be taxed to the utmost, and upon which the destinies of our people depend, we should humble ourselves before the Lord of hosts, who giveth not the battle to the strong, but upholdeth the cause of the just."

23. Richard Lowe, *Walker's Texas Division C.S.A.: Greyhounds of the Trans-Mississippi* (Baton Rouge: Louisiana State University Press, 2004), 170–177. Lowe reports that to a man, every Confederate soldier suspected an imminent invasion via the Red River. These suspicions were well founded. As part of the Federal plan, 20,000 Union troops, led by General Banks, were to move from Berwick Bay in south Louisiana toward Alexandria in the central part of the state. There they would join General Frederick Steele and 10,000 more men. Some forty miles downstream from Alexandria lay Fort DeRussy, uncompleted on the land side and, at best, a temporary stronghold for the Confederate army on the Red River. On Saturday, March 12, scouts reported the arrival of massive numbers of enemy troops, and Walker found himself outnumbered more than two to one and, in essence, surrounded on an "island," with the river to the north, and swamps and bayous to the east, west, and south. Only a small bridge that crossed Bayou Du Lac offered escape. On Monday, March 14, Walker ordered a retreat and burned the bridge behind him. He then marched his men at a furious pace, fearing that Union troops would arrive before the Texans and, capture all of the roads leading to the Red River. Corroborating Benton Brewer's letter, Lowe quotes Volney Ellis, the adjutant of the 12th Texas, who wrote, "Our men have undergone traveling 25 and 30 miles a day and sometimes all night. It is truly remarkable what man can stand!" (177).

April 10th Sunday ~ Cousin Sammy went with me out to Mr Collins this morn. Got there about a half hour after Mollie had breathed her last. Sad hearts, for 'twas hard to give her up, although we all feel she was releived from much suffering. She looks so calm and composed, and to me more as she used to, but oh so wasted.

April 12th Tuesday ~ Walked over to school this morn. Soon after I went in the room, Mack came to tell us good-bye. Stayed about a half hour. I hated much to see him start off. It seems to me like we would never see all our boys at home again though we hope to the contrary

April 14th Thursday ~ Mack passed here about half past 8~ waved his hat to us. ~ God grant your safe return ~

April 15th Friday ~ Jane and Newton came to tell us Sallie was very low and that they had sent for us girls so I left word not to expect me.

Found the Dr with her. She had taken cold and the measles did not come out as they ought.[24] They thought several times last night she would not live 'til morn. In the P.M. Jake came to tell me I must go ~ that he would send some meeting house-folks to sit up if it was necessary. But as S~ was little better I thought best to stay.

April 18th Monday ~ Arrived at Lu's. She met us at the gate with her new purple calico dress and linen apron on ~ looked so nice.

Mr Darnman set up some time, looked like he enjoyed the boys being there much. Sol C~ had run away from home ~ had his Father's horse, saddle, blankets and pistols. Every one there nearly talked to him and tried to persuade him to go back home, but did not succeed. At 4P.M. all left, causing sober looking faces. Mr W~ gave his me his watch to take home. At half past 5 all were gone.

After tea, we set up but a short time feeling low-spirited and lonsome. At half-past nine the dogs broke out like they were about to take some one. I jumped up and run to the window. Callie got out of bed, got one foot in the chamber and could n't get out until she rolled it round some time.

---

24. It was commonly believed that if a measles patient did not develop a profuse rash over much of the body, but instead internalized the lesions, grave complications, or even death, would result.

Sara Lu, Callie & I raised the window, called to find out who it was. 'Twas Sammy, H~P~W~ & Charlie U. Tom McD~ does not start until ~~thursday~~ saturday. Such a time making up beds & shiping dry-goods to Lu's room & putting our dresses over our gowns. Set up until half past eleven. Lu brought some cake and wine for the boys.

On April 19th, Lucy began to record sparse details of the fighting in Louisiana, and some of her information, this time, was correct. Most of the heaviest fighting did, in fact, occur at Mansfield and Pleasant Hill, with Banks, not Steele, commanding the Union forces at Mansfield. Generals Steele, Sherman, and Franklin had, however, supplied a substantial number of troops for what many considered a "minor mission" that diverted needed troops from the Eastern theater. According to Thomas Ayres, Grant felt that the endeavor was wasteful and agreed to it only reluctantly, preferring to press toward Atlanta and hasten the end of the war. In the end, however, he committed to "loan" 10,000 of Sherman's troops to Banks for the effort.[25]

There was similar dissension among the leadership of the Confederates, in this case, Kirby Smith, who spearheaded the Trans-Mississippi Department, and Richard Taylor, the more popular commander of the troops in Louisiana. The two were contentious about many things, not the least of which was the sale of cotton. The acquisition of cotton was basic to the rationale for invading Texas, and speculators roamed the countryside, making deals. Ayres reports that Richard Taylor had discovered that even Kirby Smith had been involved in selling cotton to Union agents, purportedly to finance the war effort.[26] In response, Ayres writes, Taylor had ordered the burning of all cotton that was not directly in the hands of Confederate troops. Tensions between the two generals waxed and waned repeatedly, and at this point in the Red River Campaign, when Taylor requested more troops, Smith was slow to respond, then slow to send the men. Taylor decided to attack, regardless. In fact, on April 8, at Mansfield, Taylor, who had not yet been given permission by Smith to engage Federal forces, sent a request to Smith, carefully worded and timed to arrive after the fighting had ensued. By the time Taylor received Smith's negative response, he declared to the courier, "Too late, the battle is won."[27]

---

25. Ayres, *Dark and Bloody Ground*, 205.

26. Ayres, *Dark and Bloody Ground*, 203.

27. Ludwell H. Johnson, *Red River Campaign: Politics and Cotton in the Civil War* (Baltimore: Johns Hopkins University Press, 1958), 142.

Fighting was brutal, pitting many combatants against each other in bloody hand-to-hand struggles. As Lucy recorded, General Mouton was one of the first to be killed, and his division lost more than one third of all killed and wounded in the battle. Walker's Division of Texans, including brigades headed by Scurry, Waul, and Randal,[28] was heavily involved. This group included many of the local boys from the Travis area, and Lucy would list some of their names as she recorded injuries in her entry of April 25. The Rebel forces took the day, even capturing a supply train, but losses were extremely heavy for both sides, as Lucy wrote. The next day, fighting resumed several miles away in Pleasant Hill, with Taylor combining forces with Tom Green's troops in an effort to capture the Union fleet situated on the Red River. Fighting was horrific, with muskets often turned into clubs. In a battle that lasted just under three hours, some 2,600 men were left dead or wounded. Only darkness stopped the carnage.

Then, despite the apparent victory, in a monumental decision, Banks ordered a retreat. Disregarding the passionate counsel of his subordinate officers, he turned away from a chance to press his advantage and demolish Taylor's troops. Leaving his wounded on the field, often to the care of Confederate surgeons, and torching the town in his wake, Banks retreated, losing the opportunity to forge on to Shreveport, and Texas. Ayres concludes: "Defying his commander and all odds, with boldness, luck and a superior force at the point of attack, [Taylor] had stopped Banks and thwarted Lincoln's plans for conquest of the Confederacy west of the Mississippi."[29]

Lucy wrote of these encounters, conflating much of the information and exercising editorial privilege over her journal, mentioning only that the beloved Texas general Tom Green had been killed on April 12. She could not know, however, that her brief entry on April 19 would encapsulate the end to Union hopes of an invasion of Texas.

April 19th Tuesday ~ Came home this morn feeling quite different from yester at 4~ P.M. Arrived at home tired and nearly wearied out. News came of more full particulars from the battle in La that took place on the 8th & 9th this month. Gen Green was killed on the 12th ~ it is said with a shell from a gun-boat. Had the top of his head blown off. Mouton also was killed and Walker wounded.

---

28. Ibid., 135.
29. Ayres, *Dark and Bloody Ground*, 234.

Heard yesterday that Capt H~, Lieut Harris & Mathews had passed through safely. It said that the enemy were routed totally, but the loss on both sides was very great. Report says Confeds took 600 prisoners captured the entire train and stores.

We are all anxious to hear particulars of our friends from this county. Sol C~ is at home. Jim Lott met him at H~ and took him back. Jake is here this eve, says news came in that Wallers B~ was to escort the prisoners to Texas.

The two hardest days' fight came off at Pleasant Hill, 20 miles from Mansfield on the road to Natchitoches. Steele commanded the Fedral forces, Kirby Smith of the Confederates.

Apr 20th Wednesday ~ Mr Wiley came there. Showed me a letter he had written home telling in it of Sara's promising some day to be Mrs W. No surprise to me however ~ wish them a long and happy life

Apr 22nd Friday ~ Our boys left again this morn. Jake was here soon in the morn to get cousin S~ to go give Mr Lott a talk about what he had said of all of them connected with Sol's going off. Uncle Pier opposed it so bitterly that he did not go, but J met Jim up near the store and went.[30]

Near 5~ Mr & Mrs Middleton came for me to go out home with them

Apr 23rd Saturday ~ Mrs M and I spent most of the day by ourselves. Learned Mrs M how to make beat biscuit[31] this eve ~ had some for tea, also a custard pie. 'Tis nine days since Mack left here. He will probably be with his command either today or tomorrow.

---

30. Lucy had written of Sol C, who had run away from home and come to Cousin Lu's house during the party on April 18. Despite pressure from his friends, Sol could not be persuaded to return home and had gone on to Hempstead, where he encountered Jim Lott on April 19. Now, Mr. Lott had apparently begun a neighborhood quarrel with words he had spoken out of turn concerning the incident. This would not be the only time that Mr. Lott would be embroiled in local controversy.

31. Abby Fisher, *What Mrs. Fisher Knows About Old Southern Cooking* (San Francisco: Women's Co-operative Printing Office, 1881), Internet Archive, December 2006, University of CA Libraries and MSN. "Beat Biscuits" or "Maryland Beat Biscuits" originated with female slaves and involved the cook beating the biscuit dough with a heavy mallet or rolling pin until it was "perfectly moist and light," writes Abby Fisher in her 1881 cookbook. Mrs. Fisher, a former slave, could neither read nor write, but was persuaded by her friends and patrons in San Francisco to publish the collection of recipes.

Apr 24th Sunday ~ Read two chapters in the Bible this morn, then commenced *The Discarded Daughter*, a tale by Mrs D E Southworth. Merely read it to pass away time 'Twas just tolerable good. Two persons died and come to life again[32]

Apr 25th Monday ~ Heard Wm Collins was wounded through the lungs in the last fight, William Brewer in the hand. Joe Blakley & Robert Minton (Jinnie's brother) are among the missing. H~ Bracey was in the hospital when he wrote.

Mr C~ came from Brenham today. Heard that a dispatch came in saying that the Fedral army under Steele was surrounded by Price and Marmaduke. They were still fighting in La and that the Infantry were to go into Ark.

Apr 26th Tuesday ~ the boys all home again. Tom McDade's child is very low, and so they will wait until it is better or dies. But if they get no word this eve, take it for granted it is better and leave tomorrow
Apr 27th Wednesday ~ The boys started again this morn. Cy was the first who came by. Went from here for Charlie U~. Then came Mr W~, Jake and Jim & Mr Torrence, Cousin S~

Apr 28th Thursday ~ No mail came ~ every-one feels disappointed. We all are anxious to hear farther from La

Apr 30th Saturday ~ Mrs C~ Campbell sent us word to come over there this morn, that Bettie's baby was dead and Lewis had brought it up. It is to be buried at ten. Little Paten was taken with diarrhea soon after they went down there, and has been so low that they have had to watch with him for near four weeks. Bettie had his dagauerreotype taken and sent up home. He was lying in the coffin but looked as though he was sleeping.

MARGINAL NOTE: *Fight in Ark ~ Mack wounded in left hand.*

---

32. Joanne Dobson and Amy Hudock, "E.D.E.N. Southworth," in *Dictionary of Literary Biography*, vol. 239, *American Women Prose Writers, 1820-1870*, ed. Katherine Rodier and Amy Hudock, 285–292 (Gale Group, 2001). *The Discarded Daughter, or the Children of the Isle*, one of Southworth's earlier works, was originally published in 1852 by Hart Co.

Even as Lucy ended her entries for April, so ended Union visions of a conquered Texas and Louisiana. Momentous events had transpired to effect this conclusion, but Lucy's emphasis, as always, was on the Travis boys. Her final remark, written in the margin of her journal, significantly singled out only one Travis boy—Lucy's beloved "Texas Brother," Mack, who had sustained a wound in the fighting, an injury that merited a special notation in her diary.

Lucy's brief comment about battles in Louisiana and Arkansas indicates the scope of fighting that was ongoing west of the Mississippi. For by the time Taylor met Banks at Pleasant Hill, General Steele had been marching from the northeast, through Arkansas, toward Banks's force for two weeks.[33] However, following decisive victories at Poison Spring and Marks' Mills, the troops under the commands of Price and Marmaduke, among others, routed Federal forces. As a result, Steele gave up all thoughts of uniting with General Banks on the Red River and realized that he had to save his army.[34]

---

33. Johnson, *Red River Campaign*, 170.

34. National Park Service, Heritage Preservation Services, *CWSAC Battle Summaries: Camden Expedition—Poison Spring and Marks' Mill, AR*.

CHAPTER 10

MAY–JUNE
1864

Two from our band are gone ~ but Neh Sara and I left. God grant we may be
spared to see the termination of this war – and all meet again.

LUCY P. STEVENS,
June 7, 1864

THE MONTH OF MAY brought with it more news from Louisiana and Arkansas, as battles continued to rage and reports continued to arrive. Like everyone else in Travis, Lucy received war news in bits and pieces, often missing and/or omitting key pieces of strategic information. Although several major skirmishes had been fought in the intervening time since her last war report, she now conflated only the most basic elements of the conflict in her diary.

In the aftermath of the Confederate victory at Mansfield in April, General Taylor had urged Kirby Smith to press their advantage by focusing on the Federal fleet situated on the Red River. The fleet had been slated to coordinate with Banks's forces, but was currently vulnerable, having been stymied by exceptionally low water levels. In essence, the fleet was a "sitting duck," and it was only when Banks was convinced of the feasibility of damming the Red River to raise water levels that the Union forces began to move. However, the delay caused by construction of the dams subjected Banks's troops to repeated attacks by Taylor's much smaller army. Outnumbered five to one,[1] Taylor and his subordinates successfully struck against Banks's men and the fleet, and as Ayres contends, "as of May 5, when the carnage ended, Dick Taylor owned the Red River."[2] The end result secured the safety of Texas and destroyed Union hopes of an invasion via the Red River. Although more fighting would follow, Lucy's friends and loved ones would be spared much danger.

---

1. Michael Forsyth, *The Red River Campaign of 1864 and the Loss by the Confederacy of the Civil War* (Jefferson, NC: McFarland, 2002), 95.

2. Thomas Ayres, *Dark and Bloody Ground: The Battle of Mansfield and the Forgotten Civil War in Louisiana* (Dallas: Taylor Publishing, 2001), 254.

MAY 1864

May 2nd ~ No news from La today. All are anxious to hear from there. News came to Hempstead on friday eve by telegraph they were fighting again on Red river. The Confederates victorious ~ had killed and wounded many and captured many more.

May 3rd Tuesday ~ Heard to day that the letter I sent to Mr Scales to be mailed in Mexico had never gone, or the one to Mrs Fowler telling of Stickney's death. Uncle Pier brought news that the Confederates lost four Generals in the last fight in La[3] ~ Mrs B's received two letters from the boys. Heard since that 'twas four wounded ~ Scurry, Randal, [Waul] and Clarke ~ Gen Scurry since died

May 4th Wednesday ~ Mrs B's letters were from Benton. He gave quite an account of the battle, says the Fedrals were defeated at every place. They had taken many prisoners. Walkers Division was on its way to reinforce Price in hopes to keep him from coming up with Banks

May 5th Thursday ~ Mrs B~ danced for joy this eve that she had news from the boys.

May 6th Friday ~ Mr B~ just returned from Houston. Says a telegraphic dispatch was received in Hempstead that morning that Gen Steeles main army had been captured by Confed forces. Had taken some 15,000 prisoners, besides killed and wounded many ~ captured many wagons[4]

3. Richard Lowe, *Walker's Texas Division C.S.A.: Greyhounds of the Trans-Mississippi* (Baton Rouge: Louisiana State University Press, 2004), 226. Although Lucy did not mention an exact location, some of the names can be found listed among casualties from Jenkins' Ferry, Arkansas, a battle that occurred on April 30. According to Lowe, three of Walker's four brigade commanders were lost in that fray: General Thomas N. Waul sustained a wound in the arm and never again commanded his troops; General William R. Scurry fell when "a minie ball pierced his lower trunk" and died the next day; General Horace Randall was mortally wounded when struck in the abdomen, dying two days later. The other commander Lucy mentioned could have been Colonel Edward Clark, who had been wounded at Pleasant Hill.

4. Ludwell H. Johnson, *Red River Campaign: Politics and Cotton in the Civil War* (Baltimore: Johns Hopkins University Press, 1958), 193–194. The complete loss of 240 supply wagons carrying provisions for Steele's men and animals proved devastating. Ludwell Johnson explains that the crucial loss of the supply train rendered Steele unable to supply his men, and in an emergency meeting after the defeat, Steele and his generals determined that they had no alternative but to retreat to Little Rock.

May 8th Sunday ~ Had word that Mr D~ [Darnman] was very low, and 'twas thought would not live through last night.

May 10th Tuesday ~ Aunt Lu and Uncle P~ returned from the Bend this morn. Mr D~ is still living, and if any thing, seems some better.

May 11th Wednesday ~ Ruf B~ came home this morn. Did not get farther than Crockett, was taken sick. Came back to his Aunt's at Huntsville and had to remain there several days. Brought Bell a present of two bales of warp from the penitentiary.[5]

May 13th Friday ~ Mr C's received a letter from Mack. He writes he was up with the command in time to be in the fight of the 30th at Caney Valley Ark ~ was well.

MARGINAL NOTE: *Fedrals left Alex~ on the 13th great rejoicing in the Confederacy*

May 15th Sunday ~ This morning while at breakfast, Johnie Chapman came in with the papers. They contain quite an account of the fight near Priceton, Ark at Jenkins landing on Sabine river. Walkers Division occupied the center. Their loss alone was near 1,000. Kirby Smith commanded Confed forces, Gen Steele Fedral[6]

Aunt H~ says Dr P~ [Peebles] is very low at Anderson ~ not expected to live. All the family have been down there. Maggie and Samie are there now ~ Mrs Clark had another spell and they came back.

May 18th Wednesday ~ In the P.M. went out to Mrs Sinclare's. How do I like her? Can not say that I am particularly [. . .] in her favor. She is one of

---

5. According to *The Handbook of Texas Online*, the state of Texas approved and constructed a penitentiary at Huntsville in 1848. To offset the costs of housing inmates and to raise revenues, in 1853 the governor requested funds to purchase equipment to establish a cotton and woolen mill to be housed within the prison compound and to be run by the inmates. The endeavor was successful, and by the late 1850s, inmates were processing as much as five hundred bales of cotton and six thousand pounds of wool a year. Ultimately, because of the naval blockade, this venture would prove vital during the war years, since the mill earned much-needed funds for the state.

6. As always, Lucy's focus was on the local boys, and she singled out their unit, Walker's Division, in her notes about losses. She wrote about the casualties, and Ayres confirms this, describing the suffering as "horrific." The count included three of Walker's four brigadier generals, of whom Lucy had written in her May 3 entry. But for Lucy, personally, the important news came in her May 13 entry: Mack had been involved and wounded in this battle, but he had survived.

these would-be grand ones, I think, but dont know how to set about it. Now ~ Mr Journal ~ you know <u>this is confidential.</u>

May 19th Thursday ~ No mail today. I begin to want a letter from my big buddies very much. Wish he would write to a body.

May 20th Friday ~ My children had speeches this P.M. All in to see them. Sallie and Newt are through their second readers now. I have had Jane commence grammar. Her and Sue get their lessons in the morn; have Steph write in the morn too.

May 21st Saturday ~ Lu had a letter from cousin Waller since he left. All were well. Report came of a great battle in Tenn between Lee and Grant. ~ Lee victorious ~ taken, killed &c 55,000.[7]

May 23rd Monday ~ E~ says she heard Mack was shot in the left arm on the 30th, Capt Hunt through the body & Lieut Mathews killed. I hope its not so though.

—⌣—

Apparently, Lucy's friend Elizabeth had had hopes of capturing Mr. Wiley's attention and had gone so far as to announce her intent to Lucy and Aunt Lu. According to Lucy's journal, however, those sentiments were not reciprocated. Mr Wiley made his feelings plainly known to Lucy, and she recorded those conversations in her entries of May 24th and 25th. The triangle that had seemed so troubling to Mr. Wiley in early April had been resolved, and he could now proceed with his courtship of Cousin Sarah.

Sarah's budding romance with Mr. Wiley serves as an excellent example of nineteenth-century romantic love. Karen Lystra reports that romantic love was by now a necessary condition for marriage within the middle class of nineteenth-century America and that this companionate marriage involved emotional bonds born of esteem and friendship.[8] She explains that two of the dominant characteristics of nineteenth-century courtship were a

---

7. Lucy had heard of "a great battle in Tennessee," and so decided to note it in her journal. The battle(s) to which she referred include the beginning of Grant's Overland Campaign during May and June of 1864. Most likely Lucy wrote about the Battle at the Wilderness, fought May 5–7, between General Robert E. Lee's troops and the combined forces of Generals Ulysses S. Grant and George G. Meade.

8. Karen Lystra, *Searching the Heart: Women, Men, and Romantic Love in Nineteenth-Century America* (New York: Oxford University Press, 1989), 31.

tendency toward excessive introspection and an analytical disclosure of the inner self to one's partner based on self-criticism.[9] Sarah's diary exemplifies just such activity. After receiving a letter from Henry P. Wiley on June 9, she wrote in her journal:

> He spoke as though if he could come home on furlough, he would like for me to marry him then. Is it possible that Sarah Pier will ever marry? He is worthy of me I know and loves me devotedly—and my love—more chastened and refined from the trial it has passed through of late—I have given to him. It is not that soul absorbing fanatical love—with which I have loved—for when the fresh pure love—the first of my young heart was rejected by who had won it by artful and designing means—it was driven back to its source there to remain inert until some more worthy object should awake it again.
>
> Mr. Wiley has been in our midst for a number of months—and I had always respected him as a friend—and regarded him as one of the noble and true hearted of earth—But never dreamed that he thought of me per-haps as more than a friend—although I often felt that there was a certain unison of thought and feeling between us two which drew me toward him . . . But he has sought my love—as a noble sincere man should—He has nothing to give me but his first pure love—In worldly goods he is poor—but rich in possessing a noble generous heart. Once I thought the same of another—but I fear not now—He knows all—that he does not possess my first love as it once bloomed forth from the throbbing more selfish heart. But it is a truer, deeper more purified love—that has been refined by its return to its natural source and that source being renovated and enobled by the fiery trial it has passed through
>
> May him to whom I have entrusted again the deepest love of my heart that is bestowed upon man be spared to me—through all the dangers and uncertainties of this cruel war—and may my longing heart find rest at last. But Oh, let him not come betwixt me and my God and may no earthly object dim for one moment the brightness of his smile for me

Analyzing and comparing her emotions to previous feelings she had experi-enced, Sarah stressed her gratitude for Wiley's love, believing that God had indeed provided a special relationship for them. She quoted Romans 8:28, "'All things work together for good to them that serve only God.' All has

9. Ibid., 31–41.

worked for good to me thus far—as undeserving as I am. May it continue to work for good" (Sarah Pier, 6/9/64) and asked God's protection for him. As Sarah's relationship with Wiley developed through the summer and fall of 1864, her reflections on the spiritual basis of the relationship continued to dominate her journal, revealing her devout Christian beliefs and reflecting the predominant nineteenth-century emphasis of a person's spiritual condition as a matter of primary importance.[10]

May 24th Tuesday ~ E~ had her picture taken in Houston. 'Tis such a good-one, I want it, but don't know but some one else has a greater claim on it. In fact, she told Aunt Lu and I so yester eve.

Well ~ Mr W~ came in the school-room this morn and spent some time. We held quite a correspondence in regard to a subject that interested me much, as it concerned one of my best friends [Elizabeth]. He told me that positively and sincerely he never had thought of paying his addresses, and such a thought was quite out of the question. He had always tried to have her understand just the contrary.

Trav C~ came here this P.M. when Mr W~ was in my school-room. As he started off, I asked him about Mack being wounded. He told me yes he was wounded in the arm ~ old hatefulness. Tried to make me believe it and that he would have to have his arm off. But afterwards, told me he was wounded in the left hand slightly, a flesh wound. I am very glad to hear it is no worse

[Mr. Wiley] asked my advice about telling E~ his feelings. I sayd no unless she came out in such plain terms that he could not well avoid it.

May 25th Wednesday ~ E~ returned this morn about 10. I believe Mr W~ took my advice, for she told me this morn that I might have her picture, but says he gave his to her. I dont believe it though. He told me posatively it was not so and said if he could get hold of it they would not get it again. She does not know that however, or will not from me

MARGINAL NOTE: *Jack Cochrane died near Evergreen La May 27th 1864*

10. Lewis O. Saum, *The Popular Mood of Pre-Civil War America* (Westport, CT: Greenwood Press, 1980), 111.

May 29th Sunday ~ Swept & dusted & cleaned up generally in Sara's room this morn, then betook myself with a book ~ *Aspirations*[11] up stairs ~ unrobed and had a good time reading. In the P.M. Mr Lee came to let me know he would make my ring and mend my ear-ring. I am so glad; wish it could be done by the 7th [Lucy's birthday].

JUNE 1864

On June 1, as Lucy recorded William Brewer's perceptions of his commanding officers, she inadvertently touched on a pervasive problem for both North and South—respect and obedience due one's officers. Gerald Linderman contends that officers "secured obedience only as their men judged them worthy to command" and that "men measured the individual . . . not the grade of his commission."[12] He explains that privates looked upon the officer's character, both on and off the battlefield, and sharply judged him as to his worthiness of emulation. When the officers were found lacking, oftentimes the privates proceeded to test them, and if they determined that the man's character did not justify his rank, they "devoted much effort to the deflation of the officer,"[13] from mockery to insubordination to outright cruelty. The officers were held accountable and taken to task.

William Brewer's comments provide an interesting perspective on camp life, but Lucy's opinions expose an even more interesting and circumspect view. She apparently knew the officers in question, and held more favorable opinions of them. She was also implicitly critical of William, possibly already knowing him as "hard to please." However, as she wrote about wanting to hear the other side of the story, she echoed phrases she had used before in writing about the philosophies of North and South, detaching herself from absolute adherence to any one stance. She would come back to these phrases from time to time, obliquely admitting that although she remained committed to the Southern boys whom she knew, perhaps she did not subscribe as fervently to the cause they embraced.

---

11. "Charlotte Mary Yonge," Contemporary Authors Online (Gale Group, 2007). *The Daisy Chain; or Aspirations: A Family Chronicle* was written by Charlotte Mary Yonge in 1856. Yonge was a prolific writer, publishing an average of three books a year, for fifty years, her most important contribution coming in the form of domestic fiction.

12. Gerald F. Linderman, *Embattled Courage* (New York: Free Press, 1987), 43–44.

13. Ibid., 48.

On her birthday, Lucy wrote again of the Federal departure from Alexandria, still ignorant of the destruction they left behind. It seems that in spite of Banks's assurances that the town would be spared, Union troops burned the town of Alexandria, Louisiana, to the ground on May 13, 1864. Ayres reports that "in less than three hours, Alexandria, the third largest town in Louisiana, had ceased to exist ... All that remained of the once vibrant city was the Catholic church and a few houses on the windward side of town, mercifully spared by nature, not man."[14] Lucy had turned back the pages of her journal to record in the margin the Union departure, stating that there was "great rejoicing in the Confederacy" (note 5/14/64), but even now, she obviously did not know of the devastation that Banks's army left in its wake.

As the retreat and torching continued, Banks's men reached the town of Simmesport, Louisiana, on May 18. There, along the Yellow Bayou, Thomas Ayers records, Union and Confederate troops engaged in the "last major battle fought on Louisiana soil," thus ending the Red River Campaign. In a fierce contest that pitted 4,500 Confederate soldiers against 30,000 Union troops, often in hand-to-hand combat, Richard Taylor's army lost 600 men.[15] Lucy wrote that Billy Fortran was among those captured.

As always, in spite of her veiled ambivalence, Lucy was committed to her Texas soldier boys, and when she heard reports of offenses against them, her Southern leanings took over, as evidenced in her June 7 entry, when she wrote, "Those Yankees are up to all kinds of tricks."

———⌄———

June 1, Wednesday ~ We had such a quiet day ~ all spoke of it. I have been ruling "Assessment" sheets for the last two days. Have 38 to rule, quite a job.

Wm's hand looks badly, but is healing. He told us a great deal of the fight. Complimented the Lieut, but hasn't any use in the round world for the Capt. Says he does not care enough for his men. Whether they want clothing ~ for eating or other attention, it matters not to him.

I think Capt considered him hard to please and for that reason did less for him than he might have done. I would like to hear the other side of the story, for of course there is two sides to every story. I hope he may have reason to change his mind and yet become an a firm friend. Am glad to hear Lieut stands high in favor. both are worthy of great esteem.

14. Ayres, *Dark and Bloody Ground*, 259.
15. Ibid.

June 5th Sunday ~ About 4~ P.M. Dick came; brought word Mr D [Darn-man] died a few moments before 11 this A.M. Cal ~ got here with the corps[e] just before dark.

Sara says Mr D~ made a profession of religion just a few days before his death. Died very easily and we all feel that he is relieved of much suffering. He arrived at Lu's the 29th of November; has been sick for six months, has been so patient.

Mr Chapman Mr & Mrs Withers all came in and offered their services to sit up. But we thought it unnecessary as the coffin was closed. All went to bed after closing up the room.

June 6th Monday ~ [Mr. Darnman's] burial was at 10 A.M. Mrs D stays until tomorrow. Heard Billy Fordtran was taken prisoner on the 18th ~ the other side of Alexandria.

June 7 Tuesday ~ My twenty-sixth birthday, the fourth I have spent in Texas.[16] Mrs Brewer had a nice dinner cooked for me. I heard such sad sad news. Poor Jack Cochrane is dead, died on the 26th of last month. I am so sorry, for he was a noble boy and so good. I loved him dearly. Two from our band are gone ~ but Neh Sara and I left.[17] God grant we may be spared to see the termination of this war and all meet again. It seems strange: on Sara's birthday, heard of Mr Bell's death in the morn ~ he was brought up and buried ~ his friends all at our house. Lu's [on Lu's birthday] ~ Mr Darnman was not expected to live, sent for Aunt Lu & Uncle Pier ~ now [on Lucy's birthday] Mr D~ just buried ~ heard of Jack's death and Callie very sick at our house, has fever.

News from La. They fought on 16th, 17th, 18th. The fedrals left Alex~ on the 13th, arrived at Sims port on the 18th where they met their gun-boats. It is said the enemies forces were 18,000, ours 8,000. I hear it said that the Fedrals built a dam below the shoals blocking up the waters until their boats were gotten down. These Yankees are up to all sorts of tricks.

Our forces admit a severe repulse on the 18th, were skirmishing for five days. Waller's Battallion lost eight in killed and wounded Col Waller had command of Green's Brigade.

---

16. Lucy miscalculated the duration of her Texas sojourn. Having arrived in Texas on Christmas Day, 1859 (per Aunt Lu's journal), Lucy had actually celebrated five birthdays in Texas.

17. When Lucy had made her initial trip to Texas at the end of 1859, her companions had been Cousin Sarah, Nehemiah Cochran, Stickney Fowler, and Jack Cochran. All three young men had enlisted in the Confederate army, and two had now given their lives.

June 10th Friday ~ This is Jane's birthday ~ In the P.M. she treated us to some cake and coffee. The latter cured my head-ache which was caused, I think, by my taking an unexpected bath yesterday eve. I started out to see the new moon, and of course was carrying such a high head as not to look where I was walking. Went to go down the steps, and put one foot into a little tub of water standing there, spattering it all over me. My chemise was wet enough to wring. I had to borrow one from Elizabeth to wear. Quite a sudden terminus to the romance. I laughed until I cried ~ 'twas so rediculus.

June 12th Sunday ~ I forgot to tell that Mr Geo Harvey brought letters from cousin Sammy and Mr Wiley. They left La on the 28th. Jack C died on the 27th was sick but a few days. Was up and walking about the morn he died, had his throat cortarized [cauterized] just a few moments before. The Dr's said he had scarlet fever and thought he must have broken a blood vessel, he died so easily. He [n]or any one else had an idea he would die. Was at a private house taking care of Hayward Smith, had every attention. Neh did not get there until after his death. The rain was so heavy yesterday that it raised Buffalo [Creek] high enough to wash Uncle Pier's fence away. And he, with the Negroes, have been busy all day putting it up again.

On June 14th, Lucy received an invitation for an outing, and she responded excitedly. Anxiety had consumed everyone, and a respite from daily toil and worry was sorely needed. With appropriate primping and preparation, Lucy departed for closing examinations and a concert in Chappell Hill, feeling "grand." In all likelihood, the examinations that Lucy and her group attended were held at Chappell Hill Female College. The school, an outgrowth of Chappell Hill Male & Female Institute, was chartered in 1856, as was Soule University for men; however, the schools were situated in different areas of the town to keep the young men and ladies separate. *The Handbook of Texas Online* lists natural philosophy among the disciplines for Soule University, but stresses that the female college was intended to "educate girls in a Christian environment and assure their acquisition of culture, discipline and oratorical skills." The school emphasized music and art; however, it can be assumed that the women were also beneficiaries of courses such as philosophy, since Lucy wrote specifically about that examination. The *Handbook* goes on to state that although most of Soule University's students enlisted in the Confederate army during the Civil War, Chappell Hill Female College continued to prosper, adding buildings during the 1870s and 1880s.

The Female College's strong emphasis on music produced the concert that Lucy and her friends attended during the evening. The concert served not only to showcase what the students had learned, but also to provide a social setting that was apparently popular and crowded. With a variety of songs and performances, one performance, in particular, highlights the accommodations that Southern women had made, thanks to the blockade. As Lucy wrote in praise of Sallie Blackshire's solo, she mentioned that Sallie not only sang about a homespun costume, she modeled it as well. Sallie's song may well have been "The Southern Girl's Song," also known as "The Southern Girl With the Home-Spun Dress," a popular tune whose author is listed only as "a Southern Lady." The lyrics clearly glorify homespun as the epitome of patriotism, as they underscore Southern supremacy in all things:

> My home-spun dress is plain, I know, my hat's quite common too;
> But then it shows what Southern girls for Southern rights will do.
> We've sent the bravest of our land to battle with the foe;
> And we would lend a helping hand—we love the South you know.
> CHORUS: Hurrah! Hurrah! for the Sunny South so dear!
> Three cheers for the Home-Spun Dress that Southern ladies wear![18]

Lucy's attention to the details of Sallie's costume serves as a reminder of Lucy's desire to dress stylishly, wherever she might be. Since homespun had been elevated from shabby to chic, and women throughout the South embraced it as a symbol of their contribution to the Cause, Lucy's compliments on both performance and costume offer a glimpse into her own costume of Southern-ness. Where once she might have belittled the dress as dowdy, she now described dress, apron, and hat with commendation.

June 14th Tuesday ~ In the P.M. as I was hearing Jane read, Ben C~ came with a horse for me. Said that Sara, Sallie Lu, Sammy & I were to go to Chapel-Hill to the concert. I was delighted at the idea, and after getting "leave of absence" from Mr & Mrs B~, borrowed E's bonnet & mantle & left.

---

18. "The Southern Girl With the Home-Spun Dress," America Singing: Nineteenth-Century Song Sheets, Library of Congress; "The Southern Girl's Song," American Song Sheets, Duke University Libraries Digital Collections. The collection shows the publication date as 1861.

Went over home. Found Sara busy as a bee getting ready, so at work I went. Washed, put on my new white coat ~ took my brage, wore my linen sack, and felt grand. Miss Sallie says that on sunday all the planters round were riding up and down the creek after their rails. Mr Murry had about a mile of fencing washed away ~ besides his cow pen ~ hog-pen & horse lot. Caney was up until it looked like a river.

June 15th Wednesday ~ Miss Sallie went with us to Chappel-Hill. Just as we went up, Mr Lee came up and he very kindly found us a nice cool seat by a window, and afterwards sent us some water. Heard a large class in Philosiphy examined ~ bore their examination with honor to themselves and teachers. Annie M and Miss L came about 11 A.M. with their blue bonnets and white-swiss dresses ~ looked as neat as wax.

Us girls got greatly scattered. I sit in the aisle; 'twas so crowded we could hardly breathe. ~~In the eve~~ Sung "Will Be Gay and Happy." "When I was Young" sung by Miss Sallie Blackshire. Had on a home-spun dress ~ no hoops, the least little home-spun white apron, a small shawl and a broad-brimed brown hat brought down like a fashionable bonnet filled in with flowers and lace. She sung first of the home-spun dress, then apron then bonnet, and afterward said the girls did not think ~~then~~ that because a gentleman came to see you they were in love, or because they asked you to ride with them that the next thing was to marry. Many other songs were sung duets played, &c &c.

June 20th Monday ~ No rain for a week 'til yesterday eve ~ a shower. E's cribs[19] were set on fire and burned by a negro yesterday. The girls went to get some one to watch out for him ~ were gone until late this P.M.

June 21st Tuesday ~ Went over home this eve. Rode Bobby ~ Ruf's pony. E went with me. Met Ans' coming back; [he] had a letter for me from Mack ~ "long looked for ~ come at last" ~ written on the 3rd of the month. Was at camp near Alexandria. Aunt Lu sent me word Miss Mary Smith was to start for home in the morn ~ so I wrote a letter to my folks and one for Mr Middleton to Mrs Georgia Reed.[20]

---

19. "Cribs" was a shortened version of "corncribs," which were small ventilated receptacles used for storing ears of corn.

20. On March 20, Lucy had learned of Miss Mary Smith's plan to leave Texas. She had apparently been successful in her attempts to secure the proper documents and was willing to take Lucy's letter to Ohio with her.

June 28th Tuesday ~ Dr. McLarin came back directly with Ruf. He says last night some negroes went to Mr Yilha's [and] stole some coffee, sugar, tobacco &c. Then when he went to follow them up to find out who they were, [they] beat him nearly to death. He and Uncle Pier were up there soon this morn and all are now interested in trying to find out the guilty party.

June 30th Thursday ~ Last night Mrs Sinclare's Abe went into Mr Brion's horse lot. Stole his horse and left, nothing been seen of him since. 'Twas not long ago Mr Ayers had one of his fine carriage horses stolen. This P.M. Sam Catlin came up on his way out to Mr Collins. As he was return-ing, saw off the road three negroes building their fire to get supper. Mr John Lott took supper here and afterward he and Uncle P~ went up to the meeting at the church to decide on what measures should be taken in regard to the Negroes. Sent for Reub Harris and dogs.

Beginning on a light note, May and June had turned into busy, worrisome months for Lucy. She had covered a wide range of topics in her diary, care-fully documenting the occurrences that framed her world. As June ended, she began to focus more heavily on the unrest in her area, but the bulk of her concern for these months had been the war. Until now, for the most part, the war had been far removed from Lucy's perspective, except for those rare occasions when a report arrived that concerned one of the local boys. Recently, however, the fighting was much nearer, and all of her friends were involved. The Red River Campaign had hit close to home, and Lucy's world felt more keenly the tremors of apprehension. Had the outcome been differ-ent, Texas could have joined the rest of the South as a conquered people, and the devastation might have been as intense.

Although not nearly as famous as the Eastern campaigns and battles, the 1864 expedition along the Texas-Louisiana-Arkansas border proved to be decisive. However, it rates merely an asterisk in many historical accounts. Thomas Ayres recaps:

The ill-fated Red River Campaign [was] one of the most ignoble defeats in this history of the United States military, and the last great victory of the Confederate States of America . . . The war in Louisiana in general and the Red River Campaign in particular stood as such an inexplicable and ignoble Union defeat that some Northern historians, in their haste to glorify the events of that great conflict after 1865, were inclined to ignore it. The Battle of Mansfield and its aftermath proved an odd piece that did not fit into the overall puzzle of Civil War, and thus they discarded it, unintentionally enshrining the Trans Mississippi conflict as our forgotten war.[21]

Though this war was perhaps forgotten by some, it captured Lucy's attention, even her heart, as she continued to record the impact of these battles in this region on the people she loved.

---

21. Ayres, *Dark and Bloody Ground*, 260.

CHAPTER 11

JULY–SEPTEMBER
1864

This morn I took a chill which lasted several hours, then had high fever all day and night.
They all wanted me to have the Dr come in and prescribe for me. And at last
I told them they could have him if they wanted to, fearing they might
some time regret it if they did not have him. ~

LUCY P. STEVENS,
August 21, 1864

THE WAR REPORTS HAD SLOWED TO A TRICKLE for the time being, and what was once the focal point of Lucy's diary was now an addendum. Local drama now dominated the pages of her journal as she detailed at length ongoing anxiety over slave issues and neighborhood feuds. Ironically, as she reported on the trial of Dr. Peebles, Lucy juxtaposed her defense of a convicted traitor on July 3 with a tribute to the early patriots the following day. On July 4, in what may be the most eloquent entry of her journal, Lucy unguardedly penned her deepest thoughts, perhaps the best indicator of her true sentiments about the conflict. Yet her words neither rebuked nor privileged either South or North. Indeed, almost as a prayer, she called on "every American who loves his country" to transcend all disputes and preserve the union forged by "noble patriots" of an earlier day.

Lucy then returned to a major concern that she had addressed at the end of June—the local violence attributed to runaway slaves in the area. Tensions were high, and no one knew what to expect in the way of future violence. Randolph Campbell reports that although runaways "generally did not use violence against their pursuers," individual examples of slaves using all manner of aggression in rebellion against their owners do exist.[1] These situations were well known among households and obviously created high levels of anxiety for slave owners. It is no wonder that Lucy wrote of Sarah

---

1. Randolph B. Campbell, *An Empire for Slavery: The Peculiar Institution in Texas* (Baton Rouge: Louisiana State University Press, 1989), 183–184.

having the "figits," and that, despite a lack of success, "all [were] interested" in a speedy resolution. Interestingly, Lucy presupposed guilt and following Abe's capture and trial, in an observation tinged with sarcasm, articulated her displeasure with the light sentence. It cannot be assumed that she would have preferred a death penalty, as the slave code allowed; what can be absolutely inferred, however, is that she was not the only person questioning the verdict.

However, as the daily dramas of life took over Lucy's thoughts, her entries concerning illness and death increasingly came to the forefront as the dominant theme. She first wrote on July 4 that little Austin Campbell had been sick for more than two weeks with typhoid fever, and she would go on to track his condition over the course of the next two weeks. His illness, typhoid fever, was of a particularly dangerous nature, as described in *The People's Common Sense Medical Adviser in Plain English* by Dr. Ray Vaughn Pierce, who wrote, "The fever is so dangerous that a physician should be summoned as soon as the disease is recognized."[2] He went on to give particulars of the disease, pointing out that the treatment involved administering doses of quinine every two or three hours. Pierce ended by indicating that the disease was highly contagious and reiterated that it was quite dangerous, warning that "its treatment should at once be confided to the family physician."[3]

Whether or not the community knew that the disease was so contagious is uncertain. It is known, however, that many friends and neighbors came regardless, to "set up" with the boy and help as they could. As participants in this standard practice, Lucy and Sarah were both fully involved during the summer as one after another of their friends fell prey to illness. Lucy wrote repeatedly about taking a turn staying with an ailing friend or loved one, and, in fact, sometimes indicated that so many were on hand that her services were not needed, signifying that for this community, at least, sitting with the sick offered a social setting as well as an opportunity to serve.

Sadly, Austin's illness was just one of many that Lucy would follow in her diary in the days to come. As the heat of summer intensified, Lucy wrote more and more despondently, as one after another of her friends and acquaintances succumbed, and the sickness spread from home to home. Young friends who were out visiting one day would be reported critically ill the next, and often, within just a short time, Lucy found herself attending their funerals.

---

2. Ray Vaughn Pierce, M.D., *The People's Common Sense Medical Adviser in Plain English; Or, Medicine Simplified* (World's Dispensary Medical Association, 1895), 407, Project Gutenberg.
    3. Ibid.

JULY 1864

July 1st Friday ~ Newt and Jane both came home with me in the eve ~ felt some what timid coming through the bottom for Mr Cyrus Campbell had a little negroe robbed of his clothes this morn.

July 3rd Sunday ~ Sister Julis twentyeth birthday ~ my good Sis, how I would like to spend it with you. but alas I can not even know that you are among the living ~ blessing on you if you may be.

Aunt Lu was telling today that Dr Peebles with three other prisoners had been remanded to ~~Houston~~ Anderson to await further orders, that Mr Baldwin was sent back previously. I thought it was very strange that Milatary had gotten to be so wonderful good. Mrs McRee says Maggie and Johnie Peebles was to have gone with their Father ~ hope they can go yet. God is all wise and will and knows best what is for the good of his children. Let us trust in him that all things will finaly end well. We can not be the judges ~ I shall try to be reconciled.

July 4th Monday ~ Hail! ~ glorious anniversary which gained our country's freedom! Long may the memory of the noble patriots who enrolled their names in assertion of our freedom be held sacred, and may their thoughts of right, unity and good will to man, be the true sentiments of every American who loves his country. Much did they suffer to gain our glorious Independence, and ought they not, for that reason if none other, be our guides now.

Sara went over to see Austin Campbell today. Found him very low, has had fever ~ typhoid ~ 17 days now.

Got to Mr Boington before dark. Johnie looks bad enough ~ I can not think he has many years to live. He stayed with Waller's Reg~ after he was sick until coming home, 'Tis terriable to think of the effects of the late battles in La as they are told us. Johnie says he was put on picket the first night after he got into camp

Spent the eve at Mrs B's, then went to Mrs Cameron's to stay all night. Had chicken & black-berry pies for our 4th of July dinner.

July 5th Tuesday ~ Just such another night as last I do not hope to spend again soon. Sara had the figets thinking of the runaways &c. Then the bugs were so bad they wouldn't let a body rest.

Mr Lee came in the school-room just before starting to Mr McRee's, and asked me didn't I want to go with him and E. to Mrs Sevintz this eve and get some water melons so this eve we went. While going, I mentioned my intended trip to Mr M's friday eve. Mr L~ says when do you return ~ I told him and he says I will have to come out and see Mrs Cleveland that day, and will come by and ride out with you. Not a word did I reply for I was not much pleased with such an arrangement.

Reub Harris came with his dog last night and Sack says I am mistakened this morn. No success yet all are interested though.

July 6th Wednesday ~ Abe was caught to day. We had quite a time this eve after tea over John['s] donkey. Sack and Hemp Edwards were going over to Mr Clevelands to help guard the negroes and went out to get their horses when they found muly gone. The children had heard a horse go at full gallop past the cow-pen, so of course the supposition was he had been taken.

Ruf got a lantern and we all went to hunt tracks and try to find out. Found horse tracks in the road but no mules. After a long search, donkey was found in the pasture. Probably had been let out by some of the servants as they went for water.

July 7th Thursday ~ Abraham left this morn. He, Mr B~ and Ruf all went over to the trial ~ at 11 A.M. came home, not at all satisfied with the result. Nearly every one was satisfied Abe was guilty of what he had been accused. Still he was let off with a whipping ~ not more than I expected after what I heard this morn.

July 8th Friday ~ Found Sara and Sis Torrence had gone to Mr Campbells to set up with Austin.

July 9th Saturday ~ In the eve went to Mr Cyrus C's to set up ~ found Sara J S~ Sue & Sallie Campbell there. Austin had very little fever this eve.

July 10th Sunday ~ Sis T went over to Mr Campbells this eve as she heard that Austin was worse.

July 11th Monday ~ E~ and I went over to Mrs Cyrus C's this eve, found Austin looking much worse than when I left yesterday

Yesterday Mr & Mrs Catlin went to see Mr & Mrs John Lott and got their written acknowledgement of having heard Mrs Cleveland talk of Sallie Lou. What is our neighborhood going to come to? You hear nothing else talked of hardly. Everyone down on the Clevelands for proof against them is so posative.

July 12th Tuesday ~ Austin had a sinking spell which lasted about two hours to day, they were afraid he would never recover from it but he looks much improved since I saw him before. Sallie C and I watched together until one. A [Austin] slept very quietly the first part of the night ~ about eleven became restless, so we called Mrs C.

Mrs Swearingen says she has seen Mr & Mrs John Lotts written statement of what the Clevelands have said about Sallie Lou and the Catlins.

July 13th Wednesday ~Mrs B~ told me Mr Cleveland was over yesterday eve after I left "to investigate the matter" found out nothing as no one had heard a word.

During this same time, a neighborhood feud had erupted in the community, and Lucy had begun to chronicle the ongoing quarrel in her diary on July 11. One neighbor, Mrs. Cleveland, had apparently spread unsavory gossip about Sallie Lou Catlin and had polarized the neighbors. However, although Lucy only now began documenting the dispute, Cousin Sarah had been recording details since late June. Both Sarah and Lucy communicated their abhorrence, indicating their disapproval of the level of vitriol in Mrs. Cleveland's words, yet neither ever divulged exactly what the rumors might be. Indeed, despite her usually conciliatory nature, Sarah expressed her condemnation far more vehemently than Lucy as she tracked the scandal in her journal:

June 26: I never heard of such a shameful story as the Clevelands have been telling on Sallie Lu Catlin—It is a perfect shame that white folks will repeat such.

July 4: I went to Mrs. Catlin's to see her this morning. She looks very badly and that horrid tale that is circulating around by Mrs. Cleveland's family makes her almost crazy. She is so mad.

July 13: The whole neighborhood is in confusion on account of Mrs. Cleveland's lies. Mrs. Catlin, I believe, is going to turn her out of the Church, I hope so at any rate—for it is a shame and disgrace to have her in it.

Sarah had revealed her indignation earlier in her journal, following Sol Cleveland's attempt to run away from home (see Lucy's entries 4/18/64 and 4/22/64). Even then, Sarah had penned her denunciation of Mr. Lott and Mrs. Cleveland, stating that Jim Lott had an "unruly tongue" and that "he [had] been talking too much of late," while "[Mrs. Cleveland was] perfectly crazy mad" (Sarah Pier, 4/20/64). Sarah's condemnation grew as the coming weeks unfolded, for the rhetoric in the community escalated, depositions were taken, violence ensued, and the diaries kept pace, chronicling the "sad affair . . . that arose from that story" (Sarah Pier, 7/14/64). Lucy returned to the "Cleveland and Catlin difficulty" in her entry of July 24, but again, it is Sarah's diary that more scrupulously details the ongoing hostilities. On the same day, Sarah wrote, "Went to church and Sabbath school. Dr. Follensby preached. Mr. Chapman divided my little class today to gratify one of Mrs. Catlin's notion of not wanting Tudie and Sukey in the same class with Caroline Cleveland." Apparently, even after bloodshed, the matter could not be resolved, and Mrs. Catlin continued to avenge her daughter's reputation.

July 14th Thursday ~ In the eve Lissie and I went over to Mr C s to set-up. Found a house full, Sara among others. They sent for her to day ~ thought A [Austin] was dying and for an hour the breath seemed to have left him. He then revived and still lives. Uncle's [Uncle Pier and Aunt Lu] have not got home yet, so I offered to go keep the house and let her stay.

Great times in our little community. A victory gained by Catlin over [Jim] Lott ~ two wounded, none killed. Mr Catlin made Mr. Lott waltz up to a new tune ~ fight took place at Mr. Rufus C's. Mr C~ was there fixing his carriage. Mr Lott and John C~ went there ~ high words passed between them. Mr L~ drew his pistol when Mr C remarked if that was his game, he was in. Run into the shop after his own, and as he came out Mr L~ peeped out from behind the shop and fired, causing a flesh wound on the right wrist. He then started on a run, Mr C after him. The latter shot three times but one of the balls taking effect. Mr L~ fell then they had it. Rolled each other over in the mud awhile but at last they were separated. Mr L~ is so badly wounded he could not be moved from Mr Campbell's. Dr is afraid he will take the lock jaw from it. Cole is their physician.

They had Dr C~ called in at Mr Cy C's [Campbell] to night he gave them no reason to hope though. Poor little Austin ~ he is perfectly raving, groans and moans all the time and throws his arms, beating his head and breast. Mrs C is almost sick she is in so much distress. It seems like Austin's every moan went to her heart.

July 15th Friday ~ Had great times this morn getting my children dressed for the last day My children did exceedingly well. Steph spoke his speech so well that Bell had to cry during the whole of it. They all talked to me so much as if I was never going to see them again. I could not keep from feeling really sad.

Found Uncle P~ and Aunt Lu had come. Left Willie sick with whooping cough and Uncle Jimmy very low with typhoid fever.

July 16th Saturday ~ Cousin S~ came from Mr Campbells about 9 A.M. Austin was still living. In the P.M. Uncle Pier had Dick take the carriage and bring us girls to Lu's. found three doctors with Uncle J~: Bailey of Hempstead, Perkins of Chapel H~ and Richie. Dr's say they do not think Uncle J~ dangerously ill. Uncle J~ shook hands with us girls as if he knew we were his friends.

July 17th Sunday ~ Dr B~ and Mr Day left after breakfast. Before starting, they told Uncle J~ they thought there was no doubt but he would soon be up but he talked quite as if he had no such hope.

During the morning, he asked for cousin Waller, Uncle Frank and Mr Day. Cousin Sara and Mrs M. Foster, who were in the room at the time, left thinking he wanted to get up. I was lying down in the room adjoining with the doors between open, and heard and saw Uncle Jimmy tell them, cous W~ & Uncle F~, he wanted cousin Lu to have Lucinda and her family.[4] Then repeated, saying he wanted cousin Lu, Waller's wife, to have Lucinda and her family, then added something to the effect he hoped his word would be sufficient. Cousin W~ and Dr [Richie] went out on the gallery and had some talk, came back, and all three tried to persuade him out of saying more at present, trying to think he would

---

4. Apparently, Uncle Jimmy owned Lucinda and her family and desired to bequeath them, as his personal property, to Cousin Lu upon his death.

soon be better. Tried my best to get cousin W~ to let Uncle J~ sayed what he wanted to, knowing all might some day regret his not having done so. And I knew very well it would be a relief and satisfaction to him to do so instead of an annoyance as he feared. Not succeeding, I told cousin Sara and tried to get her to use her influence. But after the subject had been dropped, he hated to bring it up again so delayed until after Uncle Frank had gone, then of course would not speak of it.

Lu, poor child, looks nearly worn out. We can see but little change in Uncle J~.

July 18th Monday ~ Aunt Margaret & Lu set up then 'til daylight when Sara and I got up. During the morning, Uncle J~ asked again for Uncle Frank and Mr Day. Cousin W~ sent for them, but it was late when they came and Uncle J~ seemed wearied. Cousin Lu is kept constantly on the go. Cousin Sara & I set up until past midnight then woke Uncle Frank.

July 19th Tuesday ~ Mr Day went back this morn although Uncle J~ seems no better, talks with no connection to his sentences. I have set in the room but very little today for it seems to trouble him to see so many around.

July 20th Wednesday ~ Cousin Lu and Mrs Foster set up the first part of last night, then as I could not sleep, I got up at twelve. Was by myself from three 'til half past five. Uncle J~ seems to notice everything today, about 10 A.M. Uncle J~ was so much worse that cousin W~ sent for Uncle Frank. At about half past 10 Uncle J~ thought he was dying, said "he wanted to be held up to die." We all thought he could not last longer than midnight and no one lay down until near that time.

July 21st Thursday ~ cousin Lu and Aunt Margaret set up until daylight. Uncle Jimmy seemed to notice everything that passed until seven. At half past seven his eyes were set and at ten he breathed his last. Good Uncle Jimmy ~ little did I think so sincere a friend would be the first I should see die, but so it is. We hope his spirit has gone to a brighter world where care and trouble is no more. He assured his sister that all was well with him, and we have every reason to believe so.

Mr & Mrs Buck and Mrs Day came just after he died. Mr Buck attended to dressing and laying out the corpse.

This is M'ck's [Mack's] twenty-fifth birthday. Little does he think how it is being celebrated.

July 22nd Friday ~ Cousin Sammy's twentyeth birthday

Lu sent for me soon ~ started to the grave at 9. Went by Mr Cochranes and Mr Foster's. The Foster burying ground is at Mr Banks old place, such a pretty spot enclosed with a stone wall and has several very large trees in it ~ there was a goodly number out

July 24th Sunday ~ Joe got back at noon, brought three letters for us to read, also a note from Sara. She says little Austin Campbell died on Tuesday. the Cleveland and Catlin difficulty getting worse.

25th Monday ~ Cousin Lu had Uncle Jimmy's room scoured from top to bottom ~ she and I together cleaned the windows, got nearly all the paint off from the glass. Luce cleaned over head. We had a time of it ~ took us all day, but night brought quite a change. 'Tis clean and pleasant now.

26th Tuesday ~ Lucinda cleaned the floors and scalded the bed in the room where the piano used to be. Moved the piano into Uncle Jimmy's room.

About 8 P.M. Catharine[5] took fever. Was so nervous Lu gave her two large doses of morphine, a table spoon of asfedity[6] a blister on the back of her neck and mustard poultice on her breast and stomach and sent for Dr Boyd. At 10 she seemed much better. There are five [does Lucy mean six?] negroes down now ~ black Lucinda, Aunt Betsy ~ Tilda ~ Beckie, Catharine and Aunt Violet

July 28th Thursday ~ Set up with Catharine by myself until after 1~, then slept until noon today ~ could not keep my eyes open. Luce [Lucinda] was taken with a chill this P.M. just as Catharine was Tuesday. She was so nervious, we got scared and sent for Dr Richie.

Lucinda washed yesterday and today.

---

5. Catharine was one of Cousin Lu's slave women.

6. According to the *Oxford English Dictionary*, "asafœtida" (or "asfedity," as Lucy wrote), is a bitter-tasting, foul-smelling resinous gum found in certain herbs and used as an antispasmodic.

July 31st Sunday ~ Willie is four years old ~ is telling everyone of it.

In the afternoon Lu & I went over to see Mrs Pilley. Sent Willie to Mrs B's to stay until we should return. Mr P~ had gone to Bellville election-eering ~ is running for county clerk.

AUGUST 1864

As August began, Lucy faced her own romantic dilemma. Mr. Lee, the dentist, had developed an unwanted attraction for her, and she was frustrated by his attentions. Lucy had previously recorded her displeasure in her July 5 entry, but now her irritation knew no bounds. Cousin Sarah wrote of Mr. Lee's pursuit, noting, "Mr. Lee was in to see me a few moments—had to enquire very particularly for Cous Lu. He is interested in her" (Sarah Pier, 8/1/64). Apparently, Mr. Lee felt no need for discretion as he sought intercessors for Lucy's affection. Lucy wrote scathingly of his conversation with Mrs. Middleton, then went on to inject her own caustic commentary as well-meaning friends played matchmaker.

Yet even as Lucy had unequivocally rejected the attention of Mr. Lee, her notes on August 7 may hint at an unrequited attraction of her own. Her words and tone could imply a secret affection for a local soldier boy, home on leave, but her careful phrasing gives no hint as to the identity of the young man. Neither this entry, nor any other, supplies any information that could reveal Lucy's innermost feelings. Even the confidential pages of "Mr. Journal" could not guarantee Lucy a completely trustworthy sanctuary. Thus, she kept her own counsel now, just as she had maintained her privacy when she had earlier alluded to "her old man," not willing to provide any clues as to the secret desires of her own heart.

Aug 1st Monday ~ Lu and I were just getting ready to go see Mrs O'Brion & Sue when Mr & Mrs Middleton came. Mrs M commenced joking me the first thing about Bi L. [Mr. Lee] Said she was mad at him as she could be; that he had promised to have her work ready for her last week but came there and was dissapointed in not finding "Miss Lu." She says he told he thought Miss L~ such a fine young lady was one of his favorites, and directly after told he meant soon to get a nice little home of his own. He is such a goose ~ he would soon have people believing he means to court me to listen at him. I wish he would hold his tongue. Mrs M~ brought me such a nice present of a dress from Mr M. gave $80 per yd in species for it

Aug 2nd Tuesday ~ Found out some more news about myself that I could write such a good love-letter. So someone said that professed to have seen one of my writing. I replied perhaps I could ~ but as I had never made the trial, could not answer posative. How fortunate I am to have friends so interested in my welfare.

Aug 4th Thursday ~ With Lu's perscription Mary is much better this morn. Cousin Sara tried to convince me B. L. [Mr. Lee] was intending more than friendly attention. Uncle P~ loaded Mrs B's carriage with peaches. We have had such a treat: peaches fresh ~ peaches & cream & peach cobbler.

Started for Lu's about half past 7. Called at Mrs P~. He [Mr. Pilley] is at home, has got the sulks ~ was badly beaten. Thinks the people of Austin Co do not know how to appreciate true worth;[7] did not take it as coolly as cousin W did his defeat.

Aug 7th Sunday ~ Went to church today, haven't seen so many people together in a long time before. Parson Alexander preached Uncle Jimmy's funeral sermon from the 1st chapter of Philippians 21st verse "For me to live is Christ ~ but to die is gain."

Mrs Kavanaugh & Miss Ann came still later than the others. And not long after ~ I caught a glimpse of a blue coat & white pants that I knew so well ~ my attention was riveted on the minister for the rest of the morn. John H~ brought me a letter from Mr Wiley, written the 25th of July. Gave a description of a raid they had made ~ went onto a Yankee plantation and took some negroes mules and beeves but came near being captured themselves on their backward march, had to "take to the woods."

Mollie gave me a letter from Neh to read ~ written on the 28th brought in by Billy Fordtran. He [Billy] was taken prisoner at the Yellow

---

7. "Z. W. Matthews," Austin County Abstract 270, Texas General Land Office Digital Archives. According to Austin County clerk Carrie Gregor, Z. W. Matthews won the election. Matthews had been awarded 320 acres of land by the Board of Land Commissioners for Austin County in 1839, according to records from the Texas General Land Office, having provided proof that he had "resided in the Republic 3 years and performed all the duties required of as a citizen."

bayou fight was sent to N.O. [New Orleans]. Complains of his treatment there, says if it were not for the ladies there, the prisoners would suffer. He has just been exchanged and returned home.

Spoke to mine friend [Mr. Lee] as I could not well avoid it. He was extremely friendly with cousin W~ hinting for an invite to come out here. And I was so much afraid he would succeed that I told Mrs K~ I would go home with her.

Aug 8th Monday ~ Beckie was taken with fever about half past twelve last night and has been right bad off all day. Sue Wilson came up with Lu. We started back about two. Like to have toasted, it was so warm.

Aug 10th Wednesday ~ Mrs Buck sent us word her baby was sick, so I went over and spent the day. Aunt Lu told us the sad news of Miss McH death on sunday last, was taken sick the wednesday before. Also, Fannie McLarin died on monday was dying as they drove past to bury Miss McH. I little thought when I was at Mrs L~ t'would be my last visit with Miss McH~.

Aug 11th Thursday ~ Aunt Lu & Uncle P~ visited Mrs B, her baby is worse. Miss Ann came, says Beckie is worse so she can not stay to do her coat. Wanted me to go home with her. I promised to go set up to night. She [Beckie] had had fever since we were there. Mr Holland came just as Uncle P~ was leaving, just up from Houston. [He] went down there to plead the case of a deserted soldier who had been sentenced to death. Succeeded in getting the sentence changed, but he has to be imprisoned during the war. Beckie has no fever this eve ~ they are trying to keep it off. Miss Sue Wilson is very sick.

Aug 12th Friday ~ Mrs Holland was not at all well last night, eat no supper and did not come down to breakfast this morn. [N]either did Mrs Kavanaugh, she had slept so little for three nights. Sue is indeed very sick, sent for the Dr this morn.

Aug 13th Saturday ~ In the eve went to set up with Miss Sue ~ Miss Ann was still there, had not been home. But as I was going to stay, she concluded to go and take a rest and will come back in the morning. Dr is here.

Aug 14th Sunday ~ Left Sue, as I supposed, much better. She slept for about an hour the first part of the night, and near three in the morning sayed she felt so much refreshed, was a great deal better. So I went away perfectly contented, promising to come back at night. Alas, how much deceived we can sometimes be. At half past two they sent me word she was a corpse. I could not believe it. At first it seemed so almost impossible. Went up on horse back as soon as I could; Found Mrs O'B~ in the deepest grief. Poor poor, lone woman. Would that I could be a comfort to you. but no one can ever fill the place of your affectionate daughter. Truly do I sympathize with you in your great affliction. I too have lost in Su a devoted friend. We all feel it hard to give her up.

MARGINAL NOTE: *Sue Wilson died Aug 14th 1864 ~ was 16 the 3rd of Oct 1863*

Aug 15th Monday ~ Miss Ann and I made the winding sheet. Every one seemed kind and willing to do what they could. In the morn Sue looked as natural as could be, but at half past ten, she commenced changing. Changed so very fast we feared her eyes would burst before the coffin would come, but happily they did not. All the neighbors were at the burial except Lu and Mrs Buck. They got word from Mr Burdett his wife was very low, so they went to see her

Aug 18th Thursday ~ 'Twas very unpleasant this morn. But fearing Mrs Cochrane would be uneasy about Mollie, we concluded to come home. Commenced to rain soon after we started and kept it up until afternoon. Every article of clothing I had was wringing wet. Mollie fared some better, for I thought she had taken calomel[8] and was afraid she would be salivated, so gave her the shawl and cloak. I was afraid too she might take a chill and made her drink the brandy Mr M gave us.

Aug 19th Friday ~ Mollie, Em and John Ivey all sick today. Sent for Dr Boyd for John, and this P.M., Mollie was so bad off I persuaded her to let them send for Dr Tottingham. Dr says she has no light fever that it will require strong medacine to break it up.

---

8. According to the *OED*, "calomel," or mercurous chloride, is a white, tasteless powder used widely during the nineteenth century as a purgative.

Aug 20th Saturday ~ This morn I took a chill which lasted several hours, then had high fever all day and night.

Aug 21st Sunday ~ In the afternoon, we heard Willie Cameron was dying, and Sis and Sara were going to see him, but I got so much worse they would not leave. They all wanted me to have the Dr come in and pre-scribe for me. And at last I told them they could have him if they wanted to, fearing they might some time regret it if they did not have him.

———

The soaking to which Lucy referred in her entry of August 18 may well have been the trigger for Mollie's illness, and may have set Lucy up for her own health crisis. Within days, Lucy became the patient instead of the nurse, and others rallied to her side, even as she had cared for them.

Lucy apparently suffered two serious illnesses while in Texas. Sarah had noted an anniversary of Lucy's first illness on March 25, 1863, writing: "two years ago Cousin Lue was taken sick, when she came near dying" (Sarah Pier, 3/25/63). Aunt Lu also mentioned the illness, noting that Lu was very sick (Lu M. Pier, 3/28/61, 4/8/61), but gave no other information. Lucy herself gave a name to her illness, for in her earlier diary she noted,

Tis just five weeks last eve since I was taken sick with typhus but was not very ill until the first of April—Have improved so fast for the last week that I almost feel myself well now. Dressed myself for the first time on Saturday last & Sunday went out to the dining room also et out on the gallery a half hour. No one can tell how glad I am to be able to be up & go round once more.

Lucy P. Stevens, 4/30/61

Now, a similar situation occurred, and the sickness is well documented. In her own diary, Lucy recorded that she was very sick, so sick that she allowed the family to call for the doctor. There followed a two-week gap in her diary, indicating that she was too ill to write. Here, Sarah's diary provides signifi-cant clues, with daily entries tracking Lucy's illness:

August 21: Cous Lu came home from Mr. Thos. Cochran's . . . She had a fever yesterday after a chill and it had not gone entirely off this morning . . . intending to go up but Cous Lu became so much worse I could not leave her . . . she is threatened with congestion and keeps very sick at her stomach—she also suffers much from constipation of the bowels.

August 22: Sallie Lu and the Dr. came down this morning to see Cous Lu who is quite sick—Sallie spent the day, and Sis T. is sitting up with me tonight and Ma was up until 12 Oc. The Dr. took supper here. He says Cous Lu has congestive fever.

August 23: The Dr. was here all the forenoon he is uneasy about Cous Lu—her stomach is so weak she cannot take or retain the medicine as she should. It is nothing but fan and sprinkle water in her face all the time . . . Mr. Brewer went there this afternoon for some Brandy for Cous Lu . . . Cous Lu is resting very well but her medicine does not act.

August 24: I took about two hours sleep before 12 Oc. That and an hour or so two nights ago, is all the rest I have had since Cous Lu came home. She seemed better this morning The Dr. called on his way to Hempstead this morning, and pronounced her so, but she has been very sick this afternoon—Pa sent by Mr. Middleton this evening for Dr. Key of Brenham. We gave her croton oil this afternoon but she did not retain it on her stomach long enough to benefit her. Pa then gave her salts ever few moments until they have had an effect. And now (nearly day) she is resting quietly. I feel greatly encouraged about her now. She has said from the first she would never get well but I hope she may now and believe she will.
    Sarah Pier, 8/21–24/64

Sarah and the others had good reason to worry. *The People's Common Sense Medical Adviser in Plain English* states that congestive fever was so deadly that it had been nicknamed "pernicious fever." Dr. Pierce went on to explain that this was

the most severe and dangerous form of malarial fever . . . In some instances the first paroxysm is so violent as to destroy life in a few hours, while in others it comes on insidiously, the first one or two paroxysms being comparatively mild. It is frequently characterized by stupor, delirium, a marble-like coldness of the surface, vomiting and purging, jaundice, or hemorrhage from the nose and bowels . . . This fever is so dangerous that a physician should be summoned as soon as the disease is recognized.[9]

---

9. Pierce, *Common Sense Medical Adviser*, 406–407.

Pierce's description provided an apt compilation of Lucy's symptoms, and her family and friends, for a time, rightly feared the worst.

Lucy's own diary began again on September 5, and she wrote about the severity of her illness, commenting that this was the third time in her life she had not been expected to live. She took the time to note the many visitors who had come. These personal visits were a means by which family and friends could express their love and concern, and Lucy deeply appreciated the effort. Equally worthy of mention in her diary was her appreciation of Uncle Pier, who had "set up" with her for hours one night.

Lucy's illness caused her to pause and assess her situation, brooding over the loss of so many loved ones in her life. To be sure, death was an ever-present adversary, one that frequently proved victorious. During certain periods, it seemed to Lucy and Sarah that nothing could be done to battle the ominous foe. Just before Lucy's near-fatal illness, both girls had spent much time helping other members of the community as they battled sickness. It was taken for granted that when "illness of a serious nature struck a home the neighbors were immediately informed and always there was one woman who excelled in caring for the sick in each community."[10] Sarah, despite her young age, exhibited great skill and compassion toward those who were ill. The responsibility took its toll physically and emotionally, however, for Sarah wrote on August 19, "It seems to me that tis nothing but sickness and death now days. Ella is the eighth person I have been with when they died or waited on during their last sickness, within five months. I am tired, tired, O so tired . . ." (Sarah Pier, 8/19/64).

SEPTEMBER 1864

~~ Sick ~~

Sept 5th Monday ~ As I anticipated ~ had a severe spell of sickness. the chill I had at Mr C's was congestive and I have had congestive fever until a few days ago. This is the third time in my life I have not been expected to live. Thursday was the first time I had been able to set up any, but now if it were that I am so badly salivated, I would feel much better.

Every one round has been so kind since I was sick to come see me and do what they could. This morn Mrs Chapman, thinking a ride would

---

10. Waller County Historical Survey Commission, *A History of Waller County, Texas* (Waco: Author, 1873), 113.

do me good, came by in her carriage and took us girls out to old Mrs Sam's store. Met Ellen Lott. Come out very friendly to see me; said she had not heard I was sick until a few days ago. One night Uncle P~ set up with me until after 12 ~ giving me medacine every ten to fifteen minutes ~ until it took effect.

We heard yesterday by a note from Mrs Switzer that Mrs Miller lost her little Eddy the night before. As soon as Mr Brewer heard I was sick, Mr & Mrs B~ both came over ~ he found out I wanted brandy so he would go out to Mr M's for it. Mr M~ said yes he had a little, but if he had not but one drop and I wanted it, I should have it. Although it was dark, he and Mrs M would come that night to see me ~ and he, always thoughtful, brought medacine along, fearing Uncle P's had not plenty. Such friends are to be highly prized, and I fully appreciate their worth. Next day ~~day~~ Mr M~ sent to Brenham for Dr Key if he could come. If not, for Watkins to come while he himself went to ~~Chapel H~~ for more brandy.

Sept 7th Wednesday ~ This has been a rainy day. I have spent it in writing in my Journal.

Went to the table this noon and to night, but as I can not eat anything but crackers and coffee or soup, custard, or something of the sort, did not much enjoy it.

Sept 8th ~~Friday~~ Thursday ~ Mrs Lott and Mary Cameron spent the day here ~ came about ten and not finding me up Mrs L~ declared 'twas nothing but laziness ailed me Aunt Lu had some nice strong coffee made for breakfast which I very much enjoyed then afterward had some for Mrs Cameron and Mrs L~ I drank a cup of it and at noon a third. Had chicken pie for dinner, if I had been well how much I would have enjoyed it.

Sept 10 9th ~~Saturday~~ Friday ~ Got my pay yesterday for coffee drinking ~ was sick enough soon after the ladies left and before I got over it, took a good dose of morphine. rested quietly all night, but did not sleep a minute until after five in the morn. Just as I was rising, heard a carriage drive up, looked out and saw Mr Middleton. knew at once he had come for me, but thought it impossible to go ~ but lo! Aunt Lu differed with me; said she thought it might be an advantage, so of course I went.[11]

11. In relating this anecdote, Lucy succinctly pointed out the different generational philosophies embraced by herself and Aunt Lu. Lucy was still recuperating from her serious illness and commented that even a cup of coffee had sickened her the day before. However, Aunt Lu, with her no-nonsense approach to life, put an end to any coddling and sent Lucy on an outing.

Sept 13th Tuesday ~ Mr & Mrs M do all in their power for me to feel perfectly at home and to enjoy myself. work progresses but slowly so far. I am "so, no account." This afternoon, as we were enjoy[ing] a snooze, whose but the well known voice of J~D's [John D. Harvey] should be heard. I was in no hurry to make my appearance however letting him & Mr M visit.

Sept 14th Wednesday ~ Johnie spent last night here and stayed until nearly noon to day we had a long talk about Kinch Mollie, Linda and Neh[12]

Kinch has asked and got Mr Cochrane's consent to their marriage. I am so glad for their sakes

Sept 20th Tuesday ~ Finished my calico dress ~ put a pocket in my Middleton dress[13]

News came to day confirming the report that Atlanta had fallen into the hands of the Fed~ also that John Morgan[14] was killed in Ky and that all his staff but one had been taken.

Sept 26th Monday ~ Jane & Newt are still across the creek so I begin with but three schollars.

Sept 27th Tuesday ~ Sack commenced school this morn. This eve not long after school, Mrs Stevens, Ella, Dellie (a blind child) and Lizzie came from Houston ~ ran away from yellow fever.

---

12. "Early Marriage Records 1824–1920." Kinch (Kinchen) Collins married Mollie (Mary) Cochran on December 7, 1865. Mollie's brother, Neh (Nehemiah) Cochran, married Linda (Malinda) Collins on November 11, 1865. Sadly, Linda died in 1869, and Neh subsequently married Florence Montgomery in 1872.

13. On August 1, Lucy had recorded that Mr. and Mrs. Middleton had given her the fabric for a new dress, and she had begun work on it right away. Her illness had interrupted progress, and even now, work progressed slowly. The Middletons obviously cared a great deal for Lucy, having opened their home to her on numerous occasions. Gifts such as the "Middleton dress" and expressions of deep concern for Lucy's well-being reinforce the degree of love and enjoyment the family derived from Lucy's friendship.

14. The September 24, 1864, issue of *Harper's Weekly* reported that Brigadier General John Hunt Morgan, whose likeness was featured on the magazine's cover in January, was killed in a residence in Greeneville, Kentucky, when the owner, Mrs. Williams, rode fifteen miles at night to alert Union troops of his whereabouts. "John Morgan," *Harper's Weekly* 8, no. 404 (September 24, 1864): 1, HarpWeek.

With Lucy's mention of John Morgan's death, war reports now began to creep back onto the pages of her diary. And as the months wore on, the news would become increasingly bleak. But now, as she closed her journal on September 1864, with a casual aside Lucy unknowingly acknowledged the panic that came nearly every summer to the Gulf Coast region. The Texas coast, with its warm climate, its swarms of mosquitoes, and its connections to the Caribbean, where yellow fever was endemic, was particularly vulnerable. The earliest known yellow fever epidemic in Lucy's part of Texas dates to 1833, when half of the population in Columbia on the Brazos died from the outbreak.[15] Epidemics spread with alarming regularity, and David G. McComb conveys the very real fear in his book *Galveston: A History*. He notes the 1864 epidemic of which Lucy wrote, then goes on to explain that during a subsequent epidemic in 1867, "some five thousand people fled [Galveston], probably, one-third of the population, and spread the fever along the inland train and stage routes ... there were 22 deaths in July, 596 in August, and 482 in September."[16] In one short span of time, in one coastal area, 1,150 people died from an annual scourge that struck swiftly and wreaked havoc. Lucy would detail the suffering that others had likewise experienced.

---

15. Waller County Historical Survey Commission, 289.
16. David G. McComb, *Galveston: A History* (Austin: University of Texas Press, 1986), 92–94.

CHAPTER 12

OCTOBER–DECEMBER
1864

Five years ago to day since we left Ohio. Who could have believed that this time would
have found me on Texas soil trudging off to school ~ with thoughts of home,
sweet home ~ and a determination to brave every danger in an attempt
to reach that loved spot before another year rolls round.

LUCY P. STEVENS,
December 13, 1864

DURING THESE LAST MONTHS OF 1864, the dramas of the summer had
quieted in Lucy's diary, leaving only the ordinariness of everyday life. The
long years of war had produced a weariness and a new sense of "normal" for
her, resulting in a quasi-peacetime approach to her world. Thus, the dailiness of life in and around Travis took over the pages of her diary. Only occasionally did she even mention the war, and then it was with some disdain.
Obviously other women's diaries offer a more graphic view of the times,
particularly if those women's husbands were far away fighting. The constant
anxiety they experienced produced a "significant psychological impact,"
including a numbness that eroded all sense of patriotic duty and loyalty. For
example, Drew Gilpin Faust reports that Lizzie Neblett, a Confederate wife
in another part of Texas, wrote to her husband, Will, that she felt as though
her "heart was seared, incapable of feeling as it once did."[1] However, the Pier
family enjoyed a stability that enabled life to go on much as before, and as the
end of the war approached and soldiers began coming home, local activities
assumed center stage.

Lucy did, however, keep up with some of the election news from the
North, and included several prominent names in her journal, men well
known at that time for their political views. Her inclusion of names such
as Alexander Stephens, vice president of the Confederacy, gives evidence to
the large disparity of political leanings in the Confederacy during the final

1. Drew Gilpin Faust, *Mothers of Invention* (New York: Vintage Books, 1996), 237–238.

stages of the war.[2] Additionally, the use of military information as political fodder had become commonplace, and then, as now, ordinary citizens were the intended targets of partisan power plays. Many in the North believed that McClellan's election would bring an end to the hated conflict. And many more in the South, including Lucy herself, anticipated the coming election with more than passing interest. Once again, her cryptic comments provide clues to her stance on the war, by now a sentiment shared by many. Interestingly, and as a testament to the slow transmission of news, despite her earlier references to McClellan and her interest in the upcoming election, Lucy would make no references to the election's outcome until March 4, 1865, inauguration day.

OCTOBER 1864

Sept 31 Oct 1st Saturday ~ Mended again today. Sara finished her blankets ~ has made four large ones and a small one for Willie.

Oct 2nd Sunday ~ Abb Herrick's, Sara Campbell's and Aunt Mary-Jane's birthday. Sara went to church & Mr Hoffman came home with her. This morn Uncle Pier was called on by Mr John Campbell's to go see his little sick son. John Harvey came here this eve.

Oct 4th Tuesday ~ Have been in bed all day. This morn Eliz~ Mrs Stevens & the children came to see us. Had a letter from Mack today ~ had another chill & now have fever.

Oct 5th Wednesday ~ Was in bed most of the day ~ dressed just before dinner

2. Charles F. Ritter and Jon L. Wakelyn, *Leaders of the Confederacy: A Biographical and Historigraphical Dictionary* (Westport, CT: Greenwood Press, 1998), 393. James M. McPherson, *Ordeal by Fire: The Civil War and Reconstruction,* 2nd ed. (New York: McGraw-Hill, 1992), 446–447. Alexander Stephens, vice president of the Confederacy, had become strongly opposed to the administration of Jefferson Davis, and by 1863, "the question for [him] had become, Was the struggle for a separate country worth it?" (393). Stephens and Georgia governor Joseph E. Brown actively pursued peace, and both men hoped for the defeat of Abraham Lincoln. As McPherson writes, former general McClellan, the nominee of the Democratic Party, was seen as the "peace" candidate by many in the North and South alike. However, Republicans pounced on McClellan's nomination as the "peace" candidate as capitulation, ensuring success to the Confederate cause and to military victories in Virginia as proof of the superiority of their own candidate, Abraham Lincoln.

Sara & Uncle P~ beamed a peice of negro cloth 36 yds long since N[noon]

I finished reading *The Abbot*[3] today ~ it is a continued story from *The Monastery.*

Oct 6th Thursday ~ Missed having a chill today greatly to my delight ~ shall hope to go into school on monday again. 'Tis much warmer than last eve probably preparing for another norther.

Oct 9th Sunday ~ Cousin Sara went to sabbath school. I made myself respectable, and it is well I did, for Artie & John Harvey came home with S~, and just as they came, Mr & Mrs Middleton rode up. All spent the day. Sis, Sallie Lou, Todie & Sukey came about two P.M., & Mr Hoffman about four, to go to the sing this evening as Mr Chapman had appointed for sunday school scholars to commence preparing for a concert to come off christmas.

Oct 10th Monday ~ News came yesterday confirming Dr Francis' death on the 4th of yellow fever. 'Tis still cool. In Sara's last letter from Mr W~ he urges their speedy marriage ~ she is opposed to it.

Oct 12th Wednesday ~ Uncle P~ says the Gov of Georgia & Vice President Stephens are making stump speaches for the Union, going into it on a new basis. Hurrah for McLellan ~ they say his being nominated is the cause.

Oct 13th Thursday ~ Newt came for me this morn and this eve went to the post-office ~ says Carrie told him she was coming over tomorrow to hear the children speak.

Oct 14th Friday ~ Sara & Em came to Mr B's this morn. My children did not do well at all in speaking ~ Carrie did not come ~ I'm glad. Mr M~ came for me this eve ~ we were just drinking coffee as he came ~ went by Uncle P's and changed my coat. Aunt Lu says her and Uncle P~ talk of going to Lu's tomorrow. Mr Seals took supper with us. Sara had a letter

---

3. McGhee, "Sir Walter Scott," in *Dictionary of Literary Biography*, vol. 107, *British Romantic Prose Writers, 1789–1832*, 1st ser., ed. John R. Greenfield, 247–266 (Gale Group, 1991). *The Abbott*, written by Sir Walter Scott in 1820, followed closely on the heels of its prequel, *The Monastery*, also published in 1820.

from Monticello. [from] Mr Chesley ~ came yesterday ~ written on the 27th ~ latest we have had. Waller's R~ were about 20 or 25 miles from that place. Very warm.

Oct 19th Wednesday ~ Raining and gloomy this morn. Sara is going to weave Mr Chesley an overshirt today. Rode over to school this morn and Dick came to take the pony back. Miss Ella like to have got badly burned this morning her dress and skirts got into a blaze before anyone saw it. Mr Hoffman came here today after fodder, stayed until after school. We have had a pleasant evening ~ Mollie and I danced tonight ~ Knitting seems the fashion, nine at it. Got a letter from Neh today.

Oct 21st Friday ~ By close attention to my work, was finished this noon ~ have had a great time though trying to get my heel like Sara's ~ I think these socks will be a mate, an odd one.

Sis and Mr Torrence came over this eve and spent three or four hours. Walked home tonight, came round the old way ~ the children come part-way with me, stoped and got some haws and grapes. Jane climbed a grape vine.

Sara went this morn ~ Willie came with Joe for her. Cousin Lu went across the river yesterday morning. Got a letter from Mr Wiley tonight, Sara two of them.

Oct 25th Tuesday ~ Three soldiers took dinner with us were after a deserter ~ are going over into Mr Fordtran's neighborhood. While they were out at the horse-lot, one of them saw & picked up a letter, read a little & threw it down. Steph saw it, so he took it up, read some, then he threw it away. Mr Brewer then, looked it over ~ when lo! And behold it was a love letter to Mollie from George Bell. Oh but if Mr B~ is not mad, I don't know. Every time he gets a chance he gives it to her. One would judge from the letter they were to marry soon but she *swears* she never in her life told him she would have him.

Oct 26th Wednesday ~ No norther yet. I have heard this subject of that unlucky letter brought up several times by Mr B

Oct 28th Friday ~ Mr B~ came from Hempstead this afternoon. Says a telagram came in yesterday confirming Lee's victory over Grant in front of Richmond, says he took 18,000 prisoners ~ Atlanta is again in Confederate hands. Had a fight at Rome and took there 3,000. At another place 1,800, and Price "is giving the Fed's fits in Mo." Woeful case ~

Oct 31st Monday ~ Rained last night so that Buffalo [Creek] is not crossable this morning.

In the P.M. the sky looked so dark and lowery, I concluded I'd better go over to Mr B's fearing it might be stormy in the morn. Uncle P~ went with me took them all by surprise. I am anxious for cold weather.

NOVEMBER 1864

As October faded to November, Lucy touched on primary targets of the war—the contests for Richmond and Atlanta. The Richmond Campaign, which lasted from June 1864 until March 1865, involved a series of battles designed to break the back of the Confederacy and bring an end to the war. At the same time, Sherman and Sheridan mounted campaigns to take Atlanta, "the symbol of Confederate resistance second only to Richmond" (432). Sherman's troops captured the city of Atlanta early in September 1864, and Sheridan ransacked the Shenandoah Valley, destroying military and civilian alike. By late October, Union successes had virtually crippled any Southern hope of victory.[4]

Lucy indicated that news concerning Major General Sterling Price had arrived as well. Price had been involved with the Red River Campaign earlier in the year, and was now spearheading an expedition into Missouri. He had enjoyed several victories, but by the time Lucy wrote this, on October 28, his army had suffered repeated defeats. In fact, the National Park Service reports that "Price's army was broken by this time, and it was simply a question of how many men he could successfully evacuate to friendly territory."[5]

---

4. McPherson, *Ordeal by Fire*, 429–446. During this time, Grant coordinated efforts to force Lee into a "showdown" by cutting Confederate communication and railroad supply lines. These victories would thus "crush the Army of North Virginia when it fought to protect these lifelines, as it must" (424). Yet Union forces were plagued by a number of problems, from lack of communication to indecisiveness among commanders, and the Rebel forces gained a number of victories. Regardless, both sides incurred heavy losses.

5. National Park Service. Heritage Preservation Services, *CWSAC Battle Summaries: Price's Missouri Expedition–Marmiton River, MO.*

In Travis, Texas, however, the realities of these defeats and what they meant for the Confederate cause would not be accepted for some time.

~~~~~~~~~~~~~~~~~

Nov 1st Tuesday ~ Sure enough it is raining this morn and most of last night. Dr was over sunday and engaged a turkey for the wedding that comes off tomorrow night, but this eve Sallie was here and says they will not want it as Mrs Cy. Campbell sent them one. Jimmy C~ says David had better study geography awhile longer instead of the science of Medacine ~ All agreed.

Nov 2nd Wednesday ~ It is still raining ~ Sack played for us girls to dance awhile this eve ~ then we all went into E's room and knit, sewed &c until bed time. Cleared off with a norther this P.M.

Nov 7th Monday ~ Cousin Sara's 24th birthday. Wonder where I'll be one year from today; hope in dear good old home. ~ Raining.

Nov 9th Wednesday ~ Mrs Stevens thought she saw Lissie hand Geo a letter, and they are both mad as smoke tonight. I have the whole benefit of it as they all come to me. Mrs S~ says she would swear it & Mollie that its not so

Nov 10th Thursday ~ Mrs S~ had a talk this morn before Mrs B~. Mollie begged pardon for all she had done or said

Nov 11th Friday ~ Kench was here in the night for Mr M to help get a run-away negro at Mr Edward's.

Nov 12th Saturday ~ Mr M joined the Campbell'ite church last monday ~ to night we all went to meeting.
    Mr M & Mr Seals got back just before N [noon] with the negro "Sam," belongs to Mr Shelton Bell. Kinch shot the negro in the arm last night as he was about to strike him with a bench. Mr S~ took him to Chapel Hill this P.M. Mrs B~ says the only thing she regrets is that he did not kill him. Heard of Mr Snell, owner of the Hempstead [Hotel], was shot by a

Dr Car [Kerr] who has charge of the hospital at that place.[6] the difficulty was caused by improper language used to his [Snell's] daughter by some of the waiters at the hospital.[7]

Nov 18th Friday ~ it has been raining today, almost a sleet. Steph brought me home tonight. I was glad to see the rain and cold for one, as J.D.H. [John Harvey] asked me to go out to Mr Cochrane's and I felt that I could not well spare the day, tomorrow I mean, but did not wish to refuse going thinking I might never go with him again. no telling how soon he will have to leave.

Nov 21st Monday ~ Bell came home from the Dr's after dinner ~ she says such an other love sick couple as Bolie & Silas she has not seen in many a day. This is one of the northers that will do to talk about, froze ice an inch thick last night. the wind is very high & from the north.

DECEMBER 1864

December would mark a watershed moment in Lucy's life, and new hope would emerge in her heart. News of Mary Smith's safe passage to the North had arrived, and once again, Lucy's focus shifted toward Ohio. She had only occasionally given way to her thoughts of home as anything more than a future hope, but now the possibility seemed real. Miss Mary Smith had initially appeared in the pages of Lucy's journal in September of 1863 when they first met. At that point, Lucy had written that Miss Smith had given up hope of traveling North. Months later, on June 21, 1864, Lucy wrote that Mary Smith

---

6. An advertisement in the August 6, 1859, edition of the *Hempstead Courier* indicates that Martin K. Snell opened his new hotel for business and advertised it as "inferior to none in the state." During the war, the hotel was used as a military hospital. Newspaper accessed via The Portal to Texas History.

7. *Galveston Weekly News*, November 9, 1864, Texas and Other Southern States Civil War Newspapers, 1861–1865. This time Lucy's information proved correct. The *Galveston Weekly News* reported that Captain Snell had gone to the hospital in Hempstead to confront an employee, and had himself been intercepted by Dr. Kerr. The report continues:

... angry words ensued resulting in Snell's shooting Dr. Kerr twice, or shooting at him twice with a pistol. Our informant thinks Dr. Kerr was wounded slightly by both shots. By this time Dr. Kerr seized Capt. Snell, took the pistol from him and shot him in the breast, then beat him over the head with the pistol, breaking in his skull. Capt. Snell died soon after. These are all the particulars we have received.

had left for the North, taking with her a letter that Lucy had written to her parents. Now, almost six months after her departure, news came that Miss Smith had arrived safely at her destination, a signal to all that restrictions were easing. Mail could at last reach its destination, and even more importantly, travelers could move through once impassable borders. Lucy's journal would begin to reflect her deepest longings as she, at last, gave full vent to her feelings. As December progressed, Lucy would repeatedly confide within the diary's pages that despite her love for her family and friends in Texas, she yearned for a reunion with her immediate family in Ohio. Anniversaries once marked with melancholy were now noted with determination.

———◡———

Dec 1st Thursday ~ Mr Brewer came home last night from Houston; brought word that the yellow fever was still prevailing as an epidemic[8] Miss Terry, Mrs Harris sister died of yellow fever lately in H~.

Dec 4th Sunday ~ Went up to church this morn with the intention of hearing Sara's class. It was near half past nine when I started but found no one but Mr Chapman there, waited nearly an hour before the schollars got there. Mr C took it for granted some body was offended and excused sunday school, resigning the office of superintendant.

Well our exhibition has fallen through with entirely. It is perfect foolishness I think. It will be such a dissapointment to some of the scholars.

Dec 7th Wednesday ~ A cold north came up this morn. ~

Mr Hoffman came from cousin Lu's this morn. Brought Mrs S~ a letter from her father who lives in Michigan ~ all were well. Carrie wrote a note to me yesterday saying they had received a letter from Miss Mary Smith, stating she had a pleasant trip and arrived safely at home some time since. Sent my letter immediately on ~~my~~ her arrival.

Dec 11th Sunday ~ A blustering norther blew up last night and we have to have a good big fire to keep anything like comfortable.

---

8. Mr. Brewer's account was not nearly as optimistic as the news being broadcast around the state. The *Austin State Gazette* had reported a month earlier, on November 9, that the danger had passed, stating, "We are gratified to learn that the city of Houston is now free from the contagion of yellow fever, and that visitors may go there with perfect safety," clearly a message designed to tamp down fear and encourage the resumption of travel and commerce.

Mr Hoffman came this afternoon with buckeyes[9] to use for buttons on his coat. Mr. Chapman came in this morn ~ had been up to church expecting Mr C~ Campbell to preach ~ told us all about the sunday school affair. Mrs Catlin sent word that Todie should have had as many credits as Sukie, and if they could not be made the same, she was going to take Todie out of the school.

Dec 12th Monday ~ This afternoon Carrie sent me word if I wanted to write home to do so and send it over and her Grand-pa would take it to Goliad; send it to Matamoras ~ have it mailed to Havana and from there home. I do so hope I can some time get to hear from my folks ~ wrote twelve pages of letter paper.

Dec 13th Tuesday ~ Five years ago to day since we left Ohio. Who could have believed that this time would have found me on Texas soil trudging off to school with thoughts of home, sweet home and a determination to brave every danger in an attempt to reach that loved spot before another year rolls round.

Dec 16th Friday ~ I had the reading of a letter from Mr Himan, Charles Ferris this evening. He has had yellow fever, but is well again now. Miss Mason, the daughter of the lady he has been making it his home with, died of the same disease. He proffered to send letters home for us. Has lately received letters from a mother & sister in Ohio & Mich[10]

Dec 22nd Thursday ~ Went to Mr B's by myself, us girls had a great search for my letter, found it on the mantle. 'Twas from Neh, I was so glad to hear from him, written on the 12th of Nov at Walkers Plantation, Sevier County.[11] all well but cousin Sammy.

---

9. Ohio Department of Natural Resources, ohiodnr.org. Buckeyes are the round seeds produced by the Ohio buckeye tree. The inedible seeds resemble the eye of the male deer and were viewed by many as good luck charms that warded off arthritis; their size and shape made them practical as covered buttons, particularly for such outer garments as coats. Ohioans had become known as "Buckeyes," thanks to President William Henry Harrison, and the state gained fame as the "Buckeye State."

10. Even as she continued her vigil for her own letters from Ohio, Lucy was now noting with regularity the exchange of letters from loved ones in the North.

11. "Sevier County History," Sevier County, Arkansas. Sevier County, in southwestern Arkansas, is situated above the northeast corner of Texas and shares a border with Oklahoma.

Dec 23rd Friday ~ Uncle P~ has gone to cousin Lu's ~ ~~tomorrow~~day they are to have a division of Uncle J's property. Aunt Lu is very busy making up negro clothes for Christmas, engaged my services. All passed off tolerably well in the division but Mr Frank Foster still refuses to sign away his right to Lucinda ~ although nothing was said about her.[12] Mr F Foster has little Frank, Mr Day, Willie (the blacksmith). Mrs Julia Bracey, Jake & little Charly. Mrs Joe Foster, black Lucinda & Luce, & Mrs Scurry, Tilda, Marg-Rose & Mary. Mr F Foster has Uncle Jimmy's fine watch, valued at $200. Mrs Day his ring, for Jimmy Cochrane

Dec 25th Sunday ~ Five years ago today we landed at Galveston ~ on the happy past! would that this christmas found me at good old home. Well, my christmas presents are a pair of cloth boots, two calico dresses, 5 yds of bleached domestic, 15 of unbleached, two kerchiefs, one pair of hose, paper of pins, fine comb & a silver ring, the latter from Confederate State's Jackson.

Made egg-nogg & cake this morn ~ Mr Hoffman and cousin Sara went to church. In the P.M. went with Mr H~ to Mr Catlins and [he] was married to Sallie

Rec'd an invitation to a party at Col Springs to come off tuesday eve given by Capt Davis' company, all the Travis dancers are invited. Arrived at home found Dr Alexander, and not long after-ward, John Harvey came. Brought us word cousin S~ and Hez~ would be home tuesday night or wednesday morn.

Dec 26th Monday ~ Cousin Sara went to see Parson K, who is rapidly failing they are having watches with him all the time now. Mr & Mrs Middleton came this afternoon.

We looked ~~until~~ all day for cousin Sammy, but he has not come. I had to go to bed with sick head-ache to night.

Dec 27th Tuesday ~ Mr & Mrs M. left about nine. We made certain cousin Sammy was not far off, but cousin Sara got a short note from

---

12. Lucy recorded here the distribution of Uncle Jimmy's property, including his slaves, following his death in July. Although he had wished Lucinda to remain with Cousin Lu, another man apparently held her papers and would not release her. As Lucy listed the names of the slaves with their respective owners, she gave no indication that she regarded the slaves as people with any rights, thus unconsciously reinforcing the view of the slave as property.

Mr Wiley saying the wording in cousin S~ application was not exactly right so he could not start until after it had been sent back to headquarters.

Dec 28th Wednesday ~ Just before N[oon] the negroes gave a shout. Mr Hemman had come, says cousin Sammy, Mr Wiley & Dock Cloud & Jimmy Cochrane will be here in a few days.

We were so certain cousin S~ would be home yesterday that Uncle P~ killed three turkeys. This afternoon cousin Sara and I went to see Parson Kenny ~ poor man he can not last long

Dec 29th Thursday ~ Brought down my traveling dress this morn mended the bredth, pressed it &c. Jimmy Johnson came about 3 P.M. [He] is a member of Company F Flournoy's R~ he, as well as every one else, compliments Mack highly. Says there is talk of Capt H~ being promoted to Wharton's staff and the company want M~ [Mack] for Capt in his place.

Dec 31st Saturday ~ Took my dark delain to peices and worked busy all day on it pressing cutting, peicing out sleeves have got so far along that I do not feel as if it would be much trouble to finish it up. A norther came up last night and this has been a right cold day.

No cousin Sammy yet ~

———

As Lucy ended this entry, significantly the last line of the last entry for the last full year of the war, her eagerness for Sammy's arrival could be said to typify the longings of all as they anxiously awaited the return of their loved ones and their anticipation for a new beginning. The war had taken a terrible toll, and all were ready for a new year to begin – a year with no conflict and a year with hopes of homecoming for many, Lucy included. Little did she know that within a few short weeks, that wish would be replaced by a fervent determination to somehow make the journey North. Lucy's time of exile was drawing to a close, and the coming year would be replete with anxious anticipation and bittersweet longing.

CHAPTER 13

JANUARY
1865

It is true that if it were possible, I am more
than ever anxious to go now.

LUCY P. STEVENS,
January 25, 1865

LUCY'S FIRST ENTRY FOR 1865 marked little change from the previous year.
She began the notation with bits of local gossip and the day's proceedings,
but quickly moved to the joyous news of Cousin Sammy's arrival. Then,
almost as an afterthought, she included a rumor she had heard concerning
a defeat for Sherman's army. However, her information could not have been
more erroneous. In fact, during this time, Sherman had been en route to
Savannah, conducting his "March to the Sea." James M. McPherson reports
in *Ordeal by Fire* that Sherman had at last convinced Lincoln that the psychological and material impact of a destructive march from Atlanta to the sea
would be unparalleled. Sherman's words have endured, as he claimed, "I can
make Georgia howl." During the three-and-a-half-week march, Sherman cut
a swath of destruction fifty miles wide through the heart of Georgia, inca-
pacitating the Confederacy and breaking its spirit.[1]

Lucy would continue to record the reports as she heard them, but she was
hesitant to accept them as absolute. Much of the time, the information was
incorrect, and as the last months of the war wore on, the rumors became
increasingly contradictory, so much so that she began to question their
veracity. Finally, on March 22, she acknowledged that even the newspapers
published conflicting accounts.

---

1. James M. McPherson, *Ordeal by Fire: The Civil War and Reconstruction*, 2nd ed. (New York:
McGraw-Hill, 1992), 460–463.

Even so, as the year began, much in Travis remained the same. Lucy once again confirmed in her January 8 entry that despite the second anniversary of the Emancipation Proclamation in the North, the institution of slavery was still fully functioning in Texas. She recorded that Uncle Pier had given Savilia, one of the female slaves, to Cousin Lu, as a gift, possibly in connection with the controversy over Uncle Jimmie's will concerning Lu's "inheritance" of Lucinda. Regardless, the view of slaves as property prevailed. However, despite the presence of the strictly observed hierarchy, and in spite of recurring tensions, both slave and owner in the Pier household shared an obvious affection for each other. In a letter to Sammy written in 1857, Sarah had included, "Give my love to Pa Ma Sis & Dan and all my friends—also to the Negroes tell Jane she must be a good girl and help Aunt Mary get chips and do lots of smart things" (Sarah Pier letter, 10/24/57). Then, on Christmas Day, 1862, Aunt Lu had commented that the "Negroes had quite a nice supper in Harriet's house and invited us all out to supper—roast pig" (Lu M. Pier, 12/25/62). And during the holidays of 1863, Lucy herself recorded how the family had prepared nog and best wishes for the "darkies." Now, with Sammy's return, Lucy wrote that the slaves hosted a dinner for the family in his honor.

1st Sunday ~ Uncle P~ killed a turkey for dinner hoping cousin Sammy would be here to help eat it but we were dissapointed.

This eve cousin S~ and myself had made up our minds to go to work on monday ~ she to weaving and I to school-teaching ~ was all of us setting round the fire talking, when cousin Sammy hallooed at the front gate. Oh what a happy welcome he received. We were all so rejoiced to be thus surprised. Sammy has fever to night, had a chill last night ~ rode 125 miles in three days[2] from 15 miles the other side of Crockett.[3] Cousin Sammy's arrival home has made ours truly a happy new year.

---

2. Haley Schoolfield, Head coach, Equestrian Team, Southern Methodist University, e-mail interview with Vicki Tongate, May 17, 2010. Lucy was right to be impressed by Sammy's long ride. Many sources agree that 25 miles per day via horseback is a good average, and according to Schoolfield, "125 miles in 3 days is a very impressive distance. It would surely exhaust both horse and rider."

3. Crockett, the county seat of Houston County, Texas, was established in 1837 when Andrew Edwards Gossett donated land for the town and named it in honor of a former neighbor, David (Davey) Crockett. According to *The Handbook of Texas Online*, the town became a mustering/training center for Confederate troops.

It is rumored Sherman his staff and many of his grand army have been captured near Atlanta Geo, bogged down in the swamp in an attempt to evade Ewell's[4] troops.

2nd Monday ~ Was up soon this morn and went to Mr Brewer's before breakfast to get excused from school-teaching another week on cousin Sammy's account. Finished my dark delain[5] dress this afternoon but worked faithfully to do so.

Sis Torrence was over to our house soon this morn, Sammy went home with her. Then Aunt Lu sent word for all that would to come over take dinner with us.

3rd Tuesday ~ Cousin Sara, Sammy, Sallie Catlin & I went down on the river this morn. Just before we got to Mr. Wm Brewers, J. D. H. [John Harvey] overtook us. Cousin Lu, Mr & Mrs Buck were at Mr Pilley's as we came by. He has failed very rapidly the last two days ~ they do not think he can last many hours. Cousin Sara went in and stayed a few moments found Mrs. D~ [Darnman] still at Lu's, and no danger but she will remain there for some time

4th Wednesday ~ Cousin Lu and Sara were just ready to go over to Mr P's this morn when word came that Mr Pilley was dying. They went on and, finding no gentlemen there, sent back for cousin W and the boys ~ they had intended to go hunting.

5th Thursday ~ This morn Mr & Mrs Manning ~ Mrs Kavannaugh, Miss Fanny Springfield & Mr Railey came up to the burying ~ Johnie came for me about ten.

---

4. Paul D. Casdorph, *Confederate General R. S. Ewell: Robert E. Lee's Hesitant Commander* (Lexington: University Press of Kentucky, 2004), 305–310, 336. General Richard S. Ewell had replaced Stonewall Jackson, but was ultimately removed from command by Lee. Lee did, however, place him in charge of Richmond. Ewell ultimately surrendered on April 6, 1865, at Sailor's Creek, during the Appomattox Campaign.

5. Laura Ingalls Wilder, *Little House in the Big Woods* (New York: Harper-Collins, 1960), 128. Delaine, a wool or wool/cotton fabric, often displaying a print pattern, was reserved for Sunday best. Laura Ingalls Wilder, writing of her mother's beautiful, dark green delaine dress, remarked that a dressmaker had made it and that her mother "had been very fashionable, before she married Pa, and a dressmaker had made all her clothes."

Hez K~ and Mr Bell brought word that news had been received that Sherman and his army were in front of Savannah and had no doubt taken the place before this and that Hood's army had been all cut to peices ~ such contradictory reports.[6] They also told us that a few nights ago a company belonging to Andersons Regiment had gone to Dr. Peebles, searched the quarter, then proceeded to the house. But before they got there the negroes had become very much alarmed and went to the house, frightening the ladies very much. Mr B~ says there was four gentlemen belonging to the same Regiment there, and all were in the parlor playing cards at the time. Mrs Clark had spasms & fits until they thought she would die in one. Gerrad [Jared] Groce was down at Col Blake's at the time, they sent him word and he came home very indignant and is going to report to Genl Wharton & Walker. It is said Col Kirby reported to Genl Walker that they were secreting eight Yankee deserters, found nothing or no body.

6th Friday ~ A norther came up this morn, or rather last night. Sammy is quite sick ~ chill & fever.

7th Saturday ~ Gentlemen have to sit up at Parson K's all the time, he is so bad off. We have had such a pleasant day. Cousin S~ has another chill this evening. This morning was warm and pleasant but this afternoon it is cloudy and threatens rain.

MARGINAL NOTE: *Parson K ~ died 9th 65 yrs*

8th Sunday ~ This has been a gloomy rainy day but nothing daunted. John Harvey came here before N [noon]. All of us were glad to see him to help drive dull care away or rather dull feelings. [Uncle P] gave Savilia to Lu, and she is to go down with Cal.

The darkies invited us out to a supper they gave to cousin Sammy ~ had chicken-pie, broiled ham, biscuit, two kinds of pie, tarts and peach puffs, pound cake, cookies, egg bread coffee and preserves ~ everything was as nice as could be & all enjoyed it I waited on the coffee for the first time at Aunt Lu's

---

6. McPherson, *Ordeal by Fire*, 465–466. This time, Lucy's information was correct. Sherman had, in fact, arrived in Savannah on December 10, and had taken control of the city following his epic march. In unrelated fighting in Tennessee, Hood's army had been destroyed, with horrific casualties nearly three times the number of Northern losses. Following the devastating losses of the Tennessee Campaign, Hood resigned his command.

One of my friends talked to me more seriously than I liked to have them. I would give a considerable to know their sentiments on a certain subject without their telling me.

9th Monday ~ The storm has blown with a norther. Mrs R Campbell sent us word Sis C was to be married tomorrow night. Newt says Mrs Campbell told him that "Sherman had got to the coast and Hood's army was cut all to pieces."

10th Tuesday ~ I have taken a severe cold & can not keep from shivering. Mr Brewer went [to] C.Hill [Chappell Hill] to day. Met the hearse coming to Parson K's; he died yesterday evening at 4 and was buried this afternoon. I am sorry we did not know about it in time so we could have gone to the burying. I can not feel to mourn for one who suffered so much and that lived to be so old. He was 66 [sic].

11th Wednesday ~ John H~ here. When he & Sammy went up to go to bed, cousin Sara told them to go in the girls room and get some quilts off the bed. They saw the girls gowns and put them on & slept in them ~ cousin Sammy in mine & Linda's cap & John in Sara's. Such talking as about mine being the newest fashion, having color & cuffs & the other that yokes were most fashionable.

16th Monday ~ Cousin S. says Artie, Callie & John spent last night at Mr L's. Mrs Lott put gowns & caps on the bed for the boys. I am so glad ~ I know they had a time. Mr Brewer had such a nice dinner for cousin S. John H~ was here this eve, E~ offered him a cap if he wanted to spend the night.[7]

17th Tuesday ~ This afternoon I so quietly seated myself when ~ lo! Who should walk in but Mr Chesley. I could not have received a greater surprise for we did not know he had thought of coming home. This is Aunt Lu's 51st birthday ~ she had a nice dinner and some of her cake and a turkey for supper.

18th Wednesday ~ Heard this morn Mr W [Wiley] came yesterday eve. [I] took Sara some of Aunt Lu's supper. Just as we were starting from Uncle P's, Mr Wiley came ~ I went to meet him.

---

7. Word of the prank that Cousin Sammy and John Harvey had played on the girls earlier had apparently traveled through the neighborhood.

19th Thursday ~ In the afternoon John H~ and Mr Huffman were here. Mr H~ told me of a party tomorrow night and Johnie gave me a bid.[8]

20th Friday ~ John H~ came here to night to see were we going to the party, went away in an ill humor over to Mr Catlin's ~ would not tell us when he would come back. but after he went away, got sorry & came back took supper here. Not a soul from the neighborhood have gone to the party Mrs Lott will think us kind no doubt.

21st Saturday ~ Mr Wiley came up after dinner and towards evening Artie H~ came told us all about the party. Not a girl from around Travis went and Mr Lott felt really hurt about it.

There was to be church to night but it was so cold and so late before the house was lit and warmed that Mr. Mathews & Dr. Shields concluded to let church go; came down here to spend the night. if we are not going to have one of the coldest northers we have had this winter then I am mistakened.[9]

22nd Sunday ~ As this was the day appointed for the funeral sermon of Parson K~ all his family were out. On account of the unfavoriable weather, the funeral services were postponed. Cold as Greenland ~ freezing all the time.

23rd Monday ~ John H passed by the house to day but did not come in. [He] told Mr B~ news came into H~ that Geo~ N.C. & Tenn. Had gone back into the Union.[10]

---

8. Lucy repeatedly included John (Johnie) Harvey's name in her list of visitors, and he apparently wished to pursue the friendship with romantic intent, for he now invited her to accompany him to the party at Mr. and Mrs. Lott's. However, Lucy had already registered concern about an unnamed relationship on January 8, following a conversation with a friend (quite possibly John Harvey).

9. Marissa Pazos, Undergraduate assistant, Office of Texas State Climatologist, Department of Atmospheric Science, Texas A&M University, e-mail interview with Vicki Tongate, April 5, 2010. For several days, Lucy made note of the extremely cold weather. Although few records are available from this time, the most comparable records existing for Austin indicate that January 1865 was relatively cold and wet. Ms. Pazos cites the department's online publication "Texas Weather Pre-1880," which shows that the mean temperature for January 1865, was 45 degrees, with extremes ranging from 73 degrees to 20 degrees.

10. "Reconstruction: The Second Civil War—State by State," *American Experience*. Rumors and misunderstandings abounded as the Confederacy's strength dwindled. However, no states were actually readmitted to the Union before the war ended and certain conditions had been

24th Tuesday ~ Cousin Sammy came by this morn on his way to cousin Lu's, told me cousin Sara sent word for me to come home this eve ~ she is to be married tomorrow eve.[11] I am not much surprised, for she talked as if she might do so when I came away. It does not look much like preparing for a wedding at our house. This eve Sara & I fixed over the sleeves to her brown worsted dress

---

January 25 began as a joyous day—Cousin Sarah's wedding day. However, before the day ended, Lucy's own life had irrevocably changed.

Thanks to the war, a trip to Texas that had originated as an extended visit among family had continued far longer than anyone had ever anticipated. As the conflict persisted, Lucy's isolation gradually intensified as mail delivery was cut off and news from home ceased. During the years of separation, Lucy had always noted family birthdays in her journal as a means of remembering those she missed so much. November 14 was her mother's birthday, July 14 was her brother Will's, and July 3 her younger sister Juli's. On July 3, 1863, Lucy had written, "my dear sister Juli's 19th birthday—I am in hopes it has proved a happier one to her than the day has been to me" (Lucy Stevens, 7/3/63). The following year, she penned, "Sister Juli's twentieth birthday—my good Sis—how I would like to spend it with you—but alas I can not even know that you are among the living—blessing on you if you may be."

Yet even as Lucy penned the prayers asking God's blessings on Juli, her requests were innocently tardy, for Juli had died almost two years earlier, in April 1863, at the age of eighteen. On January 25, 1865, when Lucy finally received her first correspondence from Ohio, she learned the heartbreaking news. All of her courage and resolve left her, and for the first time, her practiced composure slipped; she lost control and wrote despairingly of her loss.

Lucy's Texas family shared her suffering as they watched her endure the agony of fresh shock and grief. Although the letter had arrived on the day of Sarah's marriage to Mr. Wiley, Sarah took the time to write a moving passage about Lucy's anguish in her journal:

---

met. North Carolina was the sixth state to be readmitted, on June 25, 1868, while Georgia was the last, on July 15, 1870. Tennessee actually became the first state to be readmitted, on July 24, 1866.

11. Wilfred O. Dietrich, *The Blazing Story of Washington County* (Author, 1950), 40–41. Long engagements were rare, and wedding dates were set according to the availability of a preacher. Lucy had written of this pattern time and again throughout the pages of her diary, and in similar fashion, Sarah Pier married Henry P. Wiley on Wednesday, January 25, 1865, after finally agreeing to the marriage on Monday, January 23. Preparations commenced with a flurry, and Lucy recorded the details of the festivities.

Cous Lu recd. A letter from home this evening through the mail—the first for over three years. It contained sad news—the death of a number of friends, among them, Mr. J. D. Smith, Mr. Andrews, Mrs. Stoddard, and her much loved sister Juli. The youngest of the family and pet of the household. She was perfectly unnerved. I have sad feelings this evening—and there are but few eyes that have not shed tears of sympathy for Cous Lu this evening

    Sarah Pier, 1/25/65

25th Wednesday ~ We were all bustle and preparation for the coming wedding this morn. Making cake, pies, dressing turkeys chickens, &c &c, each one trying to look bright and cheerful as possible and to do all they could. Before noon Mrs Mary Cameron, Artie H, Cousin Lu, Waller, Willie, Mrs D [Darnman], Lula, cousin Sammy, Jimmy, Jane Edwards Bell and Mr & Mrs Middleton came. Aunt Lu and myself hardly had an opportunity to speak to them ~ too busy to be ceremonious. Surprise! and wonder! Are expressed by all.

While we were at breakfast, Ruth came in ~ says Sa-ry what are you goin to do to day because Mrs Chapman is very sick and sent word for you to come see her. So Sara went, told Mrs C~ what of the coming wedding and her guessing who was the groom to be. She was afraid it was Dr Meredith,[12] was perfectly astonished when she found it was Mr Wiley.

In the afternoon, as us girls were busy setting [the] table Cousin Sammy came to me saying he had a letter for me. No sooner did I look at the backing than I recognized the well known hand of sister Lottie. With eager but trembling hands I undid the ceil ~ but oh! How little prepared to receive the sad tidings of my beloved sister Juli's death. The household darling was rudely snatched away after an illness of but three days. Lovely girl ~ I never could think otherwise than that I would find you among the living on my return and that we would spend many happy hours together. It is so hard to know I must never never see you more. Lottie wrote "Our much loved sister has gone ~ we hope to a better world." That sentence ~ is stamped ~ with such deep heaviness ~ upon my heart. Why could it not have been otherwise ~ and my dear and aged parents ~ the trial is so great ~ must have been to them. [Juli] died

---

12. On June 7, 1863, Lucy had written scathingly of an unnamed doctor who had broken Sarah's heart. Now, on Sarah's wedding day, the doctor's name was revealed, and from Mrs. C's response, it is obvious that others shared Lucy's contemptuous opinion.

of congestion of the stomach & bowels April 23rd 1863 nearly two years since. Sister wrote [of] the death of thirteen of my friends, among the number Mrs Stoddard.[13] Brother James and Horace S~ were in Nashville Tenn, Mr Cummings in Calafornia, went a year ago the 18th of December on account of his health. Sister, Mary and Clara were at fathers ~ I am very glad that she can be there. What a broken scattered household is ours. Three years has indeed brought many and sad changes. I hope that a few more months will find me in my loved home ~ it is true that if it were possible, I am more than ever anxious to go now. But Aunt & Uncle Pier will not consent for me to start before the last of April or the first of May on account of the March winds ~ my own judgement tells me too they are right. The sad news contained in my letter has thrown a "a gloom over my feelings" ~ and that of us all that we do not feel like merry making.

In the afternoon or near dark Mr Catlin, Sue, Sara J S~ and John Harvey came. It seemed to me I could not go out but finely [finally] did so. Sara was dressed very plainly ~ wore a brown worsted bought in Ohio brown bow. Aunt Hannah gave her my collar (and under-body). It is war times and she did not feel to do different. Aunt Lu & Uncle P~ do not feel satisfied that she has such a quiet wedding and no more preparation made for it than there has been. Uncle P~ can not keep from speaking of it all the time.[14]

Aunt Lu got me to assist her in arranging beds & I thought cousin Sara was going to take the front room and so put Mrs Middleton in her bed ~ she had to leave and go into another. Mr M found it out and he and cousin W~ had a great time over it, and to cap it all after cousin W~ went up stairs told the boys of it.

MARGINAL NOTE: *Heard of sister Juli's death. Sara was married to Henry Purris Wiley.*

---

13. In a marginal note, Lucy went on to list the names of the thirteen friends who had died. Her sister Lottie had mentioned each one by name in her letter.

14. The Piers' dissatisfaction with the simplicity of Sarah's wedding provides an ample indication of the prosperity that the family continued to enjoy. Although the war had taken a toll on the magnitude of celebrations throughout the South as many had endured egregious hardships, James Bradford Pier chafed at the restrictions imposed by propriety. His pride as the patriarch of the family suffered as the festivities were reined in to comply with social expectations.

26th Thursday ~ Not satisfied last night, cousin W [Waller] told Mr part
way home with the girls. David C overtook us and told Sara her Ma sent
word for her to go set up at Mrs Chapman's to night. She is so very sick,
has Erysipelus.[15] Cousin W~ is not well this eve & I am most sick.

27th Friday Cousin Sammy & John Harvey left just before. It seemed to
me I could not tell cousin S~ good-bye ~ Never lived a better boy. This
morn before cousin W~ left, he asked me to if I would take a letter to
mail for his Uncles when I went home. How different from Mr Chesley.
He who was born & raised there preferred for me to write to his parents
than to do so himself. It is for shame that Mr C did not feel like writing,
about what any one could expect of him I knew long ago. This is a cold
gloomy day.

28th Saturday ~ A cold, gloomy, rainey morn just agreeing with my
feelings. There seems such a weight on my heart ~ I feel that I can never
again be happy and joyous as I have been

29th Sunday ~ We all made ourselves ready for church as soon as possible then started for Travis. Arrived at home, found cousin Sammy was
taken sick at Mr Collins and had to turn back, was home. Sara was in
bed, set up with Mrs Chapman last night. None of our folks but Mr Wiley
and I went to church to day. Parson Alexander preached Parson Kinney's
funeral sermon today from the 25th chapter of Mathew, 21st verse.[16]
     There was but few at church to what I had expected to see ~ some
sick, some waiting on them and others lazy.

---

15. Ray Vaughn Pierce, M.D., *The People's Common Sense Medical Adviser in Plain English; Or,
Medicine Simplified* (World's Dispensary Medical Association, 1895), 413–414, Project Gutenberg.
According to information available in 1895, erysipelas, also known as "the rose," was a condition causing fever and chills, nausea, and even diarrhea. It was characterized by a red spot "on
the face, the ear, or other part of the person" that became inflamed and tender to the touch.
The case could be serious if the inflammation extended inward to vital organs, and could even
result in death. Medical advances have since shown that the condition stems from a strepto-
coccal infection.
     16. This is an appropriate text, given Parson Kenney's lifelong ministry. The NIV (New
International Version) quotes Jesus in Matthew 25:21, as he tells the parable of the talents. In the
story, Christ commends the servant who has invested himself well, saying, "Well done, good
and faithful servant! You have been faithful with a few things; I will put you in charge of many
things. Come and share your master's happiness!"

Undoubtedly, Lucy's grief for her sister affected her perspective, as she now wrote with a somber, reflective tone. Her lighthearted spirit was now missing; in its place deep melancholy settled. Gone was her customary amusement at her own mistakes, and her propensity for the positive was noticeably absent. The frigid winter weather that had been little more than an inconvenience in the past now intensified her gloom and mirrored her own sorrow. Her sharp censure of Mr. Chesley's attitude toward his family reflects the depth of her anguish over the long separation from her own family, especially at such a critical time. To have been absent during her precious sister's illness and death—to have been totally unaware of the loss—was more than she could bear. Her sense of isolation was now complete. Yet even so, she knew that her departure was drawing closer, and with a sense of melancholy, she wrote of Cousin Sammy with deep affection, recognizing that she would soon be leaving him and her Texas family behind. While she had pursued every avenue of hope in the past, trying to find a way back home, she now redoubled her efforts. Her diary took on a new sense of urgency—the time of exile was over, and her return to the North was at hand.

CHAPTER 14

FEBRUARY-MARCH
1865

Coming home, cousin Sammy told me about being engaged, got his answer yesterday . . .
Heard today too of K's getting a white vest & telling what he was going
to marry in not too far off I judge.

LUCY P. STEVENS,
February 18, 1865

ALTHOUGH LUCY'S ENTRIES FOR 1865 had begun with much of the dailiness
that had marked the weeks and months preceding them, distinct changes in
tone had begun to emerge, even before the arrival of her sister's letter. A resignation to the eventuality of defeat now crept into Lucy's notes. War news
continued to trickle in, but Lucy recorded it as a mere aside, unworthy of
much comment.

New names found their way into the pages of the diary, and other names,
long absent from her journal, began to reappear. The machinery of war was
slowing, and unlike most of the South, where devastation had reigned, to
many in Travis there came a sense of beginnings. The young people who
had been ensnared by the years of war now sensed an end to their servitude.
Many had literally grown up in the midst of battle, but now lives that had
been interrupted by years of obligation to the Cause could be seen as their
own. Casting aside their bonds of perpetual waiting, Lucy's friends began to
plan for their futures and a resumption of their lives. Lucy now wrote regularly of first one couple, then another, announcing their engagement and
impending wedding. Even Cousin Sammy confided in Lucy concerning his
engagement. Yet all of these pairings only increased Lucy's aloneness, for
she knew that her name would not be linked with another—not now, not in
Texas.

Lucy was now much more concerned with her own plight. Still dealing with her grief, she was desperate to send word to her parents and begin preparations for her return to Ohio. In her quest to communicate with her family, she mentioned sending a letter via Galveston flag of truce, a method appropriated from the military for her own purposes. The emblem of white cloth, long signifying the temporary cessation of hostilities, had been widely used by both North and South for exchanging prisoners, information, and sometimes even mail. Since Galveston had been blockaded by Union ships for most of the war, the flag of truce had been commonly used, with proper military approval, for various exchanges. Indeed, some travelers had even been fortunate enough to secure safe passage to the North on Union ships, and Lucy fervently hoped that her letters would be allowed the same undisturbed course.

FEBRUARY 1865

1st Wednesday ~ Bell got a letter from Ruf dated the 29th says "news came yesterday that La. ~~Tenn~~ Arkansas & Missouri had gone back into the Union."[1] Cousin Sammy missed his fever today. Commenced a letter home last eve.

2nd Thursday ~ This has been a bright and beautiful day, warm as spring. Finished my letter home one to send by Galveston flag of truce, the other Mr Ferris[2] is to send.

3rd Friday ~ Sallie was in school today, Jane not well enough, Steph complaining ~ school seems some what dull when all my scholars are not in.

---

1. James M. McPherson, *Battle Cry of Freedom* (Oxford: Oxford University Press, 2003), 292–293. No states had re-entered the Union at this time. However, Lucy's inclusion of Missouri raises interesting questions about general perceptions of the Confederacy. Early in the war, Missouri had endured such fierce infighting between pro- and anti-slavery factions that "[the state] appeared headed for a civil war within its own borders" (292). Confederate-leaning leaders sent their representatives to Richmond, only to have their government become "a government in exile" (293). Confederate "bushwhackers" such as William Quantrill and Union "jayhawkers" battled each other throughout the war, but ultimately, political control remained with the Unionists. The ongoing strife obviously led to confusion in faraway rural areas like Travis, Texas, and Lucy never questioned the re-entry of seceding states, much less their exit.

2. Lucy's first mention of Mr. Ferris (12/16/64) offers an introduction and explains that he had received correspondence from the North and would be glad to assist Lucy in her endeavor to return home.

Henry got home last night, says the cars ran off the track yesterday was the reason he did not come back.[3]

5th Sunday ~ The prospect out of doors is so unfavoriable that there is no church today rained very hard part of the time. This eve I brought down Juli's letters and read them over. In every one her happy joyous nature shows its self. My dear sister how can I give you up.

8th Wednesday ~ Mr Collins was here this morn and told me Neh was home came Monday. I am so glad he is home.

9th Thursday ~ Lissie & E~ went to Bellville this morn, each one escorted by their beaux. Neh & Mr Lawrance spent the eve N~ looks so thin and badly. Is home on business. starts back Saturday but hopes to get a furlough, and if so will probably be back in two weeks. I do so hope he will come. He gave me such a pretty keepsake, a star & cresent, one he had made in La for me ever thoughtful. I shall think so much of it.

10th Friday ~ had the pleasure of being escorted by Kinch to Mr C's and back. Mollie came out to meet us in her new dress and Sack looked so neat and nice. Cousin Sammy was there, came home [from] Lu's yesterday ~ would have gone home but Em & Mollie persuaded him to stay, and when I came told him if he would wait, I'd go home with him tomorrow morn. As we came back this eve, Kinch told me Mollie said she had told me about him & her being engaged.

   Neh told me this eve that some one really was in earnest in what he had so often joked me about. I told him the truth though when I said I did not believe it or did not want to think any such a thing. Any one who will be so blinded sometimes. Well I am sorry is all I can say. I consider my note quite a presumption ~ the idea is rediculous in the extreme.

Word of Lucy's plans had begun to spread, and many would offer gifts and remembrances as tokens of their esteem. Lucy wrote of Nehemiah Cochran's special gift, and it would soon be followed by many others, from flowers to

---

3. H. Roger Grant, *The Railroad: The Life Story of a Technology* (Westport, CT: Greenwood Publishing Group, 2005). During the early years of rail travel, the railcars exacted a heavy toll on the iron tracks over which they traveled. The weight of the cars, even at low speeds of twenty miles per hour or less, eroded the tracks, causing derailments and disruptions of service.

locks of hair to poems dedicated to Lucy. Sentimental poetry had risen to the fore as an expression of one's deepest emotions during the trying years of the war, and while few books of poetry were published during this time, people from all walks of life wrote their own. After the Bible, Shakespeare was the most widely read author, and "Planters and their ladies filled diaries, correspondence, journals and even account books with their favorite printed poems as well as their own efforts."[4] Sarah made her own attempt at patriotic poetry, and Lucy copied the entire text of several poems into the back of her journal. Perhaps the best example of a personal attempt at sentimental poetry is a piece found in Lucy's diary, addressed to Miss Lue P. Stevens at Travis, Texas, and dated March 23, 1865. The poem reads:

> Friendship and Love
> Friendship is sweet to those
> Who know no purer gem;
> 'Tis like the blushing rose,
> Blown from its tender stem;
> Or like the queen of night
> That glisen in the sky;
> Her ever fading light
> Forms but a transient tie.
>
> Love is a theme that spring
> Pure in the human heart!
> 'Tis friendship decked with wings,
> A bond no-time can part.
> As the green ivy bowers
> Around the old oak tree,
> So love outlives the flowers
> That friendship culled for me.
>
> Your friend,
> Sarah Ellen Kenney

The poem, handwritten and decorated with swirls and flourishes, was a tribute presented to Lucy from Sarah Kenney not long before Lucy's departure from Texas. The verse was obviously important to Lucy, for she guarded it

---

4. Eugene D. Genovese, *The Southern Front* (Columbia: University of Missouri Press, 1995), 109.

within the leaves of her journal, along with other keepsakes such as pressed flowers and locks of hair.

The gifts and expressions of love made it all the more difficult for Lucy to say her good-byes. Throughout the last weeks of her journal, she wrote many times of the difficulty she had in parting with the people she loved so dearly. Even so, she expressed irritation, incredulity, and even despair when well-meaning friends attempted to persuade her to stay in Texas. She had made her decision, and there would be no turning back. Her poignant entry on February 5 provides perhaps the clearest view into her heart at this point. Her anguish over her sister's death anchored her thoughts and activities as she anxiously awaited the first opportunity to depart. And so, as February had begun, with Lucy's letter via flag of truce, it would likewise end with Uncle Pier interceding on her behalf with General Magruder himself.

11th Saturday ~ Wrote a little more to enclose in my letter home as it has not gone yet. Jennie told me they had lately received another letter from Mr Ferris; he has heard from home again received sad news of the death of his Mother.

14th Tuesday ~ We have [had] another pleasant day again ~ a miracle. Bolie was in my school-room yesterday morn a little while came to Uncle P's and called on the brides. I can not help thinking how lonely I will be when all the folk leave. But it will not be long, I shall be by myself ~ courage. St V's day

15th Wednesday ~ Mr W started this morn. I hated to see him start so much and I know he dreaded to leave ~ home has for him more attractions than of old. Cousin Sammy started for Lu's this morn would have me to ride behind him over to Mr B's. Went by Mr Collins of course, as that is the *nearest* way.

18th Saturday ~ Just before noon, Kinch C came. We spent a pleasant day with them then went over to Mrs Switzers to tea and did n't we have a pleasant visit. Coming home, cousin Sammy told me about being engaged, got his answer yesterday, proposed nearly a year ago. Heard today too of K's getting a white vest & telling what he was going to marry in not far off I judge.

20th Monday ~ Mr Wiley & cousin S~ started off just as I did. I so much hated to see the boys start off, yet know they realy had to go. She expected Mr W~ to go, until just as she started off, for some reason he chose to wait until tomorrow. This afternoon when school closed, Mr W~ asked us girls to go see Sallie Catlin. She had just returned from Cat Springs. Mr C~ tried to persuade I would not be contented at home, wonder what kind of a human he takes me to be.

22nd Wednesday ~ I received a letter from Jimmy Cochrane, and through the mail a letter from Ella Stevens. C says Flourney's Reg~ was near Shreves port [Shreveport, Louisiana] the last he heard so their coming to Texas seems quite a mistake. I am sorry for it for I will not get to see Mack again before I leave. Mr B's are so disappointed. they had begun to look for Bent some thinking he would come before the Reg~ for the sake of a visit at home. The children have brought me wild flowers nearly every day this & last week ~ the prairaes are covered with daisies.

24th Friday ~ A certain fact Shiloah was married last monday to Miss Maggie Brown.

25th Saturday ~ Went to the store (Have a new store).[5]

26th Sunday ~ Uncle Pier wrote an application to Gen Magruder for me to go home (this morn.) About four this afternoon, Col came to bring word Willie was very sick with typhoid fever wanted Aunt Lu & Uncle P~ to go down there. At half past four they started leaving us girls to house-keep.

28th Tuesday ~ Rode over to school again this morn and came back at night found Aunt Lu & Uncle P~ here. Left Willie improving slowly. his limbs are so badly swollen he can not sit up.
    The Indian fight to in the northern part of Texas seems quite different from what we at first heard ~ 60 Ind and some 60 Confed. the latter was scared, it is said, supposing there were many more Ind and therefore

---

5. Bellville Historical Society, "Bellville Downtown Square." Lucy may have been referring to a new enterprise selling general merchandise in Bellville. According to a brochure published by the Bellville Historical Society, Arthur Kopisch and his stepfather, Gustav Kopisch, opened a store on the square in Bellville in 1865 and operated it until the late 1870s. Lucy's mention of a new store further indicates the upturn in peacetime endeavors during the last months of the war.

retreated. The Ind tribes were supposed to be the Kickapoo's & Potawa-timo's.[6] Rained again to day

MARCH 1865

Even as Lucy's departure approached and her excitement grew, she contin-ued to realize the pain of separating from the people, young and old, whom she had come to love so deeply. With the last day of classes and the accompa-nying closing exercises nearing, her farewells to her dear "scholars" and other loved ones began in earnest, and her conflicting emotions became increas-ingly evident in her journal entries. With tenderness and genuine sorrow, she wrote of the sadness, yet admitted that she relished the freedom to look ahead to her future—a future as yet undecided and clouded with apprehension.

With alarm, Lucy devoted much space to the increase in regional violence that seemed to outpace any anticipation of peace. Indeed, the intensifying violence of which she wrote reflected the collapse of the social and political structure of the Confederacy. She sensed this upheaval following the murder of Mr. Buck, and although she was horrified by the loss, she did not seem shocked that yet another incident of this nature had occurred. Still, even as she acknowledged that Mr. Buck's family was determined to bring the killer to justice, she expressed skepticism within the privacy of her diary. She real-ized, however, that although the law might acquit, in a world of such tur-moil, the cycle of violence would continue as others sought retribution. And as Lucy began to prepare for her journey North, the violence only intensified her own sense of vulnerability in this foreign land.

1st Wednesday ~ Did not go home this eve as it was rainy and besides I have but two nights to stay with my children. I gave them the lessons they were to recite the last day just before school closed ~ and they are looking them over to night.

---

6. Lucy could be referring to the controversial Battle of Dove Creek, a clash on January 8, 1865, between Confederate forces and an alliance of Kickapoo and Potawatomi Indians. According to *The Handbook of Texas Online*, in the early 1850s, a branch of the Kickapoo tribe had combined with a segment of the Potawatomis and had settled peacefully in northeastern Texas, but were now migrating to Mexico to escape the disruption of the Civil War. Operating under the assumption that all Indians were dangerous, approximately 160 Confederate forces aligned with some 325 state militiamen to rout the Native Americans, but committed a series of fateful blunders. As Lucy reported, the military did, in fact, retreat as between 400 and 600 surprised warriors defended themselves and escaped to Mexico.

3rd Friday ~ My scholars did remarkably well in their examination and the recitation of their pieces, but came very near breaking down in some of the latter and in some of their songs. With the thoughts that they were the last we were to sing together, neither scholars or teacher could keep back the tears. My affectionate pupils ~ 'tis hard to give them up. May the All Wise be their guide and lead them in paths of virtue and usefulness.

Although it is sad for me to give up my little pupils my time here is so limited I can not but be glad too that I am free.

4th Saturday ~ Just as my school-days close, Sara's commence. She is to go down on the river tomorrow that she may begin school on the first monday of the month. I suppose the Fedral President was inaugerated today.[7]

5th Sunday ~ I went to church Parson Mathews preached. Quite a congregation out, for Travis ~ Mrs Cleveland and E. Lott was there. I'll venture it will be as Aunt Lu says, she will yet come out with higher standing than those who have put her down so much.[8] Ruth was here to night and told us Mr Catlin had just come from Mr Brewer and Mr B~ told him that on friday evening Mr Buck was killed at Hempstead by the enrolling officer Logins.

What a horriable thing to think such a good and useful man should meet with such a fate. Oh what a great loss to Mrs B~. It is said the cause of the difficulty was that Mr B~ told Logins he was not doing his duty. He was stabbed in five places had not a single weapon about him. I would not be surprised if his death caused Sara's return home.

~~10~~11th Saturday ~ yesterday Mr Slater said Mr Collins read in the paper of the 8th that the Charleston was evacuated and that the Fedrals were marching on toward Columbia. Would like to know if it was so or not. Dick brought word last thursday that the British had sent over two boats to N. Y~ to tear it all to peices. Sis T~ like to have made herself sick laughing at him, she says N.Y~ better be getting away from there. This has been such a warm day I had to have the window up.

---

7. "The Fourth of March," *Harper's Weekly*, 1865, no. 3/11, HarpWeek. *Harper's Weekly* reported the inauguration on March 11, effusively praising the president for his "spotless patriotism," and concluded: "that he is inaugurated amidst universal applause . . . is the noblest proof of the truly conservative character of that popular Government with which the name of Abraham Lincoln will henceforth be associated." Lucy, however, did not seem so impressed.

8. No doubt Aunt Lu was referencing the feud involving the Clevelands, the Catlins, and the Lotts.

Mr Buck was buried with Masonic honors.[9] Read Bent's last letter home says he was much surprised when he heard I was going home; thought I was going to marry and stay here. From what he had heard, he says if all reports are true, I have been [married] 2 or 3 times.

~~11~~12th Sunday ~ I sent word to see could I get a trunk. News came confirming the report that Charleston & Columbia was evacuated[10] and also that Richmond had been ~ [left unfinished]

~~12~~13th Monday ~ Everybody is perfectly outraged at Mr Buck being killed as he was. Logins is to be tried to-day. Telot Woods and Mr Whitworth, Mrs B's step-father and brother-in-law, they will spend $300,000 but he shall be hung. They have three eminent lawyers employed ~ Giddings of Brenham, ~~Thomas~~ Thompson or ~~Bokes~~ of Houston ~~I can not recollect the name~~ ~ and Esq Portis.

A mistake ~ Mr B's friends say they will prosecute to the extent of the law

The opposite party have ~~General Portis~~ Hiram Waller and Ben Ty Harris. If he gets clear, there is a chance for most any body to I think. But for all that, I believe he will come out cleared. I could not give much for his safety afterward though. Both Mr B & L were Masons. Mr Dabney says Mr B~ had a pistol, but never drew it, placed one hand on either shoulder and called to the lookers on to take him off, that he was cutting him. Why he did not draw his six shooter no one can tell, unless that he

---

9. Mr. Buck and Logins were both members of the Freemasons, a fraternal organization with roots in the medieval associations of stonemasons. The organization had by 1865 expanded to include men unconnected to the building trade, and was active throughout the United States. *The Handbook of Texas Online* explains that local lodges maintained prominence in Texas, having been introduced there in the 1820s. Masons espoused the ideals of brotherhood, solidarity, and justice, requiring their members to take vows of loyalty to these principles. Because of the standards they embraced, Masons exhibited a strong influence, both in their organization and in their communities. No doubt this was the case in and around Travis, since Lucy wrote that although Mr. Buck's murderer was still awaiting a criminal trial, he had already been tried by the local lodge.

10. James M. McPherson, *Ordeal by Fire: The Civil War and Reconstruction*, 2nd ed. (New York: McGraw-Hill, 1992), 473–474. In Lucy's reports of war news, fiction intermingled more and more with fact. Some reports were speedily dismissed as laughable. Others, such as the evacuation of Charleston, were quickly confirmed as fact. Charleston had surrendered on February 18, 1865, and Columbia, the capital of South Carolina, had been burned at the same time. Many in the North blamed South Carolina's fiery rhetoric for the provocation of war, and the destruction of Charleston, "Queen city of the South, [afforded] the most dramatic sign of the Confederacy's collapse" (473).

did not want to break his Masonic pledge. L~ was tried in the lodge, we have not heard the results yet. This is brother James 30th birthday, wish it could have been celebrated by my arrival home.

16th Thursday ~ Went to Lu's this morn got there about 11. Sara was in school is teaching at the school-house. Has six scholars; Em and Tallie will come next week board at Lu's. Willie looks worse than I ever saw him after a spell of sickness.

17th Friday ~ Lu was over at Mrs Buck's this morn. She has the keys and went to see to the things. Logins has been bailed. Every one says they think Logins is awol for Col Kirby ~ not the first one he has made use of from what report says.

18th Saturday ~ Bent got home thursday evening ~ I am so glad he has come, been gone 3 yrs. left his Regt at Mansfield on the 9th. [I] arrived at home, found Mrs Brewer here. Kinch and Hez were here yester today. Hez came to tell us good-bye. I am so sorry I was not at home.

19th Sunday ~ Quite a number at church Not wishing to receive the how'd'y's after church, I left while they were singing the last line. Did not write to-day ~ which shows I am not wisely improving my time.[11] Beautiful day.

22nd Wednesday ~ Set up until eleven last night talking over war times ~ it is right amusing to hear B~ tell of different circumstances make comparisons such rediculous ones and bring them in so well. But for all that I would not like my brother to talk that way.

Aunt Lu got Mrs Catlins papers this eve. The news is various and conflicting some seem to think many of the troops we have thought were coming to Texas would be sent across the Mississippi. Flourney's Regt. amongst others I am sorry. Many of the Regt's are to be dismounted. The boys will not like that much.

23rd Thursday ~ Heard G Bell was killed by B. B Lee.

11. On the title page of the 1863–1864 volume of Lucy's journal, she had included a quotation by Longfellow in which he admonishes his readers to "wisely improve the present." Lucy took this to heart and typically kept herself occupied with industrious pursuits; now, in the bustle of preparations, she guiltily, if gently, admitted that she had not fulfilled her obligation to that task.

24th Friday ~ it is a mistake about G. B. being killed, but he was wounded and a soldier killed by a groceryman, a drunken frolic from what we hear. This afternoon went out to Mr Middletons by myself. They had begun to think I did not want to come there.

25th Saturday ~ The weather is not very promising but we concluded to go to Chapel H~. Bought me a traveling dress and 2 yds of domestic. Just before we left town, it commenced raining rained all the way home. We hunted better crossings coming back and got along very well, but cold wet and muddy ~ we were glad to get to a bright fire.

26th Sunday ~ Mr M asks a blessing at the table now ~ seems so strange. No one went to church to-day 'tis so unpleasant. I wrote to Chesley then read a chapter in the bible and afterwards a in [the] Texas Almanac[12]

27th Monday ~ Arrived at home to meet with dissapointment. Nehemiah & Kinch were here yesterday today and an answer came from my application for a pass port ~ can not go by Galveston.

30th Thursday ~ Mrs P~ told me of Mrs C~ talking to her of the prisoners taking the oath of allegiance to the fed~ gov~.[13] Said as it was forced, she did not consider it binding at all (therefore it would be no disgrace for them to go into the service). No, says Mrs P~ no more than Dan's oath leaving would be, as his was a forced oath. How strange that some people can only look on one side of a question. Came home to night and Mr Slater here ~ he advises me not to return home until Peace is made. Oh, well, it is pleasant to know one has friends, but they do not know what they are asking.

---

12. The *Texas Almanac* was originally published by the *Galveston News* in January 1857. According to *The Handbook of Texas Online*, publication continued until 1873, even through the tumultuous years of the Civil War, with only a one-year break, in 1866. Following a hiatus of thirty-one years, the *Almanac* once again resumed publication, this time by the *Dallas Morning News*. In 2008, the *Dallas Morning News* donated the *Almanac* to the Texas State Historical Association, which now oversees publication.

13. "Lawmakers, Loyalty, and the 'Ironclad Oath,' 1864, US Capitol Visitor's Center." The oath that Mrs. C had declared nonbinding was known as the "ironclad oath," a pledge forswearing any previous service to the Confederacy. The "ironclad oath" had originated in the United States Congress in July 1862, and had required all federal workers to swear allegiance to the Union. However, four years later, to promote unity, the law evolved to require an oath of future allegiance to the Union.

Lucy had begun this month with both the anticipation of her leave-taking and the anguish of heartfelt good-byes. Now the farewells had become wearisome, and she had begun to avoid certain public outpourings where she could be overwhelmed by well-wishers. As strong as she was, her departure was taking a personal toll, and she attempted to reduce her own emotional upheaval.

In the midst of her own uncertainties, Lucy wrote of the disappointment of some and the bitterness of others. Yet she knew her own mind, and her reaction to Mrs. C's views may be the best gauge of her feelings about the entire conflict. Her philosophical musings convey her bafflement with Mrs. C's response to the oath. For Lucy, there had always been two sides to the question—two divergent views that she had been required to balance as a Northerner in Southern lands. But now, in spite of the turmoil that consumed the nation, in spite the bitterness of so many around her, for Lucy it was simply a matter of going home, and she would do what was necessary to get there. For this Northern girl who had put on Southernness, the bonds to both superseded any favoritism. Taking an oath seemed a small enough price, and she would soon write of seeking out that possibility. Ultimately, she would be faced with taking two oaths: first, one supporting the Confederacy, then later, one pledging her loyalty to the Union.

At this point, however, the possibilities for that journey once again seemed remote. Lucy had now learned that General Magruder had denied her passport application and that she could not go by way of Galveston. Well-meaning friends advised her to stay in Texas until a real peace was made, and although she appreciated their concern, she would not be deterred. Yet despite her resolve, the advice of friends had left its mark; her level of stress rose decidedly as she pondered her next move. Now that Magruder had said no—what would she do? If she couldn't go by Galveston, how could she get home—river travel was still far from secure—no trains/wagons were venturing North yet—the South was still ensconced in war, and word of surrender would be late in coming to Texas. Lucy's options for an impending departure were narrowing. With no passport, where would she turn?

CHAPTER 15

APRIL 1–16, 1865

I realize fully what I am undertaking. If it were not toward home,
I could not make up my mind to start such a trip

LUCY P. STEVENS,
April 13, 1865

BY APRIL 1, Lucy's apprehension was obvious. Her anxiety had penetrated her dream world, and the conflict is manifested clearly by the contrasts in her dreams. The mud that threatened to engulf her in one dream represented the uncertainty and danger associated with leaving Texas, but another dream of marriage to a longtime acquaintance from home signaled the security of a future to be found only in Ohio. Regardless of her fear, however, Lucy was determined that she would confront all risks in order to return.

Over the next few days, she began preparing her belongings and settled her account with Mr. Brewer, who, in the end, managed to renege on the terms of her teaching contract; as Sarah noted in her journal, "he consented to pay Cous Lu $5.00 a month, but charged her $5.00 a month board, something that was not in the agreement at all" (Sarah Pier, 4/11/65). Minimizing the affront, Lucy threw herself into a final round of good-byes, as she learned of Mack's impending arrival. One of her personal favorites, Mack had been deployed with his unit, and Lucy had written in February that she feared she would not see him before her departure. Now she was overjoyed to receive news that she would indeed be able to see him one last time.

1st Saturday ~ Aunt Lu says Hemman sent his particular love to me and knows that I won't marry until he comes back. I just know that was cousin Sammy sent that word ~ pay for the word I sent him.

Last night it was past twelve when I went to bed ~ I was very tired and dreamed of wading in mud so deep and black I could hardly get through it. It woke me and when I went to sleep again, dreamed of being married to Horace S~ he talked so earnestly of the future. Wish I had not had such dreams. I am not superstitious, but still they do not leave a pleasant feeling. I can not help feeling a foreboding of evil.

4th Tuesday ~ Neh came with me to Lu'. Found W~ [Waller] in the fields and 'twas so late when he returned, we could not venture over the river. Neh stayed until about two, then left will go to Mr Middleton's tonight.

5th Wednesday ~ Although it was at something of a risk, cousin W~ went with me over the river. Mrs P [Peebles] & Mrs Clark were both at home
All stand on the same old footing ~ many words of love and friendship were sent. On our return to Lu's found Mollie C~ here. My friends advise me to go down to G~ [Galveston] as soon as possible and be ready to go out the first opportunity. I shall accept their advice and go next week.

6th Thursday ~ Cousin Waller went to Bellville to-day to see about me swearing myself, concluded to do nothing for the present. This P.M. who should come walking in but Jimmy Cochrane. I am so glad he came.
Cousin S~ wrote to cousin S & Mr W~ [Wiley], told them to meet me at H~ [Hempstead] next thursday. I looked over Aunt H's trunk & took out some things mostly old pieces. Intend to start for T~ [Travis] soon tomorrow morn Sara is coming up in the eve.

7th Friday ~ Mollie and I left this morn came by Mr Cochrane's, told Mr & Mrs C~, Ann & the children good-by. Came on to Mr Collins told Mrs Burleson and Mr Slater adieux. John Harvey came to Mr Cochrane's last night. This morning he and Neh went to Mr Collins and from there to Mr Middleton's.
Mr Burleson's trial is not yet decided. At Mr Cochrane's we were told of Gen'l John Wharton's being killed yesterday by Col Baylor of the Lady ~ Rangers.[1] It is said General W~ ordered Col B~ to report to Col Terril,

---

1. According to *The Handbook of Texas Online*, Colonel George Baylor led a regiment composed of the Second Texas Cavalry, Arizona Brigade and an additional company, the "Ladies Rangers." This force saw fighting in Louisiana during 1863 and 1864, and returned to Texas in December 1864.

who was Senior. Col has a Regt made up mostly of conscripts, so col B~ refused to do so, was then ordered to go across the Miss [Mississippi River]. he replied that just suited him. Genl W~ said if that was the case he should not go, went on board the cars with his staff. but as the train did not start off in some moments, he changed his mind. went up in the city again and was killed ~ every one seems very much to regret the occurrence.[2]

8th Saturday ~ Rained most of last night and today. This afternoon John Harvey came here ~ I can not describe my feelings I was so badly plagued. To make matters worse, Aunt Lu had to speak of my receiving a letter from him.[3] Kinch Collins was also here intended to go home but I would not consent to his leaving going as I intend to leave so soon. Mr & Mrs Middleton came about 4 P.M., brought me a saw fish bill and a comb. Johnie came soon after felt a little more at my ease this eve.

9th Sunday ~ Kinch & Johnie spent last night here. They say Mack got home yesterday I am very glad to hear it.

This afternoon Jim B~, Sallie and Mrs C~ came over and stayed an hour or so. Miss Ellen C brought my china cup & saucer. E spoke to me of my school account ~ plague take people that cannot understand anything right. Sara & Joe P~ came to day say Henman was at Lu's yesterday, sent a good-by, and his love to me. Cousin W~ had Cal bring my trunk up today.

10th Monday ~ cousin Sara and Mollie worked on my dress. I trimmed my hat a present from Mollie used to be Neh's. In the afternoon, Nehemiah, Fanny and Mack came to see me. Just before they came, Bennie

---

2. According to *The Handbook of Texas Online*, the confrontation occurred much as Lucy has written. General John Wharton became embroiled in a dispute with his fellow officer, Colonel George Baylor, during a visit to General Magruder's headquarters at the Fannin Hotel in Houston: "Wharton reportedly slapped Baylor's face and called him a liar, whereupon Baylor drew his revolver and shot the unarmed Wharton." Baylor was eventually acquitted of murder charges in 1868, but expressed a "lifelong sorrow" over the incident.

3. Although Lucy had avoided viewing John Harvey as a suitor, his many visits to the Pier home and the distress of this entry imply his continued interest in her. Lucy's words indicate that she cared for him as well. However, her fondness for John was more than offset by her desire to return home. On the brink of her departure, she once again rejected any possibility of a potential courtship.

Catlin came over on horse-back and I went home with him to see Mr Catlin about getting a passport.[4] I went to Mr Clevelands this morn to see would Mr C~ pay what was coming me on the Edwards note ~ but nix-com a rouse, no such good luck. Aunt Lu and I packed Aunt H's trunk put in a great many of my things.

Mack says that he and Carrie started here yesterday, but saw so many ladies at the gate got scared out. Told Mack of his sowing his wild oats ~ he can not imagine how I found out such truths. All took supper here. Neh and myself never went to bed until after twelve o'clock talking over old & war times.

11th Tuesday ~ Neh & Mollie left about ten. Mrs Brewer and E~ came just before to settle up with me. Charged me $5 per month board ~ payed me for Judges and tuition and $10. for writing. E and I went over to Mrs Campbells & Mrs Chapman's, but only stayed a few moments at either place. Just before noon, cousin Sammy, Lu, Waller & Willie came. In the afternoon Sue Purcell came took dinner with us. Brought letters for me to take. David & Mack came to tell me good-by.

Sue P~ got up out of a sick bed, also Bettie Swearingen Jimmy came with her. In the eve Jake came, brought me a boquet. Mr & Mrs Hastings, John H & Artie & Mr Chapman Ruth Ellen were here.

Mr Campbell fixed my trunk & this afternoon I packed it. Uncle P~ gave me in specie $125 owed him before $10. but cousin W is to pay him $50. & he has my Edwards note for $40. also gave me a N. O. bill $100.

At last the day arrived, and, once again, Lucy said good-bye. Armed with the love and good wishes of family and friends, and bouquets presented by her scholars, she began her journey on April 12, 1865. As she recorded the day's events in her diary, she noted that Sammy and Jake had accompanied her part of the way. Sarah also described the day of departure in her journal:

---

4. *Journal of the Congress of the Confederate States of America*, vol. 5, March 3, 1862. Although Lucy's initial request had been denied by General Magruder, proper documentation to leave Confederate lands for a "foreign country" would undoubtedly be required. The *Journal of the Congress of the Confederate States of America* reports that a bill comparable to the bill enacted by the Union and designed to regulate the granting of passports had been introduced in Congress in early 1862 (3/3/62). It was subsequently referred to the Committee on Military Affairs for further study. It is thus no surprise that Lucy would need to obtain her passport through the offices of General Magruder and/or his representatives.

Cous Lu left us this afternoon—It was hard to part from her—and hard for her to part from us, but duty called her home—and she was anxious to go. I hope she may reach her destination in safety. Pa will meet her in Chapel Hill in the morning and go with her as far as Houston. Sammie went with her to Mr. Middleton's. Jake part of the way. Sis T., Jane B. and I watched her from the gate as long as we could see, going off escorted by two confederate soldiers, and such good friends. May God protect her on her way, for she will be alone.

    Sarah Pier, 4/12/65

Sarah's comments contained unplanned references to the dual dilemma facing Lucy. Sarah acknowledged Lucy's immediate difficulty as being that of a woman traveling alone into an uncertain future. Yet Sarah's description of Lucy bravely marching out the gate, encircled by Confederate soldiers, also paints an unconscious portrait of the long-term quandary with which Lucy would contend. To successfully negotiate her return, she needed a way to accommodate both her recent Southern life and the Northern heritage to which she was returning. Her experiences had shaped her into the woman she was, yet the question remained, just who would she become?

Lucy and Sammy stopped for the night at the Middletons' home, a place dear to Lucy's heart. And as she wrote about leaving Mrs. Middleton, her sentiment was heartfelt, borne out by her many journal entries that include this special friend. The Middleton household had been a refuge for her, where she had spent countless hours in the company of her friends. The couple had embraced Lucy and cared for her as family; thus, parting from these friends, and from her other loved ones, was almost more than she could bear. Had it not been for the beloved thought of home, that pain, plus Lucy's fear of the unknown dangers that lay ahead, would certainly have kept her in Texas.

Yet once she had taken her leave, Lucy characteristically immersed herself in her surroundings. On the train from Chappell Hill to Hempstead, she was impressed with her fellow traveler Reverend Joseph Wood Dunn, whose notable credentials gave the man some fame and must have made quite an impression on Lucy. These impressions were soon eclipsed, however, when she changed trains in Hempstead. She immediately noticed the imposing company of several high-ranking Confederate officers aboard the train, and her comments indicate that despite her apprehensions and frustrations about the war, she was even now impressed by the presence of these hardened soldiers. Yet even with her recognition of their status, she could not resist a characteristic tongue-in-cheek comment aimed at the apparent arrogance of some of the men.

But for all the observations that Lucy recorded on this first day of her journey, the most important one could easily be missed. Tucked into a short comment about a new acquaintance she had just met, Lucy mentioned for the first time the circuitous route she knew she would be required to travel to make her way home. As subsequent diary entries will reflect, she would indeed travel to Havana, Cuba, before traveling to the North. From her off-hand comment concerning her destination, it is clear that she was apprehensive about the upcoming journey, perhaps because she was already very much aware of the intricate course that she was about to travel.

12th Wednesday ~ Artie & John left this morn ~ Mrs Catlin, Jake, Sallie Lou & Sis came soon after breakfast, brought boquets from the children. Sam sent a good-bye. Mrs Campbell & Lu Alice came, brought me a pin cushion that I am to tie to my scissor-chain when I get married & a ½ $ for a ring.

Mrs Lord came by herself, Mrs Purcell sent letters for me to take. Jane Edwards is here, and Mack Campbell, and brought my album home. Mrs Catlin gave me a belt.

Cousin Sammy & Jake started with me. Bid all a last good-bye soon after dinner.

Sammy went out to Mr Middleton's with me, Jake & Sack Brewer as far as Buffalo. We called a few moments at Mr Corbans. In the eve Mr Corban & Neh came. Sent many kind messages to Aunt H & Uncle M.

13th Thursday ~ It was nearly 11 last night when we went to bed, and about 3~ we were up. Mrs M had breakfast a little past 4~. We had just got up from the table when Uncle Pier and Dick came. We started at half past five. I leave one of the truest friends I ever had in Mrs M~.

Such mud in places, it was almost impassible. Mr M~ went to Chapel H with us; took us through Dr Spen's lane & Mr Wallace's fields. By doing so, we avoided a great deal of the mud. Had to wait about a half hour for the cars. Once on board, I felt fairly embarked for home. There is little of joy in my feeling however; too many dear friends have been told farewell and my journey is fraught with too many dangers for me to anticipate much pleasure. I realize fully what I am undertaking. If it were not toward home, I could not make up my mind to start such a trip. Arrived at Hempstead. Mr Wiley was almost the first one I saw. Mr Torrence the next.

Called to Mr W~ through the window. As soon as the cars halted, he came on board and waited on me to the depot while Uncle P~ attended to the baggage. Who should come on board the train at Chapel H~ but Rev. J T Wood Dunn[5] and Mr McNese. The former made himself very agreeable. I am very glad Mr Wiley came. he had half a mind to turn back thinking something might happen to prevent my starting.

Changed cars at Hempstead. As the train started off, Mr Wiley & Torrence went loping across the square waved a good-bye to me.

Mrs Col Terry with three children are passengers. Col T's Regt are on their way to Camp Greer. also Lucken's. Major *somebody*, General Forney & staff are bound for Houston and when we got to Cypress-City, met with Terry's R~ when the Col[6] came on board.

The sight of so many *malicious* looking gents almost dazzles my eyes. Wonder if I can deign to look at common folks hereafter. Col T~ and lady occupied the seat in front of me. Are very unassuming and genteel in their appearance. Not a mark about him that he could be distinguished from a private citizen. What a contrast in General F~[7] he occupies a whole seat and hangs his hat plumed & star'd up for us to look at.

Camp Greer is much more pleasantly situated than I had supposed. The barracks look very comfortable and the grounds are kept

---

5. According to *The Handbook of Texas Online*, Dunn was well known, having helped found the respected but short-lived St. Paul's Episcopal College in Anderson, Texas, during the early 1850s. Subsequently, he had founded Emmanuel Episcopal Church in Lockhart, Texas, near Austin, in 1853.

6. Not to be confused with Benjamin Franklin Terry, the organizer of Terry's Texas Rangers who had been killed in 1861, this was David Smith Terry, Benjamin's younger brother. According to *The Handbook of Texas Online*, the younger Terry traveled to California during the gold rush of 1849 and was eventually appointed chief justice of the California Supreme Court. Terry fell into disfavor when he killed California senator David C. Broderick in a duel. In 1863 Terry returned to Texas with his family and joined the Confederate army. After the war, he eventually made his way back to California, where he was killed in 1889 in a dispute with Stephen J. Field, a U.S. Supreme Court justice.

7. General John Horace Forney, educated at West Point, resigned his commission in 1861 and aligned himself with the South. He entered the Confederate army as a colonel, and was promoted first to brigadier general, then major general. This last promotion, according to *The Handbook of Texas Online*, was "a rise in rank that probably outran his abilities," an assessment echoed by a multitude of historical accounts.

very neatly. Soldiers should bless their stars that they can have so good a place, though of course it is not pleasant to lay in camp anywhere. Arrived at Mrs Scrantons at 3 P.M. found a Mrs & Miss Hartley here.

Mr Scranton made me so welcome told me he was a man of few words but he wanted me to feel at home and make myself so.

Uncle P~ has kept himself busy running round to see what could be done toward getting a passport, but as yet has not had much encouragement.

14th Friday ~ Miss Jennie sent for a new book "Mascaria" very good so far.[8]

Uncle P~ after a great deal of running, finally succeeded in getting a passport, and in the afternoon I had to go take the oath (to give no information). Mrs Scranton kindly went for a Miss Mathews to go with me to Mrs Stevens, but as Mr Huffman came, it was unnecessary.

Addie was the first to see me, was so rejoiced she had to cry. Excitable creature! I was glad to see all. Mrs S~ [Stevens] met me, then came Ella. Lizzie has grown so much I hardly knew the child. They would not listen to my leaving that night, and as Mr Huffman told me I was not expected to Mrs Scrantons, I stayed. In the eve went with Mr Stevens, Ella & Mr Huffman to the theater. The play was the "Rich Farmer."

15th Saturday ~ Left Mrs Stevens' soon in the morn. Got to Mrs Scrantons before Mrs S~ and Jennie were up. After breakfast Mrs S~ fixed up a lunch for me and gave me some oranges had a boquet gotten for me too. Started for Galveston between eight and nine. After many delays (stopping to eat

---

8. Drew Gilpin Faust, *Mothers of Invention* (New York: Vintage Books, 1996), 117. *Macaria*, or *Mascaria*, as Lucy called it, written by Augusta Jane Evans in 1864 as a tribute to the Confederacy, was arguably the most popular novel of the Civil War South. Faust writes that Evans wrote the book as a model for Southern women struggling with their roles and identities during the war, identifying it as a departure from traditional female novels in which women's purpose and fulfillment came from romantic involvement. Instead, Faust asserts that Evans gave her main characters the choice of autonomous and public usefulness in a deliberate attempt to legitimize single life for women. Although the book met with incredible popularity, Faust reports it also faced intense criticism from the press. Many reviewers denounced the perplexing blurring of traditional gender roles, and some readers came away with an unsettling sense that while Evans took "advantage of warborn opportunity to extend the limits of the possible and of the imaginable . . . [she] may have tried to extend those boundaries too far" (177). Although Lucy gave scant mention to the book, she aligned her perspective with the many women of the South who had been thrust into the single life and had been required to forge a space for themselves in a world far different from what they had known.

dew-berries &c) we arrived in Galveston at 5 P.M.[9] Almost the first person I saw was Jimmy Clemons a happy surprise ~ we stopped at the Washington House ("Beissner" proprietor) ~ Jimmy called there to see us about an hour after we got there. Was perfectly astonished that I was homeward bound.

J~ says he is going to be married soon but would not tell me to whom.

Uncle P~ has Mr John Slate [Sleight] and Mr Jo and Wm Hendley interested in getting me off. Mr Catlin and Uncle P~ spent the eve in my room, very pleasant for me.

And Aunt Lu I am not doing it to complain, but I want to give you a description of "No 10." It has in it two beds ~ both loaded down with blankets that were, I suppose *once white*; some mosquito bars of the same material as was cousin Sammys & Mr D's No carpet on the floor and it a sight. tallow candle, with iron stick, adds beauty & light to the apartment a four legged table wash stand, bowl & pitcher four chairs and a looking glass, also one window.

16th Sunday ~ Wretched ~ what a night was last ~ [. . .] were numberless ~ the heat not hardly to be stood. Was by myself until church time ~ Jimmy came. (Miss Petty is Jimmy's girl.) Jimmy, Uncle P~ and I went up into Hendley's Lookout and took a good view of the city and of the Blockading fleet. I was expecting then to start out on the Badger this eve ~ saw it and several others lying out in the bay.

There was eleven blockaders lying off the bar, one of them is a fierce looking vessel black as midnight's darkness.

One has such a pretty view of the city here, Pillican's Pitt and beyond Boliver's Point.[10]

When we came back who should be here but Mr Ferris ~ was glad to see him. By his influence, I was persuaded to wait and try go by "Flag of

---

9. The distance from Houston to Galveston is approximately fifty miles, and Lucy expressed some frustration as she wrote about the eight or nine hours that it took to make the trip. She was impatient to be on her way and, at this point, had little patience for berry-picking excursions.

10. David G. McComb, *Galveston: A History* (Austin: University of Texas Press, 1986), 6–8. Pillican's Pitt, a natural silt catcher, had originally been a narrow marsh with only a hundred feet of dry soil. It had eventually enlarged and merged with Pelican Island. Beyond the island, and to the northeast, was the southern tip of the Bolivar Peninsula. McComb reports that the waterway between Galveston Island and the Bolivar Peninsula provides the main entrance to Galveston Bay and the channel between Galveston and Pelican Island and "formed a natural harbor for the sailing vessels and small steamers of the nineteenth century" (8).

Truce." Mr Slate also told me he thought it a better plan, so I stay. Went with Mr Ferris to Mr Masons. I feel like a tempest tossed ~~vessel~~ barque that I go with what ever wind may float me on. God grant a propitious one that I may reach my home in safety.

Mr & Mrs Mason seem very *clever* people. I am ~~sorry~~ truly sorry for Mrs Mason she lost her daughter last summer of yellow fever, and in 1863 her son died in New O~ of the same disease.

Mr Ferris had yellow fever here last summer. Mr F~ has promised to do all for me in his power. Of course I like him. I have heard so much of him before I was prepared for that. Then too he is a brother Buckeye, has lost a Mother, three sisters and a Grandmother since he left, which naturally makes me feel a sympathy for him.

———⌄———

As Lucy waited, she shifted her focus from the familiar to the new and unknown: new people, new places, and new experiences. She had now left Houston for Galveston, a city that, so far as is known, she had never visited. She took advantage of the time, assuming the role of a tourist, and recorded much information of historical significance about the city and some of its most prestigious citizens.

The Washington House, where Lucy stayed, was actually the first of two Washington hotels and was located in the heart of historic downtown Galveston. The building, typical of 1850s architectural style, still stands and is now under historical protection. According to Mr. Lesley Sommer, the former executive director of the Historic Downtown Strand Seaport Partnership in Galveston, a description of the earlier building in Howard Barnstone's 1966 book *The Galveston That Was* says it "possessed something of the charm of an old New England inn."[11] From Lucy's account of room "No. 10," however, it is doubtful that she would choose the word "charming" for the hotel.

Lucy spoke of the men Uncle Pier had enlisted to help her on her way, men who were "heavy hitters" of the day. According to Barnstone, William Hendley, along with his brother Joseph and their partner Mr. John Sleight, owned the largest shipping house of that era, and their offices were located along the Strand, the business district of downtown Galveston, across from the bay. *The Handbook of Texas Online* states that the Strand was known as the "Wall Street of the Southwest" and was "a vibrant, vital and bustling place where deals were made, goods bought and sold, ships supplied, and people served." These three men were an integral part of this commercial world, and

---

11. Howard Barnstone, *The Galveston That Was* (New York: Macmillan, 1966), 47.

it was to them that James Bradford Pier turned for help. This encounter not only introduces these three tycoons, but denotes the ease with which Pier contacted them, validating the position that James Bradford Pier enjoyed in the world of Civil War Texas.

Yet even with their assistance, Lucy waited in uncertainty. She knew neither when, nor even how, she would depart Texas. Uncle Pier remained in Galveston to oversee her plans, and to pass the time they decided to do some sightseeing, arranging to visit Hendley's Lookout. Rather than a natural vantage from which they could view the city, Hendley's Lookout was actually the rooftop of the building owned by Lucy's benefactors. Barnstone reports that the building, which received cannon fire during the Battle of Galveston in 1863, housed an observatory on its roof throughout the war years, from which "the movements of the Federal gunboats blockading Galveston were noted."[12] With J. B. Pier's connections to the Hendleys, the "lookout" was opened to Lucy and Uncle Pier, and they enjoyed a sweeping view of the city and its bay.

From her vantage atop the lookout, Lucy recorded that she saw eleven blockaders in the harbor and, for the first time, mentioned that she might consider leaving Galveston on a blockade runner's ship—an extremely risky endeavor. She had apparently, however, talked the idea over with Cousin Sarah before she left Travis, for Sarah's journal indicates that Lucy was "going to get ready and go down to Houston and stop there and wait until the boat goes out—while she tries to get a passport—Walker refused her one—and if she does not succeed in getting a passport, she intends trying to run the blockade" (Sarah Pier, 4/5/65).

Risky or not, blockading was big business in Galveston, and although blockading ships regularly ran into and out of the port throughout the war, Rodman Underwood asserts that the highest degree of activity took place from November 1864 to May 1865. He quotes historian Robert Warren Glover, who calculates that "at least thirty-seven vessels engaged in the Galveston trade" during this time frame.[13] For Lucy to count eleven, then, would not be unusual. She might not have known the names of many of the ships, save *Badger*. However, frequent visitors to the bay became well known; names such as *Wren* and *Lark* were among the most successful. Underwood reports that even Union Navy secretary Welles was cognizant of the successes of the fleet, remarking in May 1865: "It appears that blockade running at Galveston

---

12. Ibid., 36.

13. Rodman L. Underwood, *Waters of Discord: The Union Blockade of Texas during the Civil War* (Jefferson, NC: McFarland, 2003), 61.

is still carried on with much success. The following are the arrivals reported at Havana, all from Galveston, with cotton: *Lunar,* April 15; *Wren* and *Badger,* April 21; *Fox* and *Evelyn,* April 22, and *Denbigh,* May 1."[14] *Denbigh,* one of the most successful blockade runners, was, in fact, ultimately stranded at the entrance to Galveston Bay, and is today a protected archaeological site under Texas law, a study site of the Institute of Nautical Archaeology, based at Texas A&M University.[15]

In typical fashion, Lucy noted the ships, then moved on to her view of the city. As she looked northward from her vantage on Hendley's Lookout, she admired Pillican's Pitt [Spit], a marshy part of Pelican Island.[16] Beyond and to the northeast, she could also see the southern tip of the Bolivar Peninsula, known as Point Bolivar, or as Lucy termed it, "Boliver's Point," which provided a passage by which the blockade runners could sneak into the bay, a fact that did not escape Lucy's notice.

Returning from her sightseeing, Lucy remained uncertain as to her next move, and Mr. Ferris and Mr. Sleight were quick to dissuade her from the riskier alternative—running the blockade. Both men chose the more conservative path of traveling via the safer route—with permission and approval from the Confederate commanders. Lucy acquiesced, being swayed by their concern, but noted her own ambiguity with seeming frustration. We must wonder how differently Lucy's plans might have developed had anyone in Texas known of a small village called Appomattox Courthouse in faraway Virginia . . .

14. Ibid., 61–62.
15. "The *Denbigh* Project," Institute of Nautical Archaeology, Texas A&M University.
16. McComb, *Galveston,* 6.

CHAPTER 16

APRIL 17–MAY 4, 1865

...but I could not bear the thought of letting such a good *opportunity* pass ~
when there was no certainty of going By "Flag of Truce."

LUCY P. STEVENS,
April 17, 1865

MONDAY, APRIL 17, proved to be a pivotal day for Lucy. Early in the day, Uncle Pier came to bid her a final farewell as he returned to Travis, and Lucy knew this might well be the last time she would ever see him. In the five years of her sojourn in Texas, James Bradford Pier had become a father to her. He had loved her as though she were his own, and although Lucy had said her good-byes to all of her friends and family days earlier, Uncle Pier was the last link to her Texas home. He represented the love and security she had known in Texas, even during the upheaval of war, and with his departure, the chain irrevocably snapped. Lucy was now completely alone. She wrote movingly of separation, and her sister Julie, though unnamed, spurred Lucy's reflections, clearly revealing her ongoing struggles to align her sorrow with her faith.

The day passed quietly, as Lucy, who had resigned herself to waiting for permission to leave, assisted with household chores. However, at around five o'clock that afternoon, her world once again shifted. Mr. Sleight came with news of the departure of the blockade runner *Fox* and with an opportunity for Lucy. The captain, Simpson Adkins, had generously agreed to take Lucy to Havana as an unregistered passenger aboard *Fox*—if she could be ready in time!

The blockade runner *Fox* had arrived in Galveston on April 14, following a narrow escape during which she evaded a fleet of twenty-five Union warships.[1] Descriptions of the harrowing encounter were recorded in early newspaper articles and in more recent works, including W. T. Block's *Schooner*

---

1. "In Lead-Color Paint," *New York Times*, October 17, 1892, New York Times Article Archive.

The "Fox."

Bound to Nassau from Liverpool. Put into Cork to fill up coals April 26th and sailed April 27th 1864. Arrived at Nassau May 23rd.

Blockade Runner *Fox*, Watercolor, painted at Cork, Ireland, about 1864, by an unidentified artist. Courtesy of the Spurling Collection, Confederate Museum, St. George's Historical Society, Bermuda.

—

Sail to Starboard: Confederate Blockade-Running on the Louisiana-Texas Coastline.[2] Block, in fact, quotes John Mackie, a marine aboard the Union gunboat *Semi-nole* who participated in the two-hour pursuit and wrote of the event, first in the *Galveston Daily News* and later as part of a collection of memoirs titled *Under Both Flags: A Panorama of the Great Civil War.*[3] The 1896 article details the chase, speaking of cannon fire and pivot guns exploding into the side of *Fox* and adds that only when the water became too shallow for the gunboat was the *Fox* able to escape. So daring was Captain Adkins's maneuvering of the *Fox*, Mackie reported, that "as the chase came to a close, Capt. Adkins ran up the Confederate flag on his saucy, but still unknown steamer, dipped it three times, and Capt. Clarey of the *Seminole*, being a good sport even if the battle had been uneven, returned the salute."[4]

2. W. T. Block, *Schooner Sail to Starboard: Confederate Blockade-Running on the Louisiana-Texas Coastline* (Woodville, TX: Dogwood Press, 1997), 70.

3. John F. Mackie, "Running the Blockade—Escape of the Fox," in *Under Both Flags: A Panorama of the Great Civil War*, ed. George Morley Vickers, 329–332 (Veterans Publishing, 1896). Palo Alto: Stanford University Library, 1969.

4. Block, *Schooner Sail to Starboard*, 70.

It is entirely possible, however, that Lucy read about the feats of Captain Adkins in the local newspaper just hours before her life and future would become entwined with his, for the day before, the *Galveston Daily News* had reported the incident with glowing commendations for the *Fox*, Captain Adkins, and the entire crew. The article poetically links the pursuit of the *Fox* to Scottish foxhunts and borrows extensively from the writings of Sir Walter Scott. The author also appropriates a cross section of biblical allusions, even denouncing the craftiness of the Federal pursuers as "the ingenuity of Satan and his children, the Yankees."[5]

Though his foray into Galveston was his one and only trip into Texas waters, Adkins's skill was obviously well known by North and South alike. Lucy later mentioned General Magruder's high regard for the captain, his praise echoing the comments of others who more grudgingly admitted Adkins's expertise. According to the Institute of Nautical Archaeology at Texas A&M, Adkins was an old hand at running the blockade, and well known to the Federal navy. He was captured at least twice, and both times returned to his calling. After the second capture, a Federal officer described Adkins as an "old offender" and "one of the most expert pilots on the Southern coast." The officer warned his colleagues to watch Adkins carefully, but it did no good—by 1865 he was back running the blockade again, this time to Galveston.[6]

Lucy herself would write about Captain A's exploits just two days later, adding details about damage to the ship and mentioning General Magruder's high regard for the captain. However, the most exciting, if perhaps romanticized, account of the adventure comes from Captain Adkins himself. When interviewed years later by a reporter for the *New York Times*, the captain confirmed details previously reported, but by this time, many of the particulars had become considerably magnified. Both Mackie and the 1865 news article reported that of approximately one hundred shots fired, only four hit their mark. Lucy, as well, wrote that only three took effect. However, the *Times* article in 1892 vividly described the battle, recalling that "shells were bursting on the forward deck, on the main deck, overhead, close alongside . . . the ship was quivering from stem to stern . . . [it] was being literally torn to pieces." Although some discrepancies could be attributed to the captain's veiled memories during the intervening years, there is little doubt that many of the embellishments were the product of an avid reporter's linguistic zeal. However, at the end of the piece, when the correspondent asked Adkins if he would have surrendered to the Federal fleet, he received a grim response.

5. "Chasing a Fox," Institute of Nautical Archaeology, Texas A&M University.
6. Ibid.

With all seriousness, Captain Adkins somberly replied, "'I had plenty of powder aboard and before I sighted the fleet I saw to it myself that the train leading to the powder needed only a match to hurl the ship into atoms. The *Fox*,' repeated the old white-haired captain, 'would never have been taken.'"[7] It was to this man that Lucy impetuously entrusted her life, for despite Mr. Ferris's warning, within fifteen minutes she was packed and ready to leave.

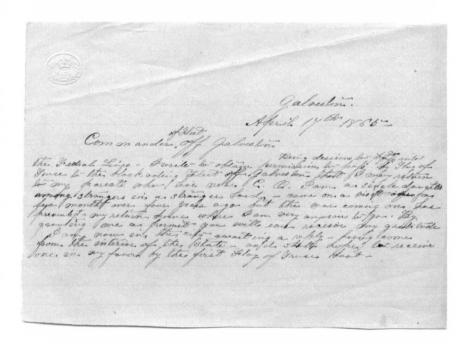

Lucy Pier Stevens' Request for Passport to Leave Texas. DeGolyer Library, Southern Methodist University, Lucy Pier Stevens Collection.

—

Galveston April 17, 1865
Commander of Fleet off Galveston

Being desirous to go into the Fedral lines—I write to obtain permission to pass by Flag of Truce to the blockading Fleet off Galveston that I may return to my parents who live near C.O. [Cleveland, Ohio]. I am a single daughter among strangers in a stranger land—came on a visit for a few months over four years ago but the war coming on has prevented my return home where I am very anxious to go. By granting me a permit you will ever receive my gratitude.

I am now in the city awaiting a reply—having come from the interior of the state— and shall hope to receive in my favor by the first Flag of Truce boat

---

7. "Running the Blockade: Exciting Experiences of Those Who Made It a Business," *New York Times*, October 2, 1892, New York Times Article Archive.

17th Monday ~ Mr F had my baggage brought up this morn. Uncle P~ came to see me this morn before I was dressed, says the cars leave soon this morn because General Magruder is going up on the train. The last good-bye to near and dear friends was said when Uncle P~ left.

The thought that we shall never all of us meet again can not but haunt me ~ for experience has taught me that those we least thought would go were the first to be taken away. Who will it be? We are taught that God does *all* things wisely but wherin that wisdom lies it is at times hard for us to see.

After my trunks were arranged my room presented quite a home-like appearance. Mrs M does her own work so of course I would not sit down and hold my hands and let her wait on me so I swept, ~~and~~ helped do the dishes, &c.

Brother Buckeye [Mr. Ferris] brought up a jar of dates for us and makes himself very generally agreeable. In the afternoon about five, Mr Slate came to Mrs Masons to let me know the "Fox" was going out that evening and Captain S~ Adkinson had proffered to take me to Havana had a comfortable room he would give up to me and Mr S~ advises for me to ~~go~~ accept the offer.

In fifteen minutes I was ready and off. Mr Ferris did not seem to think my decision a wise one, but I could not bear the thought of letting such a good *opportunity* pass when there was no certainty of going By "Flag of Truce."

I wrote to the Commander of the Fleet applying for a passport. Captain Wallace said if he had written one himself he could not have written one more to the purpose and thought I would get an answer that I would be received by the second "Truce Boat,"[8] but all that will not make it so.

Mr Slate got my passport signed again and had it ready as I went down. Mr Ferris attended to my baggage and went down to the wharf with me.

---

8. "Flag of Truce Boats," *Galveston Weekly News*, February 15, 1865, Texas and Other Southern States Civil War Newspapers/Newspaper Research, 1861–1865. The "Truce Boat" or "Flag of Truce Boat" was a common sight in Galveston Bay. In the February 15, 1865, edition of the *Galveston Weekly News*, for example, several articles mentioned the coming and going of various travelers on Flag of Truce Boats, duly noting that those departing had permission to leave the country. With the amount of traffic in the bay, Lucy's level of frustration as she attempted to obtain permission to leave Texas can only be imagined.

Was introduced to Captain A~ by Mr S~, also to Mr Watson.[9] Bid Mr S~ good-bye, then Mr Ferris ~ the last face of my Texas friends I may see in many a day.

Safely in my room at last where I found every convenience I would ask for ~ room carpeted wash-bowl water and night glass.

I sit up nearly an hour after we got started then was so sick went out on deck and threw up several times and would not have given up then had it not been [sic] for Captain A~ who acted towards me like a father. Made me loosen my clothes and assisted me in getting them off, for by that time I was almost beyond doing anything for myself. He was so gentlemanly about it too, said I must not think anything of his doing for me ~ that he was an old *married* man ~ he knew I could not wait on myself ~ that if I would take off my clothes I would feel much better, ~~for me~~ I'd not be so sick. It seemed to me at first I could not accept such assistance from a stranger and a gentleman, but was very glad afterward to accept his assistance.

18th Tuesday Was sick all night long ~ Capt A~ installed himself nurse and I could not have asked a better one.

It has been very calm since we started. Not a boat in sight ~ nothing to disturb our peace & quiet.

I did not leave my berth until afternoon then with considerable exertion, and some sickness I succeeded in dressing and getting out on deck. set there an hour or so then was so very sick I could not stay longer.

After lying down awhile could wait on myself. Not one of the men has ever entered my room unless they were sent. We can have no lights on board ~ that is a luxury blockade-runners have to dispense with.[10] It is still calm and the water as smooth as can be.

---

9. The Institute of Nautical Archaeology web page "Chasing a Fox" lists Henry Watson as the runner's pilot.

10. Thomas E. Taylor, *Running the Blockade* (1896), reprinted in *Classics of Naval Literature*, ed. Stephen R. Wise (Annapolis: Naval Institute Press, 1995). Taylor's memoir recounts the same restrictions that Lucy mentioned: "No lights were allowed—not even a cigar; the engine-room hatchways were covered with tarpaulins, at the risk of suffocating the unfortunate engineers and stokers in the almost insufferable atmosphere below. But it was absolutely imperative that not a glimmer of light should appear. Even the binnacle was covered, and the steersman had to see as much of the compass as he could through a conical aperture carried almost up to his eyes" (50).

The purser[11] Mr Havistat comes in twice a day and calls the time while Mr Murdock marks it down. Dan, the Captains waiting boy, has chills every day. Johnie a little boy about 14 ~ takes his place is so smart.

19th Wednesday ~ Did not get up to day ~ about noon Mr Murdock called out sail ho &c ~ It was supposed to be a Yankee mail-boat going towards Galveston. We were soon out of sight however without seeming to be noticed.

As the "Fox" went into Galveston, there was over 100 shots fired at her, only three of which took effect ~ they doing no particular damage. They had, however, to throw over a part of their cargo to the amount of six or seven hundred dollars. Went into to Galveston about 2 P.M. Of course the fleet were bound to notice them.

General Magruder told Capt A~ any favor he should ask of him should be granted in compliment to his bravery. *Warm* ~ why it is hot enough to toast a body ~ then sea sickness adds to ones comfort.

Such tempting dishes as are sent to me every meal ~ this noon had english peas, ham, chicken, jelly and fresh goose-berry pie. Merely tasted the ham shoved it one side ~ eat two mouth-fuls of pie and soon deposited the whole in the spitoon. Mr Murdock says if I could only go out on the Bridge I'd feel better. Drank some tea this eve.

20th Thursday ~ Tried to sit up to day, but could not. Last night slept more than any time before, in all must have slept two hours and a half.

Had the cabin door open most of the time, whenever it is closed I feel nearly suffocated. Captain A is my banker. As we were coming along to day, I was reading one of T~ S~ Arthur's work's *The Withered Heart*[12] when Captain says "that is the young man you left on the dock [Mr Ferris]." He has tried to quiz me about him several times. Like all the rest of the world because he was unmarried & seemed to take an interest in my welfare ~ of course he must be a lover a subject for conversation with

---

11. The *OED* reports that a purser is the officer on board a ship who is "responsible for provisions and for keeping accounts, or (in later use more generally) for various other administrative matters."

12. Joseph F. Goeke, "T. S. Arthur," in *Dictionary of Literary Biography*, vol. 250, *Antebellum Writers in New York*, 2nd ser., ed. Kent P. Ljungquist, 16–28 (Gale Group, 2001). *The Withered Heart* was written by Timothy Shay Arthur in 1857. As an early and avid supporter of the temperance movement, Arthur incorporated this and other moral themes into his works. His book *Ten Nights In a Bar-Room and What I Saw There* (1854), became the best-selling contemporary book of the temperance movement, second only to *Uncle Tom's Cabin*.

him. Mr Ferris payed strayage down to the boat so my whole expenses this far have been $7.00 Uncle P~ paid all other bills. I am under many obligations for favors received at the hands of friends and strangers. Mrs Mason would accept nothing for my stay there. I shall never forget the kindness from all so timely given.

21st Friday ~ Three ships in sight to day ~ a temptation to dress I could not resist. Captain A~ has given up the idea of making a sailor of me in disgust, his efforts have proved so vain. Had broiled herring, ham, eggs tomatoes and Irish potatoes sent in for my dinner; paid my compliments to the latter. And eat some tapioca pudding, although Joe said it seemed no use to bring me anything to eat.

During the first part of my trip, I mentioned in conversation that my brother was a Mason. Captain A. is also one and, if possible, he has been kinder to me for that knowledge.[13]

He was showing me his pictures of friends yesterday his wife's, Captain Brown's of the *Badger*, Capt Simms of the *S.C.*[14] and Capt Morfit of the *Florida*.[15] Mrs Adkinsons former home was in Charleston S.C., but they have moved into the country some hundred miles. Her Mother (an old lady), a sister and four children live with her. She is a fine looking lady. From her face one would think she possessed a noble heart, looks to be about the size of my mother. Capt A had a photograph of himself

---

13. Captain Adkins's connections with freemasonry, in fact, made him assume an even more protective role toward Lucy when he heard that her brother was a Mason as well. Captain A, it seems, subscribed to the same Masonic principles of brotherhood, solidarity, and justice that Mr. Buck had endorsed, and upon their arrival in Havana, he gave Lucy a Masonic pin to wear during her travels that would identify her to other Masons. According to Captain Adkins, any Mason would recognize the pin, and like himself, would render aid to her, as a family member of a fellow Mason, thus affording Lucy a higher degree of security as she traveled alone.

14. "Raphael Semmes," Naval Historical Center home page, U.S. Navy; "Rear Admiral Raphael Semmes, Confederate States Navy," Naval History and Heritage Command, Naval Historical Center home page, U.S. Navy. This is possibly Captain Raphael Semmes, who was known for his leadership of the Confederate raider *Alabama*. Semmes commanded the *Alabama* from 1862 until 1864, sinking the USS *Hatteras* off the coast of Galveston in January 1863. According to the Naval Historical Center, Semmes commanded the James River Squadron during the final months of the war, and as Richmond fell, he burned his own fleet and converted his crew to an infantry fighting force.

15. "John Newland Maffitt," Naval Historical Center home page, U.S. Navy. The *Florida* was commissioned in August 1862, and was commanded by First Lieutenant John Newland Maffitt. The Naval Center records that beginning in January 1863 Maffitt and his crew "captured twenty-two prizes [over the next eight months], striking terror in the United States' merchant marine and frustrating the U.S. Navy's efforts to catch her."

which he very kindly gave me. I shall prize it because he has been so true to my interests ~ and so gentlemanly watchful in his attention. On thursday night had to take salts, am all right now, land so near and all else considered. Sara said I would think of my friends when I got sick ~ many many is the time I have thought of them, and the knowledge that I have their warmest interest for a successful trip and their sympathy for my loneliness ~ with the thoughts of home and its loved ones helped me to make the best of what the fates send. have finished my *Withered Heart* and read most of *All is not Gold that Glitters*.[16]

In her entry of April 22, Lucy noted her arrival in Havana, then in a brief aside, recorded the historic news of Abraham Lincoln's assassination. Her information obviously came from preliminary reports that were sketchy, and ultimately, inaccurate. The news had flashed with horrific shock upon the scene of a war-weary land, and accounts varied from source to source. The April 15 edition of the *New York Times* ran an official notification from the War Department, written by Secretary of War Stanton within hours of the attacks.[17] At that point, Stanton wrote that Lincoln and Seward still lived, but that, in his estimation, their recovery was doubtful. This limited account must have spread far and wide, for this is the information, accompanied by erroneous names, that Lucy recorded. It would not be until the next day, April 23, that a more complete report reached Cuba.[18] Lucy herself would write later of the harsh reactions of "secesh" travelers she encountered. For now, however, her lack of comment could be construed as an intense preoccupation with her own plight.

After her scant mention of the news of Lincoln's death, Lucy quickly turned her attention to the next leg of her journey. A ship, the *Columbia*, stood ready to leave for New York, but Lucy's hopes were dashed when she

---

16. Jennifer L. Wyatt, "Anna Maria Hall," in *Dictionary of Literary Biography*, vol. 159, *British Short-Fiction Writers, 1800–1880*, ed. John R. Greenfield, 144–151 (Gale Group, 1996). Although there are several books from this era that contain the popular maxim "all is not gold that glitters" in their titles, given Lucy's penchant for English authors and the contemporary date of publication, it is quite possible that she was reading Anna Maria Hall's work, published in London in 1858. Hall was one of the most prolific and popular authors of her day, writing and editing numerous works about such things as the connections between economic conditions and moral failings of the Irish poor.

17. [Official] "President Lincoln Shot by an Assassin," *New York Times*, April 15, 1865, New York Times Article Archive.

18. "From Havana; Reception of the News of President Lincoln's Assassination . . . ," *New York Times*, April 27, 1865, New York Times Article Archive.

could not obtain permission in time to board. It became clear that she would stay in Havana until other arrangements could be made. Captain Adkins again came to her rescue, helping her with the necessary landing protocols and taking her to a hotel in the city. Knowing her disappointment, he kindly offered his assistance as tour guide to help pass the time and acquaint Lucy with the wonders of the city.

Now a sojourner in every sense of the word, Lucy took in the new world around her, recording with great detail her impressions of everything she saw. Over the next few days, her journal would become a travelogue, and entries would overflow with intricate descriptions and colorful stories about the people she met and the places she visited.

Travel from the United States to Cuba had apparently become increasingly popular in the years preceding the Civil War. One early diary, written by Joseph Dimock, indicates that by 1850 Cuba had become a major population center with a strong presence of North American businessmen, merchants, and plantation owners.[19] Another early traveler, Marturin Ballou, noted that Cuba had also become a resort for invalids from the North because of its climate, which "was so uniformly soft and mild, the vegetation so thriving and beautiful, the fruits so delicious and abundant, [seemed] to give it a character almost akin to that we have seen described in tales of fairy land."[20] By mid-century, in fact, the island boasted a tourist trade of almost five thousand North Americans a year,[21] and whatever the reason for travel to the island, American tourists were intrigued with the sights, sounds, and sunlight of the tropical paradise. Lucy was no exception. Visiting the Plaza de Armas with Captain A, Lucy echoed Ballou's own impressions, writing, "the prettiest spot—without exception I ever saw . . . This is such a spot as we could imagine Fairy-land to be" (4/22/65).

However captivated Lucy might have been by the city, in brief moments of solitude she struggled with her loneliness. However, she soon rallied, and in typical fashion, wrote extensively of the assortment of strangers thrown together in a foreign land and the circumstances that brought them there. Much cheered after meeting Lieutenant Baldwin, Lucy soon learned that they shared mutual acquaintances in Texas, and her mood lifted considerably. With a lighter heart, she then recounted in rich detail a story she had heard at table, another account of General Butler's abuses in New Orleans.

19. Joseph J. Dimock, *Impressions of Cuba in the Nineteenth Century: The Travel Diary of Joseph J. Dimock*, ed. Louis A. Pérez (Wilmington, DE: Scholarly Resources, 1998), xiii–xiv.

20. Marturin M. Ballou. *History of Cuba; or, Notes of a Traveller in the Tropics* (Boston: Phillips, Sampson, and Company, 1854), 68.

21. Dimock, *Impressions of Cuba*, xiv.

Matching in basic fact the account highlighted by Stephanie McCurry in her book *Confederate Reckoning*,[22] Lucy's distinctly Southern telling of Mrs. Phillips's incarceration by Benjamin Butler nevertheless underscores the perspective Lucy had adopted in the remote world of Civil War Texas.

22nd Saturday ~ Arrived at Havana at 2 A.M. Had to wait some time for a Pilot[23] The strong fortifications on either side of the channel seem perfectly impregnable The buildings are mostly of stone look to have stood for centuries.

After a good bath and change of clothes, I feel a different person. Took breakfast with the officers, was introduced to Mr Daniels and House. the latter reminds me of Mr Punchard, no more need be said for him.

Had a nice breakfast, but I enjoyed the ice water more than all else. Commenced a letter to Uncle Pier's wrote a hurried and confused one. Little boats have been coming and going all the morn.

Mr Magan, Capt A's super cargo,[24] came on board this morn. I was introduced to him. If he had not returned to Havana on the *Badger*, I could not have come on the *Fox*. I like his looks.

Almost the first news we heard on our arrival was that Lincoln ~ Seward, his son and two ~~sons~~ servants were killed by Robt Booth and his accomplices. Lincoln was at the threatre, Seward at home sick &c. We counted four U.S. vessels at half-mast.

There are a great many vessels in port: two U.S. steamers leave soon, one at noon today, the *Columbia*[25] for N. York, the other, the *Liberty*,[26] starts for N Orleans tomorrow morn at seven.

---

22. Stephanie McCurry, *Confederate Reckoning: Power and Politics in the Civil War South* (Cambridge: Harvard University Press, 2010), 113.

23. In his memoir, *Running the Blockade*, Thomas Taylor emphasizes the importance of an expert pilot when he writes, "Through the ignorance or cowardice of the pilot, vessels were frequently lost, and to obtain a good pilot was as troublesome as it was essential. The risk they ran was great, for if captured they were never exchanged; but their pay, which frequently amounted to £700 or £800 a round trip, was proportionate to the risk" (43).

24. The supercargo is the officer who is responsible for all commercial transactions of a voyage.

25. "News From Havana: Arrival of the Steamship *Columbia*, *New York Times*, August 8, 1861, New York Times Article Archive. The steamship *Columbia* had apparently traveled a regular route between New York and Havana for quite some time. A *New York Times* article, published on August 8, 1861, indicates that *Columbia* had recently arrived, bringing mail, passengers, and information from Cuba. The article also lists Captain Adams as the commanding officer and Francis D. Newcomb as the purser.

26. Jefferson B. Browne, *Key West: The Old and the New* (St. Augustine: The Record Co., 1912),

Captain A~ will not accept a dime for my passage which is usually from $150. to $300. Says it may be in my power some time to do him a favor that will be equally as great. I hope I may. If it had not been for the circumstances in which I was placed, being so long from home &c, he would not have taken me at all. Another thing he says, I am not a "*down easter*,"[27] that my passage to him was nothing "aither" here or there. he felt repaid in the knowledge that he was doing a kindness that was appreciated. He also presented me with a little Masonic pin and told me to wear it always in traveling where it could be seen. Said it might be a help to me; had it been a present of great value I could not have accepted it at the hands of one who was in reality a stranger. But as it was, I shall always prize the gift, for the givers sake.

He told me what to say was I questioned about it. Also gave me a bottle of brandy that in case I was sick, it might be useful to me.

Captain A~ went to the landing with me with the full expectation that I would get off on the *Columbia*. When lo ~ the Governor was at a dinner party and would not be seen until after 4 P.M., so I could not get a passport.

Had to get a landing passport and all baggage has to be examined before any one can enter the city limits.

Saw some U.S. naval officers going on board their little barges. They looked about as free from care as anyone I have seen.

The little boats all have an awning over the back end that remind me of Elizabeth and her ~~boats~~ maids of honor going out in their pleasure boats. The dress of the Spaniards looks odd ~ close caps, &c, but there are so many Americans here I feel a little more at home than I expected to.

Captain A's kindness did not stop here. As soon as he found I could not get off today, he took me to a hotel, the Cuban[28] where most all, landlady and boarders were American.

One lady a Mrs Howard who is on her way to Houston going to house-keeping, she was formerly from Georgia. Came here on the *Columbia* passed herself off as an English-lady all the way from New York. Such

81. The steamship *Liberty* was put into use shortly after the beginning of the Civil War by the Southern Pacific Steamship Co. The ship was fast and modern, and regularly traveled the route between Baltimore and Havana, with stops in Key West, until 1873.

27. The *OED* reports that a "down-easter" is a person or vessel that hails from coastal areas of New England, especially Maine, or the coastal regions of Canada.

28. Webmaster, Havana Guide, e-mail interview with Vicki Tongate, January 13, 2011. The oldest hotel in Havana is Hotel Inglaterra. It was located at Parque Central and was built in 1875. There is now a Tenth Street in the Havana Vedado district, but in the year 1865 this district did not exist. The building of the Vedado district started around 1900–1910. Note that if this is the correct name, the hotel Cuban might have been just a café with two or three rooms.

strange looking vehicles as they have here, valantees they call them. Covered two wheeled with shafts fourteen ft & 10 inches long and the least little ponies. Drivers riding them ~ such fine harnesses so much silver plaiting about them, the head gear nearly covers the head but there were some real American looking ones too.[29]

Well as we had got into a warm climate to work I had to go and fix something to wear out to dinner. Took the waist of my black silk tore up a handkerchief and made a band and wore it with my white swiss waist.

After dinner went into the parlor and made myself as contented as possible. Had been there but little while, when Captain came to take me a ride to see the city. At dinner, the Clerk Don Mas told me of the *Liberty* leaving tomorrow but advised me to wait until next saturday and go on the *Moro Castle* to N. York. I was undecided, but as Captain A had proved such a friend thus far, I concluded to ask and follow his advice.

He [Captain A] said my friends in Texas had placed me under his care ~ that was he going, he would not go up the river, he did not consider it safe and he did not think it would be right for me to go until I could go by way of N.Y. He was acquainted with the captain of the *Moro Castle* and his Purser and knew the boat to be a good one, that the charges would be no more to go one way than the other; so with his good reasoning I stay. Had he not been such a kind friend to me, I should have gone directly to the American consul and solicited his assistance, knowing he would have been duty bound to have given it.

Such a prison of place as this part of the city is ~ carriages can not much more than pass in the street. The buildings are high windows iron grated, and the walks so narrow, two can not walk side and side.

The tall walls have a very foreboding look to me. Another thing looked odd. The little ponies & mules packed down until it looked as if they could hardly move under their burdens.

There are more soldiers here than a few mostly for city duties and such beautiful uniforms as they have.

I went with Captain A to see the city. Its limits seem small but the prettiest part is outside. There is an immense quantity of business carried on here. the stores are so well filled; such an extensive market ~ everything that heart could wish *except apples* was to be found.

---

29. Ballou, *History of Cuba*, 130–132. Lucy was intrigued by the *volantes*, described by Ballou as being light open carriages with enormous wheels six feet in diameter and low chaises for the occupants. The horses that pulled the *volantes* wore ornate silver harnesses, and the drivers dressed in brightly colored jackets and high boots.

We went first through the business part of the city then down on the streets where the private residences were and twice passed the Governor's summer residence. the prettiest spot without exception I ever saw. It is very large (the grounds) are divided into several parts and filled with trees and flowers of every description, statues, fountains & walks that looked so cool and pleasant[30]

Capt A has promised to get me a boquet from there. This is such a spot as we could imagine Fairy-land to be.

On the street in front of the grounds are four rows of trees, look very much like the poplar only more spreading The tulip tree is very common and I saw the cocaa nut the banana and palm tree for the first time.

The houses look odd ~ most of them have such strange devices in front. There are a great many one story high with iron grating in front of all the windows.

As we went out, there was comparatively few in the streets, but on our return the streets were crowded especially on the plaza in front of the Governors summer residence.

Dressed most of them as if they were going to a ball ~ tissues, swiss, tarltons, summer silks and every light fabric that could be found of which a dress could be made. Not a bonnet worn, and very few hats. I noticed three, but it is not fashionable here for ladies to wear bonnets.[31] At nearly every window was a lady standing mostly by herself looking out, or sometimes you would see a little (naked) negroe[32] (or with slip on open all the way down in front). The ladies who stood in that way reminded me very much of the Jennies we see set up in the stores to show the fashions. Hoops big as all out doors ~ bell shaped. At a very few places we saw ladies and gentlemen sitting in their parlors looking so sociable. It was a real treat to see such a sight.

The valantees owned by private families were some of them very fine. One in particular I noticed with a great deal of silver plaiting, a dark

30. Lucy described the Plaza de Armas, a large park and promenade, across from the governor's palace, filled with beautiful walkways, gardens, fountains, and statues.

31. Ballou, *History of Cuba*, 119. Lucy, ever the fashion observer, concurred with the earlier reports of Ballou, who wrote that bonnets were entirely unknown in Cuba and that travelers who did wear them were regarded with great curiosity. He wrote that Cuban ladies sometimes wore long black veils, but most often wore no coverings on their heads at all.

32. Ibid., 94. Ballou also reports that the slave children, boys and girls, under the age of eight typically went about their days without any clothes. Even the older children and adult slaves wore only enough to be decent in order to cope with the extreme heat and humidity. He writes, "This causes rather a shock to the ideas of propriety entertained by an American; but it is thought nothing of by the 'natives'" (94).

bay pony with a silver mounted harness that nearly covered it and the negroe driver sitting up in his saddle dressed "a la Milatara," a coat with broad gilt belt cavalry boots (without feet to them) patent leather, a silver wreath and family coat of arms on them.

The city I thought looked pretty before night, but after it was lighted up, it looked splendidly.

The ladies go high on red here ~ more red head-dresses and coral ornaments than a few are seen. Returned just in time for tea of which I took a glass of ice water.

23rd Sunday ~ Oh, for a friend that I might forget my loneliness, but all are strange. The morn I spent in my room bringing up my journal so that I came near being too late for dinner ~ wore my organda and lace cape. Came to my room soon after dinner, had not been there long when the clerk Don Man came and knocked, calling "segnorita, why do you not come in the parlor and hear the music. I think you will find it pleasant."

This morn at table I was seated beside a gentleman who, finding I was just from Texas & Galveston, began to question me, and I soon found out it was Lt. Baldwin from Galveston, a gentleman who boarded at the same house Miss Mary Smith did when she was stopping there to try to get home. But wasn't I glad to meet him. he started for Europe about six weeks ago but turned back, or stopped here rather, on hearing the bad news at Galveston. I never saw the gent before, but knew him from hearsay. Capt Wallace boards at the same house he did.

As we were both acquainted with Mrs Ayers and Miss Mary, it seemed at once as if he were a friend. Although I went in the parlor and stayed awhile, I can not say that I particularly enjoyed myself, found out however that Mrs Baker is the name of the proprietress. Mr & Mrs Newcome & daughter are boarders they have spent two winters here. Mr Newcome has charge of the house at present. Just before lunch, went up on the house and took a view of the city.

In the eve three ladies, Mrs Winthrope, Mrs Avery & daughter called to see the Newcomes and Mrs Howard. Mrs N. reminds me so much of Mrs Peebles. Such another talker as Mrs Howard is; she got to giving a history of Mrs Philips being taken prisoner at N. Orleans. says she was standing on her gallery one eve dressed for a party (children's) at her next door neighbors Mrs Cone's. her & Mrs C were talking of it, when a funeral procession passed along for the burial of one of Gen'l Butler's officers. said the sun was shining brightly so they could not well look up without squinting and one of the children spoke and said Ma do look, they are all squinteyed just like Gen'l Butler ~ the idea was so ridiculous that they could not refrain from laughing "which highly insulted the Yankees officers." one who had met her in Washington recognized her and next day she was arrested and sent to Gen'l B's office.

He questioned and lectured and scolded, which she paid not the least attention to, scarcely ever answering a question, but took a peer glass and gazed round the room reading the different mottoes which according to her tell were perfectly ridiculous. At last Gen'l B~ asked her what was she laughing at ~ she replied Well ~ I dont know Gen'l ~ unless it was that I was pleased that is usually the reason of my laughing ~ and hardly answered the question before she turned to her husband, and said while the Gen'l was still talking "these are beautiful pictures."

She was sent from there into an adjoining room where was a tray of edibles and bottle of wine, a lunch for Gen'l B~. She eat and drank as much as she could, crumbed the rest of the food into the wine, then seeing pen, ink and paper wrote a very insulting note & and left it on the tray for the Gen'l.

She was consigned to Port Royal for three months! There she was shut up in a little plank cabin with the sun poring down so that she felt it not much protection, an Irish girl Eliza her only companion and she was taken sick so that Mrs P~ had her to wait on.

24th Monday ~ The *Moro Castle* which was due this morn has not yet arrived.

This afternoon just as I was beginning to feel lonely Captain A~ came and took me a drive. Went out of the city some ways.

Such a country of hills I never before saw. Some of the houses look to have been cut out of the sides of mountains. The reason of the houses being so generally low is on account of the hurricanes which sometimes sweep over the island.[33]

---

33. "Travel Cuba–Weather." Cuba is the largest Caribbean island, covering more than 110,000 square kilometers and with a topography ranging from mountains that rise more than 2,000 kilometers above sea level to flat plains and beaches. The island enjoys a subtropical climate, with an average temperature around 77 degrees Fahrenheit, and a dry season from November until April. Its rainy season, when the island is most likely to experience severe storms and hurricanes, lasts from May to October, when it receives the bulk of its average rainfall total of forty-eight inches.

It was very late when we returned home. Captain A~ promised to come for me to go get my passport tomorrow between ten & eleven. The clerk's name is Don Man He is so clever ~ I want to remember it!

25th Tuesday ~ Captain A~ came according to agreement. Before the U.S. consul would grant my passport, I had to take an oath to support the Union &c. Gave $6.50 for my passport. Engaged passage on the *Moro Castle* ~ $60.

Lt Baldwin gave me the N.Y. *Ledger*[34] to read which contained a full account of Lincoln's assassination, burial &C

In one place it told of the preparation of the body for burial. The veins were drained of their blood & filled with some chemical preparation & the brains were scooped out. Mrs Newcom says Andy J~ ought to eat them for his breakfast.

This afternoon Captain A~ came for me to go shopping and to hear the music, but as I had the neuralgia, excused myself

26th Wednes[day] ~ Lt B~ gave me *The Pilot*,[35] one of Cooper's novels to read. Spent the morn in looking it over and doing various little things.

In the P.M. went out and purchased a trunk $5.50. Capt A~ went with me. Bought such a nice present for me. Came home early as I was not feeling well. Went out and drunk a cup of tea after returning

27th Thursday ~ Spent the day in my room. Captain A~ brought me a satchel such a nice one $8.00. One more day ~ how glad I will be when saturday comes. I am so anxious to get on my home ward way once more.

28th Friday ~ The name of the street we are on is Ten, Te En Te-Bra. means Lt Governor.

At dinner Lt Baldwin invited me to go hear the music this eve. Went first and got some soda water then to the Plasia de Engle King. Saw the

---

34. Published between 1856 and 1898 in New York City, the *New York Ledger* became a wildly popular weekly paper that featured serialized stories, fashion, and current events. The publication, known as a storypaper, reached a readership of more than 375,000 and focused largely on a female audience.

35. Stephen Railton, "James Fenimore Cooper," in *Dictionary of Literary Biography*, vol. 250, *Antebellum Writers in New York*, 2nd ser., ed. Kent P. Ljungquist, 97–124 (Gale Group, 2001). James Fenimore Cooper, one of America's preeminent authors, published his fourth novel, *The Pilot: A Tale of the Sea*, in 1824. The book's success established Cooper as the creator of the genre of "sea fiction" and helped to establish his popularity among American audiences. Cooper, whose writing had already been compared to that of Sir Walter Scott, determined that he could write more knowledgeably about the sea than Scott, whom he considered a "landlubber."

statue of Queen Isabella, then down on the Plasia where the statue of King John stands. Then got some ice cream and came home. Heard such splendid music, then the final and the marching of the soldiers off the ground. But more than all that as we came back went to see the tree under which Columbus had mass said on his first arrival on the Island; saw the tomb in which his ashes were enshrined and the building in connection which has in it a number of beautiful paintings ~ different scenes in connection with him and his men. That is opened but once a year on the anniversary of the day on which the island was discovered.

Also went into the palace of the Lt Governor In the afternoon had a ride ~ was favored with kind attention today.

—⌄—

At last, the waiting ended, and on April 29 Lucy sailed for New York. She bid farewell to her newfound friends, and wrote warmly of Captain A, noting her affection and appreciation for "my captain." Then, in typical fashion, she recorded details about her departure, such as names of people she met and a brief mention about the desirability of the ship and her stateroom. Again, Capt A had gone out of his way to assure Lucy's safety and comfort as she made her way home.

Lucy's comments about the *Morro Castle* may well have been understated, for a *New York Times* article published in January 1865 reports that the ship, commanded by Captain Adams and in service only a few months, had been "built expressly for the Havana trade" and was geared toward the discriminating traveler. The article gives the speed and dimensions of the vessel, then comments, "For comfort and elegance the *Morro Castle* leaves nothing to be desired, and the traveling public of Havana, as well as its commercial classes, are under great obligations to the owners, Messrs. SPOFFORD, TILESTON & Co."[36]

Not only the ship but also the passengers aboard it caught Lucy's attention. Ever receptive to gossip, she wrote disapprovingly of the information she had heard about Miss Reed, a woman she had met aboardship. However, her own discoveries would validate the gossip, bringing Lucy's standards into sharp focus. Her observations throughout her journal indicate an unquestioning adherence to the strict moral code of her time and, at times, frame her with childlike simplicity. Yet in the closing entries of her diary, the contrast between Miss Reed and Lucy removes any doubt as to Lucy's maturity and adult values. Even as she would write of Miss Reed's nighttime

36. "Havana Correspondence," *New York Times*, January 1, 1865, New York Times Article Archive.

escapades—stopping short of outright condemnation, a day earlier she had written of Captain Adams's absolute recommendation of her own character to Mrs. Bridges. Lucy's response "What a comfort to know that although thrown among strangers ~ Yet it they know I am a lady" encapsulates the paradigm that governed her life and clearly removes any assumption of naïveté.

29th Saturday ~ I was quite amused yesterday at Lt B's description of a Bull-fight. They always come off on Sunday, the gentlemen go to the fight while the ladies go to church. He told me too of the ceremonies during Holy Week. representing Christ being sold for the 30 peices of silver, his crucifixion & the rejoicing after his resurrection the two Marys &c

The fighting ~ they would throw spears into the bull until it became perfectly enraged. Then they would let him into the ring. where two or three men would be on horseback. The bull would rush at one of the horses knock it down, and hook & some times kill the riders. Settled my bill with Mr N~ 'twas $24.

Captain A~ came for me about half past eight. Mrs Machiada gave me a basket to carry my fruit in. He and Don Man (the clerk) went to the boat with my trunks. Mr M introduced me to my room-mate, Mrs Bridges~ and to Miss Reed & her brother. Mrs B~ has been spending the winter in Matanzas. Miss Reed & brother also have been there on account of the brothers health. People say he has been crazy.

Nice boat, and Mrs B~ and I have one of the best state rooms (above).

I hated to give up my captain for a new one, but he has put me in care of the Pursor and Captain Adams seems very kind.

Bid all my new made friends an early adieux as they were obliged to attend to business Don Man is to see Mrs Howard off and Captain A~ has an appointment for ten

Our boat started off at fifteen minutes past twelve. Mrs B~ and I went up on deck to take a last look at the city as we sailed out the channel. I stayed there most of the P.M., dreading to go down lest I should be sick again.

30th Sunday ~ Was up on deck awhile this morn

Yesterday there was an Irish-woman came on board who had a very large trunk. As the sailors were drawing it in the rope broke and down it went into the water. She had her dog in her arms and went round scolding trying to get some one to notice her and have the trunk brought up. In the midst of her trouble, the land-lady sent for her dry-goods saying she had gone off in her debt 30 lbs. After about three quarters of an hour Captain Adams came and had the trunk taken up, and this morn she has her clothes strung on a line to dry chemise sleeves farthest down. I was sick this afternoon ~

Like Mrs Bridges much; she told me her husband disliked very much for her to start off alone so wrote to Captain A [Adams] to be certain to have a good room-mate for her. In reply he got word that he might be assured of one thing ~ that was, I bore a good character. What a comfort to know that although thrown among strangers ~ Yet it they know I am a lady. Captain Adkinson I see your kindness following me still.

May ~ 1st Monday ~ Did not get up today. Miss Reed & her room mate had a quarrel this morn and finely the married lady went below stairs. Both tell their own stories to us making themselves justifiable in their part of the "scene." Each one gives the other a terriable name. It is very evident that both have an awful disposition. "Mary" the chambermaid says that the married lady is right & that Miss Reed does not bear the best of characters so report tells her. Miss R~ seems to think no one ever traveled as much as she or saw so many sights.

2nd Tuesday ~ Up again this morn, although I was sick in the night. Don't think I should have been but the watch came round and closed the windows which made our room very close. I got up and tried to open the window but not succeeding opened the door. just as I did so a gentle man came from Miss Reed's room.

We feasted on oranges & pine-apple today then Mary brought us such nice dessert ~ crossed the Gulfstream last night.

On the morning of May 3, 1865, Lucy landed in New York. Her time of waiting was almost over, and she hurriedly attended to details, excitedly noting that she would be able to board a train bound for Ohio that night. Except for Miss Reed's interlude, Lucy's trip had been uneventful, her earlier anxieties assuaged by Capt A's thoughtful oversight. Upon meeting her shipboard roommate, Lucy had commented that once again the captain had extended kindness to her, and she may never have known just how far that compassion reached. According to the passenger manifest published in the May 4, 1865, edition of the *New York Times*, more than one hundred passengers debarked the *Morro Castle* on the morning of May 3, among them Mrs. E. W. Bridges and Miss Reed. Lucy is listed as well, but her name reads "Mrs. L. B. Stevens"—the middle initial perhaps a mistake in transcription on the reporter's part. However, she is notably listed as a married woman. Although this too could have been a transcription error, the title of "Mrs." could have been a deliberate attempt by Captain Adkins to further protect Lucy. As a longtime sailor aware of the unsolicited attentions targeting solitary women, he would know that by listing Lucy as a married woman, he could provide her an extra modicum of safety and security. While it is likely that Lucy never realized his provision, well did she say, "Captain Adkinson I see your kindness following me still."

Now alone in New York City, Lucy noted a city in deep mourning. Newspapers and magazines chronicled the details of Lincoln's funeral, the cortege that traveled through city after city on its way to Illinois, and the multitudes of people who thronged the paths, hoping to catch a glimpse of the procession. David Brainerd Williamson reported that in every city, black draped public buildings, bells tolled, guns fired, and masses of people gathered:

> On arriving at New York, the remains were carried in solemn procession to the City Hall, where they were placed in state. The interior of the City Hall was elaborately draped and festooned with mourning emblems, presenting a somber and solemn appearance. The room in which the remains of the President were deposited was dotted with silver stars relieved by black; the drapery was finished with heavy silver fringe and the curtains of black velvet were fringed with silver and gracefully looped. The coffin rested on a raised dais, on an inclined plane, the inclination being such that the face of the departed patriot was in view of visitors while passing for two or three minutes.[37]

The cortege left New York City on April 25, preceding Lucy's arrival by little more than a week, and the city continued in gloom. As Lucy viewed the vestiges of mourning, she leveled what was quite possibly her last blast at the North. With sarcasm and quotation marks, she made her feelings clear: "It looks to me they make a perfect God of 'the martyred President.'" Throughout the war, Lucy had indeed attempted to maintain an objective view of the

---

37. David Brainerd Williamson, *Illustrated Life, Services, Martyrdom, and Funeral of Abraham Lincoln* (Philadelphia: T. B. Peterson & Brothers, 1865), 239.

conflict, but this statement, more than any other, unmasks the degree of her isolation during her years in Texas and the depth of her Southern orientation. However, her detachment from Southern sentimentalities would now begin, and her disorientation would intensify during her train ride west as she fielded questions about Texas and Texans. Once aboard the train bound for Cleveland, she made a connection with home—and her transition from South to North began in earnest.

3rd Wednesday ~ Passed Ft Lafayette about ½ past 9. Land was in sight at daylight; landed at Pier No 4 about 10. It was a perfect hubbub getting on shore, having trunks examined &c. I check Spofford, Tileston & Co, waited until the Purser sent the ticket agent for the N. Y. Central R R to assist me. got a carriage, took me to the bank got my money exchanged, then to the office & got my ticket. by going that route I shall not have to stop in N. Y. over night, will start out at 6~

Saw the Astor House, the square in which President Lincoln's body lay in state, and passed one of the finest stores the city affords. At the depot got my own baggage checked through to Cleveland.

All the public buildings and many private residences are draped in deep mourning. Funeral services have been held all over the country. It looks to me they make a perfect God of "the martyred President."

4th Thurs ~ Passed Albany in the night The gentleman who sit opposite me found out I was from T~ and had more questions than a few to ask in regard to the sentiments of the people.

They seem to think the war would soon end, and with it slavery would go.

Got into Buffalo about ¼o past 10, there took the Cleveland train. Had only to go from one side of the depot to the other. A gentleman from Summit County O [Ohio]. found out I was from T [Texas] and a Buckeye ~ came and sit opposite me and made himself very agreeable. He was once a partner of Mr Thayers,~ a gentleman who lives in Milan.

At Buffalo he kindly assisted me in going from one car to the other & found me a good seat.

Abruptly, the diary ends. On a train bound for Cleveland, Lucy simply stopped writing. The remainder of her homecoming is shrouded in mystery, for she wrote no more entries until January 1, 1866. Thanks to Cousin Sarah's journal, however, we are allowed a slight peek into the trip's culmination, confirming Lucy's information and adding final details. Now separated by great distance and only partially aware of Lucy's situation, Sarah wrote,

> April 22—Pa came home Tuesday—left Cous Lu in Gal. At a friend of one of Jim Middleton's friends (Mr. Ferris)—She could not get her passport by flag of truce. Expects to leave soon on a blockade runner.

> April 29—Cous Lu got off the night of the 17th, on the blockade runner "Fox" so Mr. Slade of Galveston wrote Pa . . .

> May 14— Ma sent me a letter from Cous Lu written at Havanna giving a full description of her trip—she got along finely that far—the Capt. of the Fox gave her every attention. She was expecting to leave on a U.S.S. in a day or two for N.Y.

> Aug. 21—brought me a letter from Cous Lu . . . the first we have heard from her since she left Havannah. She arrived home safely on the 6th of May stopped in Cleveland and Aunt Retta went with her to Milan. Will met her, it is very gratifying to us to hear of her safe arrival home.

From here, Sarah's and Lucy's paths diverge. Sarah's life continued in Travis, as she waited with her husband for the birth of their first child. The lives of the people Lucy had loved and left behind moved on without her as Texas made the painful transition through Reconstruction back into the Union. Lucy, meanwhile, found her place in Ohio, but she left no records describing her arrival or her reunion with her parents . . . Here, the darkened diary closed the curtain to prevent prying eyes from witnessing the bittersweet return.

LUCY

Her World after Texas

ON THE TRAIN BOUND FOR CLEVELAND, Lucy Stevens found herself answering fellow passengers' questions about Texas, and those questions would undoubtedly continue. For more than five years, she had been safe with her Texas family and friends, despite her exile. Protected from the stares and comments that might otherwise have come to her as a Yankee, Lucy had acclimated herself to her surroundings and had managed quite well. In the North, however, she was quite possibly a feature attraction, offering bystanders a glimpse into a foreign world, an enemy territory. While her family assuredly rejoiced at her safe return, it is reasonable to suppose that many must have gaped and questioned her fidelity as a good Yankee girl. Certain neighbors and acquaintances in Ohio must have questioned her credibility, viewing her participation in her "captors'" culture as a forfeiture of her own civilized status.

In the volatile aftermath of the Civil War, when so many families now faced empty places at the table, Lucy's tales of life in Texas could have been construed as a capitulation to the hated enemy. Lucy had returned from her "captivity" unscathed, but certainly not unchanged. Her five years in Texas had provided a vantage from which she could view, firsthand, the admirable qualities of the enemy. Like Mary Rowlandson, the most famous of Indian captives who had discovered aspects of Indian society that created questions for her as to their "savage" existence,[1] Lucy knew with absolute certainty of

---

1. Mary Rowlandson, *The Sovereignty and Goodness of God*, ed. Neal Salisbury (Boston: Bedford Books, 1997), 28.

the good in the people of Texas. Mary Rowlandson had developed a multifaceted alienation in that she had "acquired a view of the war that [was] at odds with the orthodox histories . . . Moreover, she [had] found that the Indians [were] truly her kindred in spirit; they [were] as much capable of charity as her own people, and she [was] as capable of doing evil as they."[2] Lucy too had lived among her "captors"; she had worked and worshipped, laughed and cried with them. She had shared confidences with their daughters and danced with their sons. Lucy knew what some suspected and what some would never believe: good could be found even among the hated Rebels of the South. Now it would be Lucy's task to reconcile her past with her present, to find a way to accommodate both her life in Texas and her life in Ohio. She had heard only Southern sentiments for five years. She now would need to juxtapose those perspectives and the conflicting views of the Northern heart.

No evidence exists to definitively answer the questions surrounding Lucy's return to the North. Were it not for Cousin Sarah's diary, no information would be available to ascertain even the date of her arrival. However, some conclusions can be drawn from the entries in Lucy's diary as she again took up her pen in January 1866. The resumption of entries in the same volume, with twenty blank pages of space to separate the two segments of the diary, indicates a desire on Lucy's part to somehow connect the two phases of her life. The seven months of silence, during which nothing at all was written, must be seen as a time of reorientation for her, a rehabilitation of sorts on the part of her family, to reestablish her credibility as a bona fide member of Northern society. Lucy unquestionably needed a period of adjustment to accustom herself to the life she now resumed in the North. Even her mention of a trip "downtown" paints a picture of stark contrast to the remote locale she had so recently left (Lucy Stevens, 1/19/66). After such a lengthy absence, many such changes awaited her, and her return necessarily required modifications of attitudes, habits, and appearance.

Lucy's entries after January 1, 1866, offer subtle contrasts to her notes from her years in the South. During the seven-month silence, certain alterations in outlook apparently occurred that explain the revisions in phraseology she used. Throughout her time in Texas, Lucy referred openly to her friends there with no special classification or rank attached to their names. Once she resumed her diary in Ohio, however, her references to her friends often contained qualifiers like "Dixieland" or "Dixie," terms never once used during her sojourn in Texas. Even her recognition of differences in perceptions

---

2. Richard Slotkin, *Regeneration through Violence: The Mythology of the American Frontier, 1600–1860* (Middletown, CT: Wesleyan University Press, 1973), 112.

now seemed less pronounced. Lucy wrote in her journal on March 30, 1866, that she would love to see her Dixie friends, that it would be such a comfort to receive an occasional visit. However, having recently received a Brenham newspaper, she realized that this was a distant wish, for on March 16 she had written, "I had a Brenham paper from Jim enjoyed the reading of it much ~ 'Rebeldom' has bitter spirits yet" (Lucy Stevens, 3/16/66).

Having left Texas before the reality of a Confederate defeat settled over the state, Lucy perhaps didn't fully understand the fear and uncertainty that gripped those residents. Sarah, however, was well acquainted with the despair and had written earlier: "Oh! The unhappy state of our country! We know not what fate awaits us" (6/3/65) and "God only knows what is ahead of us. All looks dark" (6/4/65). Sarah's words powerfully convey the fear of many, a fear that Lucy was spared, for she had escaped the aftermath of defeat, and she now seemed somewhat puzzled by Southern attitudes. Instead, she stood in the unique position of having both Northern and Southern sentiments, and her diary remains neutral, displaying no preference for one or the other.

Just as the people of the Revolution had to face fundamental decisions about a British identity or an American identity,[3] so Lucy and her generation had to decide what would be the dominant theme of their identity—would it be Northern centralism or Southern regionalism? The regionalism that Lucy had witnessed had "allowed people to differentiate themselves within the nation, provid[ing] an alternative to purely local loyalties and identities."[4] Yet this same differentiation had swelled to such magnitude that it threatened to overwhelm any sense of national identity. If one were "for" the North or the South, he must be FOR the North or the South. In the end, the collision was between the right of the state and the right of the nation in a monolithic battle to determine the victory. The validity of one's patriotism as seen through Southern or Northern eyes was not in question; the matter became "one of fixing national authority. The North called for the recognition of a centralized, nationalized power that represented the majority well and was responsive to it; the South demanded a redefinition of nationalism that recognized sectional and minority rights."[5] Yet for Lucy, as for many others, the Civil War laid to rest any question of nationalism. The Union had been preserved, and transcendent ties of nationalism bound together the pieces of sectional

3. Edward Countryman, *Americans: A Collision of Histories* (New York: Hill and Wang, 1996), 70.

4. James Oliver Robertson, *American Myth, American Reality* (New York: Hill and Wang, 1980), 85.

5. Russell Blaine Nye, *Society and Culture in America, 1830–1860* (New York: Harper and Row, 1974), 7.

difference, weaving disparate scraps of unique regionalism into a blanket of variegated nationalism.

Despite the dilemma that Fort Sumter created in forcing the citizens of a nation to collectively choose sides,[6] Lucy demonstrated her own reluctance to align herself with one side or the other. Instead, she chastised Yankee and Rebel alike if, in her opinion, the cause warranted it. Her love of her adopted Texas friends gave the "enemy" a face, and this love transcended any differences she could identify. Yet with the passage of time, she gained a perspective on her own unusual situation, and as she marked the second anniversary of her departure from Travis, she wrote, "Two years today I left Uncle P's for home – am glad that trial is not to be gone through with again" (Lucy Stevens, 4/12/67). The recognition of the pain of her sacrifice and the acknowledgement of the pleasure of her sojourn in Texas knit together the aspects of that era of her life into a whole, giving it definition as well as balance.

More formally posed, the question becomes,

> What then is the American, the new man? He is an American, who leaving behind him all his ancient prejudices and manners, receives new ones from the new mode of life he has embraced, the new government he obeys and the new rank he holds . . . Here individuals of all nations [*or sections?*] are melted into a new race of men, whose labours and prosperity will one day cause great changes in the world.[7]

Historians such as Frederick Jackson Turner would agree. Turner, who asserted "a new product that is American,"[8] was produced by the rigors of the western frontier, and it was to this "product" that America owes its greatness. Others, however, have examined the attitudes and memories of a nation after the Civil War and have concluded that a massive effort of rehabilitation occurred. In the introduction of his book *Beyond the Battlefield: Race, Memory, and the American Civil War*, historian David W. Blight notes that "nations and other human groups devise, however illusively, collective memories and transmit them through myths, traditions, stories, rituals, and formal

6. Countryman, *Americans*, 215.

7. Luther S. Luedtke, ed., *Making America: The Society and Culture of the United States* (Chapel Hill: University of North Carolina Press, 1992), 3.

8. Frederick Jackson Turner, "From 'The Significance of the Frontier in American History,'" in *Rereading America: Cultural Contexts for Critical Thinking and Writing*, ed. Gary Colombo, Robert Cullen, and Bonnie Lisle, 5th ed. (Boston: Bedford/St. Martin's, 2001), 685.

interpretations of history."[9] These purposeful re-imaginings of past events serve to preserve a society's identity, or even forge a new one, depending on the cultural needs of the time.

In truth, in the years following the Civil War, a deliberate reshaping of public perception, a reconciliation of sorts, was culturally under way. Many have studied the treatment of reconciliation in the aftermath of the war, noting that frequently the memory of past events was manipulated by North and South alike—sometimes to continue the division, sometimes to bring about a renewed sense of nationalism. All manner of venues promoted this new nationalism, a nationalism that excluded/ignored blacks, but attempted to unite whites who had once fought bitterly on opposing sides. Blight tells of a carefully constructed retrospective that characterized the war "as primarily a tragedy that led to greater unity and national cohesion . . . not as the crisis of a nation deeply divided over slavery, race, competing definitions of labor, liberty, political economy, and the future of the West."[10] Alice Fahs, coeditor of The Memory of the Civil War in American Culture, agrees. In her essay "Remembering the Civil War in Children's Literature of the 1880s and 1890s," she explains that even in children's literature, a trend toward "mutual admiration" emerged in the later nineteenth century: "Political leaders and cultural commentators alike emphasized that a main meaning of the war was shared white bravery on the battlefield. Both Northern and Southern soldiers had fought heroically for their separate causes, according to the widespread interpretation, and such heroism was more important than sectional differences."[11]

Nowhere is this ideology more aptly illustrated than in the 1892 New York Times interview of Lucy's "Captain A." As the reporter narrated the story of Captain Adkins's close call in Galveston, he recounted a conversation between Commodore Sands, the commander of the Federal fleet in Galveston, and a Confederate officer in charge of a Flag of Truce Boat. In the account, the commodore had this exchange with the officer who had commanded the escaped blockade runner the previous day:

"He [Captain A] is a well-known Captain in the business," discreetly answered the Confederate.

---

9. David W. Blight, Beyond the Battlefield: Race, Memory, and the American Civil War (Amherst: University of Massachusetts Press, 2002), 2.

10. Ibid., 140.

11. Alice Fahs, "Remembering the Civil War in Children's Literature of the 1880s and 1890s," in The Memory Of the Civil War in American Culture, ed. Alice Fahs and Joan Waugh (Chapel Hill: University of North Carolina Press, 2004), 86.

"Yes, I know," said the Commodore, "but he is one of *our* people, isn't he?" and the old Commodore peered into the Confederate's face.

"He is a Confederate, Sir," said the officer, "*hardly one of your people.*"

"Oh, bosh!" said the Commodore. "He is an American, is he not? That is what I mean. Tell me, now is he not an American?"

"Yes," replied the Confederate, "he is a native-born American."

"*Good, good!*" half shouted the old Commodore. "I knew he was an American. No lime-juice Britisher could have done what that brave fellow did yesterday. Why, Sir, he took the whole fire of this fleet from one end to the other, and egad, how he did handle his ship! It was fine, fine. *No one, Sir, but an American could* have done it. It was not what was capable of a British blockade runner. The best of it is, he is one of our people. We are all one people despite this war, and we will recognize it just as soon as we get to shaking hands once more."[12]

The *New York Times* article, written twenty-seven years after the war's end, clearly exemplifies later efforts to heal a wounded nation, but Lucy Pier Stevens contended with that dilemma immediately. As soon as she emerged from the remote shelter of Travis, Texas, she was forced to examine her own position and perception of national identity. It would seem likely that although many have formally expounded on this question of the American, in Lucy's vernacular, her own explanation of her evolution as an American might read more like a recipe:

Blend Lucy's Northern heritage with the egalitarianism of the frontier, then mix with the Northeastern Puritan work economy of Aunt Lu and the Southern plantation economy of 1860s Texas. Add the Midwestern Farming ethic, then sprinkle entire mixture with racial and gender implications. Mix well, and bake in an oven of challenge and adversity to create a composite American.

Lucy Pier Stevens was just such a composite American woman. She left behind incomplete sectional identities to form an amalgamated American identity that transcended all others. She lived at the edge, experiencing occupational opportunities never before available to women and displaying independent decision-making skills seldom afforded those of the fairer sex. Her life in Texas allowed her a freedom and flexibility that a more formal and structured society might never have permitted.

12. "Running the Blockade: Exciting Experiences of Those Who Made It a Business," *New York Times*, October 2, 1892, New York Times Article Archive.

Yet while Lucy tied together the threads of her life, lacing up North with South, working woman with dependent girl, wandering adventurer with homebound traveler, she left one thread dangling until her return to Ohio. In spite of multiple opportunities for romantic involvement and plentiful candidates for matrimonial match-ups, Lucy knew that her sojourn in Texas was neither the time nor the place for an enduring alliance. She enjoyed the freedom of her single life, but reserved development of an abiding partnership for a future that awaited her in Ohio. She firmly believed that she would eventually marry, and she patiently bided her time. Then, as 1867 dawned, she met Mr. Joseph Caldwell, and their friendship soon blossomed into a deeper relationship. In one of the final entries of her journal, Lucy eloquently described her feelings about her life. To her, this remaining loose thread was soon to be tied up, as she wrote,

> I have tasted deeply from the fountain of pleasures in connection with single life and have enjoyed the draught—but now it seems a pleasure to have some one to care for me always—to love and be loved—one who can overlook follies and be a friend indeed:—such an one do I believe I have found in my Joseph—and in return—for all—I shall always try to prove myself worthy of his high regard and affection.
> Lucy Stevens, 9/22/67

Now, at last, Lucy's old life was woven into the new and her past meshed with her future. Love for her family and friends, near and far, proved stronger than the sectional variances that threatened to rend the fabric of a nation. For Lucy, the threads that bound together the pieces of her life into a whole transcended the differences that, for a time, tore the world apart.

Lucy Pier Stevens did, in fact, marry Joseph Caldwell in 1867, and they had two daughters, Mary and Caroline. Photos of Joseph and both daughters are included in Lucy's keepsake book housed in the DeGolyer Library at SMU. Sadly, however, Lucy and Joseph were married only fourteen years—Milan Cemetery records reveal that Joseph passed away in 1881 at the age of fifty-two. Lucy never remarried.

Thanks to the research of Scott Sanders, an archivist at Oberlin College, and Gil Pier, a descendant of Lucy's uncle Pier, we know that Lucy's daughter Mary became a music teacher and married Edmund Flagg, a druggist, in

Lucy Stevens Caldwell. DeGolyer Library, Southern Methodist University,
Lucy Pier Stevens Collection.

—

Joseph Caldwell. DeGolyer Library, Southern Methodist University,
Lucy Pier Stevens Collection.

Mary Caldwell. DeGolyer Library, Southern Methodist University,
Lucy Pier Stevens Collection.

—

Caroline Caldwell. DeGolyer Library, Southern Methodist University,
Lucy Pier Stevens Collection.

—

1903. They had a son, James. Tragically, Mary died, possibly in childbirth, on January 15, 1907, at the age of thirty-two. Lucy's other daughter, Caroline, married Lyman B. Hall, a professor at Oberlin College. The couple had no children of their own, but raised two nephews one of whom was James Flagg, Mary's son. According to Sanders, the 1930 Census shows that Caroline and her nephews had moved to Claremont, California, where Caroline died in Los Angeles County in June 1956. With this knowledge, the mystery of why the first volume of Lucy's diary surfaced in California is solved.

As for Lucy . . . she continued to live in Milan for several years after Joseph's death. Then, as reported in the November 1913 issue of *Oberlin Alumni Magazine*, from 1889 until her death in 1913 Lucy made her home with her daughter Caroline, who, at that time, lived in Oberlin, Ohio.[13] In late September 1913, at the age of seventy-five, Lucy fell and fractured her hip. She declined quickly, and less than three weeks later, on October 14, 1913, she passed away. Her death certificate indicates endocarditis as the cause of death, with her fall listed as a contributing factor. A brief article in the *Elyria Evening Telegram*, dated September 27, 1913, gives a better description of the events leading to Lucy's demise:

> Mrs. Lucy P. Caldwell suffered a fractured hip Tuesday just after returning from several weeks at the lake. Mrs. Caldwell was carrying her grip up the stairway at the home of her daughter, Mrs. L. B. Hall, on West College street, and thought she had another step to go after she reached the top. She became overbalanced and fell. Her hip was fractured. The injury is a painful one, but everything is being done to relieve her suffering.[14]

Thus, the years that Lucy Pier Stevens spent in Texas proved to be only a small interlude of time in a long and productive life. Once she left Texas in 1865, it is entirely possible that she never returned. However, the five years that she spent there signal a sea change in the life of one young woman, and of a nation. Forever marked by those days, Lucy, and the country, would move toward a maturing vision of inclusion.

Yet even as Lucy made her way home to Ohio, papers around Texas published a small article, a letter to the editor by "J.H.B.," urging people to save

---

13. "Necrology - Mrs. Lucy P. Caldwell," *Oberlin Alumni Magazine* 10, no. 2 (November 1913), ed. Helen White Martin (Norwalk, OH: Oberlin Alumni Publishing Co., 1913), 64.

14. Scott Sanders, Archivist, Antioch College, e-mail interview with Vicki Tongate, September 28, 2010.

their letters for future generations. Placed innocuously on the second page of the May 2, 1865, edition of the *Bellville Countryman*, the request nevertheless sounded a prophetic bell:

> I wish through your Journal and all others in Texas who may be kind enough to copy this article, to make a suggestion to a majority of this State. It is to preserve your letters received from the army, as well [as] those on hand as those hereafter to be received . . . A vast amount of most reliable history, news to be found in official documents or newspapers, is embraced in private letters from men in the army to their friends at home . . . No doubt is entertained but immediately after, if not before, the conclusion of this war, a "Texas State Historical Society" will be formed and chartered. Indeed, such a society should have been formed at the beginning of the war. This Society is the body for which all such letters should be preserved. By it they can be arranged, labeled, indexed, or extracted from as the case may be, thus preparing them as raw material for the searching analysis of our future State historians. While the general history of this war may be written from public documents and other sources, those letters will furnish a vast fund towards proper and honorable State pride, and to build up in the breasts of our descendants a genuine appreciation of both the value and cost of liberty, of manly patriotism and hatred of oppression.[15]

The writer of the article, though missing the mark by a few years, was precise in his estimation of the value of such a society, for the highly esteemed Texas State Historical Association, which was ultimately organized on March 2, 1897, describes itself as "a vast storehouse documenting the rich and complex history of the state." The TSHA explains that its mission is to "further the appreciation, understanding, and teaching of the rich and unique history of Texas through research, writing, and publication of related historical material,"[16] phrasing that is hauntingly reminiscent of that article written so long ago.

It is to this "vast storehouse," this rich repository of information, that Lucy's story may now be added. For it is not simply Lucy's story ~ it is a rich story of family, a complex story of community ~ a unique story of Texas.

---

15. "Preserve Your Letters," *Bellville Countryman*, May 2, 1865, Texas and Other Southern States Civil War Newspapers/Newspaper Research, 1861–1865.

16. "About TSHA—History of TSHA," Texas State Historical Association, December 26, 2013.

꘏

PRIMARY SOURCES

The American Journal of Dental Science 9, ser. 3. Edited by F.J.S. Gorgas, MD, DDS. Baltimore: Snowden & Cowden, 1875. Harvard University School of Dental Medicine.

"April Fool's Day." *New York Times*, April 2, 1871. New York Times Article Archive. http://query.nytimes.com/mem/archive-free /pdf?res=9902E7DC103EEE34BC 4A53DFB266838A669FDE.

Austin County, Texas. *Austin County Tax Rolls, 1860–1865*. Dallas Public Library. Microfilm.

Austin County Census 1860. Dallas Public Library, General Services. Microfilm.

Austin State Gazette. March 16, 1864. Texas and Other Southern States Civil War Newspapers/Newspaper Research, 1861–1865. www.uttyler.edu/vbetts/news-paper_titles.htm.

————. April 6, 1864. Texas and Other Southern States Civil War Newspapers/ Newspaper Research, 1861–1865. www.uttyler.edu/vbetts/newspaper_titles. htm.

————. November 9, 1864. Texas and Other Southern States Civil War Newspa-pers/Newspaper Research, 1861-1865. www.uttyler.edu/vbetts/newspaper_ titles.htm.

Ballou, Maturin. *History of Cuba; or, Notes of a Traveller in the Tropics*. Boston: Phillips, Sampson, and Company, 1854.

Barrett, Thomas. *The Great Hanging at Gainesville, Cooke County, Texas*. Gainesville, 1885.

Beecher, Catharine. "The Home: Woman's Sphere of Influence." In *Women and Religion in America*, vol. 1, *The Nineteenth Century*, edited by Rosemary Radford Ruether and Rosemary Skinner Keller, 311–312. San Francisco: Harper and Row, 1981.

Bellville Countryman, August 16, 1864. Texas and Other Southern States Civil War Newspapers/Newspaper Research, 1861–1865. http://www.uttyl.edu/vbetts/ dallas_herald.htm.

"Capture of Alexandria," *Harper's Weekly*, May 30, 1863. HarpWeek. http://app
.harpweek.com.proxy.libraries.smu.edu/IssueImagesView.asp?titleId=HW&
volumeId=1863&issueId=0530&page=339&imageSize=d.

*Catalogue of the Trustees, Faculty and Students of Baylor University, Female Department,
Independence, Texas*. Waco: Texas Collection, Baylor University, 1851–1885.

Chesnut, Mary Boykin. *A Diary from Dixie, as Written by Mary Boykin Chesnut*. Edited
by Isabella D. Martin and Myrta Lockett Avary. New York: D. Appleton and
Company, 1905.

———. *Mary Chesnut's Civil War*. Edited by C. Vann Woodward. New Haven, CT:
Yale University Press, 1981.

"Chick a Dee Dee." Boston: White, Smith & Co., 1878. American Sheet Music Collection. American Memory/Library of Congress. http://www.loc.gov/item/
sm1878.07716/.

Children of the Abbey. Literary Notices. *New York Mirror: A Weekly*, vol. 6, no. 6,
August 16, 1828. C19 the Nineteenth Century Index. http://search.proquest
.com.proxy.libraries.smu.edu/docview/136138411.

"Chitchat Up On New York and Philadelphia Fashions for September." *Godey's
Lady's Book and Magazine* (1854–1882), September 1, 1859. American Periodicals
Series Online, ProQuest. http://search.proquest.com.proxy.libraries.smu
.edu/docview/126056711/599E847ADF564126PQ/1?accountid=6667.

"Come, Come Away." Baltimore: F. D. Benteen, 1844. American Sheet Music
Collection. American Memory/Library of Congress. http://www.loc.gov/item/
sm1844.400320/.

Cormany, Samuel and Rachel. *The Cormany Diaries: A Northern Family in the Civil
War*. Edited by James C. Mohr. Pittsburgh: University of Pittsburgh Press, 1982.

Dawson, Sarah Morgan. *A Confederate Girl's Diary*. Edited by James T. Robertson, Jr.
Bloomington: Indiana University Press, 1960.

Dimock, Joseph J. *Impressions of Cuba in the Nineteenth Century: The Travel Diary
of Joseph J. Dimock*. Edited by Louis A. Pérez. Wilmington, DE: Scholarly
Resources, 1998.

Domestic Intelligence. *Harper's Weekly*, January 10, 1863. HarpWeek. http://app
.harpweek.com.proxy.libraries.smu.edu/ViewIndexEntryImage.asp?subEntry
Class=Combined&subEntryKey=500029&page=1.

———. *Harper's Weekly*, January 31, 1863. HarpWeek. http://app.harpweek.com
.proxy.libraries.smu.edu/ViewIndexEntryImage.asp?subEntryClass=Combine
d&subEntryKey=500029&page=4.

"Early Marriage Records, 1824-1920." Txgenweb.org. http://www.rootsweb
.ancestry.com/~txaustin/EarlyMarriages/Early.htm.

Embree, Henrietta Baker, and Tennessee Keys Embree. *Tandem Lives: The Frontier
Diaries of Henrietta Baker Embree and Tennessee Keys Embree, 1856–1864*. Edited by
Amy L. Wink. Knoxville: University of Tennessee Press, 2008.

"Farewell Stickney." *Bellville Countryman*, vol. 4, no. 2, August 1, 1863.

Fisher, Abby. *What Mrs. Fisher Knows About Old Southern Cooking*. San Francisco: Women's Co-operative Printing Office, 1881. University of California Libraries. https://archive.org/details/whatmrsfisherknoofishrich.

"Flag of Truce Boats." *Galveston Weekly News*, February 15, 1865. Texas and Other Southern States Civil War Newspapers/Newspaper Research, 1861–1865. www.uttyler.edu/vbetts/newspaper_titles.htm.

"The Fourth of March." *Harper's Weekly*, vol. 1865, no. 3/11. HarpWeek. http://app .harpweek.com.proxy.libraries.smu.edu/IssueImagesView.asp?titleId=HW&vo lumeId=1865&issueId=0304.

"From Havana: Reception of the News of President Lincoln's Assassination . . ." *New York Times*, April 27, 1865. New York Times Article Archive. http://www .nytimes.com/1865/04/27/news/havana-reception-president-lincoln-s-assa ssination-honors-memory-dead-mexico.html.

Galveston Weekly News, November 9, 1864. Texas and Other Southern States Civil War Newspapers/Newspaper Research, 1861-1865. www.uttyler.edu/vbetts/ newspaper_titles.htm.

"General Orders No. 8." *Tyler Reporter*, March 31, 1864. Texas and Other Southern States Civil War Newspapers/Newspaper Research, 1861-1865. http://uttyler .edu/vbetts/tyler_reporter_1861-1864.htm.

"Havana Correspondence." *New York Times*, January 1, 1865. New York Times Article Archive. http://www.nytimes.com/1865/01/01/news/our-havana-corr espondence-belgian-soldiers-en-route-mexico-shock-earthquake.html.

Hays, Will S. "The Drummer Boy of Shiloh." Augusta: Blackmar & Bro., 1863. American Song Sheets, Duke University Libraries Digital Collections. http:// library.duke.edu/digitalcollections/hasm_confo166/.

Houston Tri-Weekly Telegraph. October 31, 1863. Texas and Other Southern States Civil War Newspapers/Newspaper Research, 1861–1865. www.uttyler.edu/ vbetts/newspaper_titles.htm.

———. November 14, 1864. Texas and Other Southern States Civil War News-papers/Newspaper Research, 1861-1865. www.uttyler.edu/vbetts/newspaper_ titles.htm.

"In Lead-Color Paint," *New York Times*, October 17, 1892. New York Times Article Archive. http://query.nytimes.com/mem/archive-free/pdf?res=9506E2D61238 E233A25754C1A9669D94639ED7CF.

"The Iron-Clad Oath: Passage of a bill to repeal the law requiring it in the House— Probable Passage in the Senate." *New York Times*, December 4, 1877. New York Times Article Archive. http://query.nytimes.com/mem/archive-free/pdf?res=9 801E4DB173EE73BBC4E53DFB467838C669FDE.

"John Morgan." *Harper's Weekly*, September 24, 1864. HarpWeek. http://app.harp week.com.proxy.libraries.smu.edu/IssueImagesView.asp?titleId=HW&volume Id=1864&issueId=0924.

Journal of the Congress of the Confederate States of America, vol. 5, March 3, 1862. Library of Congress. http://memory.loc.gov/cgi-bin/query/r?ammem/hlaw:@ field(DOCID+@lit(cc00516)).

Kenney, Sarah Ellen. "Friendship and Love." Lucy Pier Stevens Diary Collection. Dallas: DeGolyer Special Collections Library, Southern Methodist University, 1865.

Mackie, John F. "A Fox Chase." *Galveston Daily News*, April 16, 1865. Maritime Texas. http://www.maritimetexas.net/Documents/FOX%20Chase%20GDN %204-16-65.pdf.

———. "Running the Blockade—Escape of the *Fox*." In *Under Both Flags: A Panorama of the Great Civil War*, edited by George Morley Vickers, 329–332. Veteran Publishing, 1896.

"Maj. Boone's Report from May 26, 1863." *Bellville Countryman*, August 8, 1863. Texas and Other Southern States Civil War Newspapers/Newspaper Research, 1861-1865. www.uttyler.edu/vbetts/newspaper_titles.htm.

"Marine Intelligence; Cleared. Arrived . . . " *New York Times*, August 8, 1861. New York Times Article Archive. http://www.nytimes.com/1861/08/08/news/mar ine-intelligence-cleared-arrived-sailed-miscellaneous-spoken-c-foreign-ports .html.

"Marine Intelligence; Cleared. Arrived. Sailed. By Telegraph." *New York Times*, May 4, 1865. New York Times Article Archive. http://www.nytimes.com/1865/05/ 04/news/marine-intelligence-cleared-arrived-sailed-by-telegraph.html.

McGinnis, O. A., ed. *Galveston Weekly News*, March 16, 1864. Texas and Other Southern States Civil War Newspapers/Newspaper Research, 1861–1865. www.uttyler.edu/vbetts/newspaper_titles.htm.

Neblett, Elizabeth Scott. *A Rebel Wife in Texas: The Diary and Letters of Elizabeth Scott Neblett, 1852–1864.* Edited by Erika L. Murr. Baton Rouge: Louisiana State University Press, 2001.

"Necrology – Mrs. Lucy P. Caldwell." *Oberlin Alumni Magazine*, vol. 10, no. 2 (November 1913): 64. Edited by Helen White Martin. Norwalk, OH: Oberlin Alumni Publishing, 1913.

"News From Havana: Arrival of the Steamship *Columbia*." *New York Times*, August 8, 1861. New York Times Article Archive. http://www.nytimes.com/1861 /08/08/news/news-from-havana-arrival-of-the-steamship-columbia.html.

"Obituary." *Bellville Countryman*, August 1, 1863.

[Official] "President Lincoln Shot by an Assassin." *New York Times*, April 15, 1865. New York Times Article Archive. http://www.nytimes.com/1865/04/15/news/ president-lincoln-shot-assassin-deed-done-ford-s-theatre-last-night-act.html ?module=Search&mabReward=relbias%3Ar.

"Passengers Sailed, Passengers Arrived." *New York Times*, May 4, 1865. New York Times Article Archive. http://www.nytimes.com/1865/05/04/news/passengers -sailed-passengers-arrived.html.

Pier, James Bradford. Pier Family Papers. Texas Collection, Baylor University, Waco.

Pier, Lu Merry, and Sarah Pier Wiley. Pier Family Diaries, 1852–1867. Texas Collection, Baylor University, Waco.

Pier, Robert J., and Cristy Pier. Bellville, Texas: Pier Family Genealogical History.
———. Pier Family Papers. Private collection.

Pierce, Ray Vaughn, M.D. *The People's Common Sense Medical Adviser in Plain English; Or, Medicine Simplified*. World's Dispensary Medical Association, 1895. Project Gutenberg. http://www.gutenberg.org/files/18467/18467-h/18467-h.htm.

Porter, Jane. *Thaddeus of Warsaw*. Boston: L. Blake, 1809. Project Gutenberg. http://www.gutenberg.org/cache/epub/6566/pg6566.html.

"Preserve Your Letters," *Bellville Countryman*, May 2, 1865, Texas and Other Southern States Civil War Newspapers/Newspaper Research, 1861–1865. www.uttyler.edu/vbetts/newspaper_titles.htm.

Richards, Brinley. "Come Dearest the Daylight is Gone." Baltimore: Miller and Beacham. 19th Century American Sheet Music Digitization Project. University of North Carolina at Chapel Hill. http://dc.lib.unc.edu/cdm/compoundobject/collection/sheetmusic/id/25090/rec/1.

"A Roar From Jeff Davis." *Harper's Weekly*, January 10, 1863. HarpWeek. http://app.harpweek.com.proxy.libraries.smu.edu/IssueImagesView.asp?titleId=HW&volumeId=1863&issueId=0110&page=19&imageSize=l.

Rowlandson, Mary. *The Sovereignty and Goodness of God*. Edited by Neal Salisbury. Boston: Bedford Books, 1997.

"Running the Blockade: Exciting Experiences of Those Who Made It a Business." *New York Times*, October 2, 1892. New York Times Article Archive. http://query.nytimes.com/mem/archive-free/pdf?res=9507E6D71238E233A25751C0A9669D94639ED7CF.

Rutledge, Thomas. "The proper use and application of riches recommended. A sermon, preached at Salters-Hall, April 15th, 1791, before the correspondent board in London of the Society in Scotland . . . for Propagating Christian knowledge. . . ." By Thomas Rutledge, A.M. Published at the request of the Society, . . . London, 1791. Eighteenth Century Collections Online. Gale Group. Southern Methodist University. http://find.galegroup.com.proxy.libraries.smu.edu/ecco/infomark.do?&source=gale&prodId=ECCO&userGroupName=txshracd2548&tabID=T001&docId=CW3319800306&type=multipage&contentSet=ECCOArticles&version=1.0&docLevel=FASCIMILE.

Schreiner, Hermann L. "God Defendeth the Right." Macon, GA: John C. Schreiner & Son, 1861. 19th Century American Sheet Music Digitization Project. University of North Carolina at Chapel Hill. http://dc.lib.unc.edu/cdm/compoundobject/collection/sheetmusic/id/20247/rec/1.

"The Southern Girl With the Home-Spun Dress," America Singing: Nineteenth-Century Song Sheets, Library of Congress. http://memory.loc.gov/ammem/amsshtml/amssTitles34.html#top.

Spaight, A. W. *The Resources, Soil, and Climate of Texas*. Galveston: A. H. Belo & Company, Printers, 1882.

Stevens, Lucy Pier. The Lucy Pier Stevens Diary. 4 vols. Dallas: DeGolyer Special Collections Library, Southern Methodist University, 1860–1867.

———. Lucy Pier Stevens Keepsake Book. Dallas: DeGolyer Special Collections Library, Southern Methodist University.

Stieler, Adolf. *Adolf Stieler's Hand Atlas*. Germany, 1896.

Taylor, Thomas E. *Running the Blockade*. 1896. Reprinted in *Classics of Naval Literature Series*, edited by Stephen R. Wise. Annapolis, MD: Naval Institute Press, 1995.

"To the Ladies of Austin County." *Bellville Countryman*, November 14, 1863. Texas and Other Southern States Civil War Newspapers/Newspaper Research, 1861–1865. www.uttyler.edu/vbetts/newspaper_titles.htm.

Williamson, David Brainerd. *Illustrated Life, Services, Martyrdom, and Funeral of Abraham Lincoln*. Philadelphia: T. B. Peterson & Brothers, 1865. New York Public Library. nypl.org/collections. http://babel.hathitrust.org/cgi/pt?id=nyp.334330 82351358;view=1up;seq=13.

SECONDARY SOURCES

Abernethy, Francis E. *The Bounty of Texas*. Denton: University of North Texas Press, 1990.

———. *The Folklore of Texas Culture*. Austin: Encino Press, 1974.

———. *Hoein' the Short Rows*. Dallas: SMU Press, 1987.

———. *Texas Toys and Games*. Dallas: SMU Press, 1989.

Aldridge, Alfred Owen. *Man of Reason: The Life of Thomas Paine*. Philadelphia: Lippincott, 1959.

Ashcraft, Allen C. *Texas in the Civil War: A Resume History*. Austin: Texas Civil War Centennial Commission, 1962.

"August the Strong." *Dresdner Christstollen*. http://www.dresdnerstollen.com/index .php?ILNK=SMenu_Stollenfest&iL=2.

"Augustus the Strong." *Encyclopedia Britannica*. http://www.britannica.com/EB checked/topic/43118/Augustus-II.

Aurin, Marcus. "Chasing the Dragon: The Cultural Metamorphosis of Opium in the United States, 1825–1935." *Medical Anthropology Quarterly* 14, no. 3 (2000): 414–441. http://www.jstor.org.proxy.libraries.smu.edu/stable/10.2307/649 506.

Austin County Texas Deed Abstracts, 1837–1852, Republic of Texas, State of Texas. Abstractor Joyce Martin Murray. Wolfe City: Henington Publishing, 1987.

Ayers, Edward. *In the Presence of Mine Enemies: War in the Heart of America, 1859–1863*. New York: W. W. Norton, 2003.

Ayres, Thomas. *Dark and Bloody Ground: The Battle of Mansfield and the Forgotten Civil War in Louisiana.* Dallas: Taylor Publishing, 2001.

Baer, Elizabeth R. "Ambivalence, Anger, and Silence: The Civil War Diary of Lucy Buck." In *Inscribing the Daily*, edited by Suzanne L. Bunkers and Cynthia A. Huff, 207–219. Amherst: University of Massachusetts Press, 1996.

Barnstone, Howard. *The Galveston That Was.* New York: Macmillan, 1966.

Bartholemew, Ed. *Kill or Be Killed.* Houston: Frontier Press of Texas, 1953.

"Battle Summaries by Campaign." *American Battlefield Protection Program.* National Parks Service. http://www.nps.gov/hps/abpp/battles/bycampgn.htm; http://www.nps.gov/hps/abpp/battles/ms011.htm.

Baym, Nina. *Novels, Readers, and Reviewers: Responses to Fiction in Antebellum America.* Ithaca, NY: Cornell University Press, 1984.

Bellville Historical Commission. *The Cemeteries of Austin County.* Author, 1990.

Bellville Historical Society. "Bellville Downtown Square." bellvilleshistoricalsociety.org.

Bemesderfer, James O. *Pietism and Its Influence upon the Evangelical United Brethren Church.* Harrisburg, PA: The Evangelical Press and published by the author, 1966.

Berkin, Carol Ruth. "Private Woman, Public Woman: The Contradictions of Charlotte Perkins Gilman." In *Women of America: A History*, edited by Carol Berkin and Mary Beth Norton, 150–176. Boston: Houghton-Mifflin, 1979.

Berkin, Carol Ruth, and Mary Beth Norton, eds. *Women of America: A History.* Boston: Houghton-Mifflin, 1979.

Betts, Vicki. "'A Sacred Charge upon Our Hands': Assisting the Families of Confederate Soldiers in Texas, 1861–1865." In *The Seventh Star of the Confederacy: Texas during the Civil War*, edited by Kenneth W. Howell, 246–267. Denton: University of North Texas Press, 2009.

Blauvelt, Martha T. "Women and Revivalism." In *Women and Religion in America*, vol. 1, *The Nineteenth Century*, edited by Rosemary Radford Ruether and Rosemary Skinner Keller, 1–9. San Francisco: Harper and Row, 1981.

Blight, David W. *Beyond the Battlefield: Race, Memory, and the American Civil War.* Amherst: University of Massachusetts Press, 2002.

Block, W. T. *Schooner Sail to Starboard: Confederate Blockade-Running on the Louisiana-Texas Coastline.* Woodville, TX: Dogwood Press, 1997.

Bloom, Lynn Z. "I Write for Myself and Strangers: Private Diaries as Public Documents." In *Inscribing the Daily*, edited by Suzanne Bunkers and Cynthia A. Huff, 23–37. Amherst: University of Massachusetts Press, 1996.

Boswell, Angela. "The Civil War and the Lives of Texas Women." In *The Fate of Texas: The Civil War and the Lone Star State*, edited by Charles D. Grear, 68–81. Fayetteville: University of Arkansas Press, 2008.

———. *Her Act and Deed: Women's Lives in a Rural Southern County, 1837-1873.* College Station: Texas A&M University Press, 2001.

Brewster, Paul G. *Children's Games and Rhymes*. New York: Arno Publishing, 1976.

Bridges over Niagara Falls. www.niagrafrontier.com.

"Brigadier General Daniel Morgan." National Parks Service. http://www.nps.gov/ cowp/historyculture/daniel-morgan.htm.

Brown, Herbert Ross. *The Sentimental Novel in America, 1789–1860*. Durham, NC: Duke University Press, 1940.

Brown, Richard Maxwell. "Historical Patterns of Violence in America." In *Violence in America: Historical and Comparative Perspectives*, edited by Hugh D. Graham and Ted R. Gur, 43–80. New York: Signet, 1969.

———. *Strain of Violence: Historical Studies of American Violence and Vigilantism*. New York: Oxford University Press, 1975.

Brown, Stephen N. "Edward Young." In *Dictionary of Literary Biography*, vol. 95, *Eighteenth-Century British Poets*, 1st ser., edited by John Sitter, 353–363. Gale Group, 1990. http://galenet.galegroup.com.proxy.libraries.smu.edu/servlet/GLD /hits?r=d&origSearch=true&o=DataType&n=10&l=d&c=1&locID=txshracd25 48&secondary=false&u=DLB&t=KW&s=4&NA=Edward+Young#MainEssay Section.

Browne, Jefferson B. *Key West: The Old and the New*. St. Augustine: The Record Co., 1912.

"Buckeyes." Ohio Department of Natural Resources. ohiodnr.org.

Bunkers, Suzanne L., and Cynthia A. Huff, eds. *Inscribing the Daily*. Amherst: University of Massachusetts Press, 1996.

———. "Issues in Studying Women's Diaries: A Theoretical and Critical Introduction." In *Inscribing the Daily*, edited by Suzanne L. Bunkers and Cynthia A. Huff, 3–20. Amherst: University of Massachusetts Press, 1996.

Campbell, Randolph B. *An Empire for Slavery: The Peculiar Institution in Texas*. Baton Rouge: Louisiana State University Press, 1989.

Caracausa, Lorelei, and Margaret Humphries, Fort Worth Weavers Guild. "Yarn Sizing." E-mail interview with Vicki Tongate. June 19, 2009.

Casdorph, Paul D. *Confederate General R. S. Ewell: Robert E. Lee's Hesitant Commander*. Lexington: University Press of Kentucky, 2004.

Cayton, Marie K., et al., eds. *Encyclopedia of American Social History*, vol. 1. New York: Charles Scribner and Sons, 1993.

"Charlotte Mary Yonge." *Contemporary Authors Online*. Gale Group, 2007. http:// galenet.galegroup.com.proxy.libraries.smu.edu/servlet/GLD/hits?r=d&origSe arch=true&o=DataType&n=10&l=d&c=1&locID=txshracd2548&secondary=fa lse&u=CA&t=KW&s=2&NA=Charlotte+Mary+Yonge.

"Chasing a Fox." Institute of Nautical Archaeology, Texas A&M University. http:// nauticalarch.org/projects/all/north_america/the_denbigh_project/denbigh _history/chasing_a_fox/.

Chicoine, Stephen. *The Confederates of Chappell Hill, Texas: Prosperity, Civil War, and Decline*. Jefferson, NC: McFarland, 2004.

Christen, Glenna Jo. "Slat Bonnet Question." Online posting. November 28, 2008. The Sewing Academy Online. http://sewingacademy.org.

Cline, Cheryl. *Women's Diaries, Journals, and Letters: An Annotated Bibliography*. New York: Garland Publishing, 1989.

Cochran, Hamilton. *Blockade Runners of the Confederacy*. Indianapolis: Bobbs-Merrill, 1958.

"Code Duello: The Rules of Dueling." *American Experience*. http://www.pbs.org/wg bh/amex/duel/sfeature/rulesofdueling.html.

Cott, Nancy F. *The Bonds of Womanhood*. New Haven, CT: Yale University Press, 1977.

Coulombe, Joseph L. "Emerson Bennett." In *Dictionary of Literary Biography*, vol. 202, *Nineteenth-Century American Fiction Writers*, edited by Kent P. Ljungquist. Gale Group, 1999. http://galenet.galegroup.com.proxy.libraries.smu.edu/serv let/GLD/hits?r=d&origSearch=true&o=DataType&n=10&l=d&c=2&locID=txs hracd2548&secondary=false&u=CA&u=CLC&u=DLB&t=KW&s=1&NA=Eme rson+Bennett.

Countryman, Edward. *Americans: A Collision of Histories*. New York: Hill and Wang, 1996.

———. Personal interview with Vicki Tongate. June 25, 2014.

Crisman, Kevin J. Faculty fellow and vice president, Institute of Nautical Archaeology, Texas A&M University. Personal interview with Vicki Tongate. May 22, 2008.

Daly, Maria. *Diary of a Union Lady*. Edited by Harold Earl Hammond. New York: Funk and Wagnalls, 1962.

"Daniel Decatur Emmett." Songwriters Hall of Fame. http://www.songwriters halloffame.org/exhibits/C196.

"Death Runs Riot." *The West*. Prod. Ken Burns and Stephen Ives. www.pbs.org/ weta/thewest/program.

DeBrava, Valerie. "Alice B. Neal Haven." In *Dictionary of Literary Biography*, vol. 25, *Antebellum Writers in New York*, 2nd ser., edited by Kent J. Lynnquist, 177–183. Gale Group. http://galenet.galegroup.com.proxy.libraries.smu.edu/servlet/ GLD/hits?r=d&origSearch=true&o=DataType&n=10&l=d&c=1&locID=txshr acd2548&secondary=false&u=CA&u=CLC&u=DLB&t=KW&s=1&NA=Alice+ Haven.

"The *Denbigh* Project." Institute of Nautical Archaeology, Texas A&M University. http://nauticalarch.org/projects/all/north_america/the_denbigh_project/ introduction/.

Derounian-Stodola, Kathryn Z. *Women's Indian Captivity Narratives*. New York: Penguin Books, 1998.

Dietrich, Wilfred O. *The Blazing Story of Washington County*. Author, 1950.

"Disciples of Christ." In *The Oxford Dictionary of the Christian Church*, edited by F. L. Cross and E. A. Livingstone. Oxford: Oxford University Press, 2005. *The Oxford Dictionary of the Christian Church* (e-reference edition). Oxford University Press.

http://www.oxfordreference.com.proxy.libraries.smu.edu/view/10.1093/oi/
authority.20110803095721427.

Dobson, Joanne, and Amy Hudock. "E.D.E.N. Southworth." In *Dictionary of Literary Biography*, vol. 239, *American Women Prose Writers, 1820-1870*, edited by Katherine Rodier and Amy Hudock, 285–292. Gale Group, 2001. http://galenet
.galegroup.com.proxy.libraries.smu.edu/servlet/GLD/hits?r=d&origSearch=tr
ue&o=DataType&n=10&l=d&c=7&locID=txshracd2548&secondary=false&u=
CA&u=CLC&u=DLB&t=KW&s=1&NA=Southworth.

Dorson, Richard Mercer. *Folklore and Folklife*. Chicago: University of Chicago Press, 1982.

"Drying Fruit." University of Georgia Extension Service. http://uga.edu/nchfp/
publications/.

Eaton, Clement. *The Mind of the Old South*. Baton Rouge: Louisiana State University Press, 1964.

Edwards, John Austin. "Social and Cultural Activities of Texans during the Civil War and Reconstruction, 1861–1873." PhD diss., Texas Tech University, 1985.

Endres, Kathleen L. "Timothy Shay Arthur." In *Dictionary of Literary Biography*, vol. 79, *American Magazine Journalists, 1850–1900*, edited by Sam G. Riley, 33–43. Gale Group, 1989. http://galenet.galegroup.com.proxy.libraries.smu.edu/servlet/
GLD/hits?r=d&origSearch=true&o=DataType&n=10&l=d&c=3&locID=txshra
cd2548&secondary=false&u=CA&u=CLC&u=DLB&t=KW&s=1&NA=Timoth
y+Arthur.

"Erysipelas." *Merck Manuals: Online Medical Library*. Fondren Library, Southern Methodist University. http://www.merck.com.

Evans, Sara M. *Born for Liberty: A History of Women in America*. New York: Simon and Schuster, 1997.

Fahs, Alice. "Remembering the Civil War in Children's Literature of the 1880's and 1890's." In *The Memory of the Civil War in American Culture*, edited by Alice Fahs and Joan Waugh. Chapel Hill: University of North Carolina Press, 2004.

Faragher, John Mack. "The Midwestern Farming Family." In *Women's America*, edited by Linda K. Kerber and Jane Sherron DeHart, 117–129. 4th ed. New York: Oxford University Press, 1995.

Farber, James. *Texas C.S.A.* New York: Jackson Co., 1947.

Faust, Drew Gilpin. *Mothers of Invention*. New York: Vintage Books, 1996.

———. *Southern Stories: Slaveholders in Peace and War*. Columbia: University of Missouri Press, 1992.

Fehrenbacher, Don E., ed. *History and American Society: Essays of David M. Potter*. New York: Oxford University Press, 1973.

Fields, William. *The Literary and Miscellaneous Scrap Book*. Philadelphia: J. B. Lippincott, 1860. http://www.brickrow.com/cgi-bin/brickrow/index.html.

Forsyth, Michael. *The Red River Campaign of 1864 and the Loss by the Confederacy of the Civil War*. Jefferson, NC: McFarland, 2002.

Frantz, Joe B., and Julian Ernest Choate, Jr. *The American Cowboy: The Myth and the Reality.* Norman: University of Oklahoma Press, 1955.

Frazier, Donald S. *Cottonclads! The Battle of Galveston and the Defense of the Texas Coast.* Abilene, TX: McWhiney Foundation Press, 1998.

"Frederick II (1712-1786)." *Encyclopedia of World Biography.* Thomson Gale, 1998. http://go.galegroup.com.proxy.libraries.smu.edu/ps/retrieve.do?sgHitCountT ype=None&sort=RELEVANCE&inPS=true&prodId=AONE&userGroupName =txshracd2548&tabID=T001&searchId=R4&resultListType=RESULT_LIST&c ontentSegment=&searchType=AdvancedSearchForm&currentPosition=6&co ntentSet=GALE%7CA148426264&&docId=GALE|A148426264&docType=GA LE&role=.

"Freemasonry." *Freemasonry for Men and Women.* co-masonry.org.

Gallaway, B. P., ed. *Texas: The Dark Corner of the Confederacy.* Lincoln: University of Nebraska Press, 1994.

"Gauging Skirts." www.elizabethstewartclark.com.

Genovese, Eugene D. *The Southern Front.* Columbia: University of Missouri Press, 1995.

———. *The Southern Tradition.* Cambridge: Harvard University Press, 1994.

Goeke, Joseph F. "T. S. Arthur." In *Dictionary of Literary Biography,* vol. 250, *Antebellum Writers in New York,* 2nd ser., edited by Kent P. Ljungquist, 16–28. Gale Group, 2001. http://galenet.galegroup.com.proxy.libraries.smu.edu/servlet/ GLD/hits?r=d&origSearch=true&o=DataType&n=10&l=d&c=2&locID=txshra cd2548&secondary=false&u=CA&u=CLC&u=DLB&t=KW&s=1&NA=timothy +arthur#MainEssaySection.

Govan, Thomas. "Americans below the Potomac." In *The Southerner as American,* edited by Charles G. Sellers, Jr., 19–39. Chapel Hill: University of North Carolina Press, 1960.

Grant, H. Roger. *The Railroad: The Life Story of a Technology.* Westport, CT: Greenwood Publishing Group, 2005.

Gregor, Carrie. County clerk, Austin County. E-mail interview with Vicki Tongate. January 29, 2010.

Hall, Jacquelyn Dowd. "Partial Truths: Writing Southern Women's History." In *Southern Women,* edited by Virginia Bernhard, Betty Brandon, Elizabeth Fox-Genovese, and Theda Perdue, 11-29. Columbia: University of Missouri Press, 1992.

Hall, Richard. *Patriots in Disguise: Women Warriors of the Civil War.* New York: Paragon House, 1993.

Haller, John S., Jr., and Robin M. Haller. *The Physician and Sexuality in Victorian America.* Urbana: University of Illinois Press, 1974.

Hampsten, Elizabeth. *Read This Only to Yourself.* Bloomington: Indiana University Press, 1982.

The Handbook of Texas Online. https://www.tshaonline.org/handbook/online.

Hardt, William. Bellville Historical Society at Bellville, Texas. Personal interview with Vicki Tongate. February 5, 2000.

———. E-mail interview with Vicki Tongate concerning "100 Years Ago in the *Times*—Samuel Bradford Pier," *Bellville Times*, March 29, 2014.

Hart, Katherine. *Pease Porridge Hot.* Austin: Friends of the Austin Public Library, 1967.

Haynes, Carolyn A. *Divine Destiny: Gender and Race in Nineteenth-Century Protestantism.* Jackson: University Press of Mississippi, 1998.

Henderson, Harry McCorry. *Texas in the Confederacy.* San Antonio: Naylor, 1955.

"Hints for Masqueraders and Others." *Buffalo Courier*, January 21, 1876. Thomas Tryniski, *Old Fulton Postcards.* http://fultonhistory.com/Newspaper4/Buffalo.

"The History of Dueling in America." *American Experience.* PBS.org. http://www.pbs.org/wgbh/amex/duel/sfeature/dueling.html.

Hodgson, Francis. *Lady Jane Grey, a Tale in Two Books.* London: T. Bensley, 1809.

Hoffstadter, Richard, and Michael Wallace. *American Violence: A Documentary History.* New York: Alfred A. Knopf, 1970.

Holman, David. *Buckskin and Homespun: Texas Frontier Clothing, 1820-1870.* Austin: Wind River Press, 1979.

———. *Letters of Hard Times in Texas, 1840–1890.* Austin: Roger Beacham, 1974.

"Hoop Skirts." *Victoriana Magazine*, December 17, 2013. http://www.victoriana.com/Victorian-Fashion/hoopskirt.htm.

Howard, Susan K. "Amelia Opie." In *Dictionary of Literary Biography*, vol. 116, *British Romantic Novelists, 1789-1832*, edited by Bradford K. Mudge, 228-233. Gale Group. http://galenet.galegroup.com.proxy.libraries.smu.edu/servlet/GLD/hits?r=d&origSearch=true&o=DataType&n=10&l=d&c=2&locID=txshracd2548&secondary=false&u=DLB&t=KW&s=4&NA=amelia+opie.

Huntington, Daniel. *Republican Court (Lady Washington's Reception Day).* Brooklyn Museum: American Art Collection. http://www.brooklynmuseum.org/open collection/objects/487/The_Republican_Court_Lady_Washingtons_Reception_Day.

Isaac, Rhys. *The Transformation of Virginia, 1740–1790.* Chapel Hill: University of North Carolina Press, 1982.

James, G. P. R. *The Smuggler.* London: Smith, Elder, 1845. Princeton University Library Manuscripts Division. http://searchit.princeton.edu/primo_library/libweb/action/dlDisplay.do?docId=PRN_VOYAGER7321801&vid=PRINCETON&institution=PRN.

"John Hunt Morgan." Civil War home page. http://www.civilwar.org/education/history/biographies/john-hunt-morgan-1.html.

"John Newland Maffitt." Naval Historical Center home page. U.S. Navy. http://www.history.navy.mil/photos/pers-us/uspers-m/j-maffit.htm.

Johnson, Ludwell H. *Red River Campaign: Politics and Cotton in the Civil War.* Baltimore: Johns Hopkins University Press, 1958.

"Johnson's Island." National Park Service. http://tps.cr.nps.gov/nhl/detail.cfm?ResourceId=1562&ResourceType=Site.

"Joseph P. 'Beadeye' Jones." Waller County page. Rootsweb.ancestry.com.

Kagle, Steven E., and Lorenza Gramegna. "Rewriting Her Life: Fictionalization and the Use of Fictional Models in Early American Women's Diaries." In *Inscribing the Daily,* edited by Suzanne L. Bunkers and Cynthia A. Huff, 38–55. Amherst: University of Massachusetts Press, 1996.

Kelley, Mary. *Private Woman, Public Stage.* New York: Oxford University Press, 1984.

Kelley, Mary, ed. *Woman's Being, Woman's Place.* Boston: G. K. Hall, 1979.

Kerber, Linda K. "The Republican Mother." In *Women's America,* edited by Linda K. Kerber and Jane Sherron DeHart, 89–95. 4th ed. New York: Oxford University Press, 1995.

Kerber, Linda K., and Jane Sherron DeHart, eds. *Women's America.* 4th ed. New York: Oxford University Press, 1995.

Kestler, Frances Roe. *The Indian Captivity Narrative: A Woman's View.* New York: Garland Publishing, 1990.

King, C. Richard, ed. *Victorian Lady on the Texas Frontier: The Journal of Ann Raney Coleman.* Norman: University of Oklahoma Press, 1971.

Kohecny, Lawrence C., and Clinton Machann. *Perilous Voyages: Czech and English Immigrants to Texas in the 1870s.* Centennial Series of the Association of Former Students: Texas A&M University, 2004.

Lacour-Gayet, Robert. *Everyday Life in the United States before the Civil War, 1830–1860.* New York: Frederick Unger Publishing, 1969.

"Lady Jane Grey." BBC Historic Figures. http://www.bbc.co.uk/history/historic_figures/grey_lady_jane.shtml.

Lasselle, Nancy Polk. *Annie Grayson, or Life in Washington.* 1853. WorldCat. http://newfirstsearch.oclc.org.proxy.libraries.smu.edu/WebZ/FSFETCH?fetchtype=fullrecord:sessionid=fsapp2-41496-hwsom4z9-5lz8fi:entitypagenum=6:0:recno=2:resultset=4:format=FI:next=html/record.html:bad=error/badfetch.html:entitytoprecno=2:entitycurrecno=2:numrecs=1.

"Lawmakers, Loyalty, and the 'Ironclad Oath,' 1864." U.S. Capitol Visitors Center. www.visitthecapitol.gov.

Leavitt, Judith W. "Under the Shadow of Maternity." In *Women's America: Refocusing the Past,* edited by Linda K. Kerber and Jane Sherron DeHart, 184–192. 4th ed. New York: Oxford University Press, 1995.

Lehuie, Isabelle. "Sentimental Figures: Reading *Godey's Ladies Book* in Antebellum America." In *The Culture of Sentiment,* edited by Shirley Samuels, 73–91. New York: Oxford University Press, 1992.

Lemolin, Robert. *Pathway to the National Character, 1830–1861.* Port Washington, NY: Kennikat Press, 1974.

Levine, Robert M. *Cuba in the 1850's: Through the Lens of Charles DeForest Fredricks.* Tampa: University of Southern Florida Press, 1990.

Linden, Glenn M., and Thomas J. Pressley. *Voices From the House Divided.* New York: McGraw-Hill, 1995.

Linderman, Gerald F. *Embattled Courage.* New York: Free Press, 1987.

Lockridge, Kenneth A. *The Diary, and Life, of William Byrd II of Virginia.* Chapel Hill: University of North Carolina Press, 1987.

Lowe, Richard. *Walker's Texas Division C.S.A.: Greyhounds of the Trans-Mississippi.* Baton Rouge: Louisiana State University Press, 2004.

Luedtke, Luther S., ed. *Making America: The Society and Culture of the United States.* Chapel Hill: University of North Carolina Press, 1992.

Lystra, Karen. *Searching the Heart: Women, Men, and Romantic Love in Nineteenth-Century America.* New York: Oxford University Press, 1989.

McCaslin, Richard B. *Tainted Breeze: The Great Hanging at Gainesville, Texas, 1862.* Baton Rouge: Louisiana State University Press, 1994.

McComb, David G. *Galveston: A History.* Austin: University of Texas Press, 1986.

McCurry, Stephanie. *Confederate Reckoning: Power and Politics in the Civil War South.* Cambridge: Harvard University Press, 2010.

McGhee, Richard D. "Sir Walter Scott." In *Dictionary of Literary Biography*, vol. 107, *British Romantic Prose Writers, 1789–1832*, 1st ser., edited by John R. Greenfield, 247-266. Gale Group, 1991. http://galenet.galegroup.com.proxy.libraries.smu.edu/servlet/GLD/hits?r=d&origSearch=true&o=DataType&n=10&l=d&c=3&locID=txshracd2548&secondary=false&u=DLB&t=KW&s=4&NA=walter+scott.

McGuffey, William Holmes. *The Second Eclectic Reader.* Cincinnati: Truman and Smith, 1836. Harvard College Library.

"McGuffey's Reader." Ohio History Central. July 1, 2005. http://www.ohiohistory central.org.

McPherson, James M. *Battle Cry of Freedom.* Oxford: Oxford University Press, 2003.

———. *Ordeal by Fire: The Civil War and Reconstruction.* 2nd ed. New York: McGraw-Hill, 1992.

Miller, Perry. *The Life of the Mind from the Revolution to the Civil War.* New York: Harcourt, Brace, and World, 1965.

Miller, Thomas. *Lady Jane Grey, an Historical Romance in Three Volumes.* London: Henry Colborn, 1840.

Mitchell, Reid. *The Vacant Chair: The Northern Soldier Leaves Home.* New York: Oxford University Press, 1993.

Moran, Ashley. Registrar, Milan Museum, Milan, OH. E-mail interviews with Vicki Tongate. March 25–April 6, 2014.

Murray, Joyce Martin. Abstractor. *Austin County Texas Deed Abstracts, 1837–1852. Republic of Texas State of Texas.* Wolfe City: Henington Public Company, 1987.

Murray, Lois Smith. *Baylor at Independence.* Waco: Baylor University Press, 1972.

Musto, David F., M.D. "Perception and Regulation of Drug Use: The Rise and Fall of the Tide." *Annals of Internal Medicine* 123, no. 6 (1995): 468–469. http://web.a.ebscohost.com.proxy.libraries.smu.edu/ehost/pdfviewer/pdfviewer?sid=912946d5-9eab-4b14-a896-f9a9f31486fd%40sessionmgr4003&vid=4&hid=4114.

Myers, Lois. *Letters by Lamplight.* Waco: Baylor University Press, 1991.

Myres, Sandra. *Westering Women and the Frontier Experience, 1800–1915.* Albuquerque: University of New Mexico Press, 1982.

National Park Service. Heritage Preservation Services. *CWSAC Battle Summaries: Camden Expedition–Poison Spring and Marks' Mill, AR.* http://www.nps.gov/hps/abpp/battles/ar014.htm.

———. *CWSAC Battle Summaries: Price's Missouri Expedition–Marmiton River, MO.* http://www.nps.gov/hps/abpp/battles/mo028.htm.

———. *CWSAC Battle Summaries: Red River Campaign–Mansfield and Pleasant Hill, LA.* http://www.nps.gov/hps/abpp/battles/la018.htm.

Neely, Joy. Bellville Historical Society at Bellville, Texas. Telephone/e-mail interviews with Vicki Tongate. May 27–28, 2008.

Nevins, Allen. *Ordeal of the Union.* New York: Scribner, 1947.

"New York Fashions: Cambric Dress Continental Basque and Long Round Over Skirt, Cambric Polonaise Walking Suit, Other Spring Dresses." *Harper's Bazaar* (1867–1912). March 18, 1876. "American Periodical Series Online," ProQuest. http://search.proquest.com.proxy.libraries.smu.edu/docview/125669174/fulltextPDF/38F9330E936F4BA4PQ/1?accountid=6667.

New York Ledger. Stanford University Libraries. http://suloas.stanford.edu/swprd_dp/pnpack.draw?pid=596.

Newman, Beth, ed. *Course Reader for English 3341: Women in the Age of Victoria.* Southern Methodist University, Dallas, Fall 1998.

North, Thomas. *Five Years in Texas; or, What You Did Not Hear During the War.* Cincinnati: Elm Street Printing Co., 1871.

Norton, Mary Beth. "The Paradox of 'Women's Sphere.'" In *Women of America: A History*, edited by Carol Ruth Berkin and Mary Beth Norton, 139-149. Boston: Houghton-Mifflin, 1979.

Norton, Mary Beth, David M. Katzman, Paul D. Escott, Howard P. Chudacoff, Thomas G. Paterson, and William M. Tuttle, Jr., eds. *A People and a Nation.* Boston: Houghton-Mifflin, 1986.

Nye, Russell Blaine. *Society and Culture in America, 1830–1860.* New York: Harper and Row, 1974.

"Oliver H. Perry." *Ohio History Central.* July 1, 2005. http://www.ohiohistorycentral.org.

Overmann, Pam. Curator, Navy Art Collection, Naval Historical and Heritage Command. E-mail interview with Vicki Tongate. January 11, 2011.

Palmer, Thomas H. *The Teacher's Manual: Being an Exposition of an Efficient and Economical System of Education, Suited to the Wants of a Free People.* Boston: Marsh, Capon, Lyon, and Webb, 1840.

Parks, Joseph H. *Joseph E. Brown of Georgia.* Baton Rouge: Louisiana State University Press, 1977.

Patmore, Coventry. "Angel in the House." *Poems.* 4th ed. London: 1890). Reprinted in *Course Reader for English 3341: Women in the Age of Victoria,* edited by Beth Newman, 55. Dallas: Southern Methodist University, Fall 1998.

Pazos, Marissa. Undergraduate assistant, Office of Texas State Climatologist, Department of Atmospheric Science, Texas A&M University. E-mail interview with Vicki Tongate. April 5, 2010.

Pennington, Mrs. R. E. *The History of Brenham and Washington County.* Brenham, TX: Author, 1915. https://archive.org/details/historyofbrenhamoopenn.

Pérez, Louis A., ed. *Impressions of Cuba in the Nineteenth Century: The Travel Diary of Joseph J. Dimock.* Lanham, MD: Rowman & Littlefield Publishing Group, 1998.

Pier, Cristy. Bellville, TX. Personal interview with Vicki Tongate. February 23, 2000.

Pier, Gil. E-mail interview with Vicki Tongate. April 9, 2009.

Pier, Robert J. Telephone interview with Vicki Tongate. February 6, 2000.

Plummer, Betty. *Historic Homes of Washington County, 1821–1860.* San Marcos: Rio Fresco Books, 1971.

"Prisoners in the Civil War." Civil War home page. civil-war.net. http://www.nps .gov/civilwar/search-prisoners.htm.

Railton, Stephen. "James Fenimore Cooper." In *Dictionary of Literary Biography,* vol. 250, *Antebellum Writers in New York,* 2nd ser., edited by Kent P. Ljungquist, 97–124. Gale Group, 2001. http://galenet.galegroup.com.proxy.libraries.smu. edu/servlet/GLD/hits?r=d&origSearch=true&o=DataType&n=10&l=d&c=1&lo cID=txshracd2548&secondary=false&u=CA&u=CLC&u=DLB&t=KW&s=1&N A=james+fenimore+cooper.

"Raphael Semmes." Naval Historical Center home page. U.S. Navy. http://www .history.navy.mil/library/online/cssalabama.htm.

"Rear Admiral Raphael Semmes, Confederate States Navy." Naval History and Heritage Command. Naval Historical Center home page. U.S. Navy. http:// www.history.navy.mil/photos/pers-us/uspers-s/r-semmes.htm

"Reconstruction: The Second Civil War—State by State." *American Experience.* http://www.pbs.org/wgbh/amex/reconstruction/states/sf_timeline.html.

Riedel, Stefan, M.D. "Edward Jenner and the History of Smallpox and Vaccination." *Baylor University Medical Center Proceedings.* January 18, 2005. http://www .ncbi.nlm.nih.gov/pmc/articles.

Ritter, Charles F., and Jon L. Wakelyn. *Leaders of the Confederacy: A Biographical and Historiographical Dictionary.* Westport, CT: Greenwood Press, 1998.

Roberts, Helene E. "The Exquisite Slave: The Role of Clothes in the Making of the Victorian Woman." *Signs: Journal of Women in Culture and Society* 2, no. 3 (1977). Reprinted in *Course Reader for English 3341: Women in the Age of Victoria*, edited by Beth Newman, 55–62. Dallas: Southern Methodist University, Fall 1998.

Robertson, James Oliver. *American Myth, American Reality*. New York: Hill and Wang, 1980.

Root, George F. "The World As It Is." Civil War Music: Battle Cry of Freedom. Civil War Trust. http://www.civilwar.org/education/history/on-the-homefront/cul ture/music/battle-cry-of-freedom/battle-cry-of-freedom.html.

Ruether, Rosemary Radford, and Rosemary Skinner Keller, eds. *Women and Religion in America*. Vol. 1, *The Nineteenth Century*. San Francisco: Harper and Row, 1981.

Saage, Wallace. Curator, Brazoria County Heritage Society. E-mail interview with Vicki Tongate. December 28, 2010.

Samuels, Shirley, ed. *The Culture of Sentiment*. New York: Oxford University Press, 1992.

Sanders, Scott. Antioch College archivist. E-mail interview with Vicki Tongate. September 28, 2010.

Saum, Lewis O. *The Popular Mood of Pre-Civil War America*. Westport, CT: Greenwood Press, 1980.

Schenone, Laura. *A Thousand Years over a Hot Stove: A History of American Women Told through Food, Recipes, and Remembrances*. New York: W. W. Norton, 2003.

Schlissel, Lillian. "Diaries of Frontier Women: On Learning to Read the Obscured Patterns." In *Woman's Being, Woman's Place*, edited by Mary Kelley, 53–67. Boston: G. K. Hall, 1979.

Schmidt, Charles F. *History of Washington County*. San Antonio: Naylor, 1949.

Schoolfield, Haley, Head coach, Equestrian Team, Southern Methodist University. E-mail interview with Vicki Tongate. May 17, 2010.

Scott, Sir Walter. *The Abbott: Being a Sequel to The Monastery*. Boston: Samuel H. Parker, 1834. Harvard University. August 28, 2009.

———. *Waverly Novels Abridged*. Edited by William Hardcastle Brown. New York: P. F. Collier and Sons, 1902.

Seeler, Barbara. E-mail interview with Vicki Tongate. June 18, 2009.

"Seven Up." *Encyclopedia Britannica*. http://www.britannica.com/EBchecked/ topic/15862/all-fours.

"Sevier County History." Sevier County, Arkansas. www.seviercountyar.com.

"Ships of the Confederate States—CSS Florida." Naval History and Heritage Command. Naval Historical Center home page. http://www.history.navy.mil/phot os/sh-us-cs/csa-sh/csash-ag/florida.htm.

Shuttleworth, Salley. "Female Circulation: Medical Discourse and Popular Advertising in the Mid-Victorian Era." *Body/ Politics: Woman and the Discourses of Society*. New York: Routledge Publishing, 1989. Reprinted in *Course Reader for English 3341: Women in the Age of Victoria*, edited by Beth Newman, 69–80. Dallas: Southern Methodist University, Fall 1998.

Silverthorne, Elizabeth. *Plantation Life in Texas*. College Station: Texas A&M University Press, 1986.

Sklar, Kathryn Kish. "Catharine Beecher: Transforming the Teaching Profession." In *Women's America*, edited by Linda K. Kerber and Jan Sherron DeHart, 162–168. New York: Oxford University Press, 1995.

Slawinski, Scott. "William Tappan Thompson." In *Dictionary of Literary Biography*, vol. 248, *Antebellum Writers in the South*, 2nd ser., edited by Kent Ljungquist, 370–377. Gale Group, 2001. http://galenet.galegroup.com.proxy.libraries.smu .edu/servlet/GLD/hits?r=d&origSearch=true&o=DataType&n=10&l=d&c=1& locID=txshracd2548&secondary=false&u=CA&u=CLC&u=DLB&t=KW&s=1& NA=william+tappan+thompson.

Slotkin, Richard. *Regeneration through Violence: The Mythology of the American Frontier, 1600–1860*. Middletown, CT: Wesleyan University Press, 1973.

Smith, Harold F. "Bibliography of American Travellers' Books about Cuba Published before 1900." *The Americas* 22, no. 4 (1966): 404–412.

Smith-Rosenberg, Carroll. "The Female World of Love and Ritual: Relations between Women in Nineteenth-Century America." In *Women's America*, edited by Linda K. Kerber and Jane Sherron DeHart, 168–183. New York: Oxford University Press, 1995.

Smithers, William W. *The Life of John Lofland: The Milford Bard, the Earliest and Most Distinguished Poet of Delaware*. Philadelphia: Wallace M. Leonard, 1894.

"Soldier's Dream." America Singing: Nineteenth-Century Song Sheets, Library of Congress. http://memory.loc.gov/cgi-in/ampage?collId=amss&fileName=hc/ hc00024c/amsspage.db&recNum=0&itemLink=D?amss:1:./temp/~ammem _HZpT::

Sommer, Lesley. Executive director, Historic Downtown Seaport Partnership, Galveston, TX. E-mail interview with Vicki Tongate. July 15, 2010.

"The Southern Girl's Song." American Song Sheets, Duke University Libraries Digital Collections. Project Gutenberg. http://library.duke.edu/digitalcollect ions/songsheets_bsvg501618/.

Southworth, E.D.E.N. *The Discarded Daughter, or the Children of the Isle*. Philadelphia: T. B. Peterson, 1855.

———. *The Missing Bride*. Philadelphia: T. B. Peterson, 1855. Project Gutenberg. http://www.gutenberg.org/cache/epub/14382/pg14382.html.

——— . *The Mother-In-Law, or the Isle of Rays*. New York: D. Appleton & Co., 1851.

"SS Liberty." Immigrant Ships Transcribers Guild. Historic American Sheet Music collection. http://www.immigrantships.net/v4/1800v4/liberty18730113.html.

St. Clair, Kathleen. *Little Towns of Texas*. Jacksonville: Jayroe Graphics, 1982.

Tautphoeus, Jemima Montgomery. *The Initials: A Novel*. 1850. WorldCat. http://
newfirstsearch.oclc.org.proxy.libraries.smu.edu/WebZ/FSFETCH?fetchtype=f
ullrecord:sessionid=fsapp7-52764-hx25y3qq-sbloua:entitypagenum=8:0:recno
=4:resultset=4:format=FI:next=html/record.html:bad=error/badfetch.html:ent
itytoprecno=4:entitycurrecno=4:numrecs=1.

Tennyson, Alfred Lord. "Locksley Hall." *Alfred Lord Tennyson: Selected Poems*. Edited
by Christopher Ricks. New York: Penguin Group, 2007.

"The Texas Hospital and Confederate Cemetery, Quitman (Enterprise), Mississippi." American Civil War home page, http://www.civilwarhome.com/texas
hospital.html.

"Texas Weather Pre-1880." Office of the Texas State Climatologist. Department
of Atmospheric Science, Texas A&M University. http://climatexas.tamu.edu/
files/osc_pubs/pre_1880.pdf.

"Travel Cuba–Weather." Travel-Cuba, http://travel-cuba.org./weather.html.

Turner, Frederick Jackson. "From 'The Significance of the Frontier in American
History.'" In *Rereading America: Cultural Contexts for Critical Thinking and Writing*,
edited by Gary Colombo, Robert Cullen, and Bonnie Lisle. 5th ed. Boston: Bed-
ford/St. Martin's, 2001.

Tyler, Ronnie C., and Lawrence R. Murphy, eds. *The Slave Narratives of Texas*. Austin:
Encino Press, 1974.

"Typhoid Fever." Mayo Clinic. http://www.mayoclinic.org/diseases-conditions/ty
phoid-fever/basics/definition/con-20028553.

Ulrich, Laurel Thatcher. *A Midwife's Tale*. New York: Vintage Books, 1990.

Underwood, Rodman L. *Waters of Discord: The Union Blockade of Texas during the Civil
War*. Jefferson, NC: McFarland, 2003.

Van Der Beets, Richard, ed. *Held Captive by Indians*. Knoxville: University of Tennessee Press, 1994.

Vest, Ladonna. Administrative director, Chappell Hill Historical Society. E-mail
interview with Vicki Tongate. June 25, 2009.

"Victorian Fashion." Apparel Search. http://apparelsearch.com/definitions/fash
ion/1860 fashion history.htm.

Waller County Historical Survey Commission. *A History of Waller County, Texas*.
Waco: Author, 1873.

Weber, David. *The Mexican Frontier, 1821–1846: The American Southwest under Mexico*.
Albuquerque: University of New Mexico Press, 1982.

Webmaster, Havana Guide. E-mail interview with Vicki Tongate. January 13, 2011.
Info@havana-guide.com.

Welter, Barbara. *Dimity Convictions: The American Woman in the Nineteenth Century*.
Athens: Ohio University Press, 1976.

White, Deborah Gray. "The Nature of Female Slavery." In *Women's America*, edited
by Linda K. Kerber and Jane Sherron DeHart, 104–117. 4th ed. New York:
Oxford University Press, 1995.

Wilder, Laura Ingalls. *Little House in the Big Woods*. New York: Harper-Collins, 1960.

Woolsey, Linda Mills. "Jane Porter." In *Dictionary of Literary Biography*, vol. 159, *British Short Fiction Writers, 1800–1880*, edited by John R. Greenfield, 265–274. Gale Group, 1996. http://galenet.galegroup.com.proxy.libraries.smu.edu/servlet/GLD/hits?r=d&origSearch=true&o=DataType&n=10&l=d&c=1&locID=txshracd2548&secondary=false&u=DLB&t=KW&s=4&NA=jane+porter.

Wordsworth, William. "We Are Seven." Poetry Foundation.org. http://www.poetryfoundation.org/poem/183927.

Wright, Marcus J., Brig. General, C.S.A., and Harold B. Simpson, Col., U.S.A.F. *Texas in the War, 1861–1865*. Hillsboro, TX: Hill Junior College Press, 1965.

Wyatt, Jennifer L. "Anna Maria Hall." In *Dictionary of Literary Biography*, vol. 159, *British Short-Fiction Writers, 1800-1880*, edited by John R. Greenfield, 144–151. Gale Group, 1996. http://galenet.galegroup.com.proxy.libraries.smu.edu/servlet/GLD/hits?r=d&origSearch=true&o=DataType&n=10&l=d&c=1&locID=txshracd2548&secondary=false&u=CA&u=CLC&u=DLB&t=KW&s=1&NA=anna+maria+hall#MainEssaySection.

Yazoo City. *Yazoo County Convention and Visitors Bureau*. Yazoo.org.

Young, Edward. *The Complaint, or Night Thoughts on Life, Death, and Immortality*.

"Z. W. Matthews." Austin County Abstract 270. Texas General Land Office Digital Archives. http://files.usgwarchives.net/tx/austin/land/abstract.txt.

"Zouave Jacket." Apparel Search. http://apparelsearch.com/definitions/fashion/1860.

INDEX

〰